International Place Branding Yearbook 2012

Also by Frank M. Go and Robert Govers and published by Palgrave Macmillan

PLACE BRANDING

INTERNATIONAL PLACE BRANDING YEARBOOK 2010
Place Branding in the New Age of Innovation

INTERNATIONAL PLACE BRANDING YEARBOOK 2011
Managing Reputational Risk

International Place Branding Yearbook 2012

Managing Smart Growth & Sustainability

Edited by
Frank M. Go & Robert Govers

Selection and editorial matter © Frank M. Go and Robert Govers 2013
Individual chapters © the contributors 2013

All rights reserved. No reproduction, copy or transmission of this publication may be made without written permission.

No portion of this publication may be reproduced, copied or transmitted save with written permission or in accordance with the provisions of the Copyright, Designs and Patents Act 1988, or under the terms of any licence permitting limited copying issued by the Copyright Licensing Agency, Saffron House, 6–10 Kirby Street, London EC1N 8TS.

Any person who does any unauthorized act in relation to this publication may be liable to criminal prosecution and civil claims for damages.

The authors have asserted their rights to be identified as the authors of this work in accordance with the Copyright, Designs and Patents Act 1988.

First published 2013 by
PALGRAVE MACMILLAN

Palgrave Macmillan in the UK is an imprint of Macmillan Publishers Limited, registered in England, company number 785998, of Houndmills, Basingstoke, Hampshire RG21 6XS.

Palgrave Macmillan in the US is a division of St Martin's Press LLC, 175 Fifth Avenue, New York, NY 10010.

Palgrave Macmillan is the global academic imprint of the above companies and has companies and representatives throughout the world.

Palgrave® and Macmillan® are registered trademarks in the United States, the United Kingdom, Europe and other countries.

ISBN 978–0–230–27952–0

This book is printed on paper suitable for recycling and made from fully managed and sustained forest sources. Logging, pulping and manufacturing processes are expected to conform to the environmental regulations of the country of origin.

A catalogue record for this book is available from the British Library.

A catalog record for this book is available from the Library of Congress.

10 9 8 7 6 5 4 3 2 1
22 21 20 19 18 17 16 15 14 13

Printed and bound in Great Britain by
CPI Antony Rowe, Chippenham and Eastbourne

Contents

List of Figures and Tables	ix
Preface	x
Acknowledgments	xii
About the Book	xiii
Notes on the Contributors	xv
Organization of the Book	xxii

Introduction   1
Frank M. Go and Robert Govers

Unraveling Place Branding: Where Do Place Brands Dwell?	2
City Hubs: Centers of Gravity in the Global Value Chain	11
Concluding Remarks	22

Part I Multidisciplinary Perspectives on Sustainable Place Branding

1 Four Readings of Place and Brand Leadership   33
Chris Mabey and Tim Freeman

A Multi-discourse Approach	34
A Functionalist Discourse of Leadership, Place Branding and Place Leadership	36
An Interpretive Discourse of Leadership, Place Branding and Place Leadership	36
A Dialogic Discourse of Leadership, Place Branding and Place Leadership	37
A Critical Discourse of Leadership, Place Branding and Place Leadership	39
Conclusion	41

2 Beyond Place Branding   45
Nicholas Ind and Erling Dokk Holm

The Problem with (Place) Branding	45
Living with Participation	47
Enabling People to Connect	50
Delivering Sustainability	51
Summary	53

3	**Crisis Communication and Sustainable Place Marketing: A Preliminary Analysis before Choosing a Restorative Media Strategy**	**56**
	Eli Avraham	
	Theoretical Background	57
	Crisis Characteristics	58
	Audience Characteristics	60
	Place Characteristics	63
	Summary	67
4	**A Perspective on Planning, Smart Growth and Place Branding**	**69**
	Kristof van Assche, Ming Chien Lo and Raoul Beunen	
	Smart Growth as Rebranded Planning	69
	Place Branding, Place Identity and Smart Growth	71
	Concluding Remarks	73

Part 2 Chapters on Particular Cases

5	**Case A Sex and the City: City Branding in Spanish Cities**	**81**
	Gildo Seisdedos and Pablo Vaggione	
	Spanish Cities: From Now on ... What?	82
	Methodology	83
	From Flagship Projects to White Elephants	84
	A Shift on City Branding	85
	Masculine versus Feminine Thinking and City Branding	87
	Implications	89
	Conclusion	90
6	**Case B A Common Agenda for Place Branding: Made in Torino**	**93**
	Alexander Otgaar	
	Fundamental Trends	94
	A Common Agenda for Industrial Tourism: How to Realize an Image Fit	95
	Made in Torino: Tour the Excellent	97
	Conclusion	100
7	**Case C Sustaining a Brand through Proactive Repair: The Case of Manchester**	**103**
	Stephen E. Little	
	Brand Manchester: From Cottonopolis to Madchester	105
	August 2011	109
	Conclusion	115

Contents

8	**Case D Social Media: An Insight into the "Public Mood" of Places? A Case Study of the City of Johannesburg**	119
	Wadim Schreiner and Frank M. Go	
	Existing Research	122
	Public Mood, Public Opinion and the Role of Social Media	123
	Methodology	124
	Results	125
	Discussion	128
	Conclusion	129
9	**Case E Turning a Gemstone into a Diamond: A Green Design and Branding Strategy for The City of Bucharest**	132
	Iulia Gramon-Suba and Chris Holt	
	International Trends	132
	The Story of Bucharest	133
	Problem and Motivation	133
	Key Question, Aim and Objectives	135
	Methodology	135
	Key Findings	137
	The Brand of Bucharest	137
	Conclusions and Recommendations	141

Part 3 Chapters on Particular Place Brand Themes

10	**Overcoming the Risk of Stereotypes: How Strategic Communications Can Facilitate Sustainable Place Branding**	147
	Roland Schatz	
	How Stereotypes Shape our Perception	148
	Media Stereotypes: Italy, Greece and France	151
	The Media Periphery: Austria, Bahrain and Vietnam	157
	What Can We Do?	161
11	**Do National Green Reputations Matter? The Global Green Economy Index and Implications for Stakeholders in the Green Economy**	164
	Jeremy Tamanini	
	Existing Indices and Underlying Methodologies	164
	Macro-trends in the Green Economy	166
	Methodology	167
	Selection of Respondents	169
	Results for 2011	170

	Managing Green Reputations	171
	Conclusion	173
12	**Branding Brazilian Slums through "Freeware" Cultural Production: The Case of Rio de Janeiro**	**174**
	Antonio Paolo Russo	
	Rio de Janeiro: The World of *favelas* vs the Corporate Tourist City	176
	The Cultural Landscape of *favelas:* Branding the Freeware	178
	Conclusions: Soft-branding Diversity for Sustainable Development	183
13	**Improved Public Infrastructure and Sustainable Place Branding**	**187**
	Keith Dinnie	
	Infrastructure and the Cityscape	188
	Cities and the Experience Economy	189
	Cases	189
	Conclusions	193

Conclusion 195

Frank M. Go and Robert Govers

Three Main Debates 195
Deficiencies 219

Index 227

List of Figures and Tables

Figures

1.1	Place brand symbolism and the interrelating socio-cultural, economic and political dynamics	3
1.1	Four discourses of leadership and place	35
5.1	Duality on urban management tools	86
9.1	Bucharest's environmental problems in citizens' opinions	139
10.1	What you know of Pisa	148
10.2	Agenda-setting at its best?	151
10.3	The whole picture	153
10.4	Topic structure of Italy's media coverage 2009–11	154
10.5	Visibility of Greece in US TV news 2008	155
10.6	Visibility of Greece in European TV news 2008	156
10.7	Topic structure of Austria's media coverage 2008–10	158
10.8	Coverage of King Hamad of Bahrain in international media, 2008–09	159
10.9	Visibility of Vietnam in international TV news, 2011	160
C.1	Model of balanced centricity as a priority for future place branding	196

Tables

5.1	City branding models	89
8.1	Top category issues: near proximity (Johannesburg)	126
8.2	Top category issues: extended proximity (Johannesburg)	127

Preface

Is life really getting better? If so, how can we tell? What are the key ingredients to improving life? Is it better education, environment, health care, housing or working hours? Does 'progress' mean the same thing to all people, to all countries, to all societies? These questions served as the basis for the Better Life Initiative, a project the OECD has worked on for almost ten years. Its purpose is to "identify the best way to measure the progress of societies – moving beyond GDP and examining the areas that impact everyday people's lives".

The previous editions in the International Place Branding Yearbook series looked at the themes of "place branding in the new age of innovation" (Go and Govers 2010) and "managing reputational risk" (Go and Govers 2011). A world in crisis is a subject that requires immediate and critical attention. Only by boycotting front-page news is it possible to ignore the fact that we live in an age of crisis. We read of climate change, global imbalances, unemployment, resource shortage and terrorism. These issues are rooted in the structure and development of the world economic system. And their manifestations are aggravated by economic and political policies, including the context and choices of place branding.

This third edition of the International Place Branding Yearbook series focuses on "managing smart growth and sustainability" and commemorates the 50th anniversary of Rachel Carson's *Silent Spring*. A biologist by training and a skilled writer, here is what this visionary observed 50 years ago: "what we have to face is not an occasional dose of poison which has accidentally got into some article of food, but a persistent and continuous poisoning of the whole human environment". In the introduction to this controversial and remarkable book Lord Shackleton wrote: "*Silent Spring* is not merely about poisons; it is about ecology or the relation of plants and animals to their environment and to one another ... Miss Carson makes a well reasoned and persuasive case for human beings to learn to appreciate the fact that they are part of the entire world inhabiting this planet, and that they must understand its conditions of existence and so behave that these conditions are not violated."

Carson's book helped to ignite the worldwide sustainability movement. Unlike the 1980s and 1990s, today's sustainability movement isn't motivated by guilt. Instead it's led by a varied group of people who see the long-term environmental, social and economic benefits of working in sustainable ways. Presently, climate change attracts increased attention from both investors and companies. A growing number of business leaders recognize that it will have a major impact on future product offerings, operations and reputation, and they are adapting their business strategies accordingly. It is also a main concern for place brands which seek to attract investors, residents and tourists to achieve and maintain place brand leadership. It therefore should not come as a surprise that increasingly businesses, territorial actors and researchers alike are interested in re-evaluating professional practice and improving the environmental footprint. The previous Yearbooks underscored the fact that place brands aren't merely logos, but represent a promise designed to empower humans to align external and internal dynamics collectively. Culture, image, symbols and vision are essential dimensions that empower the place branding process. Visionary place brands are in the temporal domain and of the future, implying a gap between the state of Carson's *Silent Spring* and the imagined state of sustainability. The "brand mission" refers to the knowledge domain of the creation of smart growth value propositions which countries and cities, in partnership with business, are either engaged in or are intending to join. "Managing smart growth and sustainability" represents a powerful concept which, given the "right" leadership, can attract the attention and energy of place brand stakeholders, experienced professionals and inspired novices and help to coordinate their actions so as to make the concept a self-fulfilling prophecy.

FRANK M. GO
ROBERT GOVERS

Acknowledgments

We are especially grateful to all the busy authors who agreed to contribute to this volume. We would also like to thank the reviewers for their valuable critiques: Simon Anholt, government advisor and author, UK; Adee Athiyaman, Western Illinois University, USA; Bill Baker, author of *Destination Branding for Small Cities* (Creative Leap Books), USA; Nicholas J. Cull, University of Southern California, USA. Keith Dinnie, NHTV Breda University of Applied Sciences, the Netherlands; Marc Fetscherin, Rollins College, USA; Joshua Fouts, Center for the Study of the Presidency and Congress, USA; Juergen Gnoth, University of Otago, New Zealand; Peter van Ham, Institute of International Relations "Clingendael", the Netherlands; Stephen Little, Open University Business School, UK; T. C. Melewar, Brunel University, UK; Nigel Morgan, Cardiff Metropolitan University, UK; Lena Mossberg, Norwegian School of Management, Norway; Professor Dipak Pant, Università Carlo Cattaneo (LIUC), Italy; Johan van Rekom, Rotterdam School of Management, Erasmus University, the Netherlands; and Peeter Verlegh, University of Amsterdam, the Netherlands. Last but not least we acknowledge the ever-present and unfailing support of the Palgrave Macmillan Business and Management, Academic and Professional Publishing staff, in particular Stephen Rutt, Editor, and Eleanor Davey Corrigan, together with Keith Povey and Nick Fox (of Keith Povey Editorial Services Ltd).

FRANK M. GO
ROBERT GOVERS

About the Book

2012 MANAGING SMART GROWTH AND SUSTAINABILITY

This Yearbook examines how place brands interrelate and configure various attributes in the place branding process to derive "smart growth". As opposed to a Darwinian type approach, which is based on the ability of a single organizational attribute to survive intensive place brand rivalry, smart growth draws from the emerging field of "quality of life". It demands research as manifested in the consumption and production practices in urban locations which emphasize ethical and aesthetic concerns around which their attributes are configured so as to achieve a consistency in their internal characteristics, a synergy in their working processes and a fitness with external contexts. The smart growth approach underscores the importance of systems or networks of interrelationships concerning a specific theme around which may be created a synergistic "soft power" that connects multisector and multilayered work processes of place brand stakeholders so as to configure the selected attributes and mediate place brands in response to the multiple demands of cultural identity, state power and capital accumulation.

YEARBOOK OBJECTIVES

This 2012 *International Place Branding Yearbook* has the following objectives:

- To increase understanding that place branding dwells within multilayered, multisector spaces, and that every situation is unique due to place-specificity, which implies that practitioners and academics must be selective in delineating brand research and projects, in contrast to applying generic approaches;

- To provide a "state-of-the art" review of research through the lens of selected individual case studies;

- To interpret the challenges that place brands face in managing smart growth and sustainability through selected themes.

OVERVIEW

This volume features perspectives of place branding that have been reviewed by an editorial board. It is not academic in the sense of laboriously expounding theory, but contributions have been screened with an eye to relevant techniques, methods and tools geared towards a focus on management for action. The final content consists of various approaches set out in three parts:

- Part 1: Examines some essential concepts and theories that underpin place branding practice.
- Part 2: Consists of a selection of chapters that addresses individual case studies of countries, regions, cities, and so on.
- Part 3: Provides state-of-the-art themes in the subject area.

We trust that the reader will appreciate the breadth of contributions and use these to view place branding through a new lens.

AUDIENCE

This Yearbook is aimed at: place branding practitioners, consultants and government agencies; ministries of economic development and cultural institutes and foundations; regional and city governments; mayoral offices; regional, cantonal, state and city tourism, investment promotion, economic and development agencies; academics and researchers in marketing, international politics, public affairs, international marketing, international relations, globalization, economics and diplomacy; and journalists who serve a wider public for debating place marketing and branding issues.

NOTES ON THE CONTRIBUTORS

Kristof van Assche is currently Visiting Associate Professor at the Communication and Innovation Studies group at Wageningen University and Research Fellow at the German Institute for Development Research (ZEF) at Bonn University. Previously, he was Associate Professor in Planning and Community Development at St Cloud State University, Minnesota. He has been a visiting senior researcher at ZEF/Bonn University and a visiting professor in planning at McGill and Wageningen universities. He is interested in spatial and environmental governance, and often uses an evolutionary and comparative perspective. He also researches, teaches and advises in North America, Europe, Central Asia and the Caucasus.

Eli Avraham is the Head of the Public Relations Program in the Department of Communication, University of Haifa, Israel. He has published more than 30 papers and is the author and co-author of eight award winning books, among them: *Campaigns for Promoting and Marketing Cities in Israel* (The Floersheimer Institute for Policy Studies, 2003); *Behind Media Marginality: Coverage of Social Groups and Places in the Israeli Press* (Lexington Books, 2003); *Media Strategies for Marketing Places in Crisis: Improving the Image of Cities, Countries and Tourist Destinations* (Elsevier/Butterworth-Heinemann, 2008). Dr Avraham's research and consulting fields include tourism marketing, place branding and ameliorating a place's image.

Raoul Beunen is Assistant Professor at Wageningen University, the Netherlands. His research in the field of spatial planning deals with policy integration and implementation, and environmental governance. He is particularly interested in the linkages between nature and landscape conservation and tourism management. He has published over 100 articles, book chapters and reports on these subjects.

Keith Dinnie is Senior Lecturer in International Marketing at NHTV Breda University of Applied Sciences in the Netherlands. He is the editor of *City Branding: Theory and Cases* (Palgrave Macmillan, 2011) and the author of the world's first academic textbook on nation branding, *Nation Branding: Concepts, Issues, Practice* (Butterworth-Heinemann, 2008). During 2009–11 he served as Academic Editor of the journal *Place Branding and Public Diplomacy*. He has published in various international journals including *International Marketing Review*, *Place Branding and Public Diplomacy*, the *Journal of Brand Management* and the *Journal of Consumer Marketing*. He is the founder of Brand Horizons consultancy and is Director of the Centre for City Branding.

Tim Freeman is Lecturer in Health Policy and Management within the School of Social Policy at the University of Birmingham. Recent publications include an ethnography of governance at a joint commissioning partnership board; a policy analysis of emerging organizational forms within health care service provision; and an analysis of leadership in health care settings. Recent projects include tracing contemporary public-sector leadership discourses through application of Q-methodology, the experience of partnership working within an inner-city regeneration project, and the governance of patient safety. Tim has an interest in interpretivist approaches to policy implementation, and with colleagues from Edinburgh University and the wider College of Social Sciences at the University of Birmingham holds an ESRC conference series award for exploring policy implementation as 'practice'. He is a governor of a local acute hospital trust, Director of Doctoral Studies at the Health Services Management Centre, and has successfully supervised PhD candidates in topic areas within health policy and health economics. He teaches on a range of MSc programs, collaborating with colleagues within HSMC and across the wider College of Social Sciences, Medical and Business Schools, where his main subject areas are quality improvement, governance and research methodology.

Frank M. Go is Professor and Director of the Centre for Tourism Management at the Rotterdam School of Management (RSM), Erasmus University, Netherlands. Prior to his present post he served within business faculties at universities in Canada and Hong Kong. His research focus is on marketing strategy, destination images and brand identity, ICT and innovation, and sustainable business development. He serves as Academic Director of a joint MSc program between the RSM and Hotelschool, The Hague, and is a visiting professor at Rikkyo University, Tokyo, Japan and the Open University Business School, UK. Go has also authored more than 125 journal articles, official reports and book chapters, in which most of his writing has focused on the need to integrate technological, market and organizational change in travel, destination and hospitality contexts to improve the effectiveness of organizations.

Robert Govers is an independent placing advisor and author on place branding. He is a visiting scholar in the Netherlands, Belgium, Italy and Dubai, and co-editor of the quarterly journal *Place Branding and Public Diplomacy* (also published by Palgrave Macmillan). He also teaches place branding on the UNESCO World Heritage at Work Master programme in Turin, Italy. Besides this, Govers is an independent place branding advisor for national, regional and city government administrations. He is co-editor of the quarterly journal, *Place Branding and Public Diplomacy*. Together with Frank Go he is the author of *Place Branding: Glocal, Virtual and Physical, Identities Constructed, Perceived and Experienced* (Palgrave Macmillan, 2009). He has also co-authored over 40 journal articles, book chapters and conference papers in the field of place branding, tourism, reputation management, e-commerce and marketing research. Govers has delivered over 60 public speeches and produced more than 20 business publications.

Iulia Gramon-Suba was born in Alexandria, Romania. She has a bachelor's degree in Business and Advertising Management at Canterbury Christ Church University and graduated with distinction from her master's degree in Design and Brand Strategy at Brunel University. She completed her dissertation on green city branding, specifically on branding Bucharest. Her fields of interest include place branding, nation branding, city branding and sustainable development. She is now working as a Marketing Planner at Nisbets.

Erling Dokk Holm is Associate Professor at the Oslo School of Management, where he also serves as the head of the Master's course in Marketing and Society. He also teaches at the Oslo School of Architecture and Design. His research interests include architectural ideologies, urban planning, public spaces and consumer behavior. Erling has also written extensive popular texts on this subject.

Chris Holt graduated from Bolton College of Art and Design (now Bolton University) in 1968. Chris has spent over 35 years in the design business: as a designer with FHK Henrion; as a senior designer with British European Airways; as a design manager with the P&O Group; as Head of Design and Publicity at the Sea Containers Group; and as Head of Design Management at British Airways. He then spent three years with the Springpoint Consultancy advising clients on the effective realization of brand identity programs and now manages his own consultancy which includes leading a range of short courses. He also holds various university lecturing posts. Much of his time nowadays is spent at Brunel University where he works on the Masters Design Strategy program.

Nicholas Ind is the author of 11 books including *The Corporate Image* (NYU Press, 1990), the best-selling *Terence Conran: The Authorised Biography* (Sidgwick and Jackson, 1995), *The Corporate Brand* (NYU Press, 1997), *Living the Brand* (Kogan Page, 2001), *Meaning at Work* (Cappelen Damm

As, 2010) and *Brand Together* (Kogan Page, 2012). He was also the editor of *Beyond Branding* (Kogan Page, 2003). Nicholas is a member of the advisory board of *Corporate Reputation Review* and of the editorial board of the *Journal of Brand Management*. He is an associate professor at the Oslo School of Management and a visiting professor at ESADE, Barcelona, Spain, and at Edinburgh Napier University, UK. Nicholas has a PhD from the European Graduate School in Switzerland.

Stephen E. Little is Senior Lecturer in Knowledge Management at the Open University Business School, UK and is a fellow of the Regional Studies Association. After graduating from the Birmingham School of Architecture he studied applied psychology at Aston University. In 1983, following a decade of practice in urban renewal in Manchester and Glasgow, he was awarded a PhD on the organizational impact of computer aided design at the Royal College of Art, London. Subsequently he held full-time appointments at Griffith University Queensland, the University of Wollongong NSW and Manchester Metropolitan University. He is a board member of Asia Pacific Researchers in Organization Studies and Chairman of the Asia Pacific Technology Network, a company limited by guarantee and established to encourage collaboration amongst the UK, Europe and Asia in the area of high technology and corporate strategy. His current research interests include the global migration of skilled labor, the contribution of large science projects to the wider economy and the role of place-branding in regional development.

Ming Chien Lo is Associate Professor of Economics at St Cloud State University, Minnesota, USA. His economic research interests include applied time series econometrics, economic institutions and economic methodology. His curiosity has allowed him to engage in several on-going, interdisciplinary projects, including a series of work with Raoul Beunen and Kristof van Assche in the area of place branding. "Planning, Preservation and Place Branding: A Tale of Sharing Assets and Heritage", which is his latest work with van Assche, has been published in *Place Branding and Public Diplomacy*. Prior to receiving his PhD in economics from the University of Washington in 2000, he studied economics and philosophy at the University of Hong Kong and the London School of Economics and Political Science.

Chris Mabey is Professor of Human Resource Management at Birmingham University, UK. He leads a multi-disciplinary, international team researching knowledge leadership in ATLAS, a global scientific collaboration comprising 3,000 physicists working in 37 countries. Chris, who is a chartered psychologist, directs the Centre for Leadership at the University of Birmingham and teaches on MSc and MBA programs in the Business School.

Alexander Otgaar is an expert in urban economics and regional development at Erasmus University, Rotterdam. He is particularly interested in the functioning of collaborative arrangements of governments, businesses and knowledge institutions. He has done research in more than 40 cities in Europe, China and North America. Alexander has a background in Business Economics (MSc, Erasmus School of Economics) and since 1997 he has worked on various projects, notably in the field of metropolitan governance, regional innovation and cross-border/cross-sector cooperation. In 2010 he finished his PhD at the Erasmus School of Economics about the development of a common agenda in industrial tourism.

Antonio Paolo Russo is Assistant Professor in the Department of Geography, Universitat Rovira i Virgili, Tarragona, Spain, and is Research Director of the Science and Technology Park of Tourism and Leisure, Universitat Rovira i Virgili, Tarragona, Spain. Previous appointments were with the Erasmus University, Rotterdam (where he received his PhD in Economics in 2002), the Universitat Autònoma of Barcelona and the IULM University Milan. He is the author of various publications in academic journals and books. His research interests range from tourism studies to cultural and urban economics and planning. He has been involved as a staff member of university departments and as an independent expert advisor in various research projects on these topics, both in specific local issues and in EU research networks and other international programs.

Roland Schatz is the founder and CEO of Media Tenor International. His interests include media impact, organizational development, cultural management and new methods in education. With over 180 employees and offices in Beirut, London, New York, Ostrava, Pretoria, St Petersburg, Windhoek and Zurich, Media Tenor is the world's leading provider of ongoing international media content analysis, including in-depth analysis of new and traditional global media content. In 2007, Schatz had the honor of opening the first Arab Media Institute at Emory University. He has also held teaching positions since 1990 in strategic communication management at universities in Augsburg, Atlanta, Berlin, Bonn, Lugano and Prague. In 2009 he opened the Global Media Impact Center in Boston. Together with Prince Ghazi of Jordan he founded the C1 Foundation in Basel, which supports dialogue amongst the three Abrahamic faiths. Aside from his background in teaching, Schatz has served as Secretary of the International

Media Monitor Association based in Washington, DC. He is also a trustee for the Education Africa Foundation in Johannesburg, the Innovation Institute in Pretoria and the Board of E-Standards in New York. Schatz has a master's degree in philosophy, economics, history and political science from the University of Fribourg and Bonn.

Wadim Schreiner is the Managing Director of Media Tenor South Africa in Pretoria and a board member of Media Tenor International in Zurich. Media Tenor's research in terms of national and international media trends has been widely published in South African and international media, in terms of both political and economic analyses. He has a master's degree in business communication and journalism from the North West University, South Africa, the topic of his thesis being 'News Flow In and Out of Africa: The Image of Africa in International Media'. He has read in media theories and communication methods at the University of Stellenbosch and the University of Cape Town, and has led a number of seminars at universities around the country. He has spoken at several media and journalism conferences in the USA, South Africa, Asia and Africa, and has published a number of research articles in international journals and books on South African and international media trends. He is a columnist for *The Media*, South Africa's media industry magazine. He is currently studying towards his doctorate at the Rotterdam School of Management, Erasmus University, the Netherlands, focusing on nation branding.

Gildo Seisdedos has a passion for cities. As a professor at the IE Business School, he combines teaching, research and consulting activities in the fields of urban planning, local policies and city marketing. He has prepared studies on urban planning and design at the London School of Economics and Political Science, the University of California in Los Angeles, the Universidad de San Andrés, Buenos Aires, and the RCC at Harvard University. He holds a PhD in Urban Economy from Madrid's Autonoma University, a bachelor in business administration (E3) from ICADE, Madrid, an MBA degree in sales and marketing management from IE Business School and he is a member of the Madrid Bar Association and a qualified estate agent.

Jeremy Tamanini is the founder of Dual Citizen Inc., a Washington DC based consultancy providing governments and international organizations with analytic tools and strategic communications consulting for advancing economic and policy agendas. Dual Citizen Inc. publishes the annual Global Green Economy Index and will launch a social media analytic tool in 2012. Tamanini has over ten years of experience working in digital and

Notes on the Contributors

traditional brand marketing as well as being a consultant to national and city governments and international organizations. He holds a bachelor's degree from Columbia University and a master's degree from Georgetown's School of Foreign Service. He was a Fulbright scholar in Dubai, United Arab Emirates, where he studied place branding and economic development. You can follow him on Twitter @DualCitizenInc and on his website www.dualcitizeninc.com, where the Global Green Economy Index executive summary can be downloaded.

Pablo Vaggione is an architect and urban planner with over 15 years of professional experience. His integrated approach to planning strives to bring together departmental programs, technical disciplines and agents of implementation. He complements skills in urban planning and spatial design with multi-stakeholder participatory processes. He has led teams preparing city-wide sustainable development strategies, plans for urban renewal that include the environmental and spatial regeneration of historic areas, and integrated plans for sustainable and scalable new districts. He is the lead author in the upcoming *UN-HABITAT Guide for City Leaders on Urban Planning*. He studied at Harvard and the United Nations University.

ORGANIZATION OF THE BOOK

This book is organized into three parts and contains 14 individual chapters. A brief description of each part and each chapter follows.

PART I MULTIDISCIPLINARY PERSPECTIVES ON SUSTAINABLE PLACE BRANDING

This section consists of four chapters and forms an introductory part that looks at multidisciplinary perspectives on sustainable place branding, including leadership, social responsibility, crisis communications, knowledge management and planning, and preservation.

Chapter 1 Four Readings of Place and Brand Leadership

Chris Mabey and Tim Freeman write from an academic perspective. The world of contemporary leadership and place-shaping is in flux. They argue that, for a host of socio-cultural, technological and political reasons a less hierarchical, more inclusive and relational model of economic development and partnership-working is gaining currency. This calls for collaborative networking, for entrepreneurship and innovation, for knowledge sharing and for cross-boundary learning – an approach that can provide neighborhoods, cities and regions with resources to improve the flow of knowledge and create branded places that are both attractive and sustainable. However, reconceptualizing "place" in this way has immediate consequences for the nature of leadership, though "place leadership" is a field which remains under-theorized to date. Mabey and Freeman propose "discourse analysis" as a fresh and theoretically informed way to explore the branding of place. By offering four different "readings", they begin to identify what is required to lead effectively in complex, sometimes chaotic, policy environments, working across institutional, professional, territorial and community boundaries.

Chapter 2 Beyond Place Branding

Nicholas Ind and Erling Dokk Holm draw on the ideas first put forward in *Beyond Branding* (London: Kogan Page, 2003), edited by Ind, and Holm's PhD study on coffee shops and the idea of soft urbanism. They have written this chapter from a practitioners' perspective. Their general focus is on how branding practice in general is changing. Social media power, the move to a more participatory culture and the recognition of the importance of sustainable growth has turned the stakeholders–brand relationship on its head thereby ceding brand control to consumers and citizens. Their co-creating of brand meaning in a conversational space has caused most of the distinctions between brand insiders and outsiders to collapse. From their work with branding organizations the authors argue that place branding needs a rethink so as to become more long-term oriented and focused on smart growth, rather than growth for its own sake. They conclude with a set of four implications which move place branding into the heart of policy-making: (1) place brands should practice democratic principles, i.e. open themselves up to more stakeholder dialogue and capture the sort of engagement as illustrated by Switzerland's direct democratic decision-making; (2) place brands must become more transparent; (3) city brands need to embrace "soft urbanism", i.e. they should diminish different stakeholders' distinctions, blend high and low culture, stimulate ideas and encourage informality; (4) place branding needs to become everyone's responsibility: creating a better community is not just the responsibility of civic leaders, rather it involves everyone working together to enhance the quality of life, both in the short and long term.

Chapter 3 Crisis Communication and Sustainable Place Marketing

Eli Avraham asks how a place's positive image can be restored after a crisis. Opposing what may be described as a one-size-fits-all approach he cautions against applying a variety of techniques and strategies and the same solutions for places that differ greatly from one another. Moreover, he suggests that the solutions proposed in the past have not taken into account the type of crisis experienced or the characteristics of the target audiences to be addressed. This chapter offers a preliminary analysis of three types of characteristics – those related to the place, audience and crisis – that must be considered before selecting a strategy to restore the positive image of a place that experienced a crisis. The discussion is both practical and theoretical. On a practical level, the analysis helps marketers in the selection of the correct strategy for restoring an image; on the theoretical level, it offers an extension to existing models for the restoration of the image of a place.

Chapter 4 A Perspective on Planning, Smart Growth and Place Branding

This chapter is by Kristof van Assche, Ming Chien Lo and Raoul Beunen, who write from an academic perspective. They argue that planning strategies that are sensitive to place branding could increase the appeal of smart growth projects by creating a value for places and the things in those places. They develop a perspective on the potential synergy between smart growth and place branding that can be valuable in various contexts – in the US, the EU and communities elsewhere – since many encounter obstacles to comprehensive planning that could be reduced by paying closer attention to how value can be affected by planning. This chapter concludes that the potential for place branding in smart growth is vast, but that it is also linked to governance in an intricate manner. The place branding literature has already moved in the direction of governance by recognizing that places are complex "products", or in fact many products, and that commodification and decommodification take place all the time. Evidence is given that the combination of visioning planning and place branding, rather than treating these as independent processes in the community, will benefit a sustainability movement such as smart growth.

PART 2 CHAPTERS ON PARTICULAR CASES

The chapters in Part 2 illustrate specific cases in the field of place branding and fall into two broad categories. Chapters 5 and 6 look at the role of gender orientation and public–private partnerships; Chapters 7 and 8 concentrate on civil disorder and public mood as sources of regeneration; while Chapter 9 examines green design for a sustainable city branding strategy.

Chapter 5   Case A: Sex and the City – City Branding in Spanish Cities

Gildo Seisdedos and Pablo Vaggione also write from an academic perspective. Through a case study, they explore the influence that gender has on city branding processes in Spain. They argue that there has been a strong shift in the way citizens assess branding efforts. That is to say, what citizenship demands of their local governments has substantially changed; what formerly was pride is now a political battlefield, which provides suspicion regarding the opportunity of branding projects. The authors suggest that a new model for city branding processes may emerge, consequent to a shift from a masculine to a feminine model, from the ethics of justice to the ethics of care. The chapter suggests that such processes in Spanish cities are adapting to this new emerging model of "openness" and concludes by describing the nature and the challenges of this change for the analysis and management of cities.

Chapter 6   Case B: A Common Agenda for Place Branding – Made in Torino

Alexander Otgaar writes from an academic perspective. Presenting a wide-ranging case study from a public sector organization – the Italian city of Turin – he considers both private and public sector perspectives that influence group decision-making. In this chapter Otgaar discusses the increasing need for a common agenda in the development of a place branding strategy and industrial tourism in particular. Furthermore, he identifies the fundamental trends that raise the importance of such an agenda. Subsequently, he focuses on the question of how to realize a fit between industrial tourism development and the intended images of both city and enterprise. The chapter concludes with an evidence-based analysis of the Made in Torino case which shows how a public–private initiative involving the local government and the chamber of commerce has developed a common agenda on industrial tourism development, has enriched the city's image and has helped to open doors and improve accessibility and visibility at relatively low costs. As has been the case with many other branding instruments it has been difficult to prove the effectiveness of the city branding program, but the fact that both initiators still support the Made in Torino initiative is an indicator of its success and could serve as inspiration for other cities.

Chapter 7   Case C: Sustaining a Brand through Proactive Repair – The Case of Manchester

Written from an academic perspective by Steve Little this chapter looks at how British cities, beyond the capital, have been affected by recent adversity and have had fewer direct control mechanisms for countering reputational risk and brand vulnerability. It focuses on the Manchester region which aspires to the role of alternative metropolitan growth pole to London and the south-east, but lacks the direct mechanisms with which to pursue this aim. Building on path dependence theory, this chapter shows Manchester's status as the international center of the cotton and textile processing industries during the 19th century, reflected in its unofficial name of Cottonopolis. Top-down government policy-making in the face of recession are the contradictory stresses that triggered the most recent civil disturbances in Manchester in August 2011. Little argues that this included the dismantling of regional policy and the substitution of poorly resourced alternative partnerships under the promotion of "localism". In the immediate aftermath of the disturbances of August 2011, Manchester local authorities deployed both traditional communication forms as well as co-opting social media, which were identified by some commentators as central to the propagation of the unrest and criminality. However, in the face of internal tensions, the extent to which the "municipalization" of social media – in campaigns such as that developed in Manchester under the immediate pressure of civil disorder – can sustain a city and region remains to be seen.

Chapter 8   Case D: Social Media – Insight into the "Public Mood" of Places? A Case Study of the City of Johannesburg

This chapter by Wadim Schreiner and Frank Go is written from a combined practitioner consultant and academic perspective. It focuses on the study of the City of Johannesburg. In particular it describes initial, exploratory research toward the development of a "public mood" index for the city. It is an exploratory study which aims at advancing understanding of the importance of mood, not just from a place branding viewpoint, but also from a future city planning perspective. Furthermore, the authors recognize that emotions are essentially subjective, and sometimes irrational. However, they play an important role in the shaping of patterns of urban regional behavior. As such, recognizing these patterns not only helps to define the roots of the City of Johannesburg, but contributes also to the critical task of managing citizen participation as part of the ongoing task of managing the brand reputation of the city.

Chapter 9   Case E: Turning a Gemstone into a Diamond – A Green Design and Branding Strategy for the City of Bucharest

Iulia Gramon-Suba and Chris Holt continue the theme of sustainability. Writing from an academic perspective, they consider socially responsible design and education to be the main factors for nullifying existing negative opinions and creating a green city brand strategy for Bucharest. This chapter presents the key findings of an audit which reveals the respondents' deep dissatisfaction and negative perception of the city's environmental situation. The same study findings also showed that a one-size-fits-all approach fails to produce the desired improvements. Instead, place-specific contexts call for tailor-made strategies. The Bucharest case study is situated against the backdrop of green city brand strategies which have been successfully implemented elsewhere. While these settings are different, they reveal a common pattern: that people need to discover for themselves that sustainable development plays an important role in the improvement of their quality of life. A place which manages to balance its economy, ecology and social equity can become sustainable and more attractive for its inhabitants, investors, businesses and tourists. The chapter concludes with the presentation of an environmental design-led city brand strategy which relies on an ongoing co-creative improvement process aimed at tackling Bucharest's current environmental issues.

PART 3 CHAPTERS ON PARTICULAR PLACE BRAND THEMES

This part shares perspectives and reflections on facilitating the implementation of place brand themes by practitioners. It covers two areas. Chapters 10 and 11 examine the risk of stereotyping and the significance of levering the green economy to build reputation, while Chapters 12 and 13 look at the branding issue of using "freeware" in the cultural production context.

Chapter 10   Overcoming the Risk of Stereotypes – Sustainable Place Branding Asks for Strategic Communications

Written by Roland Schatz, from a practitioner's perspective, this chapter presents an account of the creation and "stickiness" of stereotypes. The author describes how regions, cities or countries are typically perceived and associated with a single impression, an event or a tradition. For example, when asked, most would associate Pisa with the world-famous leaning tower, reduce Vietnam to a war which ended 40 years ago and the Middle East as a source of terror and conflict (though these have been on the wane until the recent Arab Spring uprisings). Instead, Pisa is a diverse Italian town. In 2011 Vietnam served as an eye-opener to many, as one of the "Next 11" of the world's growth regions, which is expected to experience the highest levels of economic expansion after Brazil, Russia, India, China and South Africa. And the people in Syria, Egypt, Tunisia, Libya, Bahrain, Yemen, etc. are astounding not only the experts in the White House, Paris and Berlin with respect to their steadfastness and creativity with which they made the season of spring a permanent condition. Stereotypes have always been dangerous, but surprises have increased in recent years. Not only governments, but also the media, have had to deal with the question: who is responsible for the premises that politicians, economists and the media use to underpin their decision-making? If they seemingly know so little about "the other", or if the little that they know is now more often fundamentally incorrect, what value do the measures possess that they have taken and sold to citizens as if they were concerned with responsible decision-making?

Chapter 11   Do National Green Reputations Matter? The Global Green Economy Index and Implications for Stakeholders in the Green Economy

Jeremy Tamanini also writes from a practitioner's perspective of his experiences as the founder of Dual Citizen Inc. The focus is on the tools available to country brand managers for measuring and evaluating the success, or lack thereof, of their strategic and tactical nation branding and their efforts at country reputation management. Tamanini argues that until recently measurement frameworks employed different methodologies to look at generalized conceptions of country "brands" or "reputations". The chapter highlights the perspective, methodology and results related to the Global Green Economy Index, a specialized product designed to assess both the perceptions and performance of 27 national and city green economies. Its author argues that green reputations are an increasingly important factor defining overall country brands and, as a result, that national and city leaders face a growing incentive to improve upon or consolidate their "green" reputations. The chapter concludes with the claim that nations and cities which lay the groundwork today for intelligent green strategies and develop branding and communications plans to support them will be rewarded with recognition, investment and increased tourism.

Chapter 12   Branding Brazilian Slums through "Freeware" Cultural Production – The Case of Rio de Janeiro

This chapter by Antonio Paolo Russo is from an academic perspective and reflects on a "cultural industry model" which has an important potential for local development. It examines the salient characteristics of the network of independent cultural producers of Brazilian slums. Plagued by poverty and crime *favelas* have come to encapsulate the worst aspects of chaotic urban growth in Latin American cities. Maybe more so in Rio de Janeiro than in any other Brazilian or Latin American cities, *favelas* are nevertheless important components of an urban cultural landscape of outstanding value, though they are just as difficult to conceptualize as spaces of creative expression, according to a peculiar model anchored on freeware and hacker culture and receiving the support of the federal government's cultural policy. This model made a remarkable change to the way *favelas* have come to be "legitimized" by metropolitan society over and above the criminalizing discourses of mainstream commercial media. The free cultural products of *favelas* promote community pride, recognition and visibility, and ultimately inclusion, but also job creation in its peculiar consumption filière (production for consumption), especially when the potential as "tourist brand" is taken into account. The chapter concludes that Rio's current evolution could serve as a template for other deprived urban landscapes in countries that are achieving fast growth and a transition to a post-industrial economy at the expenses of inclusion. It also opens the field to other experiments in social re-engineering "at the margin" with great potential to engender powerful brands of sustainable development, which should be considered and actively supported by progressive urban politics.

Chapter 13 Improved Public Infrastructure and Sustainable Place Branding

Keith Dinnie writes from a combined practitioner and academic perspective. This chapter examines the role that improved public infrastructure can play in sustainable place branding, demonstrating that city brands are built not only through marketing communications but more importantly through tangible evidence guided by the principles of good urban design. The author presents the case studies of Valladolid (Spain), Riyadh and the Arnhem/Nijmegen city region (the Netherlands) as illustrative examples of cities that have followed such a path. The chapter concludes that public infrastructure can play a part in sustainable place branding but so far has had an undervalued role. By way of three cases it provides tangible evidence that improved public infrastructure guided by the principles of urban design can contribute powerfully to the achieving of city branding objectives such as attracting residents, investors and tourists.

Conclusion

This is the final chapter and concentrates on future developments and areas of interest. Robert Govers and Frank M. Go write from a combined consultant and academic perspective. Which theoretical patterns can be discerned from the multidisciplinary perspectives offered in this series with regard to spatial and societal changes? And what may be their consequences which help to bridge theoretical deficiencies in the place branding debate and the gap between principles and "just place brand" practice? Our response to this query is framed in the "model of balanced centricity", including the trade-offs that need to be made between measures of performance, that is efficiency (doing things "right"), equity (doing the "right" things) and effectiveness (doing the "right" things "right").

INTRODUCTION

Frank M. Go and Robert Govers

Was Adam Smith's *Wealth of Nations* wrong? Jane Jacobs (1984) thinks so. She claims that cities rather than nations have been the constituent elements of a developing economy since the dawn of civilization through "explosive" import replacement. Cities are transformed through a variety of material, socio-economic and symbolic interventions, manifest amongst others in place brands, to become exports; and these, in turn, finance imports. For example, growth machine theory attributes the role of the capability of business elites to the use of public resources for achieving their own private objectives. In contrast, location theory is concerned with the micro-economics of space, taking input costs and transportation costs of finished goods and services to markets, particularly those with a favorable cost structure, into account as the stimulus of economic growth. On the other hand institutional theory holds that urban and regional economic activities driving growth are embedded in social networks and focus on the interactions between firms rather than within individual firms.

As inseparable as mushrooms and mycelia, place brands and networks demonstrate a reciprocity for sharing prosperity, as opposed to an economy of self-sufficient units. Therefore, economics will take investors and stakeholders only so far in valuing the place brand's growth options, prompting the question: Is the economist's or historian's model more realistic? The former "approaches choice making in terms of optimization, which conditions are rarely ever met, [whereas the latter] follows a historical actor who is grappling with intractable choices" (Offer 2007, p. 5). Kondratieff wave theory points to a relationship between innovation and the long waves of economic growth and justifies inquiry into how the "golden ages" of cities came about. Across the ages these cities differed in respect of government structure, the location of control and decision-making, but all were capitalist in nature and the global hubs of their time. Out of their network of interlinked urban economies came new artistic, technological creativity, new ways of organization and new production forms. These generated wealth and became magnets for the attraction of talented "outsiders". Not belonging to the established order of power and prestige, they gave a voice to society's discontent, sparked the creative drive and contributed to the representation of culture, which is indivisible from place branding. Fast forward and we observe how information technologies and aviation links have increased the "extensity, intensity, velocity of global flows and the impact propensity of inter-connectedness" (Held *et al.* 2000, p. 21), framed by the global value chain.

What is relevant to note here is not the basic technology per se, but how affordances of distributed, co-creative, technological, social and legal knowledge network solutions have impacted on the place branding process, turning places into creative hubs. Such hubs widen the place brand reputation over rivals, priming it for future growth, but also giving pause to rethinking the nature of rivalry in the global network context. This is particularly the case when not only the internal logic but also collaboration with a variety of stakeholders has proven important in achieving successful strategies. This raises a question regarding the direction of causality: did the place brand achieve its competitive identity consequent to systematic economic growth or, conversely, consequent to effective place branding? The answer to this issue of competitiveness depends on understanding parallel changes at both the company and regional cluster scale which, upon analysis, leads to an overarching challenge. How, despite the tensions that may exist between effectiveness and equality, between individual and collective interests, can the renaissance of the city be achieved through smart growth branding? The contributions in this volume and dedicated journals like *Place Branding and Public Diplomacy*, *Brand Management* and *Place Management and Development* suggest that three conditions under which value-upgrading is likely to happen already exist: (i) the growing significance of the knowledge-based economy; (ii) the global risk of climate change; and (iii) the increasing power of technologies and social media. Publications relating to each theme are summarized in Organization of the Book, while a linking thematic diagram is presented in Figure I.1.

UNRAVELING PLACE BRANDING: WHERE DO PLACE BRANDS DWELL?

As we travel more, cultures mingle and borders are blurring, our nationality, religion and gender should matter less. Instead, the way we perceive, live and what we fear is increasingly dictated by our identity. A corollary of this may have been that researchers shifted their focus from place marketing (Kotler and Gertner 2002; Hankinson 2004; Kavaratzis 2004; Dinnie 2010; Govers and Go 2009) to understanding places as brands and how the different demands of investment, tourism, export policy, etc. can be integrated in the place branding process. Beyond the production and consumption debate, critical cultural theorists such as Harvey, Urry and Zukin have

FIGURE I.1 | **Place brand symbolism and the interrelating socio-cultural, economic and political dynamics**

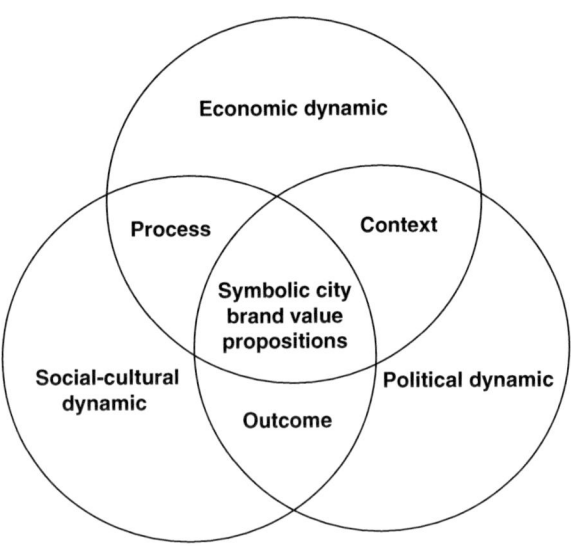

addressed social justice issues raised by differential consumer access to place, understood as a marketing commodity. They deal only incidentally with place branding issues as such and, insofar as they do so, indirectly. Instead their critiques address the impact of branding, in the broadest sense of the word, particularly referring to how capital investment and the socially constructed process generates growth and configures modern cities.

Evidence gathered by Homer-Dixon (1999) from a wide range of international research projects has resulted in the development of a detailed model of the sources of environmental scarcity. For example, he refers to water shortages in China, population growth in sub-Saharan Africa, and land distribution in Mexico to illustrate that scarcities stem from the degradation and depletion of renewable resources, the increased demand for these resources, and/or their unequal distribution. Homer-Dixon argues that these scarcities can lead to deepened poverty, large-scale migrations, sharpened social cleavages, and weakened institutions. A consequence, partly of scarcity, is the ongoing turmoil in many African and Asian countries, which may spread in due course from the periphery to the core. Faced with conditions of resource-scarce cities, nation-states and supra-national levels jockey to strengthen their positions. The latter raises direct or related issues that affect or are affected by place branding, the opportunities of geographically entangled brands, and also their contradictions (Gotham 2007) that are "closely related to spatially uneven development through the articulation of and reinforcement of economic and social inequalities and unequal and competitive socio-spatial relations and divisions of labour" (Pike 2009, p. 619). This side of branding justifies considering the ethos of smart, sustainable and inclusive growth.

Place, Branding, Smart Growth and Sustainability

The discipline of geography emphasizes that economic and material forces explain the making of place. Three phenomena have radically altered the economic, social and political dynamics (see Figure I.1) within urban regions. These are, first, the new means of consumption; second, the "signature" architecture; and third, staged mega-events. Their complex interplay of identity constructing *processes*, micro–macro relationships, representations and symbolization comes about through a "dialectic interaction between 'hard' technology/infrastructure and 'soft' concepts" (Normann 2001, p. 86). This in turn brings about spatial restructuring (*context*) as well as concerns about the disparity between public investment and private profits, and environmental and social justice critiques (*outcomes*). Though definitions of terminology of the field of interest should arise from later analysis we suggest that there is a confusion regarding the fundamental terminology. Therefore we will define the relevant terms at the start.

Space and Place

An important element of Giddens's (1991) analysis of self-identity and society is that in the pre-modern era the "when" markers (time and space) were connected to the "where" (place) not only of "social conduct but to the substance of that conduct itself" (p. 16). But in the modern age, space has become an interval of distance seen as absolutely objective in nature. It is hard to arrive at a singular definition of place, because the literature is not coherent in character. In this section we do not attempt to assess the effectiveness of these different traditions but consider the more general question of what is meant by the term "place" and how we can selectively define it for purposes of understanding how place making occurs, including beyond the process of branding.

There are different ways to define "place". The ontological perspective delineates it as the existence of a particular point or part of space or of a surface. The epistemological perspective refers to a manner of knowing or looking at a geographical point, such as a town or city. Both the natural and social sciences emphasize that the production of new knowledge is embraced or rejected in specific social, political and economic contexts (Ziman 1994).

While neither of these definitions does justice to explaining the complexity of the place concept, the latter evokes a two-pronged question consequent on possible "distance dispersion" (Van Fenema 2002, p. 21) that is relevant to defining what is meant by "local". First, to what extent do inherent place characteristics represent either a co-located situation (e.g. a workplace) or one involving considerable regional distance (in selected cases where small countries could be reasonably viewed as local)? Second, to what extent are the interests and agendas of stakeholders compatible with collaborating in the place branding process and its perceived outcomes? Yi-Fu Tuan's theory of place is positioned as "a break or pause in the movement – the pause that allows a location to become a centre of meaning with space organized around it" (1978, p. 14). Relph (1976), another geographer in the humanist tradition and Tuan's contemporary, refers to sense of place as the ability to appreciate the distinctive qualities of places, which is, in part, dependent on cultural context.

At the same time Relph opines that the prevailing medium of communication (McLuhan 2003), involving the movement of goods, people and ideas from place to place, designed to overcome the constraints of bodily space and time, undermines place, resulting in the "spread of placelessness" (Relph 1976, p. 90). In contrast, theorist Doreen Massey (1997) conceptualizes space and place in both everyday life and wider politics. She rejects the humanist geographers' introverted and exclusionary notion of place. Instead, she insists that places should not be considered in terms of boundedness but rather in a global sense as the product of processes that extend beyond the confines of a specific place. The social construction tradition addresses the changing spatiality of social practices and emphasizes the heterogeneous and multilevel nature of social exchange. That the epistemological perspective of knowledge is embodied in people and their culture is relevant to an adaptation of Zukin's (1991, p. 54) view of place as "both specific representations of a more general notion of place [which] expresses how a spatially connected group of people mediate the demands of cultural identity, state power, and capital accumulation". From Zukin's (1995) perspective, place making resembles a socially constructed process which configures cities largely through capital investment designed to generate economic growth via cultural tourism. The continued traditional growth ethos underpins and supports modern urban life. George Simmel (1911) summarized how this came to pass: "we were liberated from the chains of subjective dependence and thereby allowed a much greater degree of individual liberty. But this was achieved at the expense of treating others in objective and instrumental terms" (cited in Harvey 1989, p. 26).

Some of the intrinsic characteristics of place make it difficult to control and manage place in a direct and straightforward sense as one might a commercial organization. These characteristics include the following. First, its *inseparability*, not only from mobility as the "dynamic equivalent of place" (Cresswell 2006, p. 3) but also from urban governance, which "cannot be isolated from city politics" (Braun 2011, p. 258). Second, its *dynamism*, i.e. if we think of "space as that which allows movement, then place is pause; each pause in movement makes it possible for location to be transformed into place" (Tuan 1977, p. 6). Third, its *variety and diversity* in terms of the manifold ways in which places are experienced, which render abstract analysis unproductive (Relph 1976, p. 45). Fourth, its *ambiguity*, i.e. places tend to be ontologically conceptualized as objects, while humans use selected spatial elements to socially construct places (Boisen et al. 2011, p. 137), which is a knowledge perspective derived from practice-based epistemology. Fifth, its *susceptibility*, i.e. the identity of places can be easily expropriated "by third parties … for instance, New York has had its brand identity applied to the New York/New York casino in Las Vegas" (Roulac 1999, p. 63). Finally, its *fuzziness*, i.e. "while many place products have clear spatial definition – in terms of, for example, administrative boundaries – others can be more informally defined and often have administrative jurisdictions and elements of contestation" (Medway et al. 2008, cited in Warnaby 2009a, p. 407).

Michel de Certeau (1984, p. 117) considers, as does Lefebvre (1991), that space is produced through interaction and practical undertakings: "a place (lieu) is the order (of whatever kind) in accord with which the elements are distributed in relationships of co-existence … a place is thus an instant configuration of positions. It implies an indication of stability". While our current knowledge may not be amenable to direct control, Tuan suggests that differentiated space becomes place as we get to know it better and endow it with value. The ideas "space" and "place" require each other for definition (1977, p. 6). Tuan (1991, p. 684), particularly, underscores how the often ignored role of language in research contributes toward the making of place in a wide range of situations and cultural contexts:

> words alone, used in an appropriate situation, can have the power to render objects, formerly invisible because unattended, visible, and impart to them a certain character: thus a mere rise on a flat surface becomes something far more – a place that promises to open up to other places – when it is named "Mount Prospect".

His observation resonates with the contemporary significance of "word-of-mouth" and "word-of-mouse", acting both as solicited and unsolicited organic agents in the place branding model (Govers and Go 2009, p. 41). Rather than suggesting that place be conceptualized as a self-contained arena, we are instead advocating an approach closer to Massey's notion of place as unbounded, open and hybrid in character. The same underscores Hall's (1998) suggestion that the infrastructure of the Internet and the World Wide Web provides a foundation for new industries, enabling technology-mediated interactions of global proportions. Therefore, we emphasize the significance of developing analyses for understanding how the meaning of place branding dwells in the capability of interlocking micro-, meso- and macro-perspectives (Layton 2011), which lies beyond earlier territorialized conceptions such as "centre–periphery" and "nation–international order" binaries (Long 1997, p. 7).

Place Marketing Defined

The key assumption of marketing theory is that the customer's needs should be central and precede and inform the marketing of goods, ideas and services. It is based on the premise that no organization can survive unless customers purchase what it has on offer. Put differently, marketing uses consumer needs as its guiding principle for the operations of an organization. Translated to our field of interest place marketing seeks "to influence target audiences to behave in some positive manner with respect to products and services associated with a specific place" (American Marketing Association 1995, cited by Govers 2011, p. 228). A marketing approach which is not coordinated with brand equity building may alienate relevant multi-stakeholder representation (ibid., p. 230).

Brand and Branding

While the terms "brand" and "branding" are commonly used in everyday vocabulary, they tend also to be misinterpreted. More than a logo or a name, a brand name is ideally linked to the organization's identity (Kapferer 2004), encapsulating the full organizational personality, both of the tangible and the intangible aspects, represented by the "promise-of-value" (Kotler and Gertner 2002). Its projected image serves as the interface between the organization and its audiences and is typically applied in a narrative format to a myriad of objects, including a person (Rachel Carson), a business (VW Blue Motion), a cause (War Child), a city ("London 2012 – the most sustainable Games ever") and country (New Zealand's world-leading sustainable tourism credentials). Gradually brands have become the dominant channel of communications across the planet for products, services, ideas, celebrities, countries and cities. Cities are brands and affect the way their brand is projected and how audiences perceive and interact with it. What has changed in today's brand landscape is that shifts in global economic power and societal trends have influenced brand ubiquity. In a "sea of homogeneity" place branding is a much sought after strategic compass for informing urban/regional regeneration, strengthening a sense of local identity (Govers and Go 2010, p. 123) and complementing place marketing strategy. The growth of the social media in particular has rendered communities immersive and caused decision-makers to redraw geographical, industrial and ethical boundaries. In turn, this has caused the information order to become more "bottom up, distributed and dynamic" (Fouts 2010, p. 120). In the emerging landscape brands express ideas that can no longer be controlled. Instead, the simultaneously global and local (i.e. "glocal") context is characterized by interconnectedness affording partnerships. On an applied level brands dwell in the hearts and minds of stakeholders, citizens and consumers. Ultimately, their dialogue can serve as the potential glue to tie a place brand together in an inclusive, consistent and legitimate manner.

This raises the question as to what the salient brand attributes are and whether these may be impacted on by the emerging conditions of resource scarcity and to what extent they are sustainable. The place brand "cannot deliver value, but only offer value propositions", according to Vargo and Lusch (2008, p. 7). Their service dominant logic can be applied to integrate cultural policy and urban integration because "any form of urban planning is today, by definition, a form of cultural planning in its broadest sense, as it cannot but take into account people's religious and linguistic identities, their modes of behavior and aspirations, and the contributions they make to the urban tapestry" (Worpole and Greenhalgh 1999, p. 4; cited in Evans 2003). So, an overarching consideration is how to develop an integrated framework which involves the private and public (local, regional and supra-national) sectors in the co-creative place branding effort (Prahalad and Ramaswamy 2004; Go and Govers 2011, p. xxviii) of delivering value propositions, which refines further the scope of activity, workable processes and enumeration of the brand outcomes.

Why Look at Smart Growth Now?

Historically, two broad perspectives can be distinguished that fuel contemporary scientific and societal debates regarding the "growth" theme. On the one side there is the "anti-growth" camp which draws, among others, on the thoughts of Thomas Malthus, Richard Layard, John Kenneth Galbraith, Avner Offer and Richard Wilkinson and Kate Pickett. These thinkers claim, albeit in different ways, that the well-being of society lags its economic progress. On the other side there is the "pro-growth" camp consisting of such luminaries as Adam Smith, Joseph Schumpeter, Julian Simon, David Landes and Johan Norberg. Their ideas advocate, broadly, that capitalism and more growth is necessary to turn poverty into history. And there is a third perspective derived from physics which goes beyond earlier conceptions of social science based "anti-growth" and "pro-growth" dichotomies.

According to researchers at the Santa Fe Institute (SFI), scaling and sustainability with an emphasis on cities can be synthesized in the interdisciplinary quantitative organizational and dynamical aspects of human and social organizations. Underpinned by "hard" science perspectives the comparative studies conducted there on biological and social systems reveal insights relevant to understanding the phenomenon of growth. In particular, when organisms double in size, other factors only increase by factors of less than one. This implies that the bigger the organism, the slower its growth. For instance, while the number of heartbeats per lifespan of elephants and mice is the same, the former have a slower heartbeat. In contrast, when cities are scaled by a factor of 1.15, not only do urban areas grow on a per capita basis by 15 percent annually in terms of wealth, patents, infrastructure and traffic, but also in terms of pollution and disease. This observation has led to a universal law of urban growth: the bigger the city, the faster its growth (Bettencourt *et al.*, 2008). This law is intimately tied to economic development, driving the projected doubling of the urban population of emerging economies with profound consequences for social organization, land use and patterns of human behavior, and results in "a major challenge worldwide ... to understand and predict how changes in social organization and dynamics resulting from urbanization will impact the interactions between nature and society" (ibid., p. 7301). It is within this framework that the integrative analytical approach treats these interactions between various styles and models. It is more dynamic and considerate of history, institutions and geography, because knowledge does not move in a frictionless way among economic actors. New ideas and the adaptive conduct of societies to changing economic and technological circumstances are a precondition to sustainable growth.

One such idea is "smart growth", for which there is no single definition. Its meaning depends on context, perspective and timeframe. Van Assche *et al.* in Chapter 4 indicate that from the European perspective the smart growth concept is neither special nor unique, because of a particular tradition of urban reconstruction and development. The smart growth literature, mostly American in origin, has antecedents in different planning perspectives and therefore lacks a universally accepted definition of "smart growth". However, the Urban Land Institute defines smart growth as "growth that is economically sound, environmentally friendly, and supportive of community livability-growth that enhances our quality of life" (ULI 1999, p. 1). Smart growth is not "no growth"; it includes some of the following broad characteristics: "development is economically viable and preserves open space and natural resources; land use planning is comprehensive, integrated and regional; public, private and nonprofit sectors collaborate on growth and development issues to achieve mutually beneficial outcomes …; urban centers and neighborhoods are integral components of a healthy regional economy" and ecology (ibid., p. 3). Looking at smart growth now makes good sense given the global risks, particularly the macro-imbalances and fiscal crisis, state fragility and, especially, the economic disparity that stimulates short-term responses that undermine long-term sustainability and, in turn, endanger the reputational risk of place brands (Go and Govers 2011, p. xxviii).

Is Sustainability a Pipe Dream?

While the 1987 UN conference definition "meet present needs without compromising the ability of future generations to meet their needs" (WCED 1987) provides a vision it fails to delineate specific human and environmental parameters for modeling and measuring. The following definitions are more specific (see www.ejamn.org/defining-sustainability):

1. "Sustainable means using methods, systems and materials that won't deplete resources or harm natural cycles" (Rosenbaum, 1993);

2. Sustainability "identifies a concept and attitude in development that looks at a site's natural land, water, and energy resources as integral aspects of the development" (Vieira, 1993);

3. "Sustainability integrates natural systems with human patterns and celebrates continuity, uniqueness and place making" (Early, 1993).

From the above it follows that the *site* or the environmental context represents an important variable for working definitions of sustainability. Furthermore, the choice for smart growth is inextricably tied to social, economic and political dynamics which converge toward the place branding construct, the site-specific attributes embedded in it, and the knowledge of place branding and its relationship with sustainable development. To understand the relevance of sustainability in relation to place branding, much depends on what stakeholders have accomplished to date and how far they intend to carry their commitment, jointly. Sustainability does not have to be a pipe dream for organizations, whatever the size, sector or location, at least when it is properly reported in a tested framework for sustainability. The Global Reporting Initiative provides such a useful reporting framework (GRI 2000–11).

CITY HUBS: CENTERS OF GRAVITY IN THE GLOBAL VALUE CHAIN

Our interest in analyzing the strategies of urban regions within the context of the global rivalry of cities started in the late 1990s with an importance-performance analysis of Beijing as an International Meeting Destination (Go and Zhang 1997), followed by an investigation into how to achieve competitiveness in European tourist destinations (Go and Govers 2000) and a study on the so-called Dutch Delta-Metropolis, consisting of the spatial structure of the major cities situated in the western part of the Netherlands, including Rotterdam, Amsterdam, The Hague and Utrecht (Go *et al.* 2003). The research aims at developing tools to increase the knowledge dynamics in an effort to combine the "assets" of four medium sized cities so as to gain agglomeration advantages of a larger cluster. Under the heading of "vital cities" and in collaboration with local authorities, the research team engaged in testing the best practices and identifying the performance characteristics that emerged, in particular in round tables with local stakeholders.

Another step involved the research team building on the new measures that were developed in a wider project that addressed measures of "innovativeness" developed for Dutch circumstances. The effectiveness of the stakeholder dialog resided in its potential (amongst others) to create a "dynamic hub" in the Dutch Delta Metropolis (ibid.). In collaboration with groups of involved local stakeholders, which consisted of home-based as well as host-based companies alongside local communities, governments, trade unions and research institutes – a number of actual dialogs were organized to determine what could constitute a dynamic hub which would also display characteristics of social proficiency. While the study concerned the positioning of the Dutch Delta Metropolis in the wider context of global cities and reference was made to the term "identity", the notion of branding in the urban context hardly surfaced at the time. However, the study clearly showed how utterly disjointed and unrelated the four medium sized cities were. Their division rendered them incapable of joining forces, embracing the overall vision and exploiting advantages of scale and scope. So, this case illustrated the place-specificity of political power on the part of the four cities which declined to be seen as "sub-brands" and which kick-started a process for building trustworthy relations and identifying salient success criteria for provenance associations that could aid the levering of core values within the umbrella brand (Anholt 2004, cited in Iversen and Hem 2008).

Another action research project attempted to understand the role of local identities in the face of globalization. To this end various studies were carried out (Govers and Go 2003; 2004), which culminated in "Virtual Tourism Destination Image: Glocal Identities Constructed, Perceived and Experienced" (Govers 2005) and ultimately *Place Branding: Glocal, Virtual and Physical Identities, Constructed, Imagined and Experienced* (Govers and Go 2009). The study applied an innovative computer-supported content analysis and its results compared Dubai to other destinations, including Flanders, Florida, Morocco, Singapore and Wales. It indicated that gaps existed due to a friction between Dubai's rapid development as a global hub and its strong local identity and image.

In particular, through the integration of the local and global duality in the dynamic place image formation model a triadic tension became obvious between place identity, its projection and the perceived image of consumers. In turn, this tension, which becomes short-circuited during the travel experience in the global supply chain that we are questioning, has been driven by the goods dominant logic (Vargo and Lusch 2006), for over a century in the US and the UK, of real estate practice which has influenced such practice in other countries. It caused Maas *et al.* (2009) to ask: Are our dreams undermining the city? What is an urban vision and do we need one?

New thinking regarding temporal and spatial conventions and mobility, underpinned by technologies, render interconnectedness possible for anyone at any time for networked smart growth. This implies that potential solutions, but also threats to city brands, can only be effectively explored when the oscillating of foci are brought together within the multi-layered framework. Within this wider context, including the macro-, meso- and microscale, it would be mistaken to treat branding as a simple process of adding value by way of attaching a brand label or logo to a specific city. Instead, the branding process concerns a series of contestations and negotiations in the layered global value chain (Clancy 1998) of service provision, involving economic, socio-cultural and political dynamics which entail specific arguments. For example, is there a shared strategic vision on chain development? Is there a strategic fit in terms of brand associations among important stakeholders? And are there reputational risks involved (Go and Govers 2011, p. xii)?

These questions necessitate analysis of service flows and linkages following the creative processes of service value propositions and delivery into arenas of production, consumption and criticisms (see Conclusion) to identify those factors constituting user preferences and brand equity. Networks have brought about a defining shift in market structure and render reconceptualization of city branding from a multilevel perspective essential in both research and practice, in particular to understand the external effects of the "human capital" model (Lucas 1988) on micro-realities manifest in the practice-based city branding perspective at different knowledge and skill levels. To what extent might the latter impact on the place branding process and the place brand? Why have researchers been rather silent on the potential damage, including social inequalities that might result from city branding output? This in the face of evidence which suggests that equality is better for everyone (Wilkinson and Pickett 2010).

Why Is Smart Growth Relevant to Place Branding?

City branding is seen to function as a fundamentally affirmative device. For example, brand thinking and brand asset management have been dominant aspects of "American society and even changed the nature and dynamic of US politics" (Ham 2002, p. 250). Yet, Wilkinson and Pickett (2010) raise fundamental questions, particularly with regard to the changing relationship between material success and social failure that is increasingly characteristic of American society. In addition Pike indicates how the geographic entanglement of brands and branding intertwines with spatially uneven development consequent to their underlying dynamic of differentiation "predicated on the search for, exploitation and (re)production of economic and social inequalities over space and time" (2009, p. 620). The latter is evident in the USA and the UK which display a bigger gap between income equality and trust (Wilkinson and Pickett 2010, p. 52) than other industrialized societies. That this gap is real illustrates the image of poverty and inequality that dominated national and global news coverage of New Orleans during 2005 in the aftermath of Hurricane Katrina (Gotham 2007, p. 844):

> Like all variants of urban place promotion and marketing, urban branding is particularly silent about issues of social justice, equity, and inclusion. For tourism professionals, the question of how to represent post-Katrina New Orleans does not include poor people, the homeless and the displaced. The rebranded city increasingly reflects a series of carefully crafted branded images of rich history, delicious cuisine, and entertaining music. New logo design, brand (re) positioning, image segmentation and targeting, and other place marketing strategies fabricate an entertaining image that is insulated from the reality of life on the street.

In the globalizing society urban regions are not only becoming more reliant for opportunities on inter-regional flows, but simultaneously also more vulnerable to global risks (Go and Govers 2011). Climate change is likely to impose a toll on urban regions in the form of natural and man-made disasters. In addition, patterns of interactions between regions are experiencing rapid changes as a result of dramatic shifts in production and consumption patterns, advances in communication technologies and the emergence of new forms of harnessing knowledge and organizing collective action.

The configuration approach considers the "entangled geographies of brands and branding" from "a novel but relatively overlooked point of entry" (Pike 2009, p. 621), which bring to the fore considerations of the economic, socio-cultural and political impacts of branding.

However, the literature currently lacks "a more in-depth analysis of the governance setting in which city branding takes place, as well as the impact of specific choices made in the branding process that are particularly relevant for the implementation" (Braun 2011, p. 3). To this end Braun (ibid., p. 9) identifies eight factors that contribute to the including of spatial layers and which can (positively or negatively) affect the implementation of city branding as follows. The first four factors directly link to the context:

> the majority view on city branding; the inclusion of city branding in the political priorities; unambiguous political responsibility; and stakeholder management ... these factors are especially important for reinforcing the significance of city branding in relation to the city's traditional policies ... The remaining four factors link to the urban governance context through strategic choices regarding the substance of the brand and the approach to building the brand: genuine and credible city branding; umbrella city branding versus sub-brands; strategic co-branding with strong brands in the city; and the balancing act between distinctiveness and wide support for the brand. (Ibid., pp. 9–10)

Smart growth potential depends on, first, making the appropriate judgments according to the relevant performance measures, which lie in the overlap of three factors: efficiency (doing things "right"), equity (doing the "right" things) and effectiveness (doing the "right" things "right") (Tulder 1999, p. 25, cited in Go and Govers 2010, p. xi). Second, it depends on configuring the variables appropriately, i.e. "getting it all together" in a balanced-centric manner, which is a priority for future city branding (ibid.).

Diagnosing Metropolitan Growth and Potential City Brand Responses

While city branding from an objectivist knowledge perspective is considered a fundamentally affirmative device, we argue that the former overlooks the multi-layered interdependencies to which city branding theory and practice are subject. These are, first, a top-down legislative framework; second, participatory relations; and, third, the influence of the financial world. This raises an important question: to what extent, if any, does city branding depend on scale and scope advantages for attaining effective performance? In this section we present an empirical diagnosis based on McKinsey's MGI Cityscope (McKinsey 2011) so as to identify some important indicators and the underlying premises. The aim is to come to a selection of the most pervasive economic and institutional drivers and diagnose, where possible, to what extent these may complement or substitute one another.

We also draw on a typology of the European City (EU Commission 2007, cited by Clark and Huxley 2009) to comprehend the position of European Union cities within the emerging global system of cities and its implications for city branding practice. The rapid growth of cities around the world, now harboring more than 50 percent of the planet's population, is marked by specific characteristics. As boundaries evaporate, new challenges are raised for territorial and business actors alike. Few seem well prepared for their impact and for levering city branding as a tool kit for steering the drivers toward smart growth outcomes.

First, according to McKinsey (2011), 1.5 billion people presently reside in 600 cities, representing 22 percent of the world's population. In this top 600, measured by Gross Domestic Product (GDP), 380 cities, located in the developed world, accounted in 2007 for US$30 trillion, or 50 percent of global GDP. That same year, 100 cities in the top 600 generated $21 trillion of the world's total GDP (ibid., p. 1). Furthermore, 190 cities located in North America contributed 20 percent of the world's total GDP; the 220 largest cities in developing regions another 20 percent (China's cities 4 percent and Latin America's largest cities another 4 percent); finally 23 cities with more than 10 million residents accounted for 14 percent of the world's GDP in 2007.

Accordingly, the salient characteristics of metropolitan agglomeration are concentration in clustered network effects that, in turn, spur economic growth (McKinsey 2011, p. 11).

The historical growth of metropolitan cities has lead to issues of, most noticeably, controlling power and immigration. More specifically, 25 cities effectively control most of the world's financial transactions at the top of the hierarchy (Corbridge *et al.* 1994). The latter has its origin in special regimes that have attracted foreign direct investment since the mid-1900s and which has been adopted by 143 countries (Sassen 2006). A corollary of this can be observed in anachronistic or out-of-place activities, people and objects that are consequent on large-scale immigration, increasing income and occupational polarization. While global cities are the sites of incredible riches they also portray increasing *disparities* in income and occupation, due to increased earnings inequality.

How are cities responding to the challenge of disparities? Many employ branding strategies for purposes of differentiation aimed at international audiences. But to what extent do such strategies take into consideration insights into the "place-specific circuits of power linked to society, economy and the state" (Yüksel *et al.* 2005)? Such insights are necessary for the purposes of, first, "asset creation, asset protection and asset promotion" (Van Assche and Lo 2011, p. 116); second, planning a systematic organized response to critical issues, including those "of democracy and accountability"; and, third, "the distribution of benefits and costs from the policy processes and policy outcomes" (Yüksel *et al.* 2005).

The branding of Santa Fe in Mexico illustrates how the articulation of its brand connectedness with the world economy had an adverse effect, which caused social contrasts between the elites and marginalized groups and caused social inequalities to intensify, raising the question: to what extent does place branding as a pragmatic activity dodge "complex social forces that are shaping the urban context" (Negrete 2009, p. 33). While place brands represent the embodiment of symbolic meanings, branding serves as the process by which such meanings and symbols are reproduced. The political dynamics continue to be driven by hierarchical command and control within a silo-oriented regime of power. These are designed to serve the incumbent actors' agendas, interests and objectives and therefore often fail to capture the value-in-context, which in turn results in suboptimal, inclusive, brand performance.

Second, according to McKinsey (2011), looking for growth results in a list of the so-called middleweight cities, including around 230 that do not make it into today's top 600, all of them located in emerging regions with current populations of between 150,000 and 10 million. These middleweights include many relatively unfamiliar cities such as Ahmedabad, Huambo, Fushun, Medan and Vina del Mar (ibid., p. 2). Two characteristics can be distinguished that render the middleweight cities important. First, they outperform most megacities in terms of household growth (ibid., p. 15); second, the growth hurdle of urban centers is their inability to keep pace with and manage their expansion (ibid., p. 12).

How are cities responding to the challenge of being unable to keep pace with their growth? Networks are fundamental to the growth of cities in that they afford access and global interconnectedness supported by transport and information technologies, which can be understood as time saving devices. However, networks simultaneously enable and restrict. Presently, the hegemony of network cities is evident in for example the "global structure of the internet" (Townsend 2001). The Internet has also become the medium for technological innovation in city marketing and the city branding process. Also particularly noticeable are the traffic flows between "hub cities" linked through networks or systems of communication, in which passenger and goods transport have nurtured urban growth; though, where urban expansion has been unbridled, e.g. in Cairo, Los Angeles, Beijing, Paris, Moscow, Mumbai and São Paolo, it has led to a story of energy, transport or water systems in crisis, which impede further growth.

At another level, post-industrial conurbations, including Leeds, Glasgow and Nottingham, have been able to adapt to external changes successfully. Other cities, however, such as Stoke-on-Trent wrestle with their reported incapability of addressing a "negative parochialism", which serves as the main explanation for its economic underperformance (Hallworth and Evans 2008, p. 210).

Typically, a decline in growth is followed by high unemployment, emigration and empty buildings and neglected brown fields. This, added to a lack of investment, results in a state of collective depression, a loss of hope for "better times" and a negative city brand image, placing many medium sized cities in an unfamiliar position and in search of a new role and identity. Small and medium sized cities tend to owe their identity, at least in part, to one or few local entrepreneurs. The sudden loss of a major employer does not only imply lost jobs, but also a loss of identity and, if not arrested, may cause the city brand image to spiral downward.

Highly competitive market regions rely on their identity to remain on the map. In this regard Warnaby (2009b, p. 216) underscores the emblematic role of transport infrastructure as "gateway, flagship and symbol". So, the role of transport infrastructure goes well beyond what Kotler *et al.* (1999) referred to as "infrastructure marketing". In this regard collective symbolic values can be leveraged in marketing communications, as illustrated by Denver International Airport, with its Teflon-coated roof which echoes the shape of the Rocky Mountains (Gordon 2008, p. 254, cited in Warnaby 2009b, p. 215).

But place brands are complex in nature, i.e. in terms of organizational mechanisms and the ways in which branding theory can be applied. Place branding researchers have largely overlooked the potential of the service dominant logic of marketing and its foundational premises (Brodie *et al.* 2006; Warnaby 2009a, p. 403) as a means to respond dynamically to multi-disciplinary perspectives and multi-layered spatial challenges that may be linked, e.g. to virtual and physical identities, which are constructed, imagined or experienced in glocal brands (Govers and Go 2009). The glocal approach can serve also to frame the unfolding processes of interterritorial branding, i.e. branding that crosses administrative boundaries (Pasquinelli 2012). For instance, the case of the Cruise Baltic (Lemmetyinen and Go 2010) represents a rich array of international actors from the ten countries around the Baltic Sea. It examines the various interactions within the tourism business network with the aim of transforming the Baltic marketing approach of regionally concentrated destination to one focused on the competitive global market. It illustrates how a linear process consisting of three temporal phases (initiated, integration and identification) result in achieving three levels of network outcomes which are functional, relational and symbolic cooperational.

Third, according to McKinsey (2011, p. 28) 22 of the 25 largest cities measured by GDP are located in developed economies, though as economic power is shifting eastward this signals a defining move in market structure in the first part of the 21st century. The urban landscape of Western Europe differs from that of North America (ibid., p. 29): the 168 Western European cities in the MGI Cityscope are more broadly spread across the region than are the cities of North America. Western Europe's leading cities have a combined GDP of $10 trillion today, accounting for 18 percent of global GDP. However, this represents only 60 percent of the region's overall GDP (compared with 82 percent in North America), reflecting the fact that smaller cities and rural areas continue to have more economic weight in Europe.

The contestation of boundaries is central to identity, and the enactment of new boundaries has been a cyclical and ongoing process since ancient times. Berthon and Hulbert (2003, p. 39) demonstrate how such cycles involve stages and are nested; thus, "boundary breaking" dissolves old boundaries; "boundary shaping" creates new ones; and "cultivating boundaries" provides care and maintenance for their productive use. Such cycles overlap rather than being discrete and "boundary breaking, shaping and cultivating may coexist at the level of the firm, market, and industry" (ibid. p. 39).

At the theoretical level the "current increasingly complex political situation where new places and regions are constantly created and branded" challenges researchers to consider the "character of places" from a spatial-temporal perspective (Boisen *et al.* 2011, p. 137). In particular, by questioning the "conceptualization of places having a distinct identity", this observation renders problematic the notion of identity within this "increasingly complex political situation". In the wake of the economic crisis, debtor states and cities are trying to manage domestic and international restructuring and the type of "solutions" which these patterns typically yield, which Boisen *et al.* (2011, p. 135) refer to as the "rise of new forms of spatial identities resulting in new places, and all places can be seen as having or being new brands". The resulting spatial identities often overlap, contradict or complement each other across existing territorial administrative levels (ibid.). This also raises important questions worth pursuing in order to understand place branding, not only as a multi-actor and multi-sector (public–private) process, but also as a multi-layered one.

Multi-layers of markets oscillate foci from a specific place brand at the mesolevel to a market at the macrolevel so as to "make the scalable influence of context more salient" (Chandler and Vargo 2011, p. 35). The latter refers to a city's openness to the world for drawing on socio-cultural and political dynamics so as to build economic viability and create employment through the social inclusion of culturally diverse groups. Business involvement with the local innovative environment and strategic dialogs and social institutions can be influenced by urban governance as a vehicle for demonstrating the intensions, actions and reactions of the stakeholders. Inasmuch as cluster market dynamics have distinct characteristics (McKinsey 2011, p. 34) it may be worthwhile on a more practical scale of city brand responses to invoke Freire's (2009) plea to lever "local stakeholders, including hotel employees and taxi drivers as a critical dimension for place brand building", as stereotyping by the local people conjures much of a place's image.

Beyond this prevailing eastward shift of power, "cities play very different roles in their host economies ... The evolution of urban areas tends to have regional characteristics in both developed and developing regions" (McKinsey 2011, p. 28). These impact on the dynamics of trade transactions, technology transfer and capital flows toward change. The autonomy and authority of national states has decreased and globalization has resulted in three distinct categories of European cities, which the State of European Cities has categorized as "international hubs, specialized poles and regional poles and within this typology 13 categories of cities can be distinguished" (EU Commission 2007, cited in Clark and Huxley 2009, pp. 7–8). Against the backdrop of wider environmental, social and economic indicators the diverse characteristics of the various city types can be used for benchmarking and identifying a possible development path for defining brand value propositions.

The first group – international hubs – are international centers with pan-European or even global influence. We distinguish between:

1. Knowledge hubs: these are key players in the global economy, positioned above the national urban hierarchy, at the forefront of industry, business and financial services, and based on high levels of talent and excellent connections to the rest of the world;

2. Established capitals: these are firmly positioned at the top of national urban hierarchies, with a diversified economic base and concentrations of wealth;
3. Re-invented capitals: these are champions of transition and engines of economic activity for the New Member States.

A second broad group are the specialized poles. These play a (potentially) important international role in at least some aspects of the urban economy:

1. National service hubs: these play an essential role in the national urban hierarchy, fulfilling key national functions and often some capital functions in the (public) services sector;
2. Transformation poles: these have a strong industrial past but are well on their way to reinventing themselves, managing change and developing new economic activities;
3. Gateways: these are larger cities with a dedicated (port) infrastructure that can handle large flows of international goods and passengers;
4. Modern industrial centers: these are platforms for multinational activities as well as local companies that export abroad and involve high levels of technological innovation;
5. Research centers: these are in higher education, including science and technology related corporate activities, and are well connected to international networks;
6. Visitor centers: these handle large flows of people of national and international origin, with a service sector geared toward tourism.

The third group, a large number of regional poles, can be distinguished in many ways as the pillars of today's, yesterday's or tomorrow's European regional economies:

1. De-industrialized cities: these have a strong (heavy) industrial base, which is in decline or recession;
2. Regional market centers: these fulfill a central role in their region, particularly in terms of personal, business and financial services, including hotels, trade and restaurants;
3. Regional public service centers: these fulfill a central role in their region, particularly in administration, health and education;

4. Satellite towns: these are smaller towns that have carved out particular roles in larger agglomerations.

Under conditions of resource scarcity cities will be faced with hard choices when formulating an economy based on knowledge and innovation and which meets the three mutually reinforcing priorities within the Europe 2020 strategy for smart, sustainable and inclusive growth (European Commission 2010). However, "Without skillful planning and management, cities run the risk of diseconomies – such as congestion and pollution – starting to outweigh scale benefits, leading to deteriorating quality of life and a loss of economic dynamism" (McKinsey 2011, p. 12).

McKinsey (ibid.) also notes that "the decline in importance of megacities is neither inevitable nor irreversible. Cities can move decisively to tackle infrastructure gaps, improve planning, foster high productivity jobs, and overcome these diseconomies". As we have seen, the "functions of city economics" develop by the grace of two master economic processes that are closely related: innovation and expansion by grace of import-replacing (Jacobs 1984, p. 39). This has been a prevailing characteristic of cities for millennia as Sir Peter Hall (1998) shows by distinguishing four main stages of urban innovation: first, the stage of the artistically creative city (e.g. Athens in the 5h century BC; Renaissance Florence between 1400 and 1450); second, the technologically innovative city (e.g. Detroit around 1900; the San Francisco Bay Area in the middle of the 20th century); third, the creative innovative city (e.g. Hollywood in 1920; Memphis in the 1950s); fourth, the city of urban innovation (e.g. Stockholm in the 1950s; London in the 1980s).

Today, many "cities utilize the creative quarter and knowledge hub as the panacea to implement broader city expansion and regeneration plans" (Evans 2009, p. 1003), which in turn are increasingly linked to branding the urban (Eshuis and Edelenbos 2008). Knight (2011, p. 234) distinguishes three types of hubs: "student hub, skilled workforce hub, and knowledge/innovation hub", based on the rationales and nature of activities as opposed to the "location, level and scope of hubs". The value-creating logic embedded in knowledge and innovation hubs as multiple, price carrying, materialized manifestations can be illustrated by how the Sloan Business School of the Boston-based Massachusetts Institute of Technology (MIT) positions its brand value of knowledge embedded in place to the world: "At MIT Sloan, the leading edge is a place, not a descriptor. It's where leaders come together to work out solutions to many of the world's most complex challenges" (see http://mitsloan.mit.edu/faculty).

Singapore has since the 1980s embarked on healthcare reforms in an effort to establish itself as a medical tourism hub. But the growing private healthcare market has resulted, in the public sector, in a shortage of doctors, rising costs and user charges (Leng 2010, p. 336), which raises questions about the sustainability of such a medical tourism brand.

CONCLUDING REMARKS

The history of nations is a chronology of haves and have-nots. David Landes (1998, inside front flap) summed this view up as follows: "we live in a world divided roughly into three kinds of nations: those that spend lots of money to keep their weight down; those whose people eat to live; and those that don't know where the next meal is coming from". Inequality has deeply rooted antecedents and making it history will take some doing. In this respect, judging from the point of view of branding may be an impediment to contributing to more equality in that over the ages cities have demonstrated a strongly felt need to assert their "individuality in pursuit of various economic, political or socio-psychological objectives" (Kavaratis and Ashworth 2005, p. 506). At the same time the main consequences of rapid consumption-driven urban growth is that cities are responsible for about 70 percent of carbon dioxide emissions and also for economic disparity which results in social inequality. This raises critical research queries, which Lucarelli and Berg (2011, p. 22) formulated as follows: how "do brands and space mutually constitute and shape each other ... how do brands shape the soft and hard infrastructure of urban spaces, and to what extent are brands new semiotic spaces that re-organize the urban experience?"

The spatial dimension plays a central role of interactivity in value creation and exchange. Fully understanding these systems requires perspectives that coincide with the need to connect the local (micro) level with the region/provincial (meso) level and national (macro) level (Go and Trunfio, 2010; Layton 2011) to bridge the diversity gap and achieve a sense of governance among stakeholders, which is needed for the implementation of an integrated and balanced, centric, place branding process. The place branding approach is not solely meant to raise the degree of urban attraction but, based on the capitalist regime of accumulation, is meant, first, to influence the rules of rivalry and a mode of regulation, and, second, to comprehend how interlocking circuits of production and consumption organize political and social arrangements, e.g. in relation to income distribution. New spatial, urban interactions at multi-layered scales lead to new patterns of activities, relationships and forms of clustering and networking between regions and cause these to become increasingly fragmented in many ways: economically, socially, environmentally and also politically. In turn, their classic forms of government, based on clear-cut arrangements amongst administrative levels, policy sectors and the public and private domain, are no longer sufficient. The governance of regional branding faces multi-level, multi-actor and multi-sectoral challenges. In particular, the new spatial interactions at new scales demand new approaches for the research, analysis, consultation and coordination of regional branding. The main challenge is to design a model to ensure stability and reproduction of the economic and social system within the framework of social, economic and political dynamics so as to achieve the desired value proposition outcome of the brand symbol. Normann (2001, p. 241) summarized this succinctly: A territory

> needs over the longer term – the capability to not only adapt within an existing business model and formula, and not only the ability to change when circumstances change, but rather it needs a constant process of questioning itself, of developing preparedness so that it can react quickly and structurally rather than with marginal improvements not only once but continuously over time. We may think of this as the ability to achieve recurrent purposeful emergence.

The three levels of outcome are subsequently:

> adaptation and correction, i.e. continuous improvement within a framework; frame breaking reconfiguration, i.e. structural change of the business to match paradigmatic change in the environment; and recurrent purposeful emergence or the capacity and preparedness to achieve frame breaking reconfiguration when required. (Ibid.)

In his novel *Remembrance of Things Past*, Marcel Proust (2003) states: "the real voyage of discovery consists not in seeking new landscapes, but in having new eyes". Similarly, we argue that the realities of liquid modernity press the sedentary social sciences to adapt a new "lens" of ubiquity. Toward this end we tried to explore how mobility and dwelling in place are inextricably linked and compel researchers and practitioners alike to consider the issue of polysemy, i.e. the occurrence of different images and interpretations of changes and how these affect disciplines as diverse as geography, history, psychology, sociology, marketing and management. Place branding researchers and practitioners can either be enriched or divided by their diversity. Since Anholt launched the notion of nation branding in 1997, the field has been a hotbed of contrasting ideas and beliefs, while debate has been common, because questioning is a way of advancing our knowledge. However, improving the practice of place branding ultimately requires bringing the academic and practice communities together to generate, transfer and apply knowledge. One important step in refining the scope of this activity is identifying research efforts at agenda setting that have recently been completed or are underway. For example, Hankinson (2010, p. 309) refers to various sources "setting out agendas for future research". However, in a rapidly urbanizing world, it's rather surprising that his "inventory" of themes does not include specifically the characteristics and attributes that render the spatial dimension of place branding distinctive from commercial type branding.

Another main step is converging research toward "common ground". We tried to argue previously that a robust body of knowledge, in terms of terminology, definitions, conceptualizations and theory, is needed for developing the defining characteristics of a paradigm; namely, a "shared constellation of beliefs, values, techniques ... models and examples" (Kuhn 1970, p. 175, cited in Go and Govers 2010, p. xxv). However, the reference to the mainstream corporate branding domain seems to assume that converging toward the latter (Hankinson 2010, p. 300) will result in a universally applicable model, though this value-free view overlooks the fact that regions are marked by their internal functional integration, i.e. the way they work as opposed to internal sameness, their identity rendering every branding situation unique and therefore untenable.

Finally, we need to make two observations. First, from the beginning of this Introduction we have tried to frame the objects under investigation and indicate the nature of the issues we have been addressing. This has concerned the dynamism which characterizes place branding. Brands represent knowledge or, to paraphrase Vargo and Lusch (2008, p. 7), an "operant resource", a fundamental source for competitive advantage, which transforms cities through "explosive" import replacement, composed of a variety of material, socio-economic and symbolic interventions. That is the "what" of our story. Second, how this process manifests itself in the city context depends on the choice made for a particular discourse, which, in turn, is driven by mind pictures or "Images of Organization" (Morgan 1986). In this Introduction we have sought to assess how contemporary mobility and politics cause the need for strategies to respond to territorial pressures while constructing and levering relational networks at multilevel governance arrangements, shifting scales of statehood and redrawing boundaries. In animating the theoretical debate, several scholars observe the confrontation between state, rescaling of territories and emerging relational topologies between actors.

How the contributors to this volume treat the subject of place branding critically varies and depends in large part on their disciplinary backgrounds and personal viewpoints. Framed in Morgan's (1986) "Images of Organization" (see also the Conclusion) the contributions to this volume range in their approach from work closer to the "machine" metaphor associated with the desire of local elites to connect their city with the global economy (Burbank *et al.* 2001). Chris Mabey and Tim Freeman's reference to knowledge sharing and cross-boundary learning may be understood as an operant resource and positions them adjacent to the "brains" metaphor. Iulia Gramon-Suba and Chris Holt's environmental design-led place brand strategy relies on an ongoing co-creative improvement process and Paolo Russo's "cultural industry model" for local development – which fits the "cultures" metaphor the closest.

Nicholas Ind and Erling Dokk Holm plead for democratic policy-making. Gildo Seisdedos and Pablo Vaggione's reference to place branding processes in a political battlefield and Steve Little's chronicle of top-down government policy-making in the face of recession and recent civil disturbances situate these authors within the "political systems" metaphor. Wisely, Eli Avraham cautions against a "one-size-fits-all" approach which results from organizations clinging to the images which Roland Schatz presents as the "stickiness" of stereotypes that mimic the "psychic prisons" metaphor.

The "systems in flux and transformation" metaphor is characterized in Alexander Otgaar's common agenda for place branding strategy and industrial tourism development, and in Wadim Schreiner and Frank Go's work on the "public mood" index to enhance citizen participation. Place brand equity impact measurement can be accommodated by the "instruments of domination" metaphor, such as Jeremy Tamanini's Global Green Economy Index for intelligent green strategically based nation branding, or they can take the form of public infrastructure as Keith Dinnie shows in sustainable place branding.

Finally, the "living organism" metaphor can be recognized in the emphasis that Kristof van Assche, Ming Chien Lo and Raoul Beunen place on visioning planning and preservation. Lambooy (2002) inspired us to think of the place brand metaphorically, like a mushroom, its logo being the visible component of a larger, complex system, involving the dynamism of social, economic and political networks that give life to the city. The mushroom's task is to transform organic elements, such as leaves, into food for the nurturing of other species. But it does not carry out this task itself. Instead it is connected to the mycelium, a network of threads, which support other mushrooms that are part of the same structure. It is important to stress that place brands can be seen, of course, in different ways by any one person.

REFERENCES

Assche, K. van and Lo, M.C. (2011) "Planning, preservation and place branding: a tale of sharing assets and narratives", *Place Branding and Public Diplomacy*, 7(2): 116–26.

Berthon, P. and Hulbert, J.M. (2003) "Marketing in metamorphosis: Breaking boundaries", *Business Horizons* (May–June): 31–40.

Bettencourt, L.M.A., Lobo, J., Helbing, D., Kuhnert, C. and West, G.B. (2007) "Growth, innovation, scaling, and the pace of life in cities", *Proceedings of the National Academy of Sciences*, 104(17): 7301–6.

Boisen, M., Terlouw, K. and van Gorp, B. (2011) "The selective nature of place branding and the layering of spatial identities", *Journal of Place Management and Development*, 4(2): 135–47.

Braun, E. (2011) "Putting city branding in practice", *Journal of Brand Management*, 19: 257–67.

Brodie, R.J., Glynn, M.S. and Littel, V. (2006) "The Service Brand and the Service Dominant Logic: Missing Fundamental Premise or the Need for Stronger Theory", *Marketing Theory*, 6(3): 363–79.

Burbank, M.J., Andranovich, G. and Heying, C.H. (2001) *Olympic Dreams: The Impact of Mega-events on Local Politics*, Boulder, CO: Lynne Rienner.

Certeau, Michel de (1984) *The Practice of Everyday Life*, trans. Steven Rendall. Berkeley, CA: University of California Press.

Chandler, J.D. and Vargo, S.L. (2011) "Contextualization and value-in-context: How context frames exchange", *Marketing Theory*, 11(1): 35–49.

Clancy, M. (1998) "Commodity chains, services and development: theory and preliminary evidence from the tourism industry", *Review of International Political Economy*, 5(1): 122–48.

Clark, G. and Huxley, J. (2009) *Closing the Investment Gap in Europe's Cities*, London: Urban Land Institute.

Corbridge, S., Thrift N. and Martin, R. (1994) *Money, Power and Space*, Oxford: Blackwell.

Cresswell, T. (2006) *On the Move: Mobility in the Modern World*, London: Routledge.

Dinnie, K. (2010) "Repositioning the Korea brand to a global audience: challenges, pitfalls, and current strategy", www.keia.org/sites/default/files/publications/APS-Seo_Thorson_Final.pdf.

Early, D. (1993) "What is sustainable design?", *The Urban Ecologist*, Spring.

Eshuis, J. and Edelenbos, J. (2008) "Branding in urban regeneration", *Journal of Urban Regeneration and Renewal*, 2(3): 272–82.

European Commission (2010) "EUROPE 2020: A European strategy for smart, sustainable and inclusive growth", *European Commission*, Brussels, 3 March, http://ec.europa.eu/europe2020/index_en.htm.

Evans, G. (2003) "Hard branding the cultural city: from Prado to Prada", *International Journal of Urban and Regional Research*, 27(2): 417–40.

Fenema, P.C. van (2002) "Coordination and control of globally distributed software projects", unpublished doctoral dissertation, Erasmus University, Rotterdam.

Fouts, J.S. (2010) 'Social media and immersive worlds: why international place branding doesn't get weekends off', in Go, F.M. and Govers, R. (eds), *International Place Branding Yearbook 2010: Place Branding in the New Age of Innovation*, Basingstoke: Palgrave Macmillan, pp. 113–20.

Freire, J.R. (2009) "Local people: a critical dimension for place brands", *Brand Management*, 16(7): 420–38.

Giddens, A. (1991) *Modernity and Self-Identity: Self and Society in the Late Modern Age*. Cambridge: Polity.

Introduction

Go, F.M. and Govers, R. (2000) "Integrated Quality Management for Tourist Destinations: A European Perspective on Achieving Competitiveness", *Tourism Management*, 21: 79–88.

Go, F.M. and Govers, R. (eds) (2010) *International Place Branding Yearbook 2010: Place Branding in the New Age of Innovation*, Basingstoke: Palgrave Macmillan.

Go, F.M. and Govers, R. (eds) (2011) *International Place Branding Yearbook 2011: Managing Reputational Risk*, Basingstoke: Palgrave Macmillan.

Go, F.M. and Trunfio, M. (2010) "Twenty years of tourism development research: a strategic market forces perspective", in Keller, P. and Bieger, T. (eds), *Tourism Development after the Crisis: Poverty Alleviation*, Berlin: ESV Erich Schmidt Verlag.

Go, F.M. and Zhang, W. (1997) "Applying Importance-Performance Analysis to Beijing as an International Meeting Destination", *Journal of Travel Research*, 35(4): 42–9.

Go, F., Klooster, E., Fenema, P.C. van and Jager, W.P. (2003) *Wereldspeler van Formaat Op Weg naar de Deltametropool*, The Hague: Stichting Maatschappij en Onderneming.

Gotham, K.F. (2007) "(Re) Branding The Big Easy Tourism Rebuilding in Post-Katrina New Orleans", *Urban Affairs Review*, 42(6): 823–50.

Govers, R. (2005) "Virtual tourism destination image: glocal identities constructed, perceived and experienced", Erasmus Research Institute of Management, PhD Research in Management Series, vol. 69, Rotterdam School of Management, Erasmus University, https://ep.eur.nl/handle/1765/6981

Govers, R. (2011) "From place marketing to place branding and back", *Place Branding and Public Diplomacy*, 7: 227–31.

Govers, R. and Go, F.M. (2003) "Deconstructing Destination Image in the Information Age", *Information Technology and Tourism*, 6(1): 13–29.

Govers, R. and Go, F.M. (2004) "Cultural identities constructed, imagined and experienced: A 3-gap tourism destination image model", *Tourism Interdisciplinary Journal*, 52(2): 165–83.

Govers, R. and Go, F.M. (2009) *Place Branding Glocal, Virtual and Physical, Identities Constructed, Imagined and Experienced*, Basingstoke: Palgrave Macmillan.

Govers, R. and Go, F.M. (2010) "The E-Branding of Places". In Go, F.M. and Govers, R. (eds), *International Place Branding Yearbook 2010: Place Branding in the New Age of Innovation*, Basingstoke: Palgrave Macmillan, pp. 121–33.

GRI (Global Reporting Initiative) (2000–11) *Sustainable Reporting Guidelines*, Amsterdam: Global Reporting Initiative.

Hall, P. (1998) *Cities in Civilization*, New York: Pantheon.

Hallworth, A. and Evans, S. (2008) "Managing a third division city: negative parochialism as a restraint on urban success", *Journal of Place Management and Development*, 1(2): 199–213.

Ham, P. van (2002) "Branding Territory: Inside the Wonderful Worlds of PR and IR Theory", in *Millennium: Journal of International Studies*, 31(2): 249–69.

Hankinson, G. (2004) "Relational Network Brands: Towards a Conceptual Model of Place Brands", *Journal of Vacation Marketing*, 10(2): 109–21.

Hankinson, G. (2010) "Place Branding Research: A Cross-disciplinary Agenda and the Views of Practitioners", *Journal of Place Branding and Public Diplomacy*, 6(4): 300–15.

Harvey, D. (1989) *The Condition of Postmodernity*, Cambridge: Blackwell.

Held, D., McGrew, A., Goldblatt, D. and Perraton, J. (2000) *Global Transformations Politics, Economics and Culture*, Cambridge: Polity Press.

Homer-Dixon, T.F. (1999) *Environment, Scarcity and Violence*, Princeton, NJ: Princeton University Press.

Iversen, N.M. and Hem, L.E. (2008) Provenance associations as core values of place umbrella brands: A framework of characteristics, *European Journal of Marketing* 42(5/6): 603–26.

Jacobs, J. (1984) *Cities and the Wealth of Nations Principles of Economic Life*, New York: Viking Penguin.

Kapferer, J.N. (2004) *The New Strategic Brand Management*, London: Kogan Page.

Kavaratzis, M. (2004) "From city marketing to city branding: Towards a theoretical framework for developing city brands", *Place Branding*, 1(1): 58–73.

Kavaratzis, M. and Ashworth, G. (2005) "City Branding: An effective Assertion of Identity or a Transitory Marketing Trick?", *Tijdschrift voor Economische en Sociale Geografie*, 96(5): 506–14.

Knight, J. (2011) "Education Hubs: A Fad, A Brand, an Innovation?", *Journal of Studies in Education*, 15(3): 221–40.

Kotler, P., Asplund, C., Rein, I. and Haider, D. (1999) *Marketing Places Europe, Attracting Investment, Industries and Visitors to European Cities, Communities, Regions and Nations*, Harlow: Financial Times Prentice Hall.

Kotler, P. and Gertner, D. (2002) "Country as Brand, Product and beyond: A Place Marketing and Brand Management Perspective", *Journal of Brand Management*, 9(4–5): 249–61.

Lambooy, J.G. (2002) "Ruimte voor complexiteit over veranderende structuren, zelf organisatie en netwerken in de economische geografie", University of Utrecht, Address Faculty of Spatial Sciences, 11 October.

Landes, D. (1998) *The Wealth and Poverty of Nations: Why Some Are So Rich and Some So Poor*, New York: Little, Brown.

Layton, R.A. (2011) "Towards a theory of marketing systems", *European Journal of Marketing*, 45(1/2): 259–76.

Lefebvre, H. (1991) *The Production of Space*, Oxford: Blackwell.

Lemmetyinen, A. and Go, F.M. (2010) "Building a brand identity in a network of Cruise Baltic's destinations: A multi-authoring approach", *Journal of Brand Management*, 17: 519–31.

Leng, C.H. (2010) "Medical tourism and the state in Malaysia and Singapore", *Global Social Policy*, 10(3): 336–57.

Long, N. (1997) "Agency and Constraint, Perceptions and Practices: A Theoretical Position". In De Haan, H. and Long, N. (eds), *Images and Realities of Rural Life*, Assen: Van Gorcum, 1–20.

Lucarelli, A. and Berg, P.O. (2011) "City branding: a state-of-the-art review of the research domain", *Journal of Place Management and Development*, 4(1): 9–27.

Lucas, R.E. (1988) "On the Mechanics of Economic Development", *Journal of Monetary Economics*, 22: 3–42.

Maas, W., Swerdlov, A. and Waugh, E. (2009) *Visionary Cities*, Rotterdam: NAi Publishers and the Why Factory.

Massey, D. (1997) "A Global Sense of Place", in Barnes, T. and Gregory, D. (eds) *Reading Human Geography*, London: Arnold.

McKinsey Global Institute (2011) "Urban world: mapping the economic power of cities", www.mckinsey.com/mgi/publications

McLuhan, M. (2003) *Understanding Media: The Extensions of Man*, Berkeley, CA: Gingko Press.

Morgan, G. (1986) *Images of Organization*, Newbury Park, CA: Sage.

Negrete, M.P. (2009) "Santa Fe: a 'global enclave' in Mexico city", *Journal of Place Management and Development*, 2(1): 33–40.

Normann, Richard (2001) *Reframing Business: When the Map Changes the Landscape*. Chichester: John Wiley & Sons.

Offer, A. (2007) *The Challenge of Affluence Self-Control and Well-Being in the United States and Britain since 1950*, Oxford: Oxford University Press.

Pasquinelli, C. (2012) "Competition, Cooperation, Co-opetition: Unfolding the process of inter-territorial branding", *Urban Research and Practice*, 5(2).
Pike, A. (2009) Brand and Branding Geographies. Geography Compass, 3: 190–213.
Prahalad, C.K. and Ramaswamy, V. (2004) *The Future of Competition: Co-Creating Unique Value with Customers*, Boston, MA: Harvard School Business Press.
Proust, M. (2003) *In Search of Lost Time*, London: Penguin.
Relph, E. (1976) *Place and Placelessness*. London: Pion.
Rosenbaum, M. (1993) "Sustainable Design Strategies", *Solar Today*, May/April.
Roulac, S.E. (1999) "The Geostrategy of Place Branding", *Design Management Journal*, (Winter): 62–7.
Sassen, S. (2006) *Cities in a World Economy*, 3rd edn, Thousand Oaks, CA: Sage.
Townsend, A.M. (2001) "Networked cities and the global structure of the Internet", *American Behavioral Scientist*, 44(10): 1697–716.
Tuan, Y.F. (1977) *Space and Place the Perspective of Experience*, London: Edward Arnold.
Tuan, Y.F. (1978) "Space, time, place: a humanistic perspective", in Carlstein, T., Parkes, D. and Turnbull, D. (eds), *Timing, Space and Spacing, vol. 1*, London: Edward Arnold.
ULI (Urban Land Institute) (1999) *Smart Growth Myths and Facts*, Washington, DC: Urban Land Institute.
Vargo, S.L. and Lusch, R.F. (2006) "Service-Dominant Logic: What it is, What it is not, What it might be," in Lusch, R.F. and Vargo, S.L. (eds), *The Service-Dominant Logic of Marketing: Dialog, Debate, and Directions*, Armonk, NY: M.E. Sharpe, pp. 43–56.
Vargo, S.L. and Lusch, R.F. (2008) "Service-Dominant Logic: Continuing the Evolution", *Journal of the Academy of Marketing Science*, 36: 1–10.
Vieira, R. (1993) *A Checklist for Sustainable Developments in a Resource Guidelines for Building Connections*, Washington, DC: American Institute of Architects.
Warnaby, G. (2009a) "Towards a Service-dominant Place Marketing Logic", *Marketing Theory*, 9(4): 403–23.
Warnaby, G. (2009b) "Non-place marketing: transport hubs as gateways, flagships and symbols?", *Journal of Place Management and Development*, 2(3): 211–19.
WCED (World Commission on Environment and Development) (1987) *Our Common Future*, Oxford: Oxford University Press.
Wilkinson, R. and Pickett, K. (2010) *The Spirit Level: Why Equality is Better for Everyone*, London: Penguin.
Yüksel, F., Bramwell, W. and Yüksel, A. (2005) Centralized and decentralized tourism governance in Turkey. *Annals of Tourism Research*, 35(3/4): 859–86.
Ziman, J. (1994) *Prometheus Bound: Science in a Dynamic Study State*, Cambridge: Cambridge University Press.
Zukin, S. (1991) *Landscapes of Power From Detroit to Disney World*, Berkeley, CA: University of California Press.
Zukin, S. (1995) *The Culture of Cities*, Oxford: Blackwell.

PART I
Multidisciplinary Perspectives on Sustainable Place Branding

CHAPTER 1

Four Readings of Place and Brand Leadership

Chris Mabey and Tim Freeman

In a review of trends and conceptual models, Kavaratzis (2005) offers a reading of place branding as the application of marketing practices beyond physical goods and services, in the context of deindustrialization. Branding is conceived as a form of communication, in which brand identities mediate between the activities of brand owners and consumer perceptions. Considered as a form of place management, place branding is thus positioned as the attempt to alter the way that places are perceived by specific groups of people – to develop and disseminate a recognizable identity for a place in order to promote processes considered desirable, such as inward financial investment, tourism or the development of political capital (Kavaratzis and Ashworth 2005). These concerns inform Hankinson's (2007) principles for destination brand management and Gnoth's (2007) functional, experiential and symbolic dimensions of destination brands. While branding as place management might appeal to those charged with supporting regional growth and sustainability, the task is far from simple. Unlike product markets, notions of place exist in the minds of a wide variety of actors prior to attempts to brand them. Thus the branding of places – neighborhoods, cities, regions – as attractive and sustainable requires collaborative networking, entrepreneurship and innovation, knowledge sharing and cross-boundary learning. In short, the complexity and political dimensions of the task implies a need for leadership. While reconceptualizing "place" in this way has immediate consequences for the nature of leadership required, place leadership is itself a field which remains relatively under-theorized to date. Our intention in this chapter is to propose discourse as a fresh and theoretically informed way to explore the leadership of place branding. By offering four different "readings", we begin to identify contested assumptions of what is required to lead effectively in complex, sometimes chaotic,

A MULTI-DISCOURSE APPROACH

In order to map out the theoretical assumptions underlying different approaches to the leadership and branding of place, we refer back to previous paradigms of social and organizational inquiry (Alvesson and Deetz 2000). These authors propose that two axes or sets of assumptions should guide such inquiries: those concerning social order and those concerning epistemology. With regard to social order, some researchers start from the premise of underlying consensus and therefore "both seek order and treat order production as the dominant feature of natural and social systems ... through the highlighting of ordering principles, such existing orders are perpetuated" (ibid., p. 26). In contrast, research located toward the dissensus extreme of this axis considers conflict, tension, dilemma and struggle to be natural facets of the social world. As such, any semblance of order is to be treated with suspicion and as an indication that the full variety of human interests is in some way being suppressed. Often such research is motivated by the desire to emancipate, to reclaim conflict with a view to somehow altering the balance of power within a particular field or indeed within society more generally.

The second axis concerns epistemology, namely the nature of knowledge and how it is derived. At one extreme, researchers set out from a relatively fixed standpoint, with a priori assumptions and "either/or" thinking which prompts them to look for theoretically driven classifications and taxonomies. It is assumed that the phenomenon under investigation is frozen in time, has an identity that is separate/separable from the rest of the social world and, with appropriate research tools, can be accurately reported. In contrast, emergent epistemology highlights the unfolding nature of social phenomena rather than treating them as objectively fixed, analyzable and ultimately measurable. Because the object of study is continuously shaping and being shaped by situated practice, theorizing is associated with emergence and cyclical causality.

From these two axes four distinct perspectives or, more precisely, *discourses* can be derived: the functionalist, the interpretive, the dialogic and the critical. A discourse may be thought of as a connected set of statements, concepts, terms and expressions which constitutes a way of talking and writing about a particular issue. The idea of text (spoken or written) and other artifacts in a given space creating or constituting "reality" is a central tenet of a subjectivist thinking, since discourses may be viewed as "systems of thought which are contingent upon as well as inform material practices, which not only linguistically but also practically – through particular power techniques ... produce particular forms of subjectivity" (ibid., p. 97). As a particular historical and social mode of engagement that shapes what is thinkable, knowable and doable in its disciplinary domain, the use of *discourse* offers a valuable analytic device for exploring the leadership and branding of place (see Figure 1.1).

Discourses are not intended to be theoretically watertight boxes and their permeability allows us to be more imaginative about the way they might flow into each other. Indeed, the central point of this chapter is that a more searching understanding of the leadership and branding of place requires consideration of multiple discourses, especially those that bring a more critical edge. We will now consider each of these four "readings" in turn.

FIGURE 1.1 | **Four discourses of leadership and place**

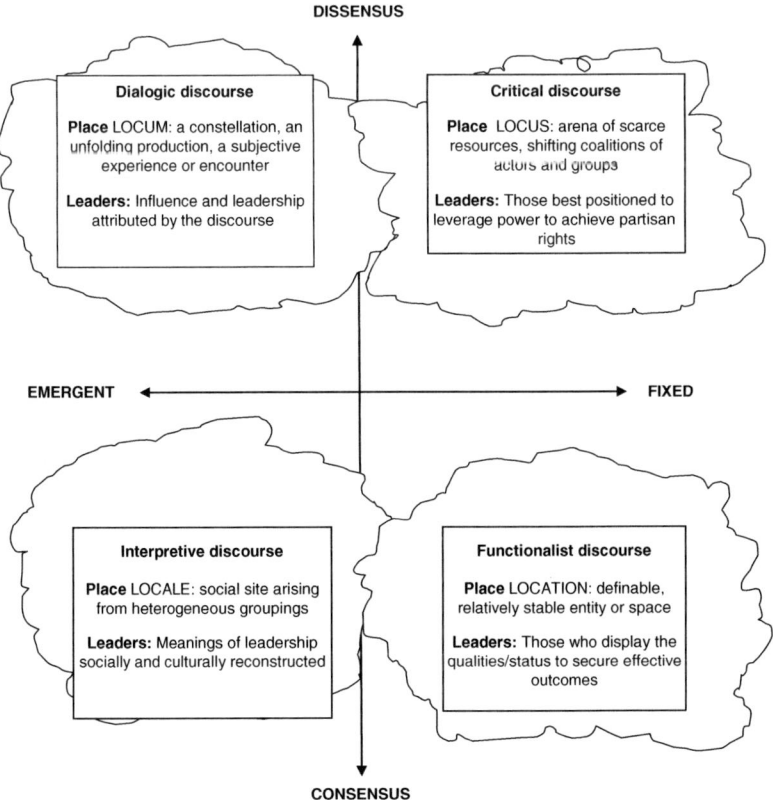

A FUNCTIONALIST DISCOURSE OF LEADERSHIP, PLACE BRANDING AND PLACE LEADERSHIP

Leadership studies informed by a *functionalist* discourse are guided by a priori (fixed) propositions and assume that social consensus is both feasible and possible. We might characterize place as a specific *location* (organizational and/or territorial) with relatively stable boundaries and definable limits. *Leaders* are those who have the capability and reputation to identify performance gaps and galvanize collective action around specified economic imperatives. Leadership research has, until recently, tended to focus exclusively on the individual leader, whether this be their situational choices, traits and psychological make-up, behavioral repertoire, relationship to followers or transformational skills. One consequence of this is that approaches to leadership development have also been predominantly individualized and attribute-based in order to identify and select those leaders capable of delivering the required policy, program or outcomes.

Anholt (2005a) provides a functionalist summary of place branding practice as the distillation of the core "essence" of a place, through reinforcement of a coherent set of "truths", to the advantage of the local community. From this perspective, place branding consists of uncovering and amplifying a pre-existing reality of place and making it available for wider consumption. Thus place branding may provide societal benefits in the form of emancipation and increased opportunities for individuals through the development of diverse markets in international tourism, the export of goods and services, or the location of corporate headquarters (Anholt, 2005b).

When applied specifically to the leadership of place, functionalist discourse highlights the changing context of leadership. This includes a shift from hierarchical professional silos to networked (Cooke and Morgan 1998) and cross-boundary working (Sullivan and Skelcher 2002). Secondly, it requires new leadership competencies/skills in partnership building across thematic, organizational, local and professional bodies (Gibney *et al.* 2009). Thirdly, it points to the need for leadership skills associated with collaborative learning (e.g. Powell 1990; Maskell 2002), with the aim of supporting and developing successful and sustainable collaborations.

AN INTERPRETIVE DISCOURSE OF LEADERSHIP, PLACE BRANDING AND PLACE LEADERSHIP

Whereas functionalists tend to regard knowledge as an objective commodity and leader capability as an individual asset, sometimes referred to as human or intellectual capital, interpretive discourse sees leadership more as a fluid consequence arising from, contributing to and shaped by social practices, thus emphasizing relational or social capital (Day 2001). Hence the term *locale* in Figure 1.1. For all their plurality, interpretive studies, like functionalist ones, remain largely consensus-oriented in the sense that they seek to portray a faithful picture of what is going on within a community, subregion or network, albeit from a particular, sectional, vantage point (e.g. residents as opposed to elected politicians, women as opposed to men, municipal government as opposed to grass-roots activists) with a strong emphasis on the language deployed by each respective grouping.

An interpretive reading of place branding emphasizes the extent to which brands exist as networks of associations in the minds of disparate target audiences (e.g. tourists, businesses and residents/workers) and is open to the likelihood that brand associations vary widely between these groups. Similarly, groups may themselves be further segmented, for example between current and potential new residents where industrial decline necessitates an influx of workers to service new creative industries. Potential conflicts and synergies between the needs of each of these groups pose challenges and necessitate the need for a careful balancing of requirements.

Leaders, or more likely, leadership informed by interpretive discourse play close attention to the cultural and symbolic in articulations of "place" – the narratives, myths and stories that are told and their use to evoke a shared sense of place. Similarly, *distributed leadership* provides an important resource for interpretive leadership of place in its orientation toward constructing a shared vision across networks lacking in hierarchical structural authority. On this reading, the "who", "what" and "how" of leadership is recast and conceptualized as a distributed and interdependent set of *practices* enacted by all rather than specific traits possessed by figureheads at the apex of a hierarchy (Gronn 2002). Embedded in social interaction, leadership is presented as a collective activity occurring in and through collaborative relationships (Spillane *et al.* 2001), centered on mutual learning, understanding and positive action and requiring the facilitation of reflection and the co-creation of ideas (Lambert 2003). The hierarchical assumption of leadership embodied in a single person at the apex of a unitary organization gives way, to be replaced by an acceptance of the importance of change agency behaviors from a broad range of collaborators, co-creating a shared vision toward which they work.

A DIALOGIC DISCOURSE OF LEADERSHIP, PLACE BRANDING AND PLACE LEADERSHIP

In common with the interpretive discourse, dialogic discourse rejects any separation of the knowing subject (e.g. the leader) and the known object (e.g. leadership capability). In contrast to functionalism's ontology of *being*, this might be characterized as subscribing to an ontology of *becoming*. Within a dialogic reading, instead of seeing individuals or social groupings as entities, organizational and individual identities are seen as constituted by ongoing human interaction. Individuals and their worlds are continuously in process. Through institutionalizing interaction in cultures and discourses, we constantly create (or constitute) a sense of who we are, of what we are doing and of where we are going, in which individuals and organizations are constantly in a process of becoming (Watson 2005, p. 223). From this we might extrapolate that there is no single and static leader of place, as such; rather there is a multi-actor process of place-making – brought about through relating and talking to a series of *locums*. Similarly, there is no *leadership* as such within this ontology, there is only leading – again accomplished through negotiation, consultation and ascription. Furthermore, the dialogic discourse rejects any notion of singular, objective and universally applicable truths. Indeed it views any attempt to produce or privilege such truths (even socially constructed ones, as in the constructivist discourse) as serving dominant interests, inherently open to challenge and ripe for deconstruction. Thus Grint (2000) rejects leadership as a concrete natural phenomenon, his constitutive theory of leadership arguing instead for the socially constructed and contested nature of a multiplicity of *accounts* of leader, follower and context. As leadership is constructed within the confines of particular social institutions it cannot exist independently of a given context and is attributed by others; leaders are those who enact the behaviors and messages required by those able to confer leadership status. Neither leader nor context may be unambiguously known since all judgments informed by particular assumptions are subject to counter-claim.

From a dialogic perspective, place branding is presented as a site for the *generative* construction of difference; "places" here are a discontinuous assemblage of people, ideas and material "things", the meaning of each of which is developed and reiterated continuously in networks of understanding (Mayes 2008). A leadership of place informed by dialogic discourse focuses on the instability of articulations of "place" and the performative nature of both "place" and "leadership". Underpinned by a performative theory of truth, in which the naming of a term brings about the existence of that which is named, Ford and Harding (2004) provide a dialogic reading of Lefebvre's critical analysis of space and place. They argue that "space" is not simply that which is there before it is filled, but is instead a production – the result of social practices – and a conceptual triad is developed to capture the physical, mental and social elements of the production of space. These constitute *spatial practice* which concerns the production and reproduction of space, *representations of space* which are images tied to the signs and codes of dominant knowledge within a society, and *representational spaces* which are directly lived, making symbolic use of physical objects. On this reading, places are characterized as articulated moments in networks of understandings:

> Individuals invest in place through their labour and the discursive construction of affective loyalties, investments that are imbricated with politics, political economy and all manner of (mis)representations arising from the fantasy of the psyche. (Ford and Harding 2004, p. 818)

A CRITICAL DISCOURSE OF LEADERSHIP, PLACE BRANDING AND PLACE LEADERSHIP

The critical discourse may be described as dualist in the sense that it tends to represent the world in terms of analytically distinct divisions, such as truth and falsity, oppressors and oppressed, agency and structure, individual and collective. Although the critical discourse does not necessarily deny processes of social construction, and hence multiple images of reality, it tends to treat these as no more than images. This contrasts with a dialogic reading that makes no distinction between *images of* reality and what it considers to be the inherently multiple *nature of* reality in itself. Ontologically, therefore, the critical discourse lays claim to the objective existence of ultimate and singular truths about the social world.

Epistemologically, however, the critical discourse considers that our means of accessing such truths will always be socially, historically and politically mediated. Hence, in Figure 1.1, we characterize place as *locus*, a contested arena of privilege, power and partisan knowledge. This also gives rise to one of the main concerns of the critical discourse, which is to expose what it sees as the *false consciousness* of individuals whenever they unthinkingly acquiesce to social dynamics or ideologies that do not serve their own *true* or *real* interests (Garrick and Clegg 2001). A stark example of this dualism, with its distinction between the oppressive holders of capital (in this case government, construction magnates and the Local Docklands Development Corporation) and the sellers of labor (i.e. employees and residents), comes from the redevelopment of the defunct docklands on the Isle of Dogs in London:

> The money central government spent indirectly to encourage this development made it an extremely expensive fiasco for the taxpayer, who subsidized big business

and also had to pay the lion's share of infrastructure costs. Instead of gaining a vibrant and humane new borough that would have taken its place within the larger framework of the metropolis and enriched the poorer communities in its vicinity, Londoners acquired a chaos of commercial buildings. (Rogers 1997, p. 109)

A salutary lesson for those seeking growth which is both smart and sustainable.

Mayes's (2008) reading of place branding incorporates critical elements, presenting culture as a manifestation of the operation of relations of power in which society is characterized by competition between rival interests with unequal access to material and symbolic resources. While functionalism positions place branding as uncovering and promoting the essence of a place for the benefit of all, critical analyses consider the selection of essential properties for branding purposes as a political act which privileges sectional interests. Thus the cultural exchange fostered by a tourist industry may operate hegemonically to reproduce and reinforce structures of dominance.

Ford *et al.* (2008) outline two challenges to functionalist leadership theory from a critical perspective. The first questions the positivist and quantitative basis of much functionalist leadership research, the point being that if the practice of leadership concerns the ability to influence social constructions of reality, its proper study requires qualitative methods capable of exploring local understandings. The second is an emancipatory challenge which rejects functionalism's supposition that leaders are required for the effective functioning of organizations. Rather, it recasts *leadership* as a political process by which certain individuals succeed in shaping the perceptions of others. The critical response identifies problems including: an exaggerated belief in the impact of the CEO; the potential destabilizing effects of charismatic leaders in a rush for change; and the negative effects of charismatic individuals, including grandiosity, distrust, suspicion and paranoia (Maccoby 2000).

Similar to dialogic discourse, a *critical* discourse of place leadership is also focused on the unstable and unfixed nature of place; however, it goes much further than the way that multiple actors seek to articulate and "name" place, by concerning itself with the emancipation of those groups which are marginalized and disempowered. It does this by seeking to surface not only the hidden narratives *between* different discourses (i.e. associated with the different views of multiple actors) but by also pointing out where there are tensions and contradictions emerging *within* these different discourses. A critical approach therefore not only offers a constructive challenge to dominant ideologies within a given place but also addresses issues of empowerment and inclusivity. It suggests the importance of moral duty toward the development of socially important ends, commitment to transformation, and communal or distributed forms of leadership as the means by which diverse voices may be harnessed to create a cultural environment consistent with principles of social justice. From a critical perspective it is important not only to analyze power distributions, but also actively to work to disrupt them in the interests of the disempowered.

CONCLUSION

The purpose of this chapter was to show that the activity of leading place for smart and sustainable growth is subject to multiple readings. By utilizing discourse, which encourages us to examine underlying assumptions, we can arrive at quite different interpretations as to how a given "place" is being branded and led. This awareness of ontological and epistemological assumptions is not merely an academic exercise. Such awareness can only improve our understanding of place leadership, in terms of both theory-building and of effective place leadership policy and practice. In contrast, fixation upon a single "reading" will lead to, at best, a partial and, at worst, a misleading prognosis. Our observation is that much of the early writing about the leadership of place falls within a functionalist discourse (e.g. Stough 2003). But with a growing emphasis upon leading processes of collaborative learning and associational working across conventional organizational, professional, territorial and community boundaries (Gibney *et al.* 2009), it is important to bring other readings into play.

With its emphasis on instrumentality and the economic imperative, functionalist research holds much promise for revealing the kinds of skills and competencies necessary for those seeking to lead place-shaping projects or networks. Indeed functionalist concerns help to reintroduce agency and the power of leadership actions to a field dominated by structural and systemic determinism. However, such competencies will be radically different from those comprising traditional leadership models and they will rarely be invested in a single leader, but rather be distributed across a range of "players". So, the quest for quantifiable outcomes (perhaps studies which seek to connect leadership impact to successful brands and place-shaping) is natural for organizations, agencies and governments seeking wise allocation of resources. The limitation, of course, is that the imposed, or in some cases elitist, nature of such branding and place-shaping is rarely questioned.

In contrast the interpretive discourse tends to shift the focus toward the social, symbolic and cultural aspects of organizational life *for their own sake*, rather than being subordinated to economic and instrumental concerns. This reading views places and their associated brands as social sites composed of distinct cultural groups, each of which are expected to have distinct ways of making sense of the organizational world. Viewed from this perspective, the significance of place leadership or branding – its purposes, implementation and effects – is considered to be a function of the sense-making of these cultural groups. A principal aim and contribution of interpretive research, then, is to provide a voice to such groups and enable the players seeking to co-create sustainable outcomes for a particular place-shaping project or organization to be viewed and interpreted through the eyes of those groups.

The dialogic discourse also has profound implications for leadership of place. This reading alerts us to the notion that, far from being a rational and/or technical process of building leadership capability, creating and sustaining vibrant places becomes a key resource in the very constitution of leadership identity. Brands are built. Places are produced. Social relations of production are continuously reinscribed within a space, thereby reproducing it. Organizational, community and regional places are characterized by their multiple natures and are not capable of being reduced to a single overarching organizational vision. Nor are such spaces capable of being unambiguously orchestrated by a single leader or leadership team. Similarly, the different cultures in organizational or regional places are not subcultures within a dominant and over-arching culture, but rather are multiple (and occasionally contesting) *organizations*. Taken to an extreme, places are considered to be devoid of material substance, having only metaphysical presence:

> The metaphysical presence of an organisation is therefore the urgent belief that something exists and is present to apprehension, and which offers the architechtonic vision that organises the work which goes on "within". (Ford and Harding 2004, p. 827)

Just as the dialogic rejects the dualism or ontological separation between subject and object, it also challenges other dualisms that are typically taken for granted within functionalism. Indeed, the very labeling of, and separation between, leaders and nonleaders is questioned, as is the expectation that to become an effective leader there is a predetermined body of knowledge or repertoire of skills to be mastered or context to be managed (Massey 2005). For this reason, we suggest that a dialogic reading may hold the key to explaining why well-marketed community projects designed to promote smart growth frequently falter and sometimes fail.

In a similar vein, but prompted more by a motive of active emancipation, place leadership research operating within a critical discourse could help to uncover the often covert power dynamics at play in place-shaping endeavors. This reading prompts a healthy suspicion of the way in which regional development initiatives and projects routinely aid and abet the dominant coalition, mask or minimize opposing interest groups and perpetuate inequalities within social spaces. We would point out strongly that learning from corporate branding in the unilateral functionalist manner implied by Kavaratzis (2005) and Hankinson (2007) risks masking the more critical stakeholder-oriented considerations of Mayes (2008). Similarly, Gnoth's (2007) model of destination brand leverage, while attending to functionalist and interpretive dimensions, risks marginalizing more critical concerns. Indeed, in practice none of the four discursive models presented above can exist in isolation, as the interactions of stakeholders will inevitably cut across the qualities of leadership implied by each of the models. Although this may sound threatening to those seeking swift and effective socioeconomic outcomes, a deeper and more considered awareness of the historical, political and ideological context of a given place-shaping project may assist a more sustained and successful leadership and branding of place in the long run.

REFERENCES

Adler, J. (1989) "Travel as performed art", *American Journal of Sociology*, 96: 1355–91.
Alvesson, M. and Deetz, S. (2000) *Doing Critical Management Research*, London: Sage.
Anholt, S. (2005a) *Brand New Justice*. Amsterdam: Elsevier Butterworth Heinemann.
Anholt, S. (2005b) "Some important distinctions in place branding", *Place Branding*, 1: 116–21.
Cooke, P. and Morgan, K. (1998) *The Associational Economy, Firms, Regions and Innovations*, Oxford: Oxford University Press.
Day, D. (2001) "Leadership development: a review in context", *Leadership Quarterly*, 11(4): 581–613.
Ford, J. and Harding, N. (2004) "We went looking for an organisation but could find only the metaphysics of its presence", *Sociology*, 38: 815–30.
Ford, J., Harding, N. and Learmonth, M. (2008) *Leadership as Identity*, Basingstoke: Palgrave Macmillan.
Garrick, J. and Clegg, S. (2001) "Stressed-out knowledge workers in performative times: a postmodern take on project-based learning", *Management Learning*, 32(1): 119–34.
Gibney, J., Copeland, S. and Murie, A. (2009) "Toward a 'new' strategic leadership of place for the knowledge-based economy", *Leadership*, 5(1): 5–23.
Gnoth, J. (2007) "The structure of destination brands", *Tourism Analysis*, 12(5): 345–58.
Grint, K. (2000) *The Arts of Leadership*, Oxford: Oxford University Press.
Gronn, P. (2002) "Distributed leadership as a unit of analysis", *Leadership Quarterly*, 13: 423–51.

Hankinson, G. (2007) "The management of destination brands: five guiding principles based on recent developments in corporate branding theory", *Brand Management*, 14(3): 240–54.

Iles, P. and Preece, D. (2006) "Developing leaders or developing leadership?", *Leadership*, 2(3): 317–40.

Kavaratzis, M. (2005) "Place branding: a review of trends and conceptual models", *The Marketing Review*, 5: 329–42.

Kavaratzis, M. and Ashworth, G.J. (2005) "City branding: an effective assertion of identity or a transitory marketing trick?", *Tijdschrift Voor Economische en Sociale Geografie*, 96(5): 506–14.

Lambert, L. (2003) "Leadership redefined: an evocative context for teacher leadership", *School Leadership & Management*, 23(4): 421–30.

Maccoby, M. (2000) "Narcissistic leaders: the incredible pros, the inevitable cons", *Harvard Business Review*, January–February: 69–77.

Maskell, P. (2002) "Social capital, innovation and competitiveness", in Barron, S. Field, J. and Schuller, T. (eds), *Social Capital: Critical Perspectives*, Oxford: Oxford University Press.

Massey, D. (2005) *For Space*, London: Sage.

Mayes, R. (2008) "A place in the sun: the politics of place, identity and branding", *Place Branding and Public Diplomacy*, 4(2): 124–35.

Powell, W. (1990) "Neither market nor hierarchy: network forms of organization", *Research in Organizational Behavior*, 12: 74–96.

Rogers, R. (1997) *Cities for a Small Planet*, London: Faber and Faber.

Spillane, J., Halverson, R. and Diamond, J. (2001) "Investigating school leadership practice: a distributed perspective", *Educational Researcher*, 30(3): 23–8.

Stough, R. (2003) "Strategic management of places and policy", *Annals of Regional Science*, 37(2): 179–201.

Sullivan, H. and Skelcher, C. 2002. *Working across Boundaries: Collaboration in Public Services*. Basingstoke: Palgrave Macmillan.

Watson, T. (2005) "Review essay: the organization and disorganization of organization studies", *Journal of Management Studies*, 43(2): 367–82.

Chapter 2

Beyond Place Branding

Nicholas Ind and Erling Dokk Holm

In spite of the long history of places promoting their virtues to visitors, commentators and investors, the concept of place branding is relatively new. In this context, the idea that there should already be a "beyond" might seem hasty. However, we will argue in this chapter that much place branding as it has been practiced has really been place marketing, concerned more with creating an image through external communication than developing the experience of a place. This has tended to make place branding seem superficial and short-termist – more concerned with visitor numbers, reputation indices and growth figures than connecting with the needs and wants of citizens. So here we will turn place branding inwards and focus on three trends that are creating the opportunity to promote citizen participation and to develop more sustainable approaches to brand building that can deliver well-being for all – the sort of benefits that Robert F. Kennedy observed in a 1968 speech and which tend to go unmeasured in statistics:

> the gross national product does not allow for the health of our children, the quality of their education or the joy of their play. It does not include the beauty of our poetry or the strength of our marriages, the intelligence of our public debate or the integrity of our public officials. It measures neither our wit nor our courage, neither our wisdom nor our learning, neither our compassion nor our devotion to our country, it measures everything in short, except that which makes life worthwhile. And it can tell us everything about America except why we are proud that we are Americans.

THE PROBLEM WITH (PLACE) BRANDING

The challenge for branding in general and place branding in particular is rooted in its orientation toward communication and the concentration of resources on building external images (Morrison and Crane 2007). Traditionally there has been an emphasis on one-way communication, whereby brands make selective promises that align with stakeholders' needs and wants. The communications led approach also tends to treat stakeholders as passive recipients of brand meaning (Prahalad and Ramaswamy 2004). However, this model is breaking down as communication becomes more interactive, organizations more transparent and relationships more focused on service. Increasingly branding is concerned with enabling dialog as the brand evolves in interaction with its stakeholders. Meaning is no longer controlled by brand managers but rather co-created in the intersection between the brand and the individual (Cova and Dalli 2010). This perspective sees stakeholders as active participants who help to create value (Vargo and Lusch 2004; Curtis et al. 2009). This is particularly notable in those arenas where brand discussion escapes the attention of brand managers, such as in naturally occurring brand communities where commentators and enthusiasts gather to discuss brands and to construct meaning together (Muniz and O'Guinn 2001). Organizations can play a supportive role in such communities and they can also learn from them, but the temptation to instrumentalize them and make them a marketing channel has to be avoided.

As brand building moves beyond the control of organizations and institutions and the importance attached to communications diminishes relative to the other components that define brand experience, so branding, as traditionally practiced, loses relevance. It could be argued that this represents the death of branding – yet brands seem to matter as much as they have always done. Rather, it is the process of brand building which is changing and becoming more open and participative. Stakeholders have a clear desire to be active in shaping what brands are and may become and they increasingly expect brands to be responsive and responsible in engaging in a dialog (Ind et al. 2012). When it comes to place branding specifically the temptation to focus on defining and communicating those attributes that are defined as unique, increasingly looks misplaced. As Anholt (2008) argues, "there appears to be no evidence to suggest that using marketing communications to influence international public perceptions of an entire city, region or country is anything other than a vain and foolish waste of taxpayers' money". This view moves brand beyond the narrow idea of communication to something that involves stakeholders in an active way in place making. In other words, the focus should be on how institutions can better connect strategy, culture and widespread involvement (Ind and Schultz 2010) and how individuals, groups and organizations can be encouraged to recognize their responsibility for making life worthwhile for themselves and for others. So, rather than just trumpeting slogans to investors, tourists and businesses, place branding should turn inwards and encourage democratization and help people to shape sustainable places that nurture wit, wisdom, courage and compassion. Here we will look at the emerging trends that signpost the changes taking place.

LIVING WITH PARTICIPATION

Our participatory culture asks "not for passive spectatorship but for active participants who share a certain responsibility towards what could be seen as the objects of our world, that is to say, the common" (de Vugt 2010). It would seem obvious that governmental and economic institutions play an important role in making a place. Governments set agendas, run budgets, create structures and systems, define strategies and play an integrative role. They determine whether a city gets a new opera house, whether there is sufficient funding for environmental initiatives and whether the transport infrastructure meets the needs of citizens. The challenge here is that these decisions can often seem remote from people. A Hobbesian view of governmentality, where the interests of the citizen and sovereign power are unified, would argue that people's views are represented. Governments are to some extent a reflection of the people they govern. However, Hobbes's approach is an abstracted ideal that focuses on the sovereign entity, whilst relying on the virtue of the sovereign power for good governance (which Hobbes himself recognized was not always the case). Foucault (2003) argues that we have to get rid of Hobbes's "Leviathan" precisely because it suggests a unity that denies the importance of individuality and difference, while Balibar (2008, p. 100), referring to the rationally conceived city, writes that it is "indeed a collective individuality, bound together by affects of friendship, morality and religion, but it is not founded on uniformity".

Instead of uniformity, places ought to welcome diversity and try to capture the energy and intellect of citizens – to draw on their skills and knowledge. It has long been an argument in the corporate world that value is created through intellectual capital (Edvinsson and Malone 1997) and that it is wasteful to ignore the creativity and knowledge of individuals. Companies such as Google, 3M, Intuit and Mozilla adopt policies specifically designed to draw on the innovation potential of their employees by creating the time and the space for the exploration of the new. Such organizations also blur the boundaries between the inside and the outside by bringing customers and partners into idea generation and development. However, with places there tends to be a belief in the primacy of expertise as embodied in politicians and administrators over the creativity of people – which is perhaps one reason why there is an alienation from democratic politics and failings in city planning. In an analysis of how New Orleans' planners failed to seize the opportunity, in the aftermath of Hurricane Katrina, to reconstruct the city for the well-being of all, Kristina Ford argues that there was a lack of participation. In *The Trouble with City Planning*, she suggests that good city plans tap into the knowledge and creativity of citizens and stimulate a "wider conversation about the city's future and spreads responsibility for bringing about what a citizenry desires" (2010, pp. 230–1).

Places do sometimes adopt a participative philosophy, but there could be far greater dialog between government and citizens, more involvement of people in co-creation and greater democratization. The value of this ought to be obvious. By tapping into the diverse skills that engineers, teachers, scientists, designers and other citizens can bring to a challenge, relevant innovations can emerge. As Steve Johnson argues concerning large groups in *Where Good Ideas Come From* (2010), it is not the crowd itself that becomes wise, but rather that connected individuals become smarter. Johnson's thinking applies both to breakthrough ideas and smaller ideas of innovation development. In an analysis of innovations since 1400, he concludes that "less than 10 percent of innovation during the Renaissance is networked; two centuries later a majority of breakthrough ideas emerge in collaborative environments".

There is an argument here about whether people really want to participate. In the corporate world, it is clear that individuals do want to take part in brand communities, because they offer opportunities for meaning making and socialization (Ind *et al.* 2012). In the case of communities of place, the importance of meaning making and socialization ought to be heightened as the environment in which we live generally matters more to well-being than the design of a yoghurt pot or the advertising for a new soft drink. If individuals fail to engage, it is because of a feeling of remoteness; that it is difficult to make one's voice heard and to have a genuine dial on things that matter. Yet, when the opportunity to participate is created there are clear benefits. For example, studies in Scandinavia demonstrate that there is a link between the ability to participate in local politics and the well-being of citizens (Baldersheim and Rose 2010). Citizens in smaller municipalities are more satisfied with the level of public services than those who live in larger municipalities. More important though is that citizens in smaller municipalities have a more solid trust in the political and administrative unit and their elected representatives – in other words in the democratic system – than those living in larger municipalities. Cities that offer citizens a real say are in a much better position to meet the demands of the future, not only because democratic activity identifies what inhabitants are interested in, but also because democratic participation produces meaning and loyalty. We can also see in Switzerland, where there is a long history of direct democracy at all levels of government, and where every municipality and canton has its own constitution, that citizens are very active in determining how they live their lives. Interestingly, where the political participation levels are highest, one finds better public services and stronger economies (Kaufmann 2007).

The underlying implication of greater involvement is a willingness to share and to practice democratization. Spinoza argued that people can only truly participate in society if they are aware of the issues. He suggested that governments often avoid sharing knowledge, because they "wish to transact everything behind the backs of citizens", while cloaking their actions in "the essential interest of the commonwealth" and in "a show of utility" (Spinoza 1998, VII, 27). Thus while there is a need for individual responsibility and involvement, governments need to create the structures and conditions for this to happen. In this context, it is interesting to note that Iceland has adopted an open approach to the creation of a new constitution. Following the financial crisis of 2008 and the seeming involvement of politicians in it, there was an agreement that a new constitution was required to avoid the situation occurring again. There was also a heightened sense of the importance of transparency and accountability in public affairs. Rather than use "experts", a group of 25 citizens was involved from the start of the process both in face-to-face sessions to set the agenda and then online to discuss and develop ideas with others. As ideas progressed, the constitutional council posted draft clauses and invited comments on its website and through Facebook. The aim was to create something made by and for the people of Iceland.

As well as officially sanctioned processes, there are also instances of empowered citizens simply seizing the initiative. Tuqan (2010) describes how a group of concerned citizens took action after the 2010 Haiti earthquake. As often happens in disasters, many groups and agencies offered help and despatched people. The problems on the ground meant though that there was a lack of coordination. The solution was a real-time Haiti crisis map, modeled from ongoing social media input, the Web, SMS and email. Interestingly, the map was not made by an official body, but by a group of students at Tufts University in Massachusetts and volunteers from Ushahidi – an open-source project that was set up to map reports of violence in Kenya. Tuqan notes, "the fact that a handful of students could mobilize so quickly to meet such a challenge speaks not only to the power of the individual, but also to the inability of governments to react faster than their citizens to a crisis".[1]

Similarly when the former industrial area around the Meatpacking District in New York was due for redevelopment, along with the High Line, a 13-mile stretch of elevated train track that used to transport meat carcasses, the assumption was that there would be demolition and redevelopment into offices. The then mayor, Rudy Giuliani, and the real estate speculators believed that the High Line would go. However, two local residents, Robert Hammond and Joshua David, formed a nonprofit organization called Friends of the High Line and argued it would be better to use the railway as a high-level urban park area. They galvanized local people and attracted high profile supporters and managed to raise the money to stop the demolition and build a new green space in Manhattan. Ten years after the project started, the first section of the High Line Park has opened, complete with grass, trees, wildlife and water features. The result of this initiative has not only been significant for New Yorkers, but as an inspiration for other would-be urban conservationists.

ENABLING PEOPLE TO CONNECT

To break down the borders between government and citizens, politicians and administrators need to encourage the sort of co-created processes as witnessed in Iceland. This concerns listening to and supporting existing online and offline communities and also creating communities of interest and expertise where people together can solve problems and innovate. This means overcoming traditional modernist thinking based on a rigid conservative societal structure that stresses the distance between governors and governed and instead promoting a soft urbanism. In place of the certainties of modernism, soft urbanism stresses the inseparability of the audience from the performance; a lessening of the boundaries such that meanings evolve in the space between as a specific type of social and cultural life emerges. This approach leads to the dissolution of the traditional oppositions that have been part of the modernist credo. Whereas once loneliness and sociality, high and low culture, production and consumption, local and global, and private and public space were seen as separate spheres, now they merge together. Nowhere better exemplifies this than the ubiquitous coffee shop (Holm 2010).

The key to the coffee shop, and other types of soft urbanism, is informality. These are places where people can go alone without feeling shy or uncomfortable. The coffee shop is somewhere where solitude is legitimate but also where more social interaction is possible. This dual capacity is a defining characteristic of many of the most important soft spots of postmodern urban life. Coffee shops represent a kind of cultural relaxation and ease. This can be seen in the fusing of low and high culture in the way that coffee bars accommodate an element of connoisseurship in the discourse on specialty coffee, while offering coffee as a normal no-brow drink which appeals to everyone.

Coffee shops are often portrayed in the media as being the domain of the white upper-middle class, closely related to gentrification and the emergence of a new social stratum labeled the "creative class". Dominant postmodern theories also produce similar claims.[2] Yet coffee shops are more diverse than that and create a space that allows for people from diverse backgrounds to occupy the same area comfortably. Coffee shop customers also become a part of the theatre of production. Employees and customers exist on a similar level. Of course, baristas still serve customers and customers do not step behind the counter to do the dishes, but the culture through which the relationship is mediated is softened. Coffee shops fuse private and public space. It is possible to sit in one for long periods without buying anything while connecting with other people both inside and on the street. While the coffee shop is the most obvious example of soft urbanity, there are a wide variety of spaces that have some of the same features: libraries, gyms, train stations, squares and parks. With a clear understanding of the concept of soft urbanity, city planners, entrepreneurs, politicians and citizens can achieve a more friendly and attractive urban environment where distinctions are played down and possibilities for well-being are enhanced.

DELIVERING SUSTAINABILITY

The third trend is the move toward sustainable thinking. Concerns about the future of the planet now occupy center stage for governments, businesses and individuals. While we might note that the rhetoric often exceeds action and that consumption now significantly exceeds resources, nonetheless environmentalism and the somewhat blurry notion of sustainability have become part of our everyday discourse and some significant steps have been taken. The Brundtland Report, first published in 1987 – at a point when demand equaled available resources – talked of sustainable development as "development that meets the needs of the present without compromising the ability of future generations to meet their own needs". This was an apt message that, like Kennedy's, tried to encourage people to think of both the present and the future; of individual needs and those of others. More recent commentators have also picked up on the theme of sustainability and the problem of the dominance of economic growth. Hamilton notes that "growth not only fails to make people contented; it destroys many of the things that do. Growth fosters empty consumerism, degrades the natural environment, weakens social cohesion and corrodes character" (Hamilton 2004), while Hakim (2011, p. 656) observes that the "consumption-based model is not sustainable. It does not positively impact our behaviours, our sense of well being or the well being of our society and the planet". In addition, there have been two emerging schools of thought around smart growth – growth that enhances lives while significantly reducing environmental risks and ecological scarcities – and degrowth. This latter concept emerged out of the First International Conference on Economic Degrowth for Ecological Sustainability and Social Equity that took place in Paris in 2008. Focusing on the idea of frugal innovation (also a theme developed by Hakim) and adjustment in resources, institutions and human behavior, degrowth challenges the "centrality of economic growth as an overarching policy objective" (Schneider 2010, p. 828).

The encouraging aspect of the growing awareness of sustainability is that some citizens and place managers are taking action. While we do live in a dominantly consumerist society where you are free to do anything, as long as it involves shopping (Böhm and de Cock 2007), it has been noted that there are increasing numbers of people who have recognized the disconnect between increased material wealth and happiness. The group known as "voluntary simplifiers" is a category of people who have made the conscious decision to reduce their consumption levels and find meaning through reducing their spend on products and services and using their time more on activities that generate meaning for them. This group is anti-consumerist and ideologically motivated (Oates *et al.* 2008; Belz and Peattie 2009). The size of this audience is difficult to estimate, but it is suggested that in the US alone there are some 60 million people who fit into the category (Sandlin and Walther 2009). These are still consuming individuals, but they are, in their eyes at least, consuming responsibly within self-defined boundaries. It can be argued that this may not be the case for the rest of the US. As one indicator of the temptation to over consume, in 1984 Americans rented 300 million square feet of self-storage space. Today the figure is 2.4 billion square feet that presumably houses all the things people thought they must, or ought to, have.

There is also some evidence at the city level of places following sustainable models. Burdett and Rode (2011) note "there is growing evidence that urban environments with higher-density residential and commercial buildings, a well distributed mix of uses and public transport reduce the energy footprint". This is a positive move away from the traditional modernist city with its problems of social alienation and environmental degradation caused not least by the love affair with the car. Sheller and Urry (2006) observe that the private car is in conflict with the humanistic aspects of urbanity in that it destroys the public aspects of a city and restricts social interaction. In the last two decades some pioneering cities have tried to alter the balance between the private car and more environmental forms of transport. This has included the promotion of shared bicycle schemes, the promotion of car pooling and car clubs, more electric and biofuel driven public transport, tariff schemes and better public transport infrastructure. For example, in the southern Brazilian city of Curitiba, which is one of the group of C40 cities focused on tackling climate change, public transport has been revolutionized. Buses have dedicated lanes, use a simple pricing system and provide safe and easy access. The service is used by 85 percent of the population and it has transformed many aspects of the city: about 1,100 buses make 12,500 trips every day, serving more than 1.3 million passengers, which is 50 times the number in 1990. This not only helps to improve air quality, but also enhances interaction and leads to improvements in the quality of life.

SUMMARY

As places become more participative, interactive, innovative and environmentally aware, they better meet the needs and wants of citizens. Place managers can and should be at the forefront of creating opportunities for democratization and engaging with the wide diversity of talents that live and work in communities, towns and cities. This is valuable for citizens because it provides an opportunity for meaning making and social interaction and is beneficial to places because they can better meet the needs of all their stakeholders. To make this change place managers need to move away from an emphasis on external brand building and turn inwards to communicate better with citizens, businesses and institutions to help people to realize their potential and to encourage innovative approaches to tackling the pressing problems of over consumption and environmental damage. At the same time, citizens, both as individuals and as part of communities, need to take responsibility in helping places maximize the well-being for all and in doing so realize Robert Kennedy's vision of the real meaning of growth.

NOTES

1. http://medinge.org/if-brands-and-governments-dont-do-their-job-someone-else-will-do-it-for-them/.
2. Lash's claim is that the producers and the relevant audience of modernist and postmodernist culture are found in particular declining and emergent social classes and class fractions (Lash 1990, ix). His perspective appears to have a wide range of followers. A study of consumption and gentrification in Sydney, Australia, illustrates how consumption practices

signify gentrification, described as a collective middle class project (Bridge and Dowling 2001, 101). A rhetoric analysis of Starbucks describes the way coffee is consumed there as a "ritual ... to cover the sins of postmodern consumer culture" (Dickinson 2002, p. 5).

REFERENCES

Anholt, S. (2008) "Place branding: is it marketing, or isn't it?", *Place Branding and Public Diplomacy* 4: 1–6.
Baldersheim, H. and Rose, L.E. (2010) "The staying power of the Norwegian Periphery", in Baldersheim, H. and Rose, L.E. (eds), *Territorial Choice: The Politics of Boundaries and Borders*, Basingstoke: Palgrave Macmillan.
Balibar, E. (2008) *Spinoza and Politics*, trans. P. Snowdon, London: Verso.
Belz, F.M. and Peattie, K. (2009) *Sustainability Marketing: A Global Perspective*, Chichester: John Wiley & Sons.
Böhm, S. and de Cock, C. (2007) "Liberalist fantasies: Žižek and the impossibility of the open society", *Organization*, 14(6): 815–36.
Bridge, G. and Dowling, R. (2001) "Microgeographies of retailing and gentrification", *Australian Geographer*, 32: 93–107.
Burdett, R. and Rode, P. (2011) "Living in the urban age", in Burdett, R. and Sudjic, D. (eds), *Living in the Endless City*, London: Phaidon.
Cova, B. and Dalli, D. (2009) "Working consumers: the next step in marketing theory", *Marketing Theory*, 9(3): 315–34.
Curtis, T., Abratt, R. and Minor, W. (2009) "Corporate brand management in higher education: the case of ERAU", *Journal of Product and Brand Management*, 18(6): 404–13.
Dickinson, G. (2002) "Joe's rhetoric finding authenticity at Starbucks", *Rhetoric Society Quarterly*, 32(4): 5–27.
Edvinsson, L. and Malone, M. (1997) *Intellectual Capital: The Proven Way to Establish Your Company's Real Value by Measuring its Hidden Brainpower*, London: Piatkus.
Ford, K. (2010) *The Trouble with City Planning: What New Orleans Can Teach Us*, New Haven, CT: Yale University Press.
Foucault, M. (2003) *Society Must Be Defended: Lectures at the College de France 1975–1976*, trans. D. Macey, New York: Picador.
Hakim, A.M. (2011) "A new model for socially responsible brand management", *Journal of Brand Management*, 18(9): 650–8.
Hamilton, C. (2004) *Growth Fetish,* London: Pluto Press.
Holm, E.D. (2010) *Coffee and the City: Towards a Soft Urbanity*, Arkitekthøgskolen i Oslo.
Ind, N. and Schultz, M. (2010) "Brand building, beyond marketing", *Strategy-Business*, July.
Ind, N., Fuller, C. and Trevail, C. (2012) *Brand Together: How Co-creation Generates Innovation and Energises Brands*, London: Kogan Page.
Johnson, S. (2010) *Where Good Ideas Come From: The Natural History of Innovation*, London: Allen Lane.
Kaufmann, B. (2007) "How direct democracy makes Switzerland a better place", *Daily Telegraph*, 18 May.
Lash, S. (1990) *Sociology of Postmodernism*, London: Routledge.
Morrison, S. and Crane, F.G. (2007) "Building the service brand by creating and managing an emotional brand experience", *Journal of Brand Management*, 14(5): 410–21.

Muniz, A.M. and O'Guinn, T.C. (2001) "Brand community", *Journal of Consumer Research*, 27: 412–32.

Oates, C.J., McDonald, S., Alevizou, P., Hwang, K. and Young, W. (2008) "Marketing sustainability: use of information sources and degrees of voluntary simplicity", *Journal of Marketing Communication*, 14(5): 351–65.

Prahalad, C.K. and Ramaswamy, V. (2004) *The Future of Competition: Co-creating Unique Value with Customers*, Boston, MA: Harvard Business School Press.

Sandlin, J. A. and Walther, C. S. (2009) "Complicated simplicity: moral identity formation and social movement learning in the voluntary simplicity movement", *Adult Education Quarterly*, 59: 298–317.

Schneider, F. (2010) "Degrowth of production and consumption capacities for social justice, wellbeing and ecological sustainability", Paper presented at the 2nd Conference on Economic Degrowth for Ecological Sustainability and Social Equity, University of Barcelona, 26–29 March.

Sheller, M. and Urry, J. (eds) (2006) *Mobile Technologies of the City*, London: Routledge.

Spinoza, B. de (1998) *Tractatus Politicus*, www.constitution.org/bs/poltreat.txt.

Tuqan, Y.T. (2010) "If brands (and governments) don't do their job, someone else will do it for them", *Journal of the Medinge Group*, 4.

Vargo, S.L. and Lusch, R.F. (2004) "Evolving to a new dominant logic for marketing", *Journal of Marketing*, 68: 1–17.

Vugt, G. de (2010) "Dare to edit! – the politics of Wikipedia", *Ephemera: Theory and Politics in Organization*, 10(1): 64–76.

CHAPTER 3

Crisis Communication and Sustainable Place Marketing: A Preliminary Analysis before Choosing a Restorative Media Strategy

Eli Avraham

In the field of image restoration, it is customary to distinguish between two types of negative destination images. The first type is a negative image caused by an unexpected crisis, such as terror attack, natural disaster or sudden epidemic. The second is a prolonged negative image generated by long-lasting problems, such as economic hardship, high crime rates, continuous war or political instability. The question of how to restore a place's positive image was dealt with in a number of academic and practical publications in the field of "crisis communication". The variety of techniques and strategies proposed were important in creating a block of knowledge in image restoration; however, the same solutions were offered for places that differ greatly from one another. Moreover, the solutions proposed did not take into account the type of crisis experienced or the characteristics of the target audiences to be addressed. This is problematic, because clearly countries that are located on the margins of global tourism, such as Somalia, for example, cannot adopt the same image-restoration strategies as that of a country that is a major world tourism player, even if each experienced the same crisis, such as a terrorist event or an epidemic. Somalia's location, its previous image, the availability of resources and its target audience are all very different elements from those characterizing that other country.

In this chapter I offer a preliminary analysis of three types of characteristics – related to the place, audience and crisis – that must be considered before selecting a strategy to restore the positive image of a place that has experienced a crisis. This discussion makes both practical and theoretical contributions. On a practical level, the analysis helps marketers in the selection of the correct strategy for restoring an image; on the theoretical level, it offers an extension to existing models of place-image restoration.

THEORETICAL BACKGROUND

Despite the growing popularity of the destination marketing field, the existing knowledge is not always relevant to the marketing of all types of destinations. Although well-known destinations like Paris, London and Frankfurt can hire an advertising agency to come up with a new tourism campaign, this tactic will not work or be feasible for destinations suffering from a problematic image (Baker 2007). In the global era, a negative image is a major obstacle to attracting tourists, high-quality residents and investors (Kotler *et al.* 1993; Beirman 2003; Baker 2007; Govers and Go 2009).

The fields of "image restoration" and "crisis communication" comprise several existing models that provide suggestions on how firms and organizations can restore their image post-crisis. For example, Stocker (1997) cites three or four steps that are included in the basic response strategy: expression of regret that the situation happened; action to resolve the situation; action to ensure that the situation will not recur; and if necessary the offer of restitution to injured parties. A more elaborate model is offered by Benoit (1995; 1997), who lists five communication strategies that can be used in response to a crisis: denial, evasion of responsibility, reducing offensiveness of events, corrective action and mortification. Similarly, Coombs (1999) identifies seven communication strategies: attacking the accuser, denial, excuse, justification, ingratiation, corrective action and full apology. One can see that most of these strategies are suitable mainly for places experiencing an immediate crisis and less for places suffering from a prolonged image crisis.

Contrary to earlier models, Avraham and Ketter (2008) proposed a new model that was designed and created exclusively for assisting localities to alter negative destination images. It offered a choice of three groups of media strategies, with the focus on the source of the message, the message itself and the target audience. Source strategies focus on affecting, influencing or replacing the sources of the negative message (mainly the mass media). Message strategies focus on the message itself, handling the problematic image components directly, and include four groups: (1) disregard for/partial acknowledgment of the crisis (ignoring the crisis, acknowledging the negative image, limiting the scale of the crisis); (2) full acknowledgment of the crisis and adoption of moderate coping measures (tackling the crisis, hosting spotlight events, hosting opinion leaders); (3) full acknowledgment of the crisis and adoption of extreme coping measures (delivering a counter-message, spinning liabilities into assets, ridiculing the stereotype); and (4) disengagement from the place's main characteristics (branding contrary to the stereotype, geographic isolation). Lastly, audience strategies focus on the target audience, its values and perceptions (for example, emphasizing cultural similarity to the target audience, use of patriotism and nationalism, and changing the target audience).

According to Avraham and Ketter (2008), media strategies in each group can be classified on a continuum between moderate and extreme. The criterion for the classification of a given strategy is the distance of its projected new image of the destination from the existing one. The more the components of the new image projected in the campaign differ from the destination's characteristics, the more extreme the strategy to be used. For example, in order to disconnect the Israeli resort of Eilat from the problematic image of Israel – during a prolonged tourism crisis that occurred in the early 2000s – marketers "relocated" it, presenting it as "Eilat on the Red Sea", disregarding the city's formal location. In this chapter I offer a preliminary analysis of the three groups of characteristics: crisis characteristics, audience characteristics and place characteristics (CAP analysis). I believe that this pre-analysis can help marketers in their decisions regarding the strategy to be chosen in order to restore a place's positive image.

CRISIS CHARACTERISTICS

When assessing a crisis, the first thing that should be analyzed is its characteristics. Crises, as we know, different greatly. Some are caused by terror attacks on tourist destinations, others, by a sudden plague; certain crises cause enormous damage and thousands of casualties, whereas others leave no casualties; there are prolonged crises and short-lived ones. Given all this variation, different recovery strategies are necessary.

Geographic Scale

The location of the region/city/resort struck by the crisis should be noted. If it is determined that it is geographically a limited-scale crisis, then the use of a media strategy called "limiting the crisis by geographical scale" can be recommended. In such a case, the country's marketers inform tourists that the crisis is limited to a certain region in the country, but that it is still safe to visit other regions. The UK, for example, employed that strategy after marketers realized that the foot-and-mouth epidemic was confined to remote areas of the country. Subsequently, the tourist campaign emphasized that the rest of the UK's areas were quite safe to visit (Hopper 2002).

Origin/Nationality of Casualties

Another issue arising from the geographical location of a crisis is the nationality or the origin of the casualties. When the victims of a crisis are tourists – especially from industrialized countries – the crisis will gain widescale media coverage. The amount of this coverage may itself affect the perception of the severity of the crisis, unfortunate as this may be. Studies of media coverage have found that the international media have a "scale of blood", according to which the odds that a crisis in a developing country will win media coverage increase as the number of foreign casualties rises (Beirman 2003).

As inappropriate as this phenomenon is, it still affects the choice of a media-recovery strategy. For example, if there were no Western casualties in a crisis that took place in an African country, it is quite likely that the crisis will receive very little media attention (tragic as the incident may be) and that the place's image will not be (severely) damaged. In such a case, place marketers are advised to ignore the negative event in their advertisements and PR campaign ("ignoring the crisis" strategy).

Duration

Time is another important factor for analyzing a crisis. How much time has passed since the crisis began? At what stage is the crisis now? The answers will help to ascertain whether the current negative events are part of an ongoing crisis or are a one-off event. The first necessary distinction is between long-term and short-term crises. With the former, we may expect many negative events, and therefore it is more likely that the target audience has heard about the crisis. By contrast, a short-term crisis may well be concluded without news of it reaching the target audience. In that case, local decision-makers might do well to ignore the crisis and adopt a "business as usual" approach.

Stage

Campaigns are affected not only by the crisis duration but also by the crisis stage. At the height of the crisis, usually in its initial stages, the marketers' message should focus on minimizing damage to the place's image, whereas the message in the final stages should focus on getting back to regular business. Such messages, geared to the stages of a crisis, can indicate that the tourism infrastructure is undamaged, attractions are fully open and that tourists are back. In any event, crisis duration and stage have an effect on the choice of a media-recovery strategy. Every stage in the crisis life cycle renders a unique message and makes different use of advertising and PR resources to alter the negative image created (Mansfeld 2006).

Type of Threat and Scale of Damage

Crises may differ also in nature, type of threat they present and the scale of damage they cause. Each of these three factors has an effect on the choice of media-recovery strategy. According to Mansfeld and Pizam (2006), each crisis type is perceived differently by the target audience, has different consequences for consumer behavior and affects a campaign's messages differently. For example, it is likely that a crisis that threatens the personal safety of tourists will be perceived as more severe than a crisis causing them disappointment or inconvenience as a result of poor infrastructure or unexpected bad whether. Another influential factor in assessing a crisis is its actual severity and the scale of the damage caused. Accordingly, it is important to examine whether the tourism infrastructure has been damaged and whether incoming tourists will be able to enjoy the same variety of attractions that the place offered prior to the crisis. Naturally, places that have sustained damage to their tourism infrastructure must employ different recovery strategies than those places not damaged. This conclusion also holds for places that have undergone a crisis and are now trying to attract investors, firms and residents. In this case, if the relevant infrastructure – telecommunication, electrical power and transportation – has been damaged, it might be better to delay the marketing process and to start with infrastructure rehabilitation.

AUDIENCE CHARACTERISTICS

Different target audiences are motivated by different needs, have different perceptions of places and are differently affected by the occurrence of a crisis event. Many studies have been conducted on the audience and its important role in the communication process (Caspi 1993). The delivery of messages is useless if the target audience does not receive, understand or accept them.

Audience Knowledge and a Place's Former Image

Images of people, products and places evolve over time (Kunczic 1997). The mind processes new information and adds it to existing images. If, for example, the media reports the murder of a tourist in a place that was considered safe, it is more likely that part of the audience will preserve that place's former positive image on the grounds that "that kind of incident can happen anywhere". However, another part of the audience, which perceived the place differently, will now consider it a "dangerous place" for tourists. Hence, a place's former image affects the way new information about it is accepted and processed (Elizur 1987). When a place has a history of involvement in conflicts, violence and negative events, one more report on disorder will be received differently than a similar report about a place that was never associated with violence and conflict. Thus, when a violent incident occurs in a place known to be risky, it will have a greater influence on that place's image than if it happened at a place free of any existing problematic image (ibid.). All this affects the marketer's decision on the choice of a strategy. An interesting example of the effect of a place's past image on its current image is presented by Krauze (1994, cited in Kunczic 1997). Krauze argued that old stereotypes of Mexico affect the present (1994) coverage of this country in the international media. He asserted that the coverage of negative events, such as murder, violence and revolts, arouse the old negative images of a "barbarous, violent and unstable country" (ibid., p. 7).

Another aspect of the impact of a place's former image is that places considered well-established brands, such as London and Paris, have a greater durability in crisis events, since the audience has many positive images associated with those places. For places with a strong positive image, the use of a more moderate media strategy is advised, sometimes even to the point of ignoring the crisis event, allowing the passage of time to reestablish the place's positive image. One more aspect of the audience's knowledge of the crisis/place is the perceived severity of the crisis. Crises that are perceived as severe and that cause booking cancelations demand an immediate and sharp response. On the other hand, if visitors continue coming to the place despite the negative events, a more moderate response strategy is advisable.

Audience Type and Size

A place should be marketed differently for different audiences. For example, an audience that visits a place for religious reasons is different from an audience seeking a sea-and-sun destination, cultural activities and historical monuments. The former will likewise be less concerned about a crisis than the latter (Mansfeld and Pizam 2006) and should be taken into account during the recovery campaign. Another important factor to be assessed is the size of the target audience and what percentage of them knows about the crisis. If, for example, the vast majority has not heard of the crisis, it might be a waste of resources to launch a campaign aimed at overcoming the negative image. In this case, the advice is to ignore the crisis (Avraham and Ketter 2008).

Proximity/distance between Target Audience and Place

Different kinds of proximity or distance – based on geography, social class, religion, political ideology and culture – may exist between the target audience and various places that have experienced a crisis (Elizur 1987). The level of proximity or distance affects our knowledge and perceptions of and our attitudes toward places. The level of proximity between two countries might also affect the amount and type of media coverage a crisis receives. Proximity generates interest, which works on newsroom considerations and routines. For example, it is reasonable to believe that a crisis in Europe involving world-class tourist attractions and harming European tourists will receive wide media coverage in the West, in contrast to a crisis erupting in a developing country in consequence of local conflicts and which affects mainly local residents (Beirman 2003). Proximity/distance also affects the way the target audience perceives, accepts and reacts to news about marketing campaigns on behalf of a certain place. A place that is geographically distant but is perceived as enjoying spiritual proximity to the target audience may use media strategies that highlight the similarity between the residents of the two places. One such example is a campaign launched by Israel with the aim of improving its image among Americans. Relying on the motif of spiritual proximity, the campaign highlighted certain apparent similarities: both countries are democracies, were founded by immigrants and are technologically advanced (Avraham 2009).

The Audience's Sources

The media provide our main source of information about distant places, though the coverage can sometimes be manipulative (Kunczik 1997). A check, therefore, should be made of whether the crisis is represented in a balanced manner, whether the causes of the crisis are being clearly explained, and whether the crisis is being dramatized to increase its news value. Place marketers should examine the credibility of media outlets that report the negative events. If the reporting is found to be questionable, the campaign managers can attempt to undermine the outlet's credibility; if they succeed in this endeavor, the negative messages and images that are delivered will be perceived as unreliable. In extreme cases, in which the media present a distorted image very different from the reality, a proper media strategy might include the use of alternative sources – a destination's website – to deliver contrary messages. Ketter and Avraham (2010) describe how African countries employed their websites to promote themselves and to fight negative stereotypes and perception.

The Social-political Environment and Essential Values

Marketing in general and delivering specific messages in particular depend on the social-political environment (Avraham 2003). The success of a campaign rests heavily on the setting: some messages can be extremely effective in one society and exert very little influence in another. Accordingly, marketing professionals try to take advantage of local values to promote certain products. For example, if the essential values in a certain society are individualism, modernity and multiculturalism, marketers will claim that their product promotes these same values (Hestroni 2000). It is only natural for marketing professionals to analyze the dominant values in a certain society and to use them to promote a place. For example, following the 9/11 terror attacks, the marketers of New York took advantage of national patriotic feelings, which usually characterize American society in any case, and which were now heightened, to promote the city after the 9/11 crisis. This approach was most successful at the time. It is doubtful, though, that the same messages can be used in other types of crisis, such as a plague or severe flood. Some response strategies may be limited to certain types of crisis and certain societies.

PLACE CHARACTERISTICS

Places naturally differ greatly. For this reason, even if two countries suffer from the same type of crisis and both aim at the same target audience, they will probably use different recovery strategies owing to their individual characteristics. These differences are especially salient in respect to developing countries, which in most cases have a lower status and fewer resources than industrialized countries, and so have to invest far more effort in altering their image.

National/International Status

Places differ in terms of national and international power and status. The common factors used to gauge a place's status or power include physical resources – such as size, economic stability and natural treasures – and abstract resources – such as a place's media or public image and cultural centrality. Given those two groups of factors, places with visible and accessible power can be distinguished from places with hidden and inaccessible power (Kotler *et al.* 2002). Similarly, Wolfsfeld (1991) distinguishes a place's general status from its status in the media. General status comprises the place's resources, physical size and ability to influence national decision-makers.

In the media, a place's status is measured by its news value and its importance in the minds of journalists and editors. Many studies have found a firm link between a place's general power and its power in the media, as the media tend to keep track of the powers that be. Headquarters of news corporations are located in the hubs of political, economic and cultural power, such as New York, London, Paris, Los Angeles and Brussels, a circumstance that only supports and magnifies media power (Avraham 2003). Such places are more durable during immediate crises, and their marketers can choose to adopt a less-drastic strategy to overcome the negative image after a crisis.

Resource Availability

A place's resources are key elements in choosing a media strategy, as altering a negative image can be costly. One reason for the high cost of campaigns is the price of media space. For example, the campaign to reattract tourism to Washington, DC, following 9/11 was estimated to be $3.37 million (Stafford *et al.* 2006), and the campaign to restore tourism to Singapore following the SARS epidemic was estimated to amount to US$33 million (Beirman 2003). It may be a truism that every place needs money to market itself effectively (Wolfsfeld 1997; Avraham 2003); however, most places cannot afford such sums, which accumulate by hiring spokespersons, conducting image surveys, buying media space and producing expensive events – hence they must adopt less costly media strategies. In other words, the choice of media strategy is directly affected by a place's resources. For example, if a place chooses to produce sports events, music festivals and other mass cultural activities to attract visitors and journalists, it requires extensive resources. Similarly, deep pockets are also needed to finance other image-altering initiatives, such as providing journalists and opinion shapers with free airline tickets, free tours and free entrance to local attractions. This was exactly what New York City did in the aftermath of 9/11, handing out free tickets to Broadway shows in order to attract tourists to the city. By contrast, places without such resources cannot afford to spend money on producing spotlight events and have to choose modest responses. To conclude, mainly rich states or cities can produce mega-events, a fact that reinforces their image (which is already positive) and facilitates their rapid management of crisis events. Still, it is also possible to rely more on

PR than on advertising, to cooperate with local firms and tourist organizations, and to create successful events without depleting the local treasury (Lahav and Avraham 2008).

Type and Variety of Tourist Attractions

Besides financial resources, places differ in the amount, type and variety of tourist attractions they offer, and in the demographic characteristics of the visitors they attract. If, for example, a place that offers sea-and-sun tourism suffers an image crisis, it will be very easy for its audience to find an alternative, since the same kind of vacation can be enjoyed at many places. However, if a crisis befalls a place that offers unique experiences, such as New York, Paris or Venice, it is reasonable to believe that those places will overcome the crisis relatively quickly because the attractions they offer are almost irreplaceable and perhaps not duplicated elsewhere. Similarly, places that offer religious sites usually have a high crisis-durability status. One such place is Mecca in Saudi Arabia, which attracts millions of pilgrims every year regardless of tragedies that take place during the pilgrimage, caused by stampedes, fires and hotels collapsing, all of which have happened in recent years. Large numbers of pilgrims likewise travel annually to Rome, Jerusalem and Nazareth, and barely consider the image of those places. In addition, places can also use the famous institutions located in their territory (for example CNN and Coca-Cola during the promotion of Atlanta) or celebrities who live in a place – as part of a campaign aim to attract back tourists and to promote the message that the place is safe. New York marketers, for example, used that strategy after 9/11 (Stafford *et al.* 2006).

Location

Without doubt, a good location is an important advantage for any country, city or tourist destination. As mentioned, a strategy applied by an image-crisis country located in Europe or North America will probably be entirely different from the strategy chosen by a country suffering from a similar crisis located in the Middle East, Asia or South America. One of the main reasons for this difference is the proximity and high accessibility of Europeans, who can easily travel to a place in Europe that has undergone a crisis. This audience will perceive the place in crisis in a much less stereotypical way and with fewer generalizations than people usually tend to make regarding remote and unfamiliar places that are engaged in crises. Another important factor arising from a place's location is its distance from the core of the crisis. Specifically, it should be assessed whether the place is at this core or only at its periphery. If the latter, it might be advisable to represent the place as an independent region or to disassociate it from the crisis area; this approach has been taken with Taba and Eilat, each of which has presented itself as an "independent" place, not located in Egypt or Israel, following a crisis.

A Place's Tourism Industry Life Cycle

Like any person or product, places have a life cycle. Some places are still at an early stage, battling for recognition and market share; others are developed and well-established, and slowly becoming irrelevant with the passage of time. The marketing of a place is affected by its life-cycle stage. Marketing an unfamiliar place or one that has a prolonged negative image is significantly different from marketing a place that is well known (Kotler and Armstrong 1989). Accordingly, crisis-response strategies for places at different stages will differ too; new and unfamiliar places (i.e. those at the start of their life cycle) are more likely to choose an extreme and bold strategy, whereas places that have gained a (positive) reputation (normally in the middle of their life cycle) can achieve the same campaign effect by employing a moderate strategy.

Regime and Local Leadership

The field of urban studies is replete with tales of failure or prosperity, which is mainly dependent on the actions of the local leadership. The upshot is that places alike in location, population and sources of income have developed differently. At the international level, the type of regime can affect the success of countries. Just as the type of regime and the actions of local leaders affect the way a place is managed and impinge on its economic prosperity, the leadership can also influence the choice of media strategy for marketing the place. For example, democracies oblige local leaders to take public opinion into consideration when a decision needs to be made about the place's well being; as a result, those leaders will tend to involve residents in their decision-making and in launching marketing campaigns (Avraham and Ketter 2008). By contrast, the role of public opinion in non-democratic regimes is less important, and those places are less likely to invite residents to participate in municipal processes. In some of those countries, the government indeed decides where the residents will live, where new factories should be located and what tourist attractions are to be developed. Discussing the choice of a marketing strategy for those places is meaningless; the decision is solely that of the government. In addition, municipalities and local authorities, democratic or not, that are governed inefficiently will probably do just as poorly when trying to run an advertising and public relations campaign. To conclude, local leadership, the local regime and its functioning exercise a direct effect on a place's image and on the choice of a marketing strategy (Avraham 2003).

SUMMARY

In this chapter, I have presented a preliminary analysis of what must be considered before marketers determine the image-restoration strategy for a place suffering from a negative image because of an immediate or prolonged crisis. The preliminary analysis included reference to three types of characteristics associated with the crisis, the audience and the place. In analyzing these three groups of characteristics, I have shown how such an analysis greatly assists place marketers with making a decision on the correct strategy to restore the place's image.

The variety of factors and characteristics that should be considered during the analysis demonstrated just how misguided was the tendency of previous publications in the fields of place marketing and branding to offer the same solution to the same places. There is no doubt that future research in place promotion should concentrate more on places that suffer from a negative image, which thus require much more knowledge and new creative ideas than do regular places to restore their image. Although most of the examples for recovery strategies presented in this chapter are from the field of advertising, it is worth remembering that there are other tools and techniques for restoring place image, such as public relations, media relations, tours for newspeople, information centers and press conferences (Avraham and Ketter 2008).

REFERENCES

Avraham, E. (2003) *Behind Media Marginality: Coverage of Social Groups and Places in the Israeli Press*, Lanham, MD: Lexington Books.

Avraham, E. (2009) "Marketing and managing nation branding during prolonged crisis: the case of Israel", *Place Branding and Public Diplomacy*, 5(3): 202–12.

Avraham, E. and Ketter, E. (2008) *Media Strategies for Marketing Places in Crises: Improving the Image of Cities, Countries and Tourist Destinations*, Oxford: Butterworth Heinemann.

Baker, B. (2007) *Destination Branding for Small Cities*, Portland, OR: Creative Leap Books.

Beirman, D. (2003) *Restoring Tourism Destinations in Crisis*, Cambridge: CABI.

Benoit, W.L. (1995) *Accounts, Excuses, and Apologies: A Theory of Image Restoration Strategies*, Albany, NY: State University of New York Press.

Benoit, W.L. (1997) "Image repair discourse and crisis communication", *Public Relations Review*, 23(2): 177–87.

Caspi, D. (1993) *Mass Communication*, Tel Aviv: The Open University of Israel. [In Hebrew]
Coombs, W.T. (1995) "Choosing the right words", *Management Communication Quarterly*, 8(4): 447–76.
Coombs, W.T. (1999) *Ongoing Crisis Communication: Planning, Managing and Responding*, Thousand Oaks, CA: Sage.
Elizur, J. (1987) *National Images*, Jerusalem: Hebrew University.
Govers, R. and Go, F. (2009) *Place Branding*. Basingstoke: Palgrave Macmillan.
Hestroni, A. (2000) "The relationship between values and appeals in Israeli advertising: a smallest space analysis", *Journal of Advertising*, 29(3): 55–68.
Hopper, P. (2002) "Marketing London in a difficult climate", *Journal of Vacation Marketing*, 9(1): 81–8.
Ketter, E. and Avraham, E. (2010) "How African countries promote themselves by using the Internet", *International Journal of Tourism Policy*, 3(4): 318–31.
Kotler, P. and Armstrong, G. (1989) *Principles of Marketing*, 4th edn, Englewood Cliffs, NJ: Prentice Hall.
Kotler, P., Haider, D.H. and Rein, I. (1993) *Marketing Places*, New York: Free Press.
Kotler, P., Hamlin, M.A., Rein, I. and Haider, D.H. (2002) *Marketing Asian Places: Attracting Investment, Industry and Tourism to Cities, States and Nations*. Singapore: John Wiley & Sons.
Kunczik, M. (1997) *Images of Nations and International Public Relations*, Mahwah, NJ: LEA.
Lahav T. and Avraham, E. (2008) "Public relations for peripheral places and national media coverage patterns: the Israeli case", *Public Relations Review*, 34: 230–6.
Mansfeld, Y. (2006) "The role of security information in tourism crisis management: the missing link", in Mansfeld, Y. and Pizam, A. (eds), *Tourism, Security and Safety: From Theory to Practice*, Burlington, MA: Butterworth Heinemann, pp. 271–90.
Mansfeld, Y. and Pizam, A. (eds) (2006) *Tourism, Security and Safety: From Theory to Practice*, Burlington, MA: Butterworth Heinemann.
Stafford, G., Yu, L. and Armoo, K. (2006) "Crisis management and recovery: how Washington, DC, hotels responded to terrorism", in Mansfeld, Y. and Pizam, A. (eds), *Tourism, Security and Safety: From Theory to Practice*, Burlington, MA: Butterworth-Heinemann, pp. 291–311.
Stocker, K.P. (1997) "A strategic approach to crisis management", in Caywood, C.L. (ed.), *The Handbook of Strategic Public Relations & Integrated Communications*, Boston, MA: McGraw Hill, pp. 189–203.
Wolfsfeld, G. (1991) "Media, protest and political violence", *Journalism Monograph*, 127.
Wolfsfeld, G. (1997) *Media and Political Conflict: News from the Middle East*, Cambridge: Cambridge University Press.

CHAPTER 4

A Perspective on Planning, Smart Growth and Place Branding

Kristof van Assche, Ming Chien Lo and Raoul Beunen

In this chapter, we argue that planning strategies sensitive for place branding could increase the appeal of smart growth projects by creating value for places and for things in those places. We develop a perspective on the potential synergy between smart growth and place branding that can be valuable in various contexts – in the US, the EU and communities elsewhere – since many encounter obstacles to comprehensive planning that could be reduced by paying closer attention to how value can be affected by planning.

SMART GROWTH AS REBRANDED PLANNING

As an intellectual movement to counter urban sprawl and other urban development that was considered undesirable in the US, smart growth literature prospered in the 1990s and continued in the 2000s in various directions (e.g. Kelly 1993; Nelson and Duncan 1995; Porter 1997; Zovanyi 1998; Beaumont 1999; Weitz 1999; Burchell *et al.* 2000; Downs 2000; 2005; APA 2001; 2002; Bengston *et al.* 2004). Although different authors define the concept differently, overlapping interests can often be found, including:

- Growth that is sustainable and environmentally sensitive.
- Growth that involves well-designed networks of transportation, housing, businesses, etc.
- An environment opposite to those that create urban sprawls.
- Restricted growth in certain areas (e.g. existing farming that is environmentally sensitive).
- Growth with multifunctional land use.

The concept of smart growth was not new. Almost all of the elements can be found in earlier planning literature, and in many cases in older practices. The American urban sprawl that was observed after World War II demonstrated that the concept and the practice had taken a break (e.g. Endicott 1993; Burchell et al. 1998; Beaumont 1999; Benfield et al. 1999). More importantly, with a different planning tradition and a skepticism against government led planning efforts, it was the academia in the US that took an activist role in the movement and championed the smart growth concept as a repackaging of what is basically comprehensive planning. In its genesis, the smart growth literature is predominantly an American one that is thoroughly grounded in the woes of American planning. After a century of planning, zoning and urban design, most planning in that country may be described as localist, legalist and lacking comprehensive spatial visioning (Knaap and Nelson 1992; Ndubisi and Dyer 1992; Weitz and Seltzer 1998; Platt 2004; Downs 2005). In other words, planning as design is a rare phenomenon (Van Assche and Lo 2011), and planners have to reassert and reconquer their position in local politics. From the European perspective, because of a different tradition of urban reconstruction and development, the smart growth concept is neither special nor unique. But in the context of American planning, putting old wine in new bottles was essential for rebranding a tradition that was lost after the war. For many American cities, comprehensive planning had been formally adopted but its implementation has proven difficult (Jacobs 1998; Arendt 1999; Platt 2004; Van Assche and Lo 2011). In this unique environment, the smart growth proponents in the US are highly aware of the obstacles in legal, political and economic systems as well as in the cultural mindsets of people. Thus, by creating the "smart growth" label, they make it more persuasive for pushing their agenda at creating desirable neighborhoods in communities to policy-makers, developers and residents (e.g. Kelly 1993; Downs 1994; Burby and May 1997; Porter 1997; Gihring 1999; Mehrhoff 1999; Gustanski and Squires 2000; APA 2001; 2002).

When it comes to making the concept a reality, non-governmental groups, planners and their backers in governments and groups of large developers all play the role of advocates according to different motives (cf. Downs 2005). Environmental lobbies and professional groups (e.g. architects) saw this as an opportunity to promote their cause or vision (Downs 1994; Benfield et al. 1999; APA 2001; 2002). Governments in major cities either believed in the intrinsic value of comprehensive planning or were interested in the cost-saving and revenue-making promises of smart growth (Zovanyi 1998; National Association of Counties 2001; Platt 2004; Downs 2005). At the Federal level, the US Environmental Protection Agency considered

A Perspective on Planning, Smart Growth and Place Branding

smart growth a way to integrate environmental and development policies (APA 2002). Motivated by potential profits, some large developers became advocates and believed that they were better positioned in the movement because they were financially and logistically resourceful (e.g. Urban Land Institute 1998; National Association of Home Builders 1999).

In spite of the efforts of the aforementioned groups of advocates, the impacts of smart growth have been limited. Starting with zoning ordinances in the 1920s that the courts upheld, local government gained more powers in regulating land uses (Arendt 1999; APA 2001; Nolon 2003; Nolon and Salkin 2006). Nevertheless, due to political pressures in local politics and the lack of expertise and resources in local governments, long-term planning perspectives were hard to articulate or implement. As a result, planning, rebranded as smart growth, had limited success in countering this environment (cf. Nolon 2003; Liverman 2004; Downs 2005).

PLACE BRANDING, PLACE IDENTITY AND SMART GROWTH

In recent years, the concept of place branding has moved from being a type of product branding to a topic of governance (Anholt 2007; 2010; Hildreth 2010; Van Assche and Lo 2011). Narrowing the view of a place as a product (Pike 2005; Pasquinelli 2010) limits our perspectives and prevents researchers and practitioners from discovering, creating and promoting the value of a place and a community. A place, with its people, is a community that has to be governed, that has its own recognition of assets and risks, and its own narratives about self, past and future (Hjortegaard Hansen 2010; Van Assche and Lo 2011). We claim that elements of place branding can be useful for implementing smart growth in both the American context and a more general context outside the US. More importantly, we will pay closer attention to value creation and destruction in and by planning (Allmendinger *et al.* 2005; Allmendinger and Haugton 2005).

A brand is a name or an image that is reputable. A well-established brand is one that will reduce the future cost of marketing as media buzz and words of mouth from informed customers to prospective customers are generated. But there are costs associated with creating a brand and maintaining the brand. To brand a product, experts must find its value and create a coherent narrative to persuade consumers. Because a place/community is more complex than a product and involves multiple organizations and groups, much of the effort of place branding is to create the unity of vision based on a new identity that is built on some existing identity narratives (Czarniawska 2002; 2008; Sonnino 2007; Hjortegaard Hansen 2010). This unity of vision is crucial to smart growth. Without this, smart growth and the related planning strategy will just be a complicated concept and process to the audience; and the idea as well as the benefits will remain costly to promote.

Anholt (2007; 2010), Hildreth (2010) and many others have already pointed out the advantages of bringing branding experts in at the early stage of planning. In a planning process, almost certainly there are a number of ways to link up different policies, concepts and assets into a coherent identity narrative (Throgmorton 1996; Soja 1997; Hillier 2002; Van Assche et al. 2012). Branding expertise can be helpful in selecting the narratives and images that can speak to the imagination and create value, while, in the other direction, planning and other experts can indicate positive or negative implications of these preferred visions for a variety of topics and policies (Van Assche and Lo 2011).

Spatial planning is about drawing conceptual boundaries. If we talk about large areas that are impacted on by smart growth, the division in neighborhoods and the lines drawn by roads, green areas and water may not be regarded as constant spatial boundaries that delineate different "products". Neither may one regard the lines between spatial scales as stable (Swyngedouw and Heynen 2003). Instead, one must realize that these boundaries and scales are not given in nature but are conceptual lines drawn by stakeholders in political, cultural and economic games (Paasi 1991; Forrest and Murie 1995; Van Assche et al. 2008). There are many ways to draw lines; but once lines are drawn, "commodities" – residential, business, transportation, recreational and natural – are delineated. The process of "line drawing" can inspire branding efforts, and that in turn allows lines to be drawn in ways that will make its commodities marketable or make it easier to promote them. In such spatial commodification, new identities and values are created.

Here, we do not consider commodification necessarily to be a negative process, as in much of the geographical and anthropological literature where it is seen as an undesirable by-product of neo-liberalism (see e.g. Jessop 1998; Peck and Tickell 2002; Swyngedouw and Heynen 2003; Lury 2004; Gotham 2007). Rather, commodification is an essential feature of capitalism. Branding is indeed more than marketing. It is the continuous changing of the boundaries of what can be considered marketable (Moor 2003; Hildreth 2010). It creates new commodities and seeks potential commodities (de Chernatony 2006). This does not mean that entities that provoke sentiments, like places, culture and nature, are reduced to lifeless physical objects for trade (Czarniawska 2002; Hjortegaard Hansen 2010; Hildreth 2010; Bellini et al. 2010). On the contrary, such an understanding of the success and failure of virtually anything in capitalist democracies – of the underlying principles of commodification and decommodification (Anholt 2007; 2010) – provides opportunities to assign value to more things, places and activities, and more opportunities to stabilize these values-in-place.

Things that are delineated, recognized as distinct from their conceptual and/or spatial environment, can more easily be valued, devalued or revalued. Very often, we first value a certain experience, then articulate it as an object or related to an object which will then become tangible for market exchanges (Appadurai 1988; Callon *et al.* 2002; Verdery 2003; Lury 2004). In space, planning can create units, neighborhoods or sites that are more clearly distinguishable from their surroundings than other parts of the landscape. Spatial differences can be observed, and the discourse among local governments, developers and media can further articulate a difference (Czarniawska 2002; 2008). These together can create an object. Planning will naturally increase this process of objectification, because it wants to make a difference and has to make a difference to legitimize itself.

From the very beginning, smart growth, as a rebranding of planning, attempted to include the developers' community because the lack of support on their part was seen as a major reason for the failure of planning in many cities and regions (cf. Urban Land Institute 1998; National Association of Home Builders 1999; APA 2001; 2002; Downs 2005; Nolon and Salkin 2006). Advocates for smart growth did not only promote the approach in the direction of residents and politicians, but also to developers. Planning repackaged as smart growth was perceived to be easier to "sell" to developers and customers. A smart growth neighborhood was perceived to be more clearly circumscribed as an identifiable product, more commodified and marketable than a neighborhood that simply followed the rules and ideas of a comprehensive plan. In that sense, the proponents of smart growth in many cases understood the power of commodification and opened the door to place branding.

CONCLUDING REMARKS

The potential for place branding in smart growth is vast, but it also linked to governance in an intricate manner. The place branding literature has already moved in the direction of governance, with a recognition that places are complex products, or in fact many products, and that commodification and decommodification take place all the time. In Van Assche and Lo (2011), using the examples of Tuscany, Missouri and northern Minnesota, we acknowledged that the creation of value by means of new identity narratives stands a much better chance if it is embedded in the identity narratives and ascriptions of value in the community. Instead of visioning planning and place branding as independent processes, sustainability movement such as smart growth will benefit from a combination of both.

REFERENCES

Allmendinger, Philip and Graham Haughton, 2005. "Spatial planning, devolution, and new planning spaces", *Environment and Planning C: Government and Policy*, 28(5): 803–18.

Allmendinger Philip, Janice Morphet and Mark Tewdwr-Jones, 2005. "Devolution and the modernisation of local government: prospects for spatial planning", *European Planning Studies*, 13(3): 349–70.

Anholt, Simon, 2007. *Competitive Identity: The New Brand Management for Nations, Cities and Regions*. Basingstoke: Palgrave Macmillan.

Anholt, Simon, 2010. *Places: Identity, Image and Reputation*. Basingstoke: Palgrave Macmillan.

APA (American Planning Association), 2001. *Policy Guide on Smart Growth*. Chicago, IL: APA.

APA (American Planning Association), 2002. *Growing Smart User Manual for the Growing Smart Legislative Guidebook: Model Statutes for Planning and the Management of Change, 2002 edition*. Chicago, IL: APA.

Appadurai, Arjun (ed.) 1988. *The Social Life of Things. Commodities in Cultural Perspective*. Cambridge: Cambridge University Press.

Arendt, Randall, 1999. *Growing Greener: Putting Conservation into Local Plans and Ordinances*. Washington, DC: Island Press.

Assche, Kristof van and Ming C. Lo, 2011. "Planning, preservation and place branding: a tale of sharing assets and narratives", *Journal of Place Branding and Public Diplomacy*, 7(2): 117–26.

Assche, Kristof van, Petruta Teampau, Patrick Devlieger and Cristian Suciu, 2008. "Liquid boundaries in marginal marshes: Reconstructions of identity in the Romanian Danube Delta", *Studia Sociologia*, 53(1): 115–33.

Assche, Kristof van, Raoul Beunen and Martijn Duineveld, 2011. "Performing success and failure in governance: Dutch planning experiences", *Public Administration*, DOI: 10.1111/j.1467-9299.2011.01972.x.

Beaumont, Costance E. (ed.), 1999. *Challenging Sprawl: Organizational Responses to a National Problem*. Washington, DC: National Trust for Historic Preservation.

Bellini Nicola, Anna Loffredo and Cecilia Pasquinelli, 2010. "Managing otherness: the political economy of place images in the case of Tuscany", in Gregory Ashworth and Mihalis Kavaratzis (eds), *Towards Effective Place Brand Management: Branding European Cities and Regions*. London: Edward Elgar, pp. 89–116.

Benfield, F. Kaid, Matthew D. Raimi and Donald D.T. Chen, 1999. *Once There Were Greenfields: How Urban Sprawl is Undermining America's Environment, Economy, and Social Fabric*. Washington, DC: Natural Resources Defense Council and Surface Transportation Policy Project.

Bengston, David N., Jennifer O. Fletcher and Kriston C. Nelson, 2004. "Public policies for managing urban growth and protecting open space: policy instruments and lessons learned in the United States", *Landscape and Urban Planning*, 69: 271–86.

Burby, Raymond J. and Peter J. May, 1997. *Making Governments Plan: State Experiments in Managing Land Use*. Baltimore, MD: Johns Hopkins University Press.

Burchell, Robert W., Naveed A. Shad, David Listokin, Hilary Phillips, Anthony Downs, Samuel Seskin, Judy. S. Davis, Terry Moore, David Helton and Michelle Gall, 1998. *The

Costs of Sprawl: Revisited. Report 39. Washington, DC: Transit Cooperative Research Program, Transportation Research Board, National Research Council, National Academy Press.

Burchell, Robert W., David Listokin and Catherine C. Galley, 2000. "Smart growth: More than a ghost of urban policy past, less than a bold new horizon", *Housing Policy Debate*, 11: 821–79.

Callon, Michel., Cécile Meadel and Vololona Rabeharisoa, 2002. "The economy of qualities", *Economy and Society*, 31(2): 194–217.

Chernatony, Leslie de, 2006. *From Brand Vision to Brand Evaluation.* Oxford: Butterworth Heinemann.

Czarniawska, Barbara, 2002. *A Tale of Three Cities or the Glocalization of City Management.* Oxford: Oxford University Press.

Czarniawska, Barbara, 2008. "Alterity/identity interplay in image construction", in *Sage Handbook of New Approaches in Management and Organization*, edited by Daved Barry and Hans Hansen. London: Sage, 49–67.

Downs, Anthony, 1994. *New Visions for Metropolitan America.* Washington, DC: Brookings Institution Press and the Lincoln Institute for Land Policy.

Downs, Anthony, 2000. *Dealing Effectively with Fast Growth.* Washington, DC: Brookings Institution.

Downs, Anthony, 2005. "Smart growth, why we discuss it more than we do it", *Journal of the American Planning Association*, 71(4): 367–77.

Duineveld, Martijn and Kristof van Assche, 2011. "The power of tulips: Constructing nature and heritage in a contested landscape", *Journal of Environmental Policy and Planning*, 13(2): 79–98.

Endicott, Eve (ed.), 1993. *Land Conservation Through Public/Private Partnerships.* Washington, DC: Island Press.

Forrest, Ray and Alan Murie, 1995. "From Privatization to Commodification: Tenure Conversion and New Zones of Transition in the City", *International Journal of Urban and Regional Research*, 19(3): 407–22.

Gihring, Thomas A., 1999. "Incentive property taxation: a potential tool for urban growth management", *Journal of the American Planning Association*, 65(1): 62–79.

Gotham, Kevin F., 2007. "(Re) Branding the Big Easy: Tourism rebuilding in Post-Katrina New Orleans", *Urban Affairs Review*, 42(6): 823–50.

Gustanski, Julie A. and Roderick H. Squires (eds), 2000. *Protecting the Land: Conservation Easements Past, Present, and Future.* Washington, DC: Island Press.

Hildreth, Jeremy, 2010. "Place branding. a View at arm's length", *Place branding and public diplomacy*, 6(1): 27–35.

Hillier, Jean, 2002. *Shadows of Power: An Allegory of Planning in Land-use Planning.* London: Routledge.

Hjortegaard Hansen, Rebecca, 2010. "The narrative nature of place branding", *Place Branding and Public Diplomacy*, 6(2): 268–79.

Jacobs, Harvey M., 1998. *Who Owns America? Social Conflict Over Property Rights.* Madison, WI: University of Wisconsin Press.

Jessop, Bob, 1998. "The Enterprise of Narrative and the Narrative of Enterprise: Place-marketing and the Entrepreneurial City", in *The Entrepreneurial City Geographies of Politics, Regime and Representation*, edited by Tim Hall and Phil Hubbard. Chichester: Wiley, 77–99.

Kavaratzis, Mihalis and Gregory J. Ashworth, 2006. "Partners in coffee shops, canals and commerce: marketing the city of Amsterdam", *Cities* 24(1): 16–25.

Kelly, Eric D., 1993. *Managing Community Growth: Policies, Techniques, and Impacts*. Westport, CT: Praeger.

Knaap, Gerrit and Arthur C. Nelson, 1992. *The Regulated Landscape: Lessons on State Land Use Planning from Oregon*. Cambridge: Lincoln Institute of Land Policy.

Liverman, Diana, 2004. "Who Governs, at What Scale and at What Price? Geography, Environmental Governance, and the Commodification of Nature", *Annals of the Association of American Geographers*, 94(4): 734–48.

Lury, Celia, 2004. *Brands: The Logos of the Global Economy*. London: Routledge.

Meek, Stuart (ed.), 2002. *Growing Smart Legislative Guidebook: Model Statutes for Planning and the Management of Change*. Chicago, IL: American Planning Association.

Mehrhoff, W. Arthur, 1999. *Community Design: A Team Approach to Dynamic Community Systems*. Thousand Oaks, CA: Sage.

Moor, Liz, 2003. "Branded Spaces: The scope of 'new marketing'", *Journal of Consumer Culture*, 3(1): 39–60.

National Association of Counties, the Joint Center for Sustainable Communities, and the Smart Growth Network, 2001. *Local Tools for Smart Growth: Practical Strategies and Techniques to Improve Our Communities*. Washington, DC: The National Association of Counties.

National Association of Home Builders, 1999. *Smart Growth Policy Statement: Building Better Places to Live, Work, and Play*. Washington, DC: National Association of Home Builders.

Ndubisi, Forster and Mary Dyer, 1992. "The role of regional entities in formulating and implementing statewide growth policies", *State and Local Government Review*, 24: 117–27.

Nelson, Arthur C. and James B. Duncan, 1995. *Growth Management Principles and Practices*. Chicago, IL: American Planning Association.

Nolon, John R., 2003. *Golden and Its Emanations: The Surprising Origins of Smart Growth*. New York: Pace University.

Nolon, John R. and Patricia E. Salkin, 2006. *Land Use in a Nutshell*. St Paul, MA: Thompson West.

Paasi, Anssi, 1991. "Deconstructing regions: notes on the scales of spatial life", *Environment and Planning A*, 23(2): 239–56.

Pasquinelli, Cecilia, 2010. "The limits of place branding for local development: the case of Tuscany and the Arno valley brand", *Local Economy*, 25(7): 558–72.

Peck, Jamie and Adam Tickell, 2002. "Neoliberalizing Space", *Antipode*, 34: 380–404.

Pike, Steven, 2005. "Tourism destination branding complexity", *Journal of Product and Brand Management*, 14(4): 258–60.

Platt, Rurtherford H., 2004. *Land Use and Society: Geography, Law and Public Policy*. Washington, DC: Island Press.

Porter, Douglas R., 1997. *Managing Growth in America's Communities*. Washington, DC: Island Press.

Soja, Edward W., 1997. "Planning in/for post-modernity", in Georges Bonko and Ulf Strohmayer (eds), *Space and Social Theory in Interpreting Modernity and Postmodernity*. Oxford: Blackwell.

Sonnino, Roberta, 2007. "Embeddedness in action: saffron and the making of the local in southern Tuscany", *Agriculture and human values*, 24(1): 61–74.

Swyngedouw, Erik and Nikolas C. Heynen, 2003. "Urban Political Ecology, Justice and the Politics of Scale", *Antipode*, 35: 898–918.

Throgmorton, James A., 1996. *Planning as Persuasive Story-telling: The Rhetorical Construction of Chicago's Electrical Future*. Chicago, IL: University of Chicago Press.

Urban Land Institute, 1998. *Smart Growth: Economy, Community, Environment*. Washington, DC: Urban Land Institute.

US Environmental Protection Agency, 2002. *About Smart Growth*. Washington, DC: US EPA.
Verdery, Kathryn., 2003. *The Vanishing Hectare. Property and Value in Post-Socialist Transylvania*. Ithaca, NY: Cornell University Press.
Weitz, Jerry, 1999. "From quiet revolution to smart growth: state growth management programs, 1960 to 1999", *Journal of Planning Literature*, 14(2): 266–37.
Weitz, Jerry and Ethan Seltzer, 1998. "Regional planning and regional governance in the United States 1979–1996", *Journal of Planning Literature*, 12(3): 361–92.
Zovanyi, Gabor, 1998. *Growth Management for a Sustainable Future: Ecological Sustainability as the New Growth Management Focus for the 21st Century*. Westport, CT: Praeger.

PART 2
Chapters on Particular Cases

Chapter 5

Case A Sex and the City: City Branding in Spanish Cities

Gildo Seisdedos and Pablo Vaggione

The concept of place branding has been pervasively adopted by communities, cities, regions and nations (Gertner 2011); branding and brand management can be said to have been one of the leading areas of focus both for marketing academics and practitioners during the final two decades of the 20th century (Hankinson 2001). There is, however, an evident confusion in the use of the term (Kavaratzis 2004; 2005). Branding and marketing are managerial tools precisely defined in business management literature (Aaker 1991; Kotler *et al.* 1993). Both tools share a common philosophy: to connect certain positive values to a product in order to make it unique and, through this, to gain relevance in a competitive environment. As globalization has increased competition between cities, marketing and branding have broadened their scopes from the corporate world to urban management, expanding the design of public policies for sustainable urban growth (Kotler and Levy 1969). Initially, the application of branding and marketing to cities took the form of a simple promotion of the city but, very soon, more complex and sophisticated approaches were developed, including spatial-functional, organizational and financial measures (Ashworth and Voodg 1990).

However, thinking that marketing practices of cities necessarily involve the development of a media campaign, the logo and tagline is still one of the most common misconceptions about place marketing (Hospers 2010). A wider definition of city branding would include "the means both for achieving competitive advantage in order to increase inward investment and tourism and also for achieving community development, reinforcing local identity and identification of the citizens with the city and activating all social forces to avoid social exclusion and unrest" (Kavaratzis 2004).

Tourism has quickly and successfully adopted destination marketing: destinations are seen as mere amalgams of tourism products, offering an integrated experience to consumers in an extremely competitive global market (Buhalis 2000) for tourism. Agriculture, foreign direct investment and skilled labor (or talent) are also other well consolidated fields for place marketing and branding (Papadopoulos 2004).

It is obvious that city branding and promotion is an important activity for cities around the world (Lucarelli and Berg 2011). The 28 responses from 12 different countries included in the Eurocities Questionnaire revealed, for example, that the average city marketing budget allocated for city branding in these cities was €400,000 per city, ranging from €130,000 to 10 million per year (Seisdedos 2006).

Although promotional expenditure is the most visible part of city branding efforts, bidding for events or building iconic cultural equipment could also be considered as part of city branding strategies. As place branding identifies the core brand, preferably based on a unique identity of place and competitive advantage and tries to align the image, identity and experience (Hulleman and Govers 2011), these flagship projects are seen as the standard bearer of the new values the city wants to appropriate, as the quickest way to manage the level of hospitality in a place as they link place identity, product offering and perception together through consumption experience (Govers and Go 2009).

SPANISH CITIES: FROM NOW ON ... WHAT?

Thirty five years ago, Spanish cities were not really part of modern Europe. In the last four decades, they have transformed themselves into the urban fabric of a modern European democracy, repositioning themselves through an ambitious promotional program using Joan Miró's sun to symbolize the step change in the modernization of Spain. This modernization program was accompanied by advertising on a national, regional and city level, the impact of hosting the Barcelona Olympics and the rebuilding of great cities like Bilbao with the Guggenheim Museum (Gilmore 2001). In 1999, Spain was said to be "amongst the best examples of modern, successful national branding" (Preston 1999, p. 23). Spain initially reaped important benefits from its membership of the single European currency and access to credit. As a result, a surge of foreign investment set off an economic boom that raised living standards and attracted migrant workers. But, nearly at the same time as the national team won the Euro 2008 football championship, international economic press headlines stated that, after two decades of economic growth, the party was over (Catan 2008). Since 2010, Spain has been among a handful of European economies that have been in the line of fire of investors because of budget deficit and economic weakness in terms of low growth and high unemployment.

This radical shift has affected city branding in Spain. The reasons behind this shift are related to the new economic environment and, closely linked to this, the need for institutional reforms (financing, competence attribution, or even an in-depth redesign of the existing territorial model) that are under debate and consideration in an environment marked by crisis and austerity. In the wake of the financial crisis Spanish cities are gripped by the economic asphyxia linked to the burst of the real estate bubble. This situation is affecting city branding and new patterns seem to be emerging.

METHODOLOGY

This chapter is based on a set of 35 interviews with public officers in charge of the marketing and branding strategies of major Spanish cities. Size in terms of population was the selection criteria, and the following cities were part of the sample: Madrid, Barcelona, Valencia, Seville, Saragossa, Malaga, Murcia, Palma de Mallorca, Las Palmas, Bilbao, Alicante, Cordoba, Valladolid, Vigo, Gijón, Hospitalet, La Coruña, Granada, Vitoria, Elche, Oviedo, Santa Cruz de Tenerife, Badalona, Cartagena, Tarrasa, Jerez de la Frontera, Sabadell, Móstoles, Alcalá de Henares, Fuenlabrada, Pamplona, Almería, Leganés and San Sebastián y Castellón de la Plana.

The method of research chosen was the semi-structured interview. The framework of themes to be explored covered a broad spectrum of city domains with an emphasis on urban services, governance, housing and local environment, work, health, work–life balance, subjective well-being, social participation, quality of social services, quality of society and city branding.

The framework of interviews, in common with previous editions of mercoCIUDAD, was reviewed and improved in close cooperation with the IE Business School. While the priority was to retain core themes to enable trend analysis, a certain number of new areas were identified where the survey's scope could be usefully extended. The draft version of the master framework was tested in the pilot survey.

The diversity of the organization charts made every city a particular case, so these interviews were granted by directors of strategic planning, communications directors, councilors in charge of local economic development, PR managers, research directors and other managers, under a wide range of denominations, in crafting urban branding policies.

The reason for this round of interviews was the preparation of the third edition of mercoCIUDAD,[1] a study of Spanish cities. These interviews brought to the table a shift in city officers' thinking, exemplified through the following three brief case studies.

First, Barcelona is the Spanish city with the most powerful global brand, which is in the process of being redefined. Paradoxically, this project with an innovative approach has turned into a low profile project. The reason is that a key project to keep up Barcelona's competitiveness is now seen as a source of vulnerability from a political perspective.

Second, L'Hospitalet de Llobregat is a fascinating city, noted for its high social diversity, the densest population in Spain and for being a living laboratory for urban and social policies. In recent years, the city undertook an ambitious process of urban regeneration. As a result, a new skyline emerged, including the luxurious Hesperia Hotel, designed by Richard Rogers and aimed at being the new icon for the recovered self-esteem of the city, which is trying hard to communicate this project as a strategic asset for addressing growing social demands and unrest.

Third, but probably the most illustrative case, is Saragossa. On 14 September, International Expo Zaragoza 2008 ended and the city completed the most ambitious process of urban transformation in Spain, jumping ahead through an impressive renovation of all its infrastructure. The city had all the ingredients in terms of branding to succeed, which it projected to the world through this impressive event. Paradoxically, the following day, Lehman Brothers filed for bankruptcy and the world has not been the same since. Talking with the Saragossa team for city branding, a meaningful sentence came to the table: "when we got to the finishing line, the rules of the race had changed". The perception behind this sentence has been unanimously endorsed by all the city officers interviewed; their inferences for city branding are listed in the following sections.

FROM FLAGSHIP PROJECTS TO WHITE ELEPHANTS

A star project is a flagship development project which aims to market a certain area of a city as a whole. The development as an entity in itself is important, yet it is the wider promotional value that makes the flagship distinctive. It is clear that the greater the investment in an area, the greater the rent that can flow, providing, of course, that the overall level of economic activity permits this (Smyth 1994). Flagship developments are at the forefront of testing concepts for marketing a city. They are also an important part of the armory for regenerating areas and employment.

Many were privately led, many were initiated by local public agencies, and a large number were undertaken as partnerships between the public and private sectors. This occurred when urban regeneration projects were being property-led in policy terms. Central government was "reducing" intervention and endeavoring to contain the efforts of local government, while local government was trying to recreate ways of intervening in the local economy and property markets. Flagship developments have been an entrepreneurial solution for many authorities and a way of creating development opportunities for the private sector (Hospers 2010).

In the aftermath of a property boom, within recessive conditions and a changing political milieu, it is appropriate and relevant to evaluate flagships, both as developments and as vehicles for regenerating urban areas, for promoting cities and therefore for regenerating local and regional economies (Smyth 1994).

One of the conclusions of the set of interviews is that flagship developments are turning into white elephants. The term derives from the sacred white elephants kept by Southeast Asian monarchs: possessing a white elephant was regarded as a sign that the monarch reigned with justice and power. So far, urban projects used to follow this pattern, maximizing the number of white elephants to increase urban competitiveness in the global arena. These projects fitted into a wide typology, ranging from iconic buildings to hosting global events. But, because white elephants were considered sacred and laws protected them from labor, receiving a gift of a white elephant from a monarch was a blessing but also a curse. It was a sign of the monarch's appreciation but a curse because the animal had to be fed and could not be put to work to offset the cost of keeping it. Interviews show a growing awareness by Spanish citizens about the final bill being presented to the public for flagship developments and star projects conceived by overzealous developers in conjunction with power-driven politicians. Star projects are now seen in many cases as white elephants; or, at least, it is now felt necessary that an in-depth and detailed explanation is provided regarding the return on the investment made. In particular, who benefits from such investment? Politicians and developers must ensure that urban policies follow a sense of equitability, i.e. that they contribute to "doing the right things" in regard to urban development.

A SHIFT ON CITY BRANDING

Urban policies constantly evolve and change. Before the new economic cycle, town planning was the main engine for urban economic growth in

Spanish cities (Gilmore 2001). When the engine began to overheat, the reaction was more emphasis on city branding, more ambition and an exponential growth of star projects. We could mention plenty of breeds of white elephants, which in many cases were the products of a forced real estate market. Ecodistricts, financial cities, museums, film cities, cultural events, bidding for hosting global events, a high speed train and exhibition centers are only some of them. Hosting the Olympic Games was the dream (Waitt 1999) but, if this was not possible, a mega-cultural event, Guggenheim-style, would fill the role (Zukin 1995).

From the perspective of managerial tools, there was a strong duality at work here. Officers from the town planning department issued master plans, cutting the cities into parts of a real estate ecosystem and, simultaneously but uncoordinatedly, making city branding a key issue in strategic plans oriented at generating a consensus and selling the city.

When the real estate bubble burst, the model depicted in Figure 5.1 was unfeasible for two reasons. First, it turned out to be financially unsustainable. The factor "land" ceased to be an economic asset for Spanish cities and probably will remain like this in the near future. Second, even if affordable, it would be an opportune time for civil society to start pressuring the government for a new set of urban policies, for a more realistic paradigm: one which would place more focus on the prevailing socio-economic conditions

FIGURE 5.1 | **Duality on urban management tools**

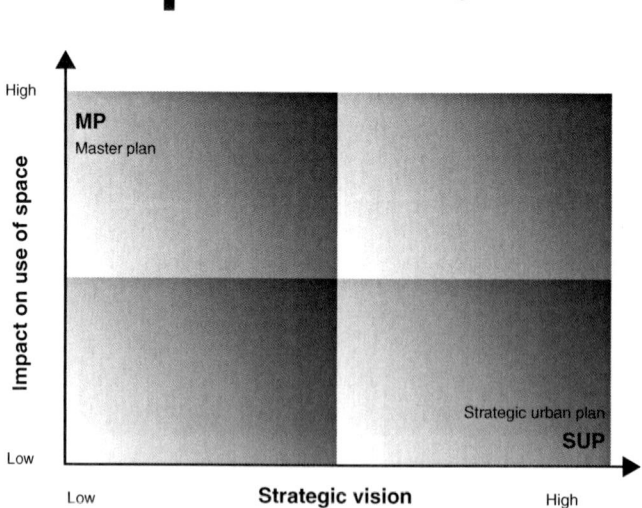

Source: Based on Seisdedos (2008).

and particular problems at the local level, and less emphasis on ambition in terms of "putting the city on the map" or in constructing iconic buildings (Krantz and Schätzl 1997).

This fact has strong implications for city branding as the challenge is to meet these new expectations and create a new narrative around them. The contrast between masculine and feminine thinking, between masculine ethics of justice and feminine ethics of care, offers some interesting possibilities for explaining the new paradigm in the design of urban strategies.

MASCULINE VERSUS FEMININE THINKING AND CITY BRANDING

Gender has been recently introduced in urban theory; for instance, Rotterdam uses femininity as a branding strategy to "cleanse" the city of its working-class mythology. Gentrification is most often approached in theory and research as a class issue. However, it has been argued that gentrification is essentially a product of the dissolution of the patriarchal family (Lees *et al.* 2008) and the formation of relatively new ways to live and new combinations of paid and nonpaid work. And people often tend to think of cities as gendered: Rotterdam is a muscleman; Frank Sinatra sang "LA is my lady" (Van den Berg 2012).

A quick review of the state of the art in this field shows its potential to explain what is going on with cities today and to create a powerful narrative explaining the differences between the new situation and the previous one (MacDowell 1999). Debate on ethics and gender is a huge field that is used here to get a very simplified model to apply to Spanish cities in order to understand what is going: understanding and modeling the new situation is a *sine qua non* for choosing the right policies.

Plato made no distinction between men and women when referring to "the life of the soul", to thinking and ethically acting. He concluded this from his distinction of soul and body. Gender remains in the body; ethics and morals lie in the soul. Consequently, there is no masculine or feminine ethics or thinking. Nowadays, many authors share Plato's perspective and defend gender as not being an essential factor; from this perspective, education could explain most of the existing nuances (Davis 2008).

But there is not a peaceful consensus on this point. According to other authors, there are intellectual and moral differences whose roots are genetic and, consequently, related to gender (Gilligan 1982). The ethics of care emphasize the emotional dimension of relationships and some authors have linked ethics of care with a way of typical feminine thinking and acting. From this viewpoint, it will make sense to distinguish between a masculine and a feminine ethics. For the purpose of this chapter, I have simplified the huge theoretical debate on the issue under two main labels: masculine versus feminine thinking; and ethics of justice versus ethics of care. Under the label of "masculine ethics" or "ethics of justice", I will gather ethical approaches giving preponderance to formal criteria (as in Kantianism), legal aspects (as in legal ethics) or decision-making to maximize social utility (as in utilitarianism).

On the other side, I will place "feminine ethics" or "ethics of care" – which is more centered in the individual, in his or her relationships and affections, in his or her way of getting into a particular moral dilemma, in his or her willingness to taking care of his fellow's well-being – and I will jump over the existing abstract rules that do not provide an understanding of the emotional dimensions of a particular situation. According to this, men tend to underline the importance of rights and justice, of abstract values, while women emphasize the sense of responsibility that comes from human relations, which is especially strong between parents and sons (Gilligan 1982).

I will use this model to draw an analogy between gender thinking and the shift on city branding in Spanish cities I have identified. Following this analogy, cities have been defining their strategies from a masculine perspective oriented toward abstract values: city managers offer their citizens a set of projects following a global and depersonalized analysis of the social utilities linked to each one of them (Baier 1985).

The economic crisis is generating important new social needs; this fact brings to the table new feminine patterns where looking face to face at the citizen is critical for understanding their specific problems and providing warm and emotional answers to them. The "cold" management of social utilities gives way to policies adapted to the emotional dimensions of every particular situation (Fretter 1993).

This shift in urban policies could be explained away by the introduction of the ethics of care. The city switches from the eyes of the father to those of the mother, focusing on taking care, being attentive to the diversity of the children, to their different needs and sensibilities. Let's take a closer look to consider what this means.

Ethics of Care: A New Paradigm for Urban Policies and City Branding

So, the emerging model is feminine and based on the ethics of care: city branding becomes less aggressive and ambitious. New challenges for urban policies (and branding) are protecting my citizens with loving care, taking into account their different needs, emphasizing social policies, using

TABLE 5.1 City branding models

	Model in crisis	Emerging model
Stereotype	Masculine	Feminine
Ethics	Justice	Care
Objective	Put city on map	Protect
Password	Ambition	Closeness
Emphasis	Star project	Social policies
	Urban hardware	Urban software
Orientation	Outwards	Inwards
Communication	Mass media	Segmented
Focus	Globalization	Diversity

an introspective approach, and showing an interest in providing services adapted to the citizenship's diversity that demands custom-made attention. The consequences for city branding are important as the new paradigm has very different implications. From the ethics of care, learning about the context in a more detailed way becomes critical as applying the same rule everywhere could be unfair. Holding tight to the rules without taking into account context involves ignoring the citizenship's diversity.

The ethics of care appeal to the specificity of each citizen and his or her context. The powerhouse of the feminine thinking would be rejecting impartiality, separation and depersonalization and taking into account the demands of every particular citizen when delivering a service. At the same time, the risk of marginalizing social groups will be offset with processes of participation, negotiation and the debate of public policies.

The citizen should be addressed as a specific individual and not as an abstract concept. City managers should be committed to people, not to a generic idea. This is one of the most important contributions of the ethics of care when applied to cities: the citizen should be seen as an individual because that is necessary to make right decisions on how much, when and to whom care should be delivered. In the new paradigm, city branding requires not only thinking from the citizen's point of view but also establishing an open dialog with all of them. The idea of citizens as passive and dependent, and the city government as the only active agent, should be overcome. The main features of each one of the models are schematized in Table 5.1.

IMPLICATIONS

Revisiting the ethics of care in the present situation can be extremely inspiring because of its implication for city branding in Spanish cities.

Caricaturing diagnosis, we could state that the importance of social policies for crafting a powerful brand will be pivotal. Urban stakeholders will attribute a higher value to messages whose core is closer to the role of a loving mother than to those, prevailing until recently, focusing on making us proud about how powerful and strong our father is. Consequently, star projects run a growing risk of being perceived as white elephants, as a burden, instead of as a source for pride and joy.

Signs of this shift were identified in all the city councils interviewed and are also present on the streets of our cities, and growing every day. There is a common feeling about this change, although putting forward a theory is risky, above all since the change is so recent and incipient. Reading wisely what is going on would throw some light on how cities can make the most of this change.

CONCLUSION

The process of building mercoCIUDAD – a comprehensive study on urban management and city branding in Spain – has provided a very detailed insight through personal interviews on how city branding and tools for urban strategy are evolving. Out of this insight, three main conclusions could be drafted.

First, there is a strong shift in the way civil society assesses urban policies and city branding efforts, based on a collective action perspective. What unites citizens nowadays within the civil society context is embraced in a demand for a voice, i.e. to be heard loud and clear by local government – this can be considered a "sea change".

Second, this change is recent but is also powerful and has come to stay. This shift is radical: what formerly was pride is now a political battlefield, a source of suspicion regarding the alleged opportunity of a project. Instead, civil society seeks trust.

Third, a new model for urban strategy and city branding has arrived; a shift from a masculine to a feminine model, from the ethics of justice to the ethics of care, has taken place. City branding needs to adapt its further developments to this new emerging model, otherwise citizens will turn their backs on it: the proposed conceptualization aims to be a useful tool to understand the nature of this change and adapt to it. Here, Spain's scores on Hofstede's "power distance" (high) and "uncertainty avoidance" (high) may present barriers to adaptation, whereas "masculinity" (low) presents hope for progress (Hofstede 1991).

NOTE

1. On a year to year basis, mercoCIUDAD analyses 78 major Spanish cities from four convergent perspectives: compiling data on 154 objective variables, meeting with 100 experts and city managers, 10,000 interviews with citizens and, in addition, a questionnaire to every city council to learn about the best practices in their judgment. See www.merco.info/es/countries/4/rankings/3

REFERENCES

Aaker, D. (1991) *Managing Brand Equity: Capitalizing on the Value of a Brand Name*, London: Macmillan.
Ashworth, G.J. and Voodg, H. (1990) *Selling the City: Marketing Approaches in Public Sector Urban Planning*, London: Belhaven Press.
Baier, A. (1985) *Postures of the mind*, Minneapolis, MN: University of Minnesota Press.
Berg, L. van den and Braun, E. (1999) "Urban Competitiveness, Marketing and the Need of Organising Capacity", *Urban Studies*, 36(5–6): 987–99.
Berg, M. van den (2012) "Femininity as a city marketing strategy: gender behind Rotterdam", *Urban Studies*, 49(1): 153–68.
Buhalis, D. (2000) "Marketing the competitive destination of the future", *Tourism Management*, 21: 97–116.
Catan, P. (2008) "The party is over in Spain", *The Economist*, 15 November.
Davis, K. (2008) "Intersectionality as buzzword: a sociology of science perspective on what makes a feminist theory successful", *Feminist Theory*, 9(1): 67–85.
Fretter, A.D. (1993) "Place marketing: a local authority perspective", in Kearns, G. and Filo, C. (eds), *Selling Places: The City as Cultural Capital, Past and Present*, Oxford: Pergamon Press, pp. 163–74.
Gertner, D. (2011) "Unfolding and configuring two decades of research and publication on place marketing and place branding", *Place Branding and Public Diplomacy*, 7(2): 91–106.
Gilligan, C. (1982) *In a Different Voice*, Cambridge, MA: Harvard University Press.
Gilmore, F. (2001) "A country: can it be repositioned? Spain: the success story of country branding", *Brand Management*, 9(4–5): 281–93.
Govers, R. and Go. F.M. (2009) *Place Branding: Glocal, Virtual and Physical Identities, Constructed, Imagined and Experienced*, Basingstoke: Palgrave Macmillan.
Hankinson, G. (2001) "Location branding: a study of the branding practices of 12 English cities", *Brand Management*, 9(2): 127–42.
Hofstede, G (1991) *Cultures and Organizations: Software of the Mind*. New York: McGraw Hill.
Hospers, G.-J. (2005) "Creative Cities in Europe: Urban Competitiveness in the Knowledge Economy", *Intereconomics*, 38(5): 260–9.
Hospers, G.-J. (2010) "Four of the most common misconceptions about place marketing", *Journal of Town and City Management*, 2(2): 167–76.
Hulleman, B.-A.B.F. and Govers, R. (2011) "The Hague, International City of Peace and Justice: a Relational Network Brand", in Dinnie, K. (ed.), *City Branding: Theory and Cases*, Basingstoke: Palgrave Macmillan.
Kavaratzis, M. (2004) "From city marketing to city branding: Towards a theoretical framework for developing city brands", *Place Branding*, 1(1): 58–73.

Kavaratzis, M. (2005) "Place branding: a review of trends and conceptual models", *The Marketing Review*, 5: 329–42.

Kavaratzis, M. (2007) "City marketing: The past, the present and some unresolved issues", *Geography Compass*, 1(3): 695–712.

Kotler, P. and Levy, S.J. (1969) "Broadening the concept of marketing", *The Journal of Marketing*, 33(1): 10–15.

Kotler, P., Haider, D.H. and Rein, I. (1993) *Marketing Places*, New York: The Free Press.

Krantz, M. and Schätzl, L. (1997) "Marketing the city", in Jensen, C., Shashar, A. and van de Weesep, J. (eds), *European Cities in Competition*, Aldershot: Ashgate, pp. 468–93.

Lees, L. Slater, T. and Wyly, E. (2008) *Gentrification*, New York: Routledge.

Lucarelli, A. and Berg, P.O. (2011) City branding: a state-of-the-art review of the research domain", *Journal of Place Management and Development*, 4(1): 9–27.

MacDowell, L. (1999) Gender, Identity and Place: Understanding Feminist Geographies. Minneapolis, MN: University of Minnesota Press.

Papadopoulos, N. (2004) "Place branding: evolution, meaning and implications", *Place Branding*, 1(1): 36–49.

Preston, P. (1999) "Branding is cool", *The Guardian*, 15 November.

Seisdedos, G. (2006) "State of the art of city marketing in European cities", paper presented at the 42nd IsoCaRP Congress, Istanbul.

Seisdedos, G. (2007) *Managing 21st-Century Cities*, Madrid: Prentice Hall.

Seisdedos, G. (2008) "Más allá del POM y del PEU: la EDU como herramienta para el diseño de estrategias urbanas", *Análisis Local*, 78(III): 17–23.

Seisdedos, G. and Mateos, M.C. (2010) "From global Madrid to Madrid Global", in Ashworth, G.J. and M. Kavaratzis (eds), *Towards Effective Place Brand Management: Branding European Cities and Regions*, Cheltenham: Edward Elgar.

Smyth, H. (1994) *Marketing the City: The Role of Flagship Developments in Urban Regeneration*, London: E & FN Spon.

Waitt, G. (1999) "Playing Games with Sydney: Marketing Sydney for the 2000 Olympics", *Urban Studies*, 36(7): 1055–77.

Ward, S. (1995) *Selling Places: The Marketing and Promotion of Towns and Cities (1850–2000)*, London: E & FN Spon.

Zukin, S. (1995) *The Culture of Cities*, Cambridge, MA: Blackwell.

Chapter 6

Case B   A Common Agenda for Place Branding: Made in Torino

Alexander Otgaar

The image of a place is a co-creation of public and private stakeholders. Local authorities, businesses and citizens share a collective interest in having an attractive place brand, since soft, intangible location factors become increasingly decisive in the global competition between regions. In line with behavioral location theories residents, firms, investors and tourists choose particular locations because of their *perceived* qualities, though these are often different from the actual qualities.

Every region faces the challenge of developing an attractive place brand that corresponds with the actual qualities of a place. While some regions such as Paris and New York benefit from a very appealing and a maybe even too positive image, others are struggling with an image that is too negative (an image gap), or is biased and incomplete, or – worst of all – there is no image at all. This should not only be a concern for policy-makers, but also for businesses and other organizations who have a stake in the region's future.

One way to improve and to enrich the image of a place is to open the doors of companies. The development of *industrial tourism* presents "opportunities for city and enterprise" to enhance and enrich the image of a city and its industries (Otgaar *et al.* 2010). In contrast with industrial *heritage* tourism, industrial tourism can be defined as "visits by tourists to operational sites where the core activity of the site is non-tourism oriented" (Frew 2000, p. 1). Industrial tourism enables visitors to learn about a city's economic activities. In a broader definition it also encompasses company museums, communication centers and brand parks such as Volkswagen Autostadt in Wolfsburg (Marcon *et al.* 2000; Steinecke 2001). Industrial tourism is a small but growing segment of the tourism industry that facilitates the demand of tourists for unique, authentic and real experiences (Speakman and Bramwel 1992; Otgaar 2010).

In this chapter I discuss the increasing need for a common agenda in the development of a place branding strategy and industrial tourism in particular. I first identify the fundamental trends that raise the importance of such an agenda. I then focus on the question of how to realize a fit between the development of industrial tourism and the intended images of city and enterprise. I then discuss the feasibility of a common agenda on industrial tourism by analyzing the case of Made in Torino. This case study is based on a literature review and interviews with local stakeholders (see the list of discussion partners at the end of this chapter).

FUNDAMENTAL TRENDS

Several fundamental trends change the environment in which cities and their industries are operating. These are: globalization; the shift to an information and knowledge economy; the increasing concern about the environment and climate change; the growing attention to corporate citizenship; and the transition to an experience economy. These trends raise the importance of a common agenda for place branding and the development of industrial tourism.

At the present time sustainability has become a leading paradigm in the competitiveness of cities, industries and individual firms. Sustainable urban development (SUD) takes into account the interests of future generations which is not only a matter of securing the ecosystem but also requires social and economic stability. SUD not only depends on the intervention of (local) government, but on that of private actors as well. Many scholars agree that SUD requires the involvement of citizens and businesses, arguing that the knowledge, power and resources to secure sustainability are distributed among various stakeholders (Bryson and Crosby 1992). There is an increasing need for cooperation and coordination between governments, businesses, knowledge institutions and civic organizations.

The future of cities depends on the actions of firms, but the reverse is true as well: businesses have a stake in an attractive, well organized environment (cf. Logan and Molotch 1987). In a globalizing world firms need to build good relations with the communities in which they operate: to try to become a "neighbor of choice" (Burke 1999). Kaptein and Tulder (2003) advise companies to adopt a model of "consultation and cooperation" instead of "competition and confrontation". It is not a coincidence that the three pillars of the "Triple P Bottom Line" (People, Planet, Profit) correspond with the three dimensions of SUD. Companies are expected to be accountable for their contributions to social, environmental and economic place performance ("urban competitiveness") indicators such as hiring minorities, reducing carbon emissions and creating jobs at other local firms.

The mutual dependence of city and enterprise also reveals itself in the marketing and branding of places and industries, as I have already briefly mentioned. And this is where industrial tourism comes to the fore. Company tours can be used by firms to communicate with stakeholders in a more direct way: demonstrating that their corporate social responsibility (CSR) policies are more than window dressing. In more general terms, industrial tourism can help to establish a bond between stakeholders (e.g. consumers, suppliers, employees, neighboring residents) and a brand (Mitchell and Orwig 2002): this not only applies to corporate brands but to place brands as well. According to this "involvement theory", brand loyalty increases if stakeholders can witness economic activities. Industrial tourism can thus be used to strengthen the image of a single firm, the industry to which it belongs and the city in which it is located. Industrial tourism can assist cities to communicate a more realistic, up-to-date image of their industries: not only manufacturing industries, but also creative industries and service-oriented firms.

A COMMON AGENDA FOR INDUSTRIAL TOURISM: HOW TO REALIZE AN IMAGE FIT

The development of industrial tourism can be seen as a collective action problem: individual firms and actors at the level of a city may recognize common or compatible interests, but they do not necessarily cooperate to reach shared objectives. From urban regime theory we know that a common policy agenda requires consensus on the main objectives and strategies to reach these goals (Stone 1993; Mossberger and Stoker 2002). Austin (2000) refers to a connection based purpose that engages people. This purpose should be clear, ensuring congruency between the missions, strategies and values of the participating actors. According to the concept of organizing capacity (Van den Berg *et al.* 1997) the challenge for cities is to involve all relevant stakeholders and to define a common vision for sustainable development. Alignment and coordination in place branding and the development of industrial tourism not only make it easier to gain political and societal support, but also to reduce transaction costs which allows stakeholders to use their scarce resources (e.g. budgets for marketing campaigns) in a more efficient way.

One of the key issues for which consensus needs to be reached regarding the development of a common agenda on industrial tourism is the fit between industrial tourism and the intended image of a firm and the city in which it is located: the "image fit". The intended image is defined here as the values and strengths a company or a city wants to communicate.

For an individual firm, company tours could be used, for example, to demonstrate good citizenship, a care for quality and an attractive working environment (a good employer). Industrial tourism can benefit the firm if company tours help to create good ambassadors (Rudd and Davis 1988): visitors are not only (potential) consumers, but also investors, employees, business partners and neighboring citizens. For companies the key question is not so much *if* they want to open their doors, but who they allow to enter the workfloor or a visitor center. What matters is the relevance of these groups for the continuity of the firm (minimizing wastage in marketing terms) and whether industrial tours actually raise their loyalty. To give an example: tours to factories in the food industry are sometimes less effective at attracting consumers as a confrontation with the production process is likely to reduce their appetite (Mader 2003). Another condition for firms is the cost efficiency of industrial tourism compared to other forms of marketing and public relations. The director of Celestial Seasonings once said that "one visit has more value than one hundred commercials when guests rate their positive experiences to friends and family" (Brumberg and Axelrod 1995), though this may not be a valid argument for all CEOs.

A city could see industrial tourism as an instrument for promoting itself as a good business location for particular industries or clusters of activities. The question, however, is whether cities are actually willing to connect tourism with industry in their marketing activities. Some cities are reluctant to use industrial tourism as a tool for place marketing, arguing that leisure tourists associate industry with negative values such as pollution and noise (Schmidt 1988; Fontanari and Weid 1999). A solution could be to replace the term "industrial tourism" with neutral terms such as "company visits" or positive terms such as "economic discoveries" (Morice 2006). In addition, organizations at the level of a city could try to facilitate the development of industrial tourism in industries and firms that fit in with the desired image of the city (cf. Pechlaner *et al.* 2006). In this way industrial tourism can become an instrument of cobranding, assuming a two-way relationship between corporate brands and place brands (Azevedo 2004; Kavaratzis and Ashworth 2005). In other words: (1) the city wants to be associated with host firms and their products; and (2) the host firm appreciates the association with the city in which it is located.

The increasing need for SUD and a "sustainable reputation" for cities and their industries provides opportunities to align the interests of public and private actors through industrial tourism as an instrument of cobranding.

Company tours can be used to connect the image of a place with attractive and responsible firms: demonstrating care about their local and global environment, the quality of their products, a safe and healthy environment for employees, etc. It may be even more interesting for cities to open the doors of companies that actually make a contribution to SUD: firms in the emerging "green economy" (e.g. recycling, clean energy, climate adaptation, sustainable transport). From the company's point of view industrial tourism helps to strengthen the branding association between a firm and a city. The argument presented here is that if a city becomes known as a "center of excellence" for a particular cluster of activities, the members of this cluster (the firms) will also benefit: it will be easier to attract supporting industries and human capital and to sell products and services to businesses and consumers.

MADE IN TORINO: TOUR THE EXCELLENT

Turin is one of the most active European cities in the development of industrial tourism. In 2005 they launched a program called "Made in Torino: Tour the Excellent", hereafter abbreviated to "Made in Torino". Through this program residents and tourists get the opportunity to visit companies that demonstrate the economic vitality and diversity of the region. It is a joint initiative of the City of Turin's tourism agency (Turismo Torino) and the Chamber of Commerce for the Turin Province, in close cooperation with the participating firms. In our view Made in Torino is an interesting example of a public–private initiative to use industrial tourism for cobranding the city and its industries. This single case study can help us to gain some understanding if it is feasible to develop a common agenda, notably in view of the "image fit".

First, let us briefly introduce the city. Turin is an industrial city (population: 2.2 million) with an economy that used to be dominated by one single firm: at the end of the 1950s approximately 80 percent of all industrial activity was related to the production of cars. Like many other industrial cities, Turin has been confronted with industrial decline but also with a diversification of the economy (Symcox and Cardoza 2006). Compared to other Italian and European cities, the share of industry in employment is still high: more than 30 percent. Apart from the automotive industry, several other industries have been earmarked as "key industries": aerospace, ICT, life sciences and biotechnology, logistics, nanotechnology, environment and renewable energy, artistic handicraft, contemporary art, writing tools, agro-food and the movie industry (Chamber of Commerce for the Turin Province 2008).

While the economic structure of Turin has changed over the years, the image has remained about the same (City of Turin 2000). Before the Olympic Winter Games took place in 2006 many people had a biased perception of the city as one dominated by the automotive industry and Fiat, while other people had no perception of the city at all. Like many other hosts of the Olympic Games Turin considered the mega-event as a tool for improving its image: promoting the city as a business location and tourist destination (Van den Berg et al. 2002). Although the development of industrial tourism was not mentioned in the strategic plan formulated in 2000, the launch of the industrial tourism program in 2005 was clearly in line with the ambitions that were formulated in this plan.

The objective of Made in Torino is to demonstrate the "excellence" of Turin and its companies, not only to tourists, but to residents as well: they are the ambassadors of the city. After 2005 the initiators gradually developed a package of company tours to firms that are symbolic of the region's economic diversity and strength. They started with the automotive industry, including not only car manufacturers (Fiat, Iveco, New Holland) but also famous car designers (Bertone, Giugiaro, Pininfarina). Furniture designer Gufram was also added to the program.

Another cluster promoted by Made in Torino concerns the production of luxurious pens, including brands such as Aurora, Lecce and Stilolinea. In 2006 the aerospace cluster opened its doors enabling people to visit Alenia Aeronautica, Thales Alenia Space and Galileo Avionica. In 2008 the program was expanded with the so-called "taste makers" industry, which involved producers of coffee (e.g. Lavazza), beverages (Martini and Rossi), bread, chocolate and sweets (Pastiglie Leone). Recently the program has been updated and organizes company visits in five categories: (1) The Delight of Luxury; (2) Producers of Taste; (3) Automotive and Design; (4) The Aerospace Adventure; and (5) The Art of Printing (see www.turismotorino.org).

As the main sponsor of this program the Chamber of Commerce has managed to open the doors of "key industries" that represent the regional economy and contribute to a richer image for the city. The strategy is to expand and update the program step by step. Apparently the City and the Chamber of Commerce see industrial tourism as a tool to improve and enrich the city's image. But does this also apply to the participating companies and other stakeholders? Below we briefly discuss the views of three companies and the regional authorities.

Fiat receives more than 20,000 visitors a year, but most of these visits are organized by the public relations department. Less than 1 percent of the visitors are delivered by Made in Torino. The car manufacturer sees factory tours as a way of improving customer loyalty but also as a way of demonstrating good citizenship and attracting future employees. By showing the working conditions Fiat wants to convince young people that factories are not the gray, dark and sad places their parents talked about. In this way the global company indirectly contributes to city branding, although the relation between Fiat and Turin is not as strong as it used to be.

Gufram accepted the invitation to participate in Made in Torino to improve its visibility, particularly regarding the production of special design objects for consumers. Company tours are considered less relevant for the other core business: the production of armchairs for public venues such as theatres. An additional reason to open their doors was to build and maintain good relations with the City of Turin and other local authorities, thus providing evidence of good citizenship. For visitors with a leisure motive, Made in Torino is the only supplier of tours to Gufram. Tours for professional visitors and students are organized by the firm's marketing department. Gufram considers the company tours of Made in Torino not the most effective but certainly a cost-efficient tool for promoting the Gufram brand. The individuals who book a tour to the firm are not necessarily potential customers or employees, which implies a high level of wastage. Nevertheless the company appreciates participation in the program because the brochures and website of Turismo Torino help to promote its corporate brands (i.e. free publicity).

Pen producer Aurora receives visitors via Made in Torino but also through other channels. Company tours fit in with the firm's outward-looking strategy which aims at building good relations with relevant stakeholders. Moreover, industrial tourism is considered an instrument for communicating the connection between the company and its products on the one hand and the company and the region on the other. The fact that pens are produced in Italy adds a premium to the brand and the products that carry the brand.

While the City of Turin and the Province support the industrial tourism program, the regional authorities of Piedmont are less enthusiastic about Made in Torino. The regional strategy identifies four product categories: the mountains (skiing); the lake area; the hills with their wine, castles and culture; and the City of Turin (meetings, incentives, conferences and exhibitions). There are two reasons why the region ignores industrial tourism. First, it is a relatively small segment of the tourism market, generating only a few bednights, which is an important performance indicator for determining the budget allocated by the Italian government. Although it is difficult to count industrial tourists (no data is available) the region certainly has much more to offer than company visits. Second, because industry does not fit in with the desired image of the region, policy-makers are afraid that tourists will not appreciate the association of tourism with industry. There is clearly some resistance to connecting industry with tourism in place marketing.

CONCLUSION

The case of Turin shows that the City and the Chamber of Commerce (as a representative of the private sector) have developed a common agenda on the development of industrial tourism. It is an example of a public–private initiative for enriching the image of a city using a cluster-oriented approach. It will be difficult to prove the effectiveness of the program (as with many other branding instruments), but the fact that both instigators still support the initiative is an indicator of its success. Made in Torino could inspire other cities to take similar initiatives, notably because the required investments are limited (approximately €100,000 a year). Industrial tourism can be developed at low costs, because the attractions have already been developed: it is mainly a matter of opening doors and improving accessibility and visibility.

The participating companies are positive about the program because they expect an improved reputation, promotion of their brands and strong relations with local stakeholders, notably with the City of Turin itself. Although many visitors that enter the firms via Made in Torino are less relevant as stakeholders, companies do expect reputation benefits, mainly because the program itself generates a lot of free publicity. The city wants to be associated with the companies. But does it also work the other way around? Yes, but not always! In the case of Aurora we saw that the company expects added value from the brand association with the region. For the two other firms we found no evidence. In general we could say that many firms (including Fiat) appreciate the association with Italy (not specifically with Turin) because Italy is a strong brand connected with design and quality.

We expected that companies would also recognize an interest in a strong city brand and a good reputation of the cluster. It is difficult, however, to find supporting evidence for this hypothesis in the case of Turin. One explanation could be that the firms we analyzed actually do not belong to the clusters as defined by Porter (2000) but to industries that consist of individual firms not necessarily connected to each other. For Fiat this is certainly not true: many suppliers (including car designers) are located in the region. An alternative explanation is that the Chamber of Commerce acts as a representative of the private sector concerning issues of cluster and city development, making individual firms less aware of their interests and less inclined to take action.

REFERENCES

Austin, J.E. 2000. *The Collaboration Challenge: How Non-Profits and Businesses Succeed through Strategic Alliances*. San Francisco, CA: Jossey-Bass Publishers.

Azevedo, A. 2004. "Image transference from product branding to place branding: the case study of Marinha Grande Glass", *International Review on Public and Non Profit Marketing*, 1(2): 101–11.

Berg, L. van den, Braun, E. and Meer, J. van der 1997. *Metropolitan Organising Capacity: Experiences with Organising Major Projects in European Cities*. Aldershot: Ashgate.

Berg, L. van den, Braun, E. and Otgaar, A.H.J. 2002. *Sports and City Marketing in European Cities*. Aldershot: Ashgate.

Brumberg, B. and Axelrod, K. 1995. *Watch It Made in the USA: A Visitor's Guide to the Companies That Make Your Favorite Products*, 1st edn. Santa Fe, NM: John Muir Productions.

Bryson, J. and Crosby, B. 1992. *Leadership for the Common Good: Tackling Public Problems in a Shared Power World*. San Francisco, CA: Jossey-Bass.

Burke, E.M. 1999. *Corporate Community Relations: The Principle of the Neighbor of Choice*. Westport, CA: Quorum Books.

Chamber of Commerce for the Turin Province, 2008. *Invest in Piemonte*.

City of Turin 2000. *The Strategic Plan of Torino 2000–2010*. www.recs.it/en/upload_pdf/The_Strategic_Plan_of_%20Torino.pdf

Fontanari, M.L. and Weid, M. 1999. "Industrial tourism as a tool for positioning in the competition between destinations." In Fontanari, M., Treinen, M. and Weid, M. (eds), *Industrial Tourism in the Competition among Regions*. Trier. ETI Publications.

Frew, E.A. 2000. "Industrial tourism: a conceptual and empirical analysis". PhD thesis, Victoria University.

Kaptein, M. and Tulder, R. van 2003. "Toward effective stakeholder dialogue", *Business and Society Review*, 108(2): 203–24.

Kavaratzis, M. and Ashworth, G.J. 2005. "City branding: an effective assertion of identity or a transitory marketing trick?" *Tijdschrift voor Economische en Sociale Geografie*, 96(5): 506–14.

Logan, J.R., and Molotch, H.L. 1987. *Urban Fortunes*. Berkeley and Los Angeles, CA: University of California Press.

Mader, T. 2003. *Produzierende Betriebe als toeristische Attraktionen im Ruhrgebiet: Grundlagen, Erscheinungsformen, Probleme*. Magisterarbeit, Heinrich-Heine Universität Düsseldorf, Hamburg.

Marcon, A., Preuilh, P. and Ksouri, S. 2000. *Tourisme de découverte économique et visites d'entreprises*. Conseil national du tourisme, pp. 10–16.

Mitchell, M. and Orwig, R.A. 2002. "Consumer experience tourism and brand bonding", *Journal of Product and Brand Management*, 11(1): 30–41.

Morice, J.R. 2006. "La visite d'entreprise en Europe: un champ à explorer." In Morice, J.R. (ed.), *Visite d'entreprises: Actes du premier Colloque Européen de la Visite d'entreprise*. Paris: Les Cahiers Espaces, p. 92.

Mossberger, K. and Stoker, G. 2002. "The evolution of urban regime theory", *Urban Affairs Review*, 36(6): 810–35.

Otgaar, A. 2010. *Industrial Tourism: Where the Public Meets the Private*. Rotterdam: ERIM, Erasmus University.

Otgaar, A.H.J., Berg, L. van den, Berger, C. and Feng, R.X. 2010. *Industrial Tourism: Opportunities for City and Enterprise*, Aldershot: Ashgate.

Pechlaner, H., Fischer, E. and Go, F.M. 2006. Identity-creating values as basis for the integrated promotion: the case of Ingolstadt–Audi AG Partnership, in Keller, P. and Bieger, T. (eds), *Marketing Efficiency in Tourism: Coping with Volatile Demand*. Berlin: Erich Schmidt Verlag.

Porter, M. 2000. "Location, Competition, and Economic Development: Local Clusters in a Global Economy", *Economic Development Quarterly*, 14: 15–34.

Rudd, M.A. and Davis, J.A. 1988. "Industrial heritage tourism at the Bingham Canyon Copper Mine", *Journal of Travel Research*, 36: 85–9.

Schmidt, D. 1988. "Industrie-Tourismus: Moeglichkeiten und Grenzen einer Anwendung auf ausgewaehlte Gemeinden der Landkreise Coburg, Kronach und Lichtenfels, Bayreuth", *Arbeitsmaterialen zur Raumordnung und Raumplanung*, 63.

Speakman, L. and Bramwell, B. 1992. *Sheffield Works: An Evaluation of a Factory Tourism Scheme*. Sheffield: Centre for Tourism Research, Sheffield City Polytechnic.

Steinecke, A. 2001. Industrieerlebniselten: zwischen Heritage und Markt: Konzepte – Modelle – Trends. In: Hinterhuber, H.H., Pechlaner, H. and Matzler, K. (eds), *IndustrieErlebnisWelten: vom Standort zur Destination*. Berlin: Erich Schmidt.

Stone, C.N. 1993. "Urban regimes: a political economy approach", *Journal of Urban Affairs*, 15(1): 1–28.

Symcox, A.L. and Cardoza, G.W. 2006. *A History of Turin*. Turin: Einaudi.

Discussion Partners

Marzia Baracchino, Piedmont Region.
Cristina Cerutti, Turismo Torino e Provincia.
Fabrizio Gardella, Gufram.
Gianpiero Masera, Chamber of Commerce Turin.
Gabriella Ragazzone, FIAT Group.
Maria Elena Rossi, Sviluppo Piemonte Turismo.
Cesare Verona, Aurora.

CHAPTER 7

Case C Sustaining a Brand through Proactive Repair: The Case of Manchester

Stephen E. Little

The current global recession has created economic and social pressures on governments at national and local level. Currently regional and urban governments in England are under pressure from two directions – the national government's rejection of regional development mechanisms in the form of regional development agencies and their replacement with ad hoc "local enterprise partnerships", and the bottom-up dissatisfaction and unrest resulting from the consequences of severe austerity measures.

In August 2011 the bottom-up reaction was expressed in an extreme form in London, with the civil unrest which spread from the north to the south of the capital with considerable damage to property, before erupting in four other major cities. Five lives were lost in addition to the fatal shooting by police which triggered the initial Tottenham riot. These disturbances preceded the London "Occupy" movement, part of a wider and more focused international expression of dissatisfaction with the governance of financial institutions and national government austerity programs.

In the run up to the 2012 Olympics, and as the main tourist destination for the UK, as well as being the financial center, London was most widely affected by the perceived loss of confidence in urban governance and the consequent damage to its brand image, a situation not helped by the draconian sentencing of a range of minor offenders. *The Guardian* newspaper reported that a Manchester mother of two was jailed for five months for receiving a pair of shorts given to her after they had been looted from a city center store; while in London, a 23-year-old student was jailed for six months for stealing £3.50 worth of bottled water from a supermarket (*The Guardian* 2011a). While satisfying some elements of public opinion these sentences gave the impression of a deeply threatened system of government.

Unlike the other affected cities, London has had a Greater London Assembly (GLA) since 2000. This is the successor to the Greater London Council, which was abolished in 1985 along with other English metropolitan county authorities. The GLA enjoys jurisdiction across the whole London conurbation and has powers over the regulation of public transport and strategic policy that are denied to other English authorities. The other cities affected have had fewer direct controls with which to counter reputational risk and brand vulnerability.

At the time of previous extensive unrest in 1981 several cities were attempting to develop forms of "municipal socialism" (Cochrane 1988) in opposition to the policies of the national government. By the following decade, budget reductions and compulsory outsourcing of services had removed many of the means to pursue alternative strategies from the direct control of local authorities. While the Manchester region still aspires to the role of alternate metropolitan growth pole to London and the south-east (e.g. Peel Holdings 2010), it has fewer direct mechanisms with which to pursue this aim than the capital city.

With such limited governance options, reputational risk assessments might help to facilitate place brand sustainability. However, Cartmell (2010) reports a hostile reaction from NGOs to the Burson-Marsteller consultancy's Brand Vulnerability Index (BVI), which is aimed at "identifying emerging risks, allowing pre-emptive engagement and mediation; and assessing comparative risk against competitor brands". This is achieved through a database of 3,000 NGOs and a summary of the issues they are currently talking about in reports, online and in the media. Burson-Marsteller argue that trends toward overt campaigns can be predicted through the monitoring of building momentum around the issues 12–18 months before mainstream media coverage begins. The BVI is intended primarily to assess and counter threats from NGOs which might target any number of areas and issues from supply chains to marketing strategies. However, the developers and managers of place brands must monitor an even broader range of potential threats. While Knowles (2006) suggests that the British Prime Minister Harold Macmillan may not actually have characterized the key uncertainties of a political environment as "events dear boy events", it is events like those of August 2011 which can unsettle a carefully planned brand strategy and demand a rapid response.

Immediately after the civil unrest of 9 August 2011 Manchester launched a set of campaigns and coordinated events to repair the city brand. The same social media alleged to have been used by rioters were combined with traditional channels to coordinate innovative and established events. The context of this reaction to the events of that month in the defense of the city and region brand is the subject of this chapter.

BRAND MANCHESTER: FROM COTTONOPOLIS TO MADCHESTER

Place brands, whether for countries, cities or regions, retain a strong element of path dependence. Braun (2011) explores this in relation to Rotterdam. Liverpool leveraged its status as 2008 EU Capital of Culture to consolidate a strong and positive culture brand. In doing so it produced a selective narrative of the city's recent past, and significant events were only re-acknowledged in subsequent years (Little 2009). Nevertheless, when seeking visibility in north-west England's knowledge economy of science and life sciences, the Liverpool First agency found that Merseyside, beyond the Liverpool city core, retained older negative connotations. To escape these, new brands with different and wider spatial references, such as the "Mersey Corridor" or "Atlantic Gateway", were required.

Manchester's path dependence has a literal element, as the city pioneered a number of key transport innovations in its industrialization and is currently a strong supporter of the HS2 high speed rail proposal recently approved in principal by the UK national government.

Manchester's status as the international center of the cotton and textile processing industries during the 19th century was reflected in its unofficial name, "Cottonopolis". For the author Charles Dickens the archetypal northern industrial textile city was CokeTown through which he satirized the more extreme forms of utilitarianism which led the economic development of north-west England (Dickens 1854). While Dickens is thought to be referencing the Lancashire city of Preston, Manchester's present day pragmatism owes something to these origins, as when a 1996 IRA bomb attack in the city center was leveraged into effecting a review and a completion of the post-war redevelopment of the area (Quilley 2000). This commercial and civic robustness coupled with technical innovation constitutes the mainstream narrative of Manchester's development.

The visit of the Iwakura mission from Japan in 1872 was a significant step in the global diffusion of the Manchester brand. The principal focus of this mission was on military and transportation technology. Manchester factories subsequently delivered over 350 out of 1,023 railway locomotives between 1890 and 1911 (Checkland 1998), but more significantly a cotton industry was established around Osaka, utilizing the best Manchester technology. Over 100 years later the term "Manchester" is still used to indicate cotton and fabric goods in Australian department stores.

Three major innovative projects were landmarks in the creation of the infrastructure which supported this global presence. In contemporary terms they would qualify as "megaprojects" under the rubric of Flyvbjerg *et al.* (2003), and they characterize the 19th-century vision of Manchester.

The Bridgewater Canal

Manchester's 19th-century prominence was derived from a range of innovations in both technology and transport infrastructure. The switch from water and steam power in Manchester and its surroundings gave an advantage over locations to the north and east in the Pennine valleys which provided the superseded waterpower. The demand for coal to generate steam led to the construction of the Bridgewater Canal, the first component of what became a national canal transport system. Developed by the Duke of Bridgewater to transport coal from his mines at Worsley to the Manchester mills, the canal opened in 1761, becoming the first not to be based on an existing watercourse, crossing the river Mersey on the first aqueduct of the modern era.

The Liverpool and Manchester Railway

The improvement of technology in the first decades of the 19th century increased output dramatically. This in turn led to a bottleneck in the importation of raw materials and export of finished textiles. Manchester was reliant on the Port of Liverpool, and by the 1820s the capacity of existing roads and canals was inadequate. Proposals for a railway between Liverpool and Manchester gained approval from Parliament in 1826. The choice of locomotive over stationary steam haulage using cables to haul trains was made relatively late in the planning, but, when completed, the railway contained a range of innovations which became commonplace in subsequent railway construction.

The Manchester Ship Canal

By the end of the 19th century port to rail transhipment between Liverpool and Manchester were regarded as restricted and expensive in a time of prolonged recession. The project to create a 36 mile (58 kilometer) long ship canal utilizing the rivers Mersey and Irwell and incorporating sets of locks to lift vessels some 60 feet (18 meters) to Manchester was completed in January 1894. The 18th-century Bridgewater aqueduct was replaced with the Barton swing aqueduct that permitted ocean-going ships to pass. Its construction made extensive use of mechanical equipment alongside the navvies or navigators – the labor force that had constructed the narrow canal system and the railways by hand.

Opposition from Liverpool delayed the passage of the necessary Act of Parliament by three years, but the £15 million investment made Manchester, 40 miles (64 kilometers) inland, Britain's third busiest port.

The Parallel Narrative: Social Infrastructure

The technocratic narrative of commerce, transport and manufacturing technology set out in Manchester's Museum of Science and Industry (www.mosi.org.uk) is paralleled by a different pathway depicted in the People's History Museum (www.phm.org.uk), one which is framed by unrest from the 18th to the 20th century.

Manchester has a history of social and political dissent and innovation. The city raised a company in support of the Jacobite uprising of 1745–46 which sought to restore the Stuart monarchy. In the following century it was the locus of a succession of social campaigns.

On 16 August 1819, in what is now St Peter's Square, Manchester, over 60,000 peaceful campaigners for parliamentary reform gathered and were attacked by armed cavalry, an event which became known as The Peterloo Massacre. Although this event is a key moment in the emergence of popular democracy in England, the memorial plaque at the site was amended from "subsequent dispersal by the military" to "men, women and children … attacked by armed cavalry resulted in 15 deaths and over 600 injuries", only after a campaign this century. The narrative remains sensitive after almost 200 years. These events occurred during a period of immense political tension and mass protests when fewer than 2 percent of the population could vote and agricultural protection had made bread unaffordable.

Subsequently Manchester became the center of the Co-operative movement. The North of England Co-operative Wholesale Industrial and Provident Society Limited was created in 1867 by 300 individual cooperatives in Yorkshire and Lancashire, becoming in 1872 the Co-operative Wholesale Society. The successor organization remains a major UK retailer.

Manchester was the home of the Pankhurst family and a center for the women's suffrage movement of the late 19th and early 20th century. A campaign based in Manchester organized the Kinder Scout mass trespass in 1932 which led to legislation on countryside preservation and access, including a system of national parks being established after the Second World War and a legislated "right to roam" implemented in 2005.

Moss Side and "Madchester"

In July 1981 riots returned across British cities, including Manchester, with unrest in and around Moss Side, south of the city center, lasting for some 72 hours. Local shops and others in Rusholme to the east were burned and looted. Moss Side had been a migrant destination, particularly for Caribbean immigrants, over the previous decades. Contemporary commentary blamed, alternatively and in combination, racial tension, mass unemployment and policing methods. At the time, the government insisted that the disturbances were criminal and not political. However, in August 2011 Prime Minister David Cameron contrasted the 1981 "political" riots with the 2011 "criminal" disturbances.

The opening of the Haçienda nightclub, an initiative of Factory Records, in May of the following year, marked a turning point for Manchester's popular music culture, providing the basis for a favorable comparison with neighboring rival Liverpool. The strong club culture that grew up around this initiative gave rise to the term "Madchester" and was instrumental in attracting students to the city's growing universities, as well as in underpinning pride and identity for the region's youth.

Such key informal and counter-cultural initiatives were eventually included in the corporatist narrative of a shifting local government ethos. The "Gay Village", which is now a key sub-brand within Manchester's leisure sector, was initially a political response to the policing policies of the chief constable associated with the 1981 riots. Binnie and Skeggs (2004) describe the contradictions of its current situation and suggest that this reflects Žižek's (1997) identification of the division and incorporation of previously marginalized groups by late capitalism.

Cochrane (1988) suggests that, following the re-election of Margaret Thatcher's conservative government in 1983, the post-riot period of the 1980s saw a shift away from building "municipal socialism" as a bulwark against a neoliberal national government and toward an alignment with private sector interests in order to achieve relatively limited policy objectives. Quilley (2000) suggests that Manchester is the most interesting case of transformation from municipal socialism, not least because of its relative success in the physical and cultural transformation of the city. This shift paralleled the rebranding of the national Labour Party as "New Labour".

Official attempts to raise the positive profile of Manchester went ahead strongly in this period. The city bid for the 1996 Olympic Games, eventually hosted by Atlanta, was eliminated in the first round of voting, but Manchester reached the third round in 1994 with a bid for the 2000 games, eventually held in Sydney. These unsuccessful bids forged regional networks and built the confidence which underpinned successful bids for high profile Millennium lottery funded projects and for a successful bid for the Commonwealth Games.

Cochrane *et al.* (1996) argue that the politics of Manchester's Olympic bids powerfully symbolize many of the supposedly transformative features of the new urban politic presented more widely as "New Public Management" (e.g. Boston *et al.* 1996):

> as the old images of municipal welfarist (bureaucratic) politics have apparently been superseded by those of a dynamic and charismatic (entrepreneurial) business leadership. But while there are superficial similarities between these developments

and those highlighted by analysts of US "growth coalitions", the Manchester case reveals how they are as much about struggles over the role, meaning and structure of the state, as they are about urban growth. Manchester's Olympic bid committee resembles not so much a growth coalition as a grant coalition. This said, it is important not to underestimate the significance of the new urban imperative to talk about growth in order to get grants.

To borrow a phrase later adopted by the City Council as its new slogan, the new politics he symbolised had to be about "Making it happen". This was portrayed as a common-sense and apolitical approach. (Cochrane et al. 1996, pp. 1319, 1324)

Following the successful Commonwealth Games bid Manchester was one of eight cities to host the 1996 UEFA European soccer cup. It was also the target of a massive truck bomb detonated by the IRA. This devastated a substantial area of the city center, fortunately with no fatal injuries, largely due to the significantly increased level of policing for the tournament.

The 2002 Commonwealth Games represented the culmination of the physical renewal efforts that Manchester had driven forward in the wake of the bombing. The main athletics stadium was designed for conversion to the new home ground of Manchester City, the "other" soccer team, and formed the centerpiece of a regeneration corridor into east Manchester. This was intended to be reinforced by an extension of the city's "Metrolink" light-rail system which was eventually scheduled to open in 2012:

This (the 1996 bombing) cleared the way for a £1.2 billion root and branch redevelopment which has transformed the cityscape, opening out the River Irwell for the first time since the industrial revolution, and allowing for the construction of palatial new developments (the world's biggest M&S opposite an equally superlative Boots). But if the IRA inadvertently created the opportunity, it is also true that the speed and imagination of the subsequent redevelopment was only the logical extension of the previous ten years of regeneration – both in terms of the sustained vision of what the city could be like, but also the high-level partnerships which have been further consolidated with each development and with each phase of boosterish hype. (Quilley 2000, p. 610)

AUGUST 2011

The most recent civil disturbances in Manchester reflected the contradictory stresses created by top-down government policy-making in the face of recession. This included the dismantling of regional policy and the substitution of poorly resourced alternative partnerships under the banner of "localism".

> Riots began in Tottenham on Saturday 6th August following a specific incident – a fatal shooting by police. This had spread to 12 areas of London by the 7th and nationally to 44 areas by Monday 8th August, lasting five days in total. (Riots Communities and Victims Panel 2011, p. 44)

Between 6 and 10 August 2011, an estimated 13,000–15,000 people were actively involved in the riots across England. By the time the interim report of the Panel had been drawn up, more than 4,000 suspected rioters had been arrested. Nine out of ten were already known to the police. In total, more than 5,000 crimes were committed, including five fatalities, 1,860 incidents of arson and criminal damage, 1,649 burglaries, 141 incidents of disorder and 366 incidents of violence against the person.

In Salford reported crimes totaled 186, in Manchester 388, although there were differences between the two areas. In Salford looting and arson at a local shopping precinct accompanied an almost ritual stand-off between youths and police outside a local police station. In Manchester it was the core of the city retail area which was subject to attack. The disturbances of 1981 were confined to inner suburbs associated with deprivation and to the destruction of relatively local resources (Newburn *et al.* 2011).

As an eyewitness I can confirm that the febrile atmosphere in the city center on the night of 9 August was strongly reminiscent of that in the city center on the Monday following the IRA bombing during the Euro 96 soccer tournament. The prompt reaction of Manchester city council in closing down the city center saw the bemused patrons of the venues there mingling with potential rioters as one group replaced the other.

Taken together, the interim report of the Riots Communities and Victims Panel (2011) established by the national government, and *The Guardian* and London School of Economics joint inquiry into the August disturbances which involved 270 interviews with rioters (*The Guardian* 2011b), place the summer disorder in context:

> The rioters were not a homogenous group of people all acting for the same reasons. They acted differently depending on why they decided to riot and what they wanted to get out of it. We break down those present at the riots into five broad categories:
>
> - Organized criminals, often from outside the area.
> - Violent aggressors who committed the most serious crimes, such as arson and violent attacks on the police.

- "Late night shoppers" – people who deliberately travelled to riot sites in order to loot.
- Opportunists – people who were drawn into riot areas through curiosity or a sense of excitement and then became caught up in the moment.
- Spectators – people who came just to watch the rioting. (Riots Communities and Victims Panel 2011, p. 11)

A difference from the events of 1981 was arguably the speed with which unrest spread across England over four nights, with the media highlighting the BlackBerry messaging service that enabled "flashmobs" to congregate at prearranged locations (*The Guardian* 2011). In 1981, serious riots in Brixton, south London, pre-dated by four months similar disturbances in Liverpool, Leeds, Manchester and Birmingham. However, these later disturbances then spread to a further five cities within a week.

The Guardian and the London School of Economics' joint inquiry argues that the rush to blame communication technology is nothing new:

> The government mistakenly blamed social media such as Twitter and Facebook for the "viral" spread of the August 2011 riots. During the LA riots, rolling TV coverage was the scapegoat, while riots in France in 2005 were partly explained by reference to young people communicating via text message, email and blogs. (Newburn et al. 2011)

The Guardian/LSE report cites scare stories from 1981 that, in Manchester and London, rioters were communicating using "£10 radios" – the Citizens Band radio fad which pre-dated cellphones by a decade. It argues that social media were as significant in the coordination of community resistance to robbery and arson as they were to the organization of disorder. The Riots Communities and Victims Panel (2011, p. 12) also argues that social media networks should not be shut down during any future disturbances. Evidence from several cities that social media were used to coordinate grass-roots "clean-up" campaigns in the immediate aftermath of the violence supports this position.

Riots and Brands

In contrast to the 1981 riots, attacks on retail and commercial premises were not confined to the inner city areas of high relative deprivation, and arguably this visibility in the commercial urban core triggered the subsequent punitive sentencing.

The Riots Communities and Victims Panel (2011) reflected on the rise of consumer brands and their impact on aspirations and as markers of individual self-esteem. They argue that we live in a society where conspicuous consumption and self-worth have become intrinsically interlinked. In interviews the desire to own goods which give the owner high status (branded trainers and digital gadgets) was seen as an important factor behind the looting, with certain brands and products repeatedly targeted:

> Businesses and brands do not operate in a moral vacuum where right and wrong do not apply. We want to explore how ethical thinking influences the way business operates, especially given the challenging economic times we are now experiencing. Brands have a special relationship with their customer and the Panel is keen to explore how brands could use their powerful influence positively for the good of the community. (Riots Communities and Victims Panel 2011, p. 104)

There is an equal imperative for civil authorities to consider their own brand and identity; and Manchester responded to this.

I ♥ MCR

Immediately after the civil unrest of 9 August 2011, "Love Manchester" appeared. The city had launched a campaign utilizing the slogan derived from I ♥ NY. This widely imitated campaign originated as an initiative taken in a troubled decade for that city, in which local government debt impacted on services and perceptions. Countless cities, including Manchester, had already created their version of the iconic slogan, but the city council now placed it at the core of a campaign which also co-opted the same social media alleged to have been used by the rioters to avoid police and to coordinate attacks.

I ♥ Manchester was only one of a number of complementary initiatives emerging immediately in the aftermath of the disturbances in Manchester and Salford:[1]

> The I ♥ MCR campaign launched at the end of last week in response to the disturbances that took place on Tuesday 9 August, with the aim of promoting civic pride across Greater Manchester.
>
> There are a number of events and initiatives going on in the city to encourage people to come into the centre and make the most of the shops, restaurants and bars and show their love for Manchester. (Comment at http://beproudlovemanchester.com, 22 August 2011)

Free parking on street and off street in the city center was offered, along with free tram travel, vouchers offered on-line and in the city's evening newspaper.

Sustaining a Brand through Proactive Repair

In addition to free entertainment across the central business district, the site promoted the "Manchester Moment", in effect a local authority sponsored flashmob at the center of the unrest in the Market Street shopping area:

> If you are taking advantage of this Sunday's free travel into the city why not participate in the "Manchester Moment"?
>
> The "Manchester Moment" will be a simple way of bringing people together to show the world the true face of the city. Shoppers will be given posters to hold aloft for the Moment, which takes place at 2 p.m. on Market Street. There will also be music and entertainment.
>
> It is our way of showing the world that Manchester is back in business. All proud Mancunians are invited to Market Street, near American Apparel, to gather from 1.45 p.m. on Sunday to take part in the Manchester Moment at 2 p.m. (Comment at http://beproudlovemanchester.com, 22 August 2011)

Friday 26 August was designated "We Love MCR" day and those unable to attend were urged to take party by tweeting "messages of love for the city by including the hashtag #ILoveMCR in your message – and help put Manchester on the global trending map".

More traditional events and branded apparel were also promoted, but the city had in effect co-opted the social media used both by both the rioters and the community resistors, building on a grass-roots community-level reaction to events. The co-optation of such spontaneous events by both authorities and media led to a heated on-line debate on the level of genuine as opposed to manipulated activity. Critics used terms such as "broom fascism" to describe the televized clean-up activities in affected locations, while some active volunteers made a point of displaying notices to the effect that they were not subscribing to the government's "Big Society" slogan and agenda.[2]

New Infrastructure and New Momentum

Manchester maintains a strong affection for large infrastructure projects, and the £35 billion HS2 high speed rail project qualifies as a megaproject (Flyvbjerg *et al*. 2003). Construction could begin in 2017, following completion of the major Crossrail project in London, with the first trains running as far as Birmingham by 2025.

Manchester's continuing aspirations are still evident. With the completion of its orbital motorway in 2000, the section of the M62 Mersey to

Humber motorway, utilized to form the complete circuit, was renumbered to create the M60 in imitation of the M25 London orbital motorway.

Air transport and aerospace have been strong presences in the regions, with the opening of Barton Aerodrome in 1928 as the first municipal airport in the UK, to the present Manchester Airport, opened as "Ringway" just prior to the outbreak of the Second World War. A second runway was added in 2001 in face of environmental activist opposition and site occupation. It is now the largest UK airport outside the London region and remains in public ownership through a holding company representing the ten local authorities of Greater Manchester, with Manchester City Council as the largest shareholder.

The Manchester ship canal is now privately owned by Peel Ports, whose plans include redevelopment, expansion and an increase in shipping from 8,000 containers a year to 100,000 by 2030, as part of their Atlantic Gateway project. The framework for this, agreed between Liverpool and Manchester and supported by the North-West Regional Development Agency (NWDA), aims to boost the economic potential of a region spanning from Merseyside to north Cheshire, Chester, Halton, Warrington and into Greater Manchester. With the abolition of the NWDA in April 2012, the private Peel Holdings has become a major proponent of these strategic plans for the region (Peel Holdings 2010). However, Peel's interests and objectives are not entirely in accord with those of the local authorities. As owners of the Trafford shopping center they opposed the adoption of a congestion charging system in Manchester, which was promoted vigorously by the city council, and as owners of Liverpool airport they have campaigned for the privatization of Manchester airport.

The Atlantic Gateway framework has been used to link a number of significant projects, including the Media City UK development. Situated on the banks of the Ship Canal, in neighboring Salford and close to Manchester city center, this development is reaching a critical mass after a long gestation with the arrival of significant departments of the BBC during 2011. The relocation of BBC radio news resources and other programming to Salford began in 2010 and greater visibility of Manchester and north-west England is evident at a national level.

The importation of a model used in both Dubai and South Korea, complete with the deputy director of the Seoul Media city, represents a traditional approach to job and capacity creation, building on existing but relatively limited capacities. However, the leveraging by local higher education institutions, with a faculty of the University of Salford relocated within the development, reflects an understanding of the role of intellectual capital in the so-called "knowledge economy". The expansion of the region's capacity in the mass media and social media through this support suggests the possibility of a convergence of the strands of social and technical innovation that have characterized Manchester's past.

Such a globally connected initiative fits with Kraetke's (2003) concept of an urban hinterworld which he defines as "the pattern of a city's relations with other cities across the world". He measures this by aggregating the level of service provision that is available in a city for doing business in another city. As a second tier city in the context of the UK, Manchester's creative media industries are linked to those in London which are in turn linked to the United States. Since the 1990s, high capacity information and communication technologies have allowed the almost instantaneous transfer of digital media for post-production work. Building on a long tradition of north-west media production, the visibility of Media City UK provides the prospect of more direct global networking that could transcend the territorial trap (Agnew 1994) of the national government's emphasis on "localism" and reassert Manchester's historic global prominence.

The local authorities have recovered some of the tools that had been denied them since the 1980s. The former Greater Manchester Council, abolished by the Thatcher administration in 1985, along with all other metropolitan county authorities, has been reconstituted on a new, lean legal basis. A new single legal entity allows coordination between the Greater Manchester authorities, which previously had been done through the voluntary Association of Greater Manchester Authorities.

The Combined Authority which came into being on 1 April 2011, complements the recent announcement of the Greater Manchester Local Enterprise Partnership and will ensure a coordinated approach is delivered in the ten local authorities that make up the Manchester City Region. This sits alongside the agreement of local government across north-west England to continue to operate as "North-West England" following the abolition of the NWDA at a European level, where DG Regio deals in such levels of aggregation for funding purposes. These complementary initiatives are indicative of the level of proactive and reactive interventions necessary to the maintenance of a place brand in times of uncertainty.

CONCLUSION

In many ways Manchester retains its historic aspirations. The presence of nationally and internationally significant universities and research institutions in and around the city, and the convergence of technical and social innovation through the vehicle of Media City, indicate that the city retains its capacity for innovation and impact.

The city council has been close to successive Labour governments but remains very good at negotiating with all comers. Involvement in an abortive referendum on road charging, which promoted a more sophisticated but more complex version than the central London scheme, reflected its metropolitan aspirations. Despite the logic of the road charging scheme – that it would fund the completion of the embryonic Metrolink light rail system – this is now being completed across the Greater Manchester region.

In the immediate aftermath of the disturbances of August 2011 Manchester local authorities deployed traditional communication forms as well as co-opting the social media identified by some commentators as central to the propagation of the unrest and criminality (Ball and Lewis 2011). These were combined into the existing repertoire of public events such as the "Manchester Mela" (www.manchestermela.co.uk/) and smaller local events.

These efforts sit within a continuing process of brand management and development in which Manchester, as a city within the reconstituted greater Manchester region and within the broader context of north-west England, was able to call upon a related set of nested brands and identities. Wider messages, directed at external audiences, continued through large-scale projects with which the city has long been associated. The shifts in local politics described by Cochrane (1988) and Quilley (2000) continue, and both public and private resources are now entwined in urban governance and service delivery, although not necessarily closely aligned.

This is exemplified at the street level by the privatized for-profit enforcement of council regulations. A significant part of Manchester's "offer" to citizens to reoccupy the city center was the suspension of parking regulations which were only recently extended into the evening and weekends. The continued outsourcing of front line services and the ceding of enforcement to for-profit entities carries a logic which can undermine the wider objectives of local authorities, leading to a focus on rent-seeking behavior directed at replacing former financial resources. This is exemplified by the pre-Olympic environment in London where the enforcement of parking regulations for the entire city is being undertaken by a German based and French financed multinational corporation. Vigorous enforcement by a profit driven external agency creates a very different visitor experience than that sought through the impression management and branding initiatives of local authorities such as the "Olympic Borough of Hackney", one that is no longer under the direct control of local authorities.

The process of corporatization and depoliticization continues with the familiar forms of corporate communication replacing democratic discourse. The cumulative effect of this continuing erosion of this aspect of legitimation is falling voter turnout and ill-considered remedies such as directly elected mayors and police chiefs.

In the face of these internal tensions, the extent to which the "municipalization" of social media in campaigns, such as that developed in Manchester under the immediate pressure of civil disorder, can help a city or region to maintain a coherent brand becomes a research topic of some significance.

NOTES

1. See http://beproudlovemanchester.com, www.ilovemcr.com, www.i-love-manchester.co.uk/ and www.facebook.com/IloveManchesterOnline.
2. See for example the heated discussions at http://universityforstrategicoptimism.wordpress.com/2011/08/10/riotcleanup-or-riotwhitewash/.

REFERENCES

Agnew, J. (1994) "The territorial trap: the geographical assumptions of international relations theory", *Review of International Political Economy*, 1(1): 53–80.

Allen, J. and Cochrane, A. (2007) "Beyond the territorial fix: regional assemblages, politics and power", *Regional Studies*, 41(09): 1161–75.

Ball, J. and Lewis, P. (2011) "The politicians and police rushed in to condemn. Twitter helped clean up", *The Guardian*, 8 December: 14–15.

Barca, F. (2009) *An Agenda for Reformed Cohesion Policy: A Place Based Approach to Meeting European Union Challenges and Expectations*. Independent report to the Commissioner for Regional Policy, www.eurada.org/site/files/Regional%20development/Barca_report.pdf

Binnie, J. and Skeggs, B. (2004) "Cosmopolitan knowledge and the production and consumption of sexualized space: Manchester's gay village", *Sociological Review*, 52(1) February: 39–61.

Boston, J., Martin, J., Pallot, J. and Walsh, P. (1996) *Public Management: The New Zealand Model*. Auckland: Oxford University Press.

Braun, E. (2011) "History matters: the path dependency of place brands", in Go, F.M. and Govers, R. (eds), *International Place Branding Yearbook 2011: Managing Reputational Risk*. Basingstoke: Palgrave Macmillan, pp. 39–46.

Cater, H. (2011) "Rioters' stories: I thought of it like a battle, like a war", *The Guardian*, 6 December: 6.

Cartmell, M. (2010) "NGOs denounce Burson-Marsteller's Brand Vulnerability Index", www.prweek.com, 22 June.

Checkland, O. (1998) "The Iwakura Mission, industries and exports". Discussion Paper No. IS/98/349, March, *Suntory and Toyota International Centres for Economics and Related Disciplines, London School of Economics and Political Science*, pp. 25–34.

Cochrane, A. (1988) "In and against the market? The development of socialist economic strategies in Britain 1981–1986", *Policy and Politics*, 16(3): 159–68.

Cochrane, A., Peck, J. and Tickell, A. (1996) "Manchester Plays Games: exploring the local politics of globalisation", *Urban Studies*, 33(8): 1319–36.

Dickens, C. (1854) "Hard Times", *Household Words*, 1 April.

Flyvbjerg, B., Bruzelius, N. and Rothengatter, W. (2003) *Megaprojects and Risk*. Cambridge: Cambridge University Press.

Kapulsky, J.R. (2011) *Brand Resilience: Managing Risk and Recovery in a High-Speed World*. New York: Palgrave Macmillan.

Knowles, E.M. (2006) *What They Didn't Say: A Book of Misquotations*. Oxford: Oxford University Press.

Kraetke, S. (2003) "Global media cities in a worldwide urban network", *European Planning Studies*, 11(6): 605–28.

Little, S. (2009) "Regional identity and regional development: the role of narratives in the European Capital of Culture programme". Paper presented at the Third Central European Conference in Regional Science, Kosice, 6–9 October.

Little, S. (2010) "In the shadow of Bangalore: place branding and identity or Chennai", in Go, F.M. and Govers, R. (eds), *International Place Branding Yearbook 2010: Place Branding in the New Age of Innovation*, Basingstoke: Palgrave Macmillan, pp. 88–96.

Newburn, T., Lewis, P. and Metcalf, M. (2011) "A new kind of riot? From Brixton 1981 to Tottenham 2011", *The Guardian*, 9 December, www.guardian.co.uk/uk/2011/dec/09/riots-1981-2011-differences.

Peel Holdings (2010) "A response by the private sector to the Government's request for outline proposals in relation to Local Enterprise Partnerships (LEPs) in respect of Atlantic Gateway Peel Holdings". www.peel.co.uk/media/News/Peel_LEP_Submission_vFinal.pdf.

Quilley, S. (2000) "Manchester First: From Municipal Socialism to the Entrepreneurial City", *International Journal of Urban and Regional Research*, 24(3): 601–5.

Riots Communities and Victims Panel (2011) *Five Days in August: An Interim Report on the 2011 English Riots*. www.5daysinaugust.co.uk

The Guardian (2011a) "Riots: magistrates advised to 'disregard normal sentencing'". 15 August, www.guardian.co.uk/uk/2011/aug/15/riots-magistrates-sentencing.

The Guardian (2011b) "Travelling for trouble", 6 December: 6–7.

Žižek, S. (1997) "Multiculturalism, or, the cultural logic of multinational capitalism", *New Left Review*, I(225): 28–51.

CHAPTER 8

Case D Social Media: An Insight into the "Public Mood" of Places? A Case Study of the City of Johannesburg

Wadim Schreiner and Frank M. Go

Traditionally, the reputation of a location is measured by considering how individuals, organizations and "external" stakeholders feel, think and make decisions. "Reputation of place" measurement, including country and city, is emerging as a domain for inter-disciplinary analysis. While all these have absolute merits and are an integral part of any place's efforts to improve its global reputation, what is often overlooked is the importance of "domestic reputation management", including "public mood".

Traditionally, the "mood" of the people has been measured via qualitative research and surveys. While these methods have a certain degree of value, they also display a number of major disadvantages, particularly within an emerging market context. In particular, their relative high cost leads to irregular – annual and in some cases biennial – measurement. Furthermore, the time allocated to respondents' interviews has a direct bearing on survey results. This does not serve as a criticism or argument against the need for qualitative research, which often provides in-depth answers to questions. Rather, it suggests that it may not be the best instrument through which to establish a robust "public mood" database, one that is accessible to a wider group of affected stakeholders. It is for this reason that social media have begun to revolutionize the way in which information about people's thoughts can be utilized. Presently, there is a dearth of research which actively responds to the social media trend and its affordance to involve society in place brand development (Widler 2007; Tatevossian 2008; Gilmore 2008), particularly on a regional basis. In a relatively short period of time, the social media have taken the world by storm. For instance, Twitter just turned five in March 2011 (Dorsey 2006). Facebook, in its original form, started on 4 February 2004 (Seward 2007) but only really became commercial on 26 September 2006 (Abram 2006).

Undoubtedly, these past five years have changed the way in which people communicate and share their opinions. The way in which the media industry operates, the way journalists obtain information and quote sources, and the way that business and politicians view their respective "constituencies" have been revolutionized. Although online media have been available for much longer, making news and information available more immediately than traditional media, social media, particularly Twitter and Facebook, have added a never before experienced dimension: the immediate commentary opinion.

On the back of Facebook and Twitter came the increased number of blogs, with personal opinions expressed on subjects at the macro and microlevels to both large and niche audiences. It has also led to the creation of the term "citizen journalism" (Borman and Willis 2003) where everyone with a camera and access to the Internet can be a source of news and opinion.

With an increasing number of people expressing their opinion through the Internet, many tools have been developed that are able to harvest the information, monitor its content and help to streamline the large volumes of it. These tools are called "feeds". Over 200 online organizations are offering services that "crawl" the Internet for relevant opinions and thoughts expressed in blogs and social networks (Burbary 2011). Many corporate organizations use the information to gather insight into customer attitudes, opinions of products and competition.

Most software includes algorithms to measure "sentiment" around key words or brands, allowing organizations to gauge attitudes. However, this type of "sentiment analysis" is rudimentary, often incorrect and hardly a reliable indicator of such opinions. Although there are a number of considerable technical improvements currently taking place, sentiment analysis may only be considered as a valuable opinion variable once these technical obstacles have been overcome. In this study, and for the aforementioned reasons, we have abstained from analyzing the concept of "sentiment".

There are additional reasons for our focus on social media. These are, first, it allows for the unedited and unstructured assessment of peoples' opinions, as opposed to traditional opinion surveying. The latter involves answers to prepared questions, often linguistically structured to lead to a specific answer. Put in other words, whilst the comments conveyed through social media are unstructured, they reflect, albeit not in depth, a spontaneous sense of otherwise unnoticed emotional human feelings. The lack of structure, however, makes the interpretation of results emerging from social media research much more difficult and open to interpretation.

Second, social media elicit a "sense-and-response" feeling among users and therefore generate immediate, emotional and often to-the-point responses. For example, the social media, particularly Twitter, has far less "pointless babble" as it is popularly conceived (De Beer *et al.* 2011). An analysis of international tweets regarding the 2010 FIFA World Cup showed that "pointless babble" only comprised 22 percent of the total discussion, just marginally higher in comparison to the international print media coverage.

Third, the properties of social media afford an immediate and reactive measuring of people's moods. Fourth, and importantly, establishing a social mood polling system based on social media would be considerably better value for money than traditional surveys, a fact exceptionally relevant in emerging markets and which is the main purpose addressed in this chapter.

This chapter describes initial research toward a possible "public mood" index for the City of Johannesburg, based on the analysis of selected social media. The city is the largest in South Africa and is one of the largest metropolitan areas on the continent, identified by the Monitor Group (2011) as one of the three African Growth Opportunities. But it suffers from the consequences encountered by many business hubs in emerging markets: overpopulation, deterioration of public services, increasing crime levels and a lack of social delivery.

The city also lacks an effective citizen feedback system, with its complaints call center being largely ineffective. In this context, the relationship between independent hubs and the collective decision-making process can turn to one of tensions and conflicts from known dichotomies and differing objectives. To understand both the process and the underlying, invisible forces that shape relations requires constant assessment. This need for assessment to provide effective citizen feedback renders the present research project relevant both in academic and pragmatic terms. The research is theory based and, as such, describes the selection of relevant social media, together with the establishment of an analysis framework that can capture conversations and the development of a database of issues, stakeholders and "influencers" relating to social delivery in Johannesburg.

Based on the evidence presented, we examine a possible business model for a framework that would allow stakeholders from the private sector, as well as local government, to monitor the public mood through local conversation patterns and to engage with relevant opinion makers on topical issues that arise. Importantly, we analyze the extent to which social media may serve as a useful tool and be substituted for traditional market research in budget-constrained organizations. Further, an indication of "public mood" could serve for the critical task of managing citizen participation as part of the ongoing process of managing the reputation of a city brand.

EXISTING RESEARCH

Existing research on the use of social media as a way to gauge public opinion or public mood is rare, which is perhaps not surprising considering that social media have only been in existence for a short duration. While the number of academic research studies clearly demonstrates a paucity of results, the number of newspaper or online articles on commercial "solutions" are abundant. However, the fundamental methodologies used in the commercial propositions remain vague. At least 300 online references over the past 24 months were found using the Factiva/Dow Jones search engines that contain information about the launch of various "trackers" by enterprises that were able to detect attitude and "mood" toward various issues on the basis of social media – though none refer specifically to the exact methodologies used, perhaps for reasons of competition.

It appears, however, that academic research repeatedly points to Twitter as a relatively reliable way of gauging public opinion. Carnegie Mellon University fellows O'Connor *et al.* presented a paper in May 2010, during the International Association for Advancement of Artificial Intelligence (AAAI) Conference on Weblogs and Social Media, in which they compared surveys on consumer confidence and political opinion in 2008 and 2009 to the frequency with which selected words appeared in Twitter messages. Their results highlighted the "potential of text streams as a substitute and supplement for traditional polling". Overall, their analysis of Twitter in comparison to other surveys showed a good result correlation, and the authors state that "while the results do not come without caution, it is encouraging that expensive and time-intensive polling can be supplemented or supplanted with the simple-to-gather text data that is generated from online social networking" (p. 7).

Cummings *et al.* (2011) undertook a similar experiment on the use of Twitter to measure US presidential approval ratings, economic confidence and the generic Congressional ballot, while in the business environment a group of researchers published findings of their analysis on the use of Twitter to predict the stock market (Bollen *et al.* 2011). These recent studies underline the increased interest in the use of social media, not purely as a conversation tool, but, through more structured approaches, for leveraging the information to develop tools that address the growing need for an ongoing measurement of "public mood". Such research findings might serve as relevant input to underpinning the process of building the reputation of "internal" place brands.

PUBLIC MOOD, PUBLIC OPINION AND THE ROLE OF SOCIAL MEDIA

A number of global events over recent months have increased the debate regarding a better understanding of "public mood". Even before the 2011 London riots or the emergence of the Occupy Wall Street Movement, politicians around the world had made statements indicating their support for a better understanding of the concept.[1] Rahn *et al.* (1996, p. 31) define public mood as a "diffuse affective state, having distinct positive and negative components that citizens experience because of their membership in a particular political community". Smith and Darlington (2010, p. 113) argue that "place branding is effective only if it is affective ... Thoughts and images of places are really feelings about them and a policy is nothing if it is not felt (otherwise, it will not be enacted)." While the authors state that "local emotions are public feelings, fashioned collectively and made real over very long periods of time", Rahn *et al.* (p. 32) argue that there are differences between private feelings and public feeling and that "public mood is not the aggregation or the average of the moods people experience in their everyday lives". Instead, public mood needs also to take into account the fact that some people are genetically happier than other people (Seidlitz and Diener 1993) and that individuals "often have emotional experiences because of their membership in a particular national community" (Smith 1993, p. 299) or "class". An increase in a person's mood seems to be correlated with an increased harmony or balance between personal preferences and the environment, or, conversely, people perceive environmental features according to the salience of their needs (Kahana *et al.* 1999). As a result, when people's expectations clash with a place's reality the degree of positivity or negativity of their mood is influenced. In turn, the notion of "mood" appears to have a direct effect on the reputation of a place, as people interact, either as a one-off, repeatedly or ongoingly, with it and also with outsiders, such as tourists or investors who define the character and atmosphere of the place (Insch and Florek 2008). City residents with positive perceptions of their city reinforce and communicate favorable associations with their place and, conversely, unhappy and dissatisfied residents can harm the brand image through negative word of mouth.

One can perhaps argue that the difficulties emerging from the global economic downturn have exerted greater pressure on policy-makers and businesses to achieve strategic goals by listening more to their respective constituencies. In the past, constituencies had few channels through which to voice their concerns. The traditional media have been playing the role of agenda-setters and gate-keepers by allowing only some citizens' concerns to be broadcast. With the rise of social media, more people have access to channels through which to raise their opinions, either to niche audiences and/or wider recipients, with exponential gains in influence on both accounts. In a recent article, Ripberger (2011, p. 240) makes interesting observations about the definitions of public opinion and public attention. He states that "public attention, though related, is not the same as public opinion". Public opinion is "what people think", whereas public attention is "what people think about" (see also Newig 2004). What initially may seem to be miniscule differences can turn out to be significant attributes for understanding the context of mining opinions (or attitudes) in social media.

In essence, Ripberger (2011) argues that traditional opinion polls only answer the questions asked, whereas an understanding of the "mood of the people" should ideally be obtained through a system of direct access to people's thoughts, their thought processes and their information-seeking behavior.

As such, a few recent studies in the field of sociology are pointing to some interesting observations. Golder and Macy (2011) as well as Dodds *et al.* (2011) have found that social media hold potential power for studying social phenomena on a massive scale and provide results in the form of indicators that could help to break new ground in resolving questions about how information and influence flow through social networks (Miller 2011).

If we assume that social media correlate with public sentiment or public mood, as highlighted by the previous studies, then any systematic analysis framework should cater for both the aspect of public attentiveness and public opinion (Ripberger 2011). Conclusions about the "mood" drawn should be based on a combination of expected and open-mined information. In our methodology for the use of social media monitoring as a platform for effective regional reputation management, we have aimed at including both mechanisms, namely a set of issues we are potentially expecting to be discussed as well as topics that emerged from the open-minded mining of available commentary.

METHODOLOGY

In designing a system to measure "public mood" for the City of Johannesburg, relevant information from social media sources was collected with the assistance of specialized social media monitoring companies. References to the city, including abbreviations and terms commonly used by people living in Johannesburg, were leveraged as keywords. Taking into account that Twitter, for instance, limits conversations to 160 characters, the following search string was created: "Johannesburg" OR "Joburg" OR "Jo'burg" OR "Jozi" OR "Johanesburg". Jozi and Joburg are common references to Johannesburg. With the help of the sentiment analysis platform GATE (General Architecture for Text Engineering), the coverage was further analyzed according to its content, particularly the linguistic assessment of topic selections. Items with Johannesburg/Joburg/Jozi, in English only, were tagged as one method for eliminating foreign commentary on the city and were combined in one "Johannesburg" category.

The rules were defined so as to guarantee that topics and issues found in the proximity of Johannesburg were really related to "Johannesburg" and were not coincidentally associated. Since the ultimate goal of this research project was to establish an assessment of social media mood for the city as an organization, world-cloud software was applied to various City of Johannesburg strategy documents (which were available on its website: www.joburg.org.za/documents). From these, service issues important to the city were determined for their inclusion in a list of "policy" categories used to distinguish between conversations that dealt with non-organizational matters. Finally, all individual issues were grouped into predefined higher-end policy categories.

RESULTS

For the month of June 2011, 43,140 mentions of Johannesburg were observed in English language social media coverage. Of these, 7,119 were found to be in close proximity (within ten words) and linked to one or more of the policy group issues, topics or entities. All keywords in the 36,021 mentions of Johannesburg that were *not* in the proximity of any of the policy categories were examined to establish if they needed to be added to the initial issue codebook. However, it was evident that the discussion in these feeds had little impact on the city. Coverage not in close proximity to Johannesburg, largely centered around touristic aspects, such as the weather, a visit to South Africa by US First Lady Michelle Obama and local football games taking place in the city. Overall, the researchers were satisfied that the 36,021 mentions that did not fall within the topic structure contained no significant value to the actual City of Johannesburg as an administrative entity.

Thereafter, 7,119 relevant mentions of Johannesburg between close-proximity (within ten words) and extended-proximity (within two sentences before or after "Johannesburg") were categorized. In the first group (close-proximity) 2,542 references were assigned to main themes and sub-themes. From the above classifications, a list of the highest referenced issues by social media commentators on the City of Johannesburg was generated (see Table 8.1).

Although the results might shed some light on the issues of largest concern to those expressing an opinion on Johannesburg, we must reiterate that the above results are based on issues that have been found in the *direct* proximity of the keyword "Johannesburg" (within ten words). We must put into context the fact that those expressing opinions might be reiterating their concerns using different styles and media. Twitter, for instance, is limited to 160 characters and is therefore likely to inform the bulk of the above assessment. Yet, in order for us to take into account social media formats where people might be expressing their opinions extensively, the proximity parameter was extended to two sentences before and after the umbrella keyword "Johannesburg" to include more information from the likes of blogs (extended-proximity). There were 5,787 topics identified in the extended-proximity of the keyword, including sub-categories (see Table 8.2).

The comparison of "top-of-mind" results from the close-proximity and extended-proximity topic categories highlights that the traffic situation and

TABLE 8.1 Top category issues: near proximity (Johannesburg)

Traffic	346	Animals	27
Events	250	Awards	26
Billings and payment	224	Burglary/robbery	16
Electricity	175	Response to queries	15
Trains	161	Communication	14
Taxis	148	Waste removal	14
Crime	140	Xenophobia	14
Media coverage	136	Construction	12
Water	106	Sustainability	12
Accident	80	Provision of houses	10
Building	79	Public transport	9
Leadership	76	Procurement	8
Administration	64	Green	8
Health services	59	Licenses and permits	7
Protests	45	Emergency services	7
Theft	35	Infrastructure	7
Corruption	35	Capacity	7
Road safety	32	Environment	6
Finances	32	Apologies	5
Flood	28	Call center	5

TABLE 8.2 Top category issues: extended proximity (Johannesburg)

Billings and payment	579	Response to queries	59
Traffic	564	Burglary/robbery	57
Event	553	Road safety	55
Leadership	407	Provision of houses	50
Health services	375	Administration	48
Media coverage	322	Corruption	48
Electricity	316	Infrastructure	47
Water	235	Xenophobia	43
Trains	229	Construction	42
Taxis	228	Waste removal	39
Crime	211	Green	39
Finances	172	Environment	35
Building	135	Flood	34
Accident	128	Capacity	32
Animal	108	Apologies	27
Theft	103	Sustainability	22
Awards	102	Procurement	19
Elections	91	Call center	17
Communication	83	Public transport	15
Protests	83	General interaction	13

problems relating to the billing system were of the greatest concern. In the extended-proximity category, an extensive focus is placed on discussing the leadership and management aspects of the City of Johannesburg, a subject rarely mentioned in the close-proximity list. Similarly, issues such as health and media coverage play a significant role in the extended list.

It is likely that, when provided with more commentary space, opinion makers are discussing issues picked up in the traditional media. Notably, the close-proximity list seems to be an indicator of higher emotional issues based on personal experiences (and hence perhaps is the closest to Ripberger (2011) observation of public mood), while the extended-list brings complex topics to the fore. Both lists share a lack of environmental, public transport and infrastructure coverage. Although extended-proximity results indicate slightly more discourse on some of the topics, the overall list of issues is similar.

Overall, the results demonstrate that it is possible to conduct selected "top-of-mind" research based on social media coverage on clearly defined subject matter (in our case the City of Johannesburg). For reasons already mentioned, we did not undertake any sentiment analysis, but we are certain that in the future, with improvements to this automated technique, it might be possible to add the results of such an analysis to the above assessed top-of-mind issue responses so as to have an even better understanding of the mood of a city's population.

DISCUSSION

Although the results from the preliminary analysis of social media coverage on the City of Johannesburg deliver a number of interesting results, they lead to even more questions. This is particularly the case when using data generated by social media as a potential replacement of surveys or polls, which were the traditional instruments used to conduct mood research, which involved slow, laborious sampling methods and high costs.

What is evident from the results is that social media analysis in its current format still poses myriad challenges. First, it presents one with a completely unknown audience universe. The anonymity of the Internet allows only for a limited identification of the actual people behind the comments. It is almost impossible to draw any representative samples, as very little can be established in terms of demographics. Statistics as to who is using social media and who is accessing social media remain vague and under-researched, especially within an emerging market such as South Africa.

Second, we attempted to isolate social media feeds to those either living in Johannesburg or being affected by the City of Johannesburg, but we were unable to secure a reliable method that would guarantee this. While geo-location is a feature in many social media such as Twitter, it is voluntary and could easily be manipulated. Unless demographic and location information becomes more freely available, "national" samples are unlikely to be selected. Importantly, these concerns do not mean that the results are not representative in terms of those commenting on social media.

Third, it must be noted that the results are not representative of the population of Johannesburg in that only English feeds were analyzed. Additionally, the results of the top-of mind issues seem to be representative of a population characterized by a higher living standard, i.e. a segment, which uses private means of transport, for example; hence the manifestation of "traffic" concerns in the data. Although this may pose a challenge to the interpretation of the results as reflective of all citizens of Johannesburg, it should not be dismissed due to the importance of such a group for the future performance of the city.

Lastly, the project faced critical linguistic challenges. In a country and city with multiple mother tongues, commonly available lexica to detect phrases, words and expressions will continue to be a challenge. Future research in this field must take into account not just specific regional language nuances, but the ever changing way of commonly used language expressions.

CONCLUSION

This exploratory study sheds light on the question as to whether social media as a survey medium provide us with a better understanding of the mood of groups of people. Provided that key challenges within social media analysis are overcome, we believe that a robust methodology, together with appropriate software and the appropriately trained human factor, could, in a few years, pave the way for social media to be used in collaboration with other means of survey gathering and be used to establish a public mood indicator that is useful for both regional as well as national place branders. Considerable improvements are needed in the field of sentiment analysis to address the subject of public opinion relation. It must also be understood that social media will remain a tool for those who voluntarily express opinions and, as such, any results derived will always have to be considered in this context.

In an article published by the *Nieman Reports*, Ashbrook (2004, p. 48) refers to media as "a mirror. A mirror of society's hopes and fears, of its obsessions and conceits and, even, its illusions." While we perhaps assume what media-consuming people are thinking, we are however not sure how these thoughts culminate in raw, emotional and often subjective expressions of mood. Social media are in many cases the expressions of such emotional and irrational thoughts, unfiltered by the gatekeeping mechanisms of traditional media. And while traditional surveys and opinion polls are set up to eliminate this subjectivity to allow for better categorization, it takes away the fact that it is exactly this lack of structure, this expression of emotions and this irrational behavior that represents the mood of people in its purest form.

From our assessment of social media discussions about the City of Johannesburg we can deduce the degree of importance that certain issues have in the life of an economically active group of citizens and which in turn influences how they feel about the place they live and work in. Our research is an attempt to make a small contribution to advance the knowledge domain of regional reputation management, most notably through a better understanding of the cost benefits of social media versus traditional polling. As much as this knowledge could serve for an understanding of future policy development and execution for the city it could also be utilized as an insight into future town planning and urban development priorities.

NOTE

1. See www.guardian.co.uk/lifeandstyle/2010/nov/14/happiness-index-britain-national-mood.

REFERENCES

Abram, C. (2006) "Welcome to Facebook Everyone". Retrieved from http://blog.facebook.com/blog.php?post=2210227130, 26 September.

Amatomu (n.d.) Retrieved from www.amatomu.com.

Ashbrook, T. (2004) "Journalism mirrors the public mood". *Nieman Reports*, 58(4): 48, http://search.proquest.com/docview/216751841?accountid=13598.

Beer, A. de, Schreiner, W. and Vos, N. (2011) "Tweeting 'South Africa' during FIFA World Cup 2010: a news country image study". Paper presented at the International Association for Mass Communication Research Conference, Istanbul, 13–17 July.

Bollen, J., Mao, H. and Xiaojun, Z. (2011) "Twitter mood predicts the stock market", *Journal of Computational Science*, 2: 1–8.

Borman, S. and Willis, C. (2003). Retrieved from The Media Center at the American Press Institute: www.hypergene.net/wemedia/weblog.php.

Burbary, K. (2011) "A Wiki of social media monitoring solutions", http:wiki.kenburbary.com.

Cummings, D., Oh, H. and Wang, N. (2011) "Stanford University". Retrieved from Who needs Polls? Gauging Public Opinion from Twitter data: www.google.co.za/url?sa=t&source=web&cd=1&ved=0CBYQFjAA&url=http%3A%2F%2Fnlp.stanford.edu%2Fcourses%2Fcs224n%2F2011%2Freports%2Fnwang6-davidjc-harukioh.pdf&ei=Sul3TurOGKTzmAWe1qGUAg&usg=AFQjCNFvor6IQ-zkMxBobaJdmtWzys0jCA.

Dodds, P., Harris, K., Kloumann, I., Bliss, C. and Danforth, C. (2011) "Cornell University Library". Retrieved from *Physics and Society*: http://arxiv.org/abs/1101.5120, 12 June.

Dorsey, J. (2006) "Just setting up my twttr". Retrieved from twitter.com/#!/jack/status/20, 21 March.

Gilmore, F. (2008) "A country: can it be repositioned? Spain: the success story of country branding", *Journal of Brand Management*, April, 281–93.

Golder, S. and Macy, M. (2011) "Diurnal and seasonal mood vary with work, sleep, and daylength across diverse cultures", *Science*, 333(6051): 1878–81.

Insch, A. and Florek, M. (2008) "A great place to live, work and play: conceptualising place satisfaction in the case of a city's residents", *Journal of Place Management and Development*, 1(2): 138–49.

Kahana, E., Lovegreen, L., Kahana, B. and Kahana, M. (1999) *Foundations of Hedonic Psychology: Scientific Perspectives on Enjoyment and Suffering*, New York: Russel Sage Foundation.

Miller, G. (2011) "Social scientists wade into the tweet stream", *Science*, 333(6051): 1814–15.

Monitor Group (2011) *Africa from the Bottom Up: Cities, Economic Growth and Prosperity in Sub-Saharan Africa*. Johannesburg: Monitor Group.

Newig, J. (2004) "Public attention, political action: the example of environmental regulation", *Rationality and Society*, 16(2): 149–90.

O'Connor, B., Balusabramanyan, R., Routledge, B. and Smith, N. (2010) "Stanford University". Retrieved from From Tweets to Polls: Linking text Sentiment to Public Opinion Time Series: www.google.co.za/url?sa=t&source=web&cd=1&ved=0CBYQFjAA&url=http%3A%2F%2Fnlp.stanford.edu%2Fcourses%2Fcs224n%2F2011%2Freports%2Fnwang6-davidjc-harukioh.pdf&ei=ydY3ToKml-3PmAW97LGhAg&usg=AFQjCNFvor6IQ-zkMx-BobaJdmtWzys0jCA, May.

Rahn, W., Kroeger, B. and Kite, C. (1996) "A framework for the study of public mood",. *International Society of Political Psychology*, March: 29–58.

Ripberger, J. (2011) "Capturing curiosity: using Internet search trends to measure public attentiveness", *Policy Studies Journal*, 39(2): 239–59.

Seidlitz, L. and Diener, E. (1993) "Memory for positive versus negative life events: theories for the differences between happy and unhappy persons", *Journal of Personality and Social Psychology*, 64: 654–64.

Seward, Z. (2007) "Judge expresses skepticism about Facebook lawsuit". *Retrieved from Wall Street Journal* Online: http:..online.wsj.com/article/SB118539991204578084.html?mod=googlenews_wsj, 25 April.

Smith, E. (1993) "Social identity and social emotions: toward new conceptualizations of predudice", in Mackie, D. and Hamiliton, D. (eds), *Affect, Cognition and Stereotyping: Interactive Processes in Group Perception*, New York: Academic Press, pp. 297–315.

Smith, S. and Darlington, K. (2010) "Emotional ecologies as brands: towards a theory of occasioned local feelings", *Place Branding and Public Diplomacy*, 6(2): 112–23.

Tatevossian, A. (2008) "Domestic society's (often-neglected) role in nation branding", *Place Branding and Public Diplomacy*, 4(2): 144–50.

Wahl, H. and Weisman, G. (2003) "Environmental gerontology at the beginning of the new millenium: reflections on its historical empirical and theoretical development", *The Gerontologist*, 43(5): 5–22.

Widler, J. (2007) "Nation branding: with pride against predudice", *Place Branding and Public Diplomacy*, 3(2): 144–50.

CHAPTER 9

Case E Turning a Gemstone into a Diamond: A Green Design and Branding Strategy for The City of Bucharest

Iulia Gramon-Suba and Chris Holt

INTERNATIONAL TRENDS

Today, more than half of the world's population are urban dwellers, this number being forecast by the United Nations to increase to 69 percent by 2050. Cities are the biggest consumers of electricity, gas and heat (Urban Investment Network 2011). This, along with demographic change and the fact that 80 percent of world economic growth is powered by cities and that 75 percent of the emissions are coming from urban locations (Fox-Martin 2009), have made city leaders realize the importance of sustainable development and that the fate of our global climate lies in the future actions of cities (Tyndall Center for Climate Change Research 2008). As Frank Lee (2011), Head of Holding Funds and Advisory, states: "cities ought to play a crucial role in accomplishing climate change objectives and energy efficiency, so the new trend is directed towards sustainability".

It is therefore not surprising to observe that cities around the world have increasingly engaged in a fierce competition to attract attention, talent, innovation and creativity (Konijnendijk 2010) by proving that they offer a healthy and sustainable environment. That is, an environment that facilitates "development that meets the needs of the present without compromising the ability of future generations to meet their own needs" (Rees and Mark 1991) with a high quality of life.

As this is also about perceptions, city branding has become integrated in sustainable city management activities (Kavaratzis and Ashworth 2007) and is a recurrent subject in economical and urban policy debates (Stevens 2011). Increasingly important is the fact that designers have been employing socially responsible means to "address a range of quality-of-life issues" (Cooper et al. 2009).

THE STORY OF BUCHAREST

Every place, even if it has not undergone a branding process, already has an image created through different kinds of communication which ultimately determine people's perceptions of a city. Bucharest is such a city, whose general perception is predominantly negative and associated with the dreadful communist era and the lack of strength to develop into a modern and civilized metropolis. Having arrived as a newly minted national capital in the 20th century, drawing on its association as the "Paris of the East" through its belle époque architecture, the Romanian city of Bucharest is now best known for its socialist realism era, the bloody scenes of 1989 and a difficult transition to a modern metropolis in spite of the country's accession to the European Union. It is the sixth largest city in Europe with its population of 1,950,000 inhabitants (National Institute of Statistics 2010). Bucharest is not only Romania's capital city but also its industrial, commercial and political center. Despite *The Economist* (2009) categorizing Eastern European capitals as "troublesome cripples whose views can't be ignored", they are often very popular attractions for visitors, investors, multinational companies and creative talent (Dinnie 2010). Bucharest is a city of contrasts, an amalgam of tradition and the avant-garde, blended in a unique way, a rough-cut gemstone waiting to be transformed into a highly polished diamond. Today, incoherent governance arrangements and a lack of political will or maturity have seen the city's brand neglected amid crucial indifference by its authorities.

PROBLEM AND MOTIVATION

In this chapter we aim to analyze Bucharest's current situation, investigate how environmental design can be used to change people's perceptions and identify the issues that need to be addressed by using design. We then can depict the brand promise along the lines advocated by Anholt (2004, p. 12): "to be persuasive, we must be believable; to be believable we must be credible; to be credible we must be truthful. It is as simple as that." We will also construct an environmental design-led brand strategy that would allay people's negative perceptions about Bucharest and promote it as a place to invest, visit, work and study and which will generally enhance the quality of life of its inhabitants.

In an attempt to sketch a general panorama of Bucharest's brand, the following aspects were brought to light:

- It is the second worst online brand, ranked 129 of 130 (City Mayors 2004).
- It is ranked 107 out of 221 EU capitals, still lagging behind most of them with regard to the quality of life (Mercer 2010).
- Regarding workforce qualifications, it is near the bottom, ranked 30 out of 34 (Cushman and Wakefield 2009).
- It is ranked bottom for its low human capital (the percentage of people working there has started to decline due to the increasing ageing of the population and the migration of young, capable people to other countries that offer better professional development) (Cushman and Wakefield 2009).
- There is a low quality of life for employees, being ranked 30 out of 34 (Cushman and Wakefield 2009).
- It is ranked at the bottom of the European Green City Index (30 out of 30 cities), according to the Siemens (2010) index of environmental governance, because it is the most polluted European capital due to gas emissions , the lack of recycling systems, the traffic, the lack of green spaces and stray animals.
- There is degradation of its cultural inheritance.
- There is continuous degradation of its landscape and a lack of involvement and civic pride.

However, there are also positive things associated with the city:

- It is ranked first as the ideal place for the relocation of businesses from the labor-cost point of view (Cushman and Wakefield 2009).
- It looks good in terms of attracting investors: 30 companies want to move to Bucharest over the next five years, while the top two such places, Warsaw and Moscow, have 36 and 35 companies respectively that want to move to them (Cushman and Wakefield 2009).
- Bucharest is the biggest cultural center in Romania on account of its universities, theaters, museums, monuments, etc.
- There is a wide range of tourist attractions in Bucharest (historical monuments, quality hotels, restaurants).
- It holds a variety of cultural events.

Consequently, there is an opportunity for a branding project that would help to solve the predominant perception problems and improve actual current conditions. Mitchell (2008) as cited in Salman (2009) states that "the brand has to be based on what is already there in a city or else it is just like giving someone a nice haircut – it might look good for a while, but it doesn't give you a new personality". A good brand should continue to promote the city both internally and externally.

KEY QUESTION, AIM AND OBJECTIVES

The key question of the project is: how could environmental design be used to create a brand strategy that would help change people's perceptions of Bucharest? The aim is: to develop a design-led brand strategy that would help to change people's perceptions about Bucharest through an improvement program based on tackling the city's current environmental problems. In order to achieve this aim, the following objectives were set up:

1. To investigate all relevant available material on city branding and environmental design in order to establish parameters for the research.

2. To analyze why some "green" branding strategies are more successful than others.

3. To audit Bucharest's current brand and environmental situation, with emphasis on design-related issues.

4. To identify how environmental design can educate people and change their perceptions.

5. To create an environmental design-led city brand strategy for Bucharest.

METHODOLOGY

The research was undertaken in four main phases:

Stage 1: Discovery and Planning

This phase was comprised only of secondary research, using a literature review, case studies, city rankings and broadcast documentaries, and set the foundations of the research by appraising current theories on city branding, sustainable cities, environmental design and green city branding and the concepts associated with them.

Stage 2: Investigation

Building on the knowledge set of the first phase, by use of primary research, insights were gathered into the mindset of the city's stakeholders. In order to retrieve exclusive information and gain useful insights, interviews were conducted with: the president of the biggest environmental NGO (Niculae Radulescu-Dobrogea, ECO-Civica); people from the National Environment Protection Agency (including Ioan Baceanu); the City's Town Hall and Ministry officials (Razvan Murgeanu, the Secretary of State of the Ministry of Regional Development and Tourism; Emanuel Papagheorghiu, the director for the Direction of Culture, Education and Tourism); academics from all over the world (including John Simmons, director of "The Writer" and co-author of *Brands and Branding*); and brand consultants.

What's more, a better understanding of the current environmental situation of Bucharest was gained by means of observational research. Questionnaires were used to investigate the general opinion of Bucharest's inhabitants using: two focus groups; a party group (a small gathering of people where they can talk freely while having a drink, which represents a fun and creative way to benefit from deep, thoughtful discussions and which can add important dimensions to the topic); and a Facebook discussion group.

Stage 3: Analysis and Integration

Following the assessment of the results of the previous two stages, the integration of the main findings was carried out in order to compare and contrast distinctive views on the subject and craft a thorough analysis.

Stage 4: Conclusions

Subsequent to the analysis, the design-led Environmental Brand Strategy was created and, along with this, some further recommendations with regard to short-term, medium-term and long-term solutions were provided. Secondary research was used in order to investigate relevant theories and literature on city branding, sustainable cities, environmental design and green city branding, so as to gain an insight into the prevailing problems that the city is currently confronted with.

KEY FINDINGS

The key findings of the research enabled us to create a definition of city branding, sustainable cities and green city branding to see how these three fields overlap. "City branding" is neither product branding, nor city marketing nor corporate branding and, thus, a different form of branding is required (Kavaratzis and Ashworth 2007). The root of this whole process is portrayed by the city's image, which is the interaction point between the "external city" – the city's physical appearance – and the "internal city" – or the "inner-directed mnemonic city" as Graham (2002) calls it; that is, as "the link between real, objective space and its perception" (Kampschulte 1999).

A sustainable city has a long-term vision to stay healthy and preserve current resources for future generations, its primary aspiration being epitomized by the betterment of the quality of life in concordance with the health improvement of ecological systems, supported by a healthy economical base (Indigo Development 2006). The field of green city branding is still underdeveloped as there is not much theory currently available in the public domain. Branding a city as "green" requires green city goals, such as improved air quality, reduced infrastructure spending, waste reduction and access to green space (Dinnie 2010).

Additionally, key elements of successful city branding include: involving the people, creating public–private partnerships between the community, governmental sectors and business organizations, and positioning the city in people's minds. Moreover, in order for a city successfully to develop in a sustainable way, it has to create a balance between the economy, the ecology and social cohesion, all of these having people at the center of the ideas. However, in order to create a successful green city brand there has to be a lot of pro bono work involved and communication should only be one of the pillars of the strategy. Recent research into the field indicates that socially responsible design is being more and more employed for solving quality of life issues and as a catalyst for change.

THE BRAND OF BUCHAREST

> Bucharest as a brand is hard to digest.
> (Razvan Murgeanu, Former State Secretary and Mayor of Bucharest)

As stated already, previous research done amongst Bucharest's inhabitants has uncovered some general brand problems which are detracting from the city's glamor. There is an evident absence of a clear brand identity because it lacks that "sui generis" which epitomizes the kernel of every city: "when

I think of Bilbao, I think of Frank Gehry's Modern Art Museum" (John Simmons, personal communication, April 2011), whereas "Bucharest is the city of contrast, diversity and change" (Emanuel Papagheorghiu, personal communication, April 2011).

Bucharest as a brand is a raw, unpolished product, doomed to failure if proper correction programs are not implemented beforehand, as its brand promise has to be based on facts. Should this fail to "match up with the true identity of place, it can create a place brand strategy gap" or a self-perpetuating "system of illusions" (Govers and Go 2009, pp. 71–2) which alienates both inhabitants and visitors.

However, as every coin has two sides, so does Bucharest's brand. Thus, besides the bad and the ugly mentioned above, there is also the good and a big disparity between what people think about Bucharest and its wonderful facets that are hidden under the negative layers. Bucharest brags a blend of various architectural styles, ranging from French influences, through which it acquired the name of "The Little Paris", to baroque styles, to massive communist constructions (e.g. the Palace of Parliament which is the second largest building in the world after the Pentagon). It is the place where one can never get bored and where one can find something to suit every taste – for example, with food, it might be Indian cuisine from 2011 or a traditional Romanian meal from the 19th century, served on plates made of clay and with drinks in wooden cups: "1920 or 2010, everything is authentic" (Razvan Murgeanu, personal communication, April 2011). This city is, in fact, an inexhaustible source of inspiration. It is a vibrant city where new elements appear and disappear very quickly, where the benchmarks are constantly changing and where one can find one's true self. It is a bit chaotic, incoherent in some places, but it has a certain "style", an impressive appearance and a percussive rhythm (see www.bucharestbyhand.ro). However, "the most important asset that Bucharest city has is its invaluable gem, its people" (Razvan Murgeanu, personal communication, April 2011) and their heterogeneity. The strata of its society is made up of ten different communities which are spread throughout.

The main environmental problems that Bucharest is faced with are shown in Figure 9.1, which contains the results of our primary research and which is confirmed by market research report statistics (IRSOP 2009).

As can be seen, the fundamental environmental issues are a high level of pollution, accompanied by congestion, waste and garbage, a clear lack of green spaces and too much dust, along with a mixture of many other small problems. Nevertheless, the city managers' opinions concur with the above findings; Murgeanu (personal communication, April 2011) agrees that there are some infrastructural problems such as "the sewerage system, the traffic,

FIGURE 9.1 | Bucharest's environmental problems in citizens' opinions

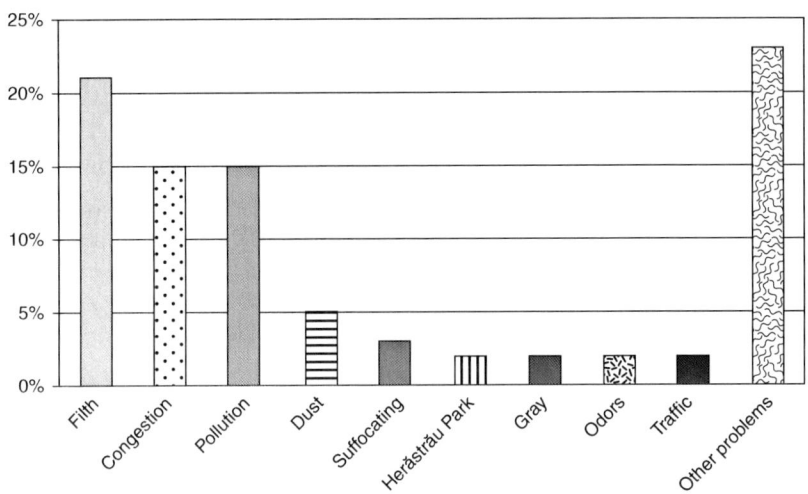

Note: Citizens were asked what the first word was that came to mind when considering the main problems in Bucharest's environment.

the liaison between the motorways and a big lack of square meters per person". Adding to what Murgeanu said above, Niculae Radulescu-Dobrogea (personal communication, April 2011) declared that "instead of having 26 square meters per person, we are now way below the guidelines, having 8 square meters per person". In addition, the quantity of dust per person is way above the standards set in the official documents. Ioan Baceanu (personal communication, April 2011) agrees with all this and additionally mentions the increased level of noise pollution and the really bad organization of bicycle paths which are swamped with cars. According to the European Green City Index, Bucharest is not even near the average in comparison with other European capital cities in sectors such as carbon dioxide emissions, energy efficiency, buildings, transport, water, waste, air quality and environmental governance.

However, there is a common belief that the underlying cause of these problems is people's lack of education, ignorance and indifference toward the environment and the quality of life. Besides these, there is the degradation of the cultural inheritance which is a very important aspect of Bucharest's environment that is clearly highlighted in the observational research done amongst its inhabitants and which is mainly due to inconsiderate human actions, such as being careless with garbage and cigarettes or stealing iron from old, degraded museums in order to sell it to get food. Globalization and climate change, overlapping the vulnerability of an insufficiently prepared society, together with an acute lack of environmental education, has severely altered the cultural patrimony. Economic pressures may well lead to its irreversible destruction (The Presidential Administration, cited in The Platform for Bucharest 2008).

As reported by the environmental NGO Eco-Europe (2011), Bucharest is the only European city that does not have a modern drinking water treatment plant or a public recycling system and that also still uses leaded gasoline. Also, there is a very low level of environmental information system management, reduced investment in industrial pollution control and poor environmental monitoring equipment.

Unfortunately, there is no recipe for successful green city branding: it all depends on the city's state of affairs and the circumstances which lead to the call for action. But what all of the successful green city brands have in common is their focus on conceiving a single strategy for one or two problematic areas, such as developing a green economy, transportation and promoting healthy living. Also important is the community's involvement, the most valuable resource, as it embodies the identity of the place – they know best what the city stands for, what it wants to achieve and who it wants to attract. The community knows what its strengths and weaknesses are and what makes it tick and gets it involved, all of which leads to trust in the brand, treating it as a shared common goal which will bring about common benefits for everyone. The community should be emotionally connected to the "infrastructure of love", otherwise the infrastructure becomes disposable, as people usually get rid of invaluable things (TheInfrastructurist 2011): "things do not pass for what they are, but for what they seem. Most things are judged by their jackets" (Gracian 1991).

However, the case study analysis revealed some successful factors in the green city branding process which encompass people's education concerning sustainable development: that of a collaborative planning of the green concept where the citizens have the biggest contribution (as the soul of the city, representing its values). This is based on: the commitment to improve the quality of life; the implementation of an environmental legislation and a taxation for those disobeying it; and having a long-term vision materialized in an environmental strategy developed by a relational network which brings all the city's stakeholders together (including organizations from around the world, e.g. the Canadian NGO Sustainable Cities). However, as Interbrand (2011) stated in a recent presentation, for a brand to be really successful, it has to comply with the following: "Be it! Do it! Say it!". Thus, some of the most pressing and critical brand issues that should be addressed by the use of design are: pollution; the lack of balance between government, the economy and society; a lack of sustainability; and a lack of environmental education and trust toward the higher authorities.

CONCLUSIONS AND RECOMMENDATIONS

Taking everything into account, today's accelerated rhythm of life (along with the speed of globalization and the increasing urbanization of the population) has led to a greater focus on the city's sustainable development and the reduction of its impact on climate change. City branding and green city branding have become a recurrent theme in the development of urban policies and have been integrated in the city management process. Today, being involved in such a process is no longer an option, it's a prerequisite.

Bucharest's current brand image is composed of all of its actions up to date, its history, policies, the way in which it has depicted itself to the world and the way in which the world has perceived it. Unfortunately, the dominating results of the research emphasize a prevailing bad perception due to the variety of problems which disturb its inhabitants. This gap can only be filled by making real improvement in the city, together with an image improvement, in order to instigate a change of the negative perceptions and strengthen the future brand. That is why the developed design-led environmental brand strategy is based on an ongoing environmental improvement program that underpins both short, medium and long-term solutions. This would entail solving all the critical problems based on a plan with actions to be taken for a larger period of time, i.e. pollution can be easily reduced in the short term by using design to make people aware that a small change in their behavior can be a big step for humanity (such as changing to energy-efficient light bulbs, using brushes around doors to reduce draughts, using e-shopping to reduce carbon dioxide emissions, insulating cavity walls, turning appliances off when not in use, and switching to direct debits and paperless billing). All this can easily be done through the use of posters, leaflets and design-led environmental campaigns.

On the other hand, the lack of balance between the government, the economy and society, and the awful consequences that this broken relationships have on Bucharest's brand, can be improved and fixed in the medium term by creating public–private partnerships between the community (environmental NGOs such as Eco-Civica and ProNature), the governmental sector (such as the members of parliament and all the public institutions) and business organizations (such as recycling and waste companies, the National Health Service (NHS) and other big companies, e.g. Niro Investment Group, which is one of the biggest investment groups in Romania, that could easily sponsor this project as a part of its own corporate social responsibility (CSR) plan). This would teach people about the importance of the quality of life and the repercussions of their actions on climate change.

In the long term, people's environmental education can only be accomplished through more force, an alliance that would gather its resources for educational purposes. For example: the creation of a relational network (a charity organization) between the best design agencies and government (the secretary of state of each public sector) and other businesses (such as The National Association of Environmental Protection, student organizations like AIESEC, and the biggest Romanian Banks, i.e. The Romanian Commercial Bank and The Romanian Bank of Development, which are really involved in these kinds of projects and are very supportive of the community). This would inspire the best use of design to "improve quality and well being" (Bichard 2011).

This is not the usual branding process as design will be used throughout to solve the current issues, improve the status quo and educate people. This is because its citizens will only be able to take pride in it if a real change is happening. It is vital that this should be a joint action of all the city's stakeholders, reflected in a collective message and reproduced in the set of brand guidelines.

Despite its ubiquitous negative associations, Bucharest has many wonderful things to offer, most of them being hidden under the veil of dissatisfaction. Turning a gemstone into a diamond is very difficult, especially when there are so many facets which need to be polished. Behind the shadows of deprecating opinions, the city possesses all the necessary characteristics required to attract investors, businesses, tourists, students and of course its inhabitants. But beauty is in the eyes of the one who knows how to appreciate things for their true value and can see behind the mask. For a change to be truthful, it has to come from within, from the core of the city, but for that Bucharest's citizens have to be educated to appreciate the real value and importance of the environment they live in and realize the potential quality of their lives.

In conclusion, Bucharest is an imposing traditional city with a remarkable history, great opportunities and a derailed image caused by an unfriendly environment and unfavorable historical settings (that position it as traditional and ungreen). These aspects can only be altered through a constant correction program and the implementation of an environmental design-led brand strategy (that would help to reposition it as traditional and green). Crafting a brand which would differentiate the city from others, fulfill the citizen's needs and gain the stakeholder's sustenance requires patience, collaboration, strategic perspective and a common vision. Thus, the alchemy will only be fully complete when the effect of the brand is perceived at every level and people's mentality has changed.

REFERENCES

Anholt, S. (2004) *Brand New Justice*, 2nd edn, Oxford: Butterworth-Heinemann.
Anholt, S. (2006) *Competitive Identity: The New Brand Management for Nations, Cities and Region*, Basingstoke: Palgrave Macmillan.
Anholt, S. (2009) *Places: Identity, Image and Reputation*, Basingstoke: Palgrave Macmillan.
Bichard, Michael (2011) Presentation to the Design Council, Brunel University, West London, 18 February.
City Mayors (2004) "European eCity Award 2003", www.citymayors.com/features/e-cities.html.
Cooper, R., Evans, G. and Boyko, C. (2009) *Designing Sustainable Cities*, West Sussex: Blackwell.
Cushman Wakefield (2009) "European Cities Monitor", www.europeancitiesmonitor.eu/.
Dinnie, K. (2010) *City Branding: Theory and Cases*, Basingstoke: Palgrave Macmillan.
Eco-Europe (2011) "The most active, numerous and nonconformist ecological organization of Bucharest", www.eco-civica.20m.com/.
Economist, The (2009) 'Walls in the mind', 5 November, www.economist.com/node/14793753?story_id=E1_TQSJPSVP.
Economist Intelligence Unit (2009) "European Green City Index", www.commoncurrent.com/notes/2009/12/european-green-city-index-rele.html.
fDi Magazine (2010) "European Cities & Regions of the Future 2010/11", www.scribd.com/doc/28444403/European-Cities-and-Regions-of-the-Future-2010-11.
Fox-Martin, A. (2009) "Building sustainable cities: reality check", http://egovasia.enterpriseinnovation.net/content/building-sustainable-cities-reality-check.
Govers, R. and Go, F. (2009) *Global, Virtual and Physical Identities, Constructed, Imagined and Experienced*. Basingstoke: Palgrave Macmillan.
Gracian, B. (1991) *The Art of Worldly Wisdom*, Whitefish, MT: Kessinger.
Graham, B. (2002) 'Heritage as knowledge: capital or culture?', *Urban Studies*, 39(5–6): 1003–17.
Indigo Development (2006) "The unsustainability of cities", www.indigodev.com/Sustain.html
Interbrand (2011) Presentation made at the Interbrand Venue, London, August.
IRSOP (2009) *Calitatea mediului din Bucuresti in opinia cetatenilor*, www.agenda21.org.ro.
Kampschulte, A. (1999) 'Image as an instrument of urban management', *Geographica Helvetica*, 54(4): 229–41.
Kavaratzis, M. and Ashworth, G. (2007) 'Beyond the logo: brand management for cities', *Brand Management*, 16(8): 520–31.
Konijnendijk, Cecil (2010) *The Forest and the City*, Berlin: Springer.
Lee, F. (2011) Presentation made at the Intelligent Cities Expo, Hamburg, Germany, 8–11 November.
Mercer (2010) "Quality of Living Global City Rankings", www.mercer.com/press-releases/quality-of-living-report-2010.
National Institute of Statistics (2010) "Settled population at 1 January 2009", www.insse.ro.
Platform for Bucharest (2008) "Together for a better Bucharest", http://bucurestiulmeu.ro/index.php?option=com_content&view=article&id=14&Itemid=91.

Rees, William E. and Roseland, Mark (1991) "Sustainable Communities: Planning for the 21st Century. Plan Canada", http://archive.rec.org/REC/Programs/SustainableCities/What.html.

Salman, S. (2009) "Brand of Gold", *The Guardian*, 1 October, www.guardian.co.uk/society/2008/oct/01/city.urban.branding.

Siemens (2010) "European Green City Index", www.siemens.co.uk/events/pool/home/EFEF/sustainable-cities-european-green-city-index.pdf.

Stevens, A. (2011) "City branding must reflect on the past and point to the future", www.tourism-review.com/fm1563/p1.pdf.

TheInfrastructurist (2011) "Why aren't we building emotionally connected cities?", www.infrastructurist.com/2011/05/17/why-arent-we-building-emotionally-connected-cities-a-guest-post/.

Tyndall Centre for Climate Change Research (2011) www.tyndall.ac.uk/.

Urban Investment Network (2011) "Public–Private Partnerships in Sustainable Urban Development", www.urbaninvestmentnetwork.com/_assets/client/images/collateral/ULI%20InfoBurst%20%20Public%20Private%20Partnerships%20in%20Sustainable%20Urban%20Development%20June%202011.pdf.

PART 3
Chapters on Particular Place Brand Themes

CHAPTER 10

Overcoming the Risk of Stereotypes: How Strategic Communications Can Facilitate Sustainable Place Branding

Roland Schatz

In this chapter I will illustrate how quickly individual events or clichés can destroy reputation and have a major influence on further economic development. In other words, how tourism and investments can fail to materialize in the economy in the wake of highly negative headlines. The chapter contains examples from three countries with a relatively high degree of media perception (Italy, Greece and France), as well as three countries with a low level of media interest (Bahrain, Austria and Vietnam). First, I will portray the behavior patterns of our six examples and how they are connected. Then I will propose a way as to how countries can effectively free themselves from their dependency on headlines in the future.

How a region, city or even a country is perceived is often characterized by an impression, an event or a tradition. Despite its diversity, most people still only know Pisa as a tower (see Figure 10.1). Vietnam has been reduced to a war that ended 40 years ago. Until the start of the Arab Spring the Middle East had suffered under the banner of terror and conflict. Walter Lippmann (1922, p. 7) was among the first to highlight the connection between perception of countries and media coverage when he said, "the world that we have to deal with politically is out of reach, out of sight, out of mind. It has to be explored, reported, and imagined. Man is no Aristotelian god contemplating all existence at one glance".

The year 2011 was an eye-opener for many, as Vietnam is now a growth region and has been accepted by economic experts as one of the "Next 11", those countries that are expected to experience the most growth after Brazil, Russia, India, China and South Africa. The people in Syria, Egypt, Tunisia, Libya, Bahrain, Yemen and elsewhere surprised experts in the White House, Paris and Berlin with their steadfastness and creativity with which they made the season of spring a permanent condition.

FIGURE 10.1 | **What you know of Pisa**

Source: Ghigo Roli (2004) *Serie Speciale 360*, Priuli & Verlucca.

HOW STEREOTYPES SHAPE OUR PERCEPTION

Stereotypes have always been dangerous, but surprises of this kind have increased in recent years. Realizing this, governments and the media alike have asked the question: who is responsible for the premises that politicians, economists and the media use to underpin their decision-making? If we know so little about "the others" or, even worse, if the little that we do know is fundamentally incorrect, how valuable and responsible can our politics be considered?

Anastasio *et al.* (1999, p. 152) contend that "by showing only a tiny and unrepresentative portion of the world through its window, the media may help to create the very world it seeks to reflect". It's clear from this statement that the authors share Lippman's (1921) view of media agenda-setting, but they add an interesting caveat to this model:

> Neutral media coverage of a controversial event, such as an election, often results in members of both sides of the controversy perceiving the media as hostile to their own group. Because coverage of both sides of an issue tends to emphasize differences between sides, the perceiver's own group membership is made salient and thus sets in

motion the motivation to perceive the in-group as superior and the out-group as inferior. Thus, neutral coverage of the in-group is perceived as unfair and hostile in comparison with the inflated perceptions of the correctness of one's in-group. (p. 153)

The assertion here is that, even in the instances where media coverage is objectively neutral, consumers of that news perceive it as biased because they think it misrepresents/inadequately represents their worldview. Anastasio *et al.* (1999, p. 154) refer to this phenomenon as "social identity":

> Social identity is a powerful sculptor not only of perceptions, but of opinions as well. Research has shown that opinions are often influenced by other members of the in-group. Even when an in-group member presents an opinion that is unpopular and goes against one's natural inclinations, the in-group member still remains a persuasive force, much more so than any out group member.

This suggests that the source of information invariably decides how well that information is received within a specific social identity classification. For example, Americans might trust an American broadcaster more on the Afghanistan War than someone working for Al Jazeera. Anastasio *et al.* (1999) also contend there are two major routes of persuasion through which attitudes and opinions are changed: the central and peripheral routes. The central route is one where an individual weighs all sides of the debate before coming to a conclusion. The authors (1999, p. 154) define the peripheral route in the following way:

> The perceiver lacks either the motivation or the ability (e.g. because of time constraints or other pressing issues that drain cognitive resources) to fully process much of the message's information. When this is the case, any number of peripheral cues contained within the message may provide "mental shortcuts" that the perceiver can use to arrive at an opinion or decision.

They set out to answer whether coverage emphasizing intergroup differences and intragroup similarities fueled the tendency to side with one's in-group. They found that the homogeneity of coverage greatly influences opinion to coincide with that coverage, but heterogeneous coverage results in heterogeneous opinion. The implication of their findings suggests that the media, when acting in unison, have an overwhelming influence on public opinion. They conclude (p. 155):

> Not only do the media bias people's perceptions by offering an unrepresentative view of the world at times, but it may also facilitate biased processing of accurate information by presenting that information with an emphasis on intergroup

differences ... In summary, on the one hand, multiple news broadcasts that dissect the world into distinct social categories and emphasize group differences have the ability to perpetuate actual differences. On the other hand, news that obscures intergroup boundaries may have an equally great potential to diminish group differences and forge necessary connections. The media, which disseminates information and creates social norms, most likely has the power to build bridges as well as destroy them.

The implication for agenda-setting is that the influence of media coverage is relative to the consumer's sense of self – how (and with whom) one self-identifies. In turn, the media can either feed or diffuse the divisiveness of perception through the relative divisiveness of coverage.

Frank Go set the overall frame back in 2010:

> The 11th International Agenda Setting Conference in the face of the TRUST MELTDOWN begs many questions. To paraphrase Immanuel Kant: What can we know? What ought we to do? What can we hope? First, with regard to research we possess knowledge about the powerful impact of the media on the human race. Or to paraphrase Shaw and McCombs (1977): "Here may lie the most important effect of mass communication, its ability to mentally order and organize our world for us. In short, the mass media may not be successful in telling us what to think, but they are stunningly successful in telling us what to think about." In fact, the media have been so successful that publics follow its messages like the "Pied Piper's" song.
>
> Second, faced with a myriad of complex challenges, including pollution, biodiversity, abject poverty, and a myriad of other issues, what we ought to do represents a major challenge. Presently, many decision makers rely for their navigation on a set of screens, including the laptop, Blackberry, and mobile telephone. Due to their focus on news events it is easy for boardroom members to lose touch with reality, including the consequences from child abuse, burqa discussions and resignations. All are sourced in a specific spatial location where stakeholders mobilize social relations and try to engage in community. (Address to the 11th Agenda-Setting Conference, Rapperswil, 2010)

Decisions are always based on matters as they stand, and unfortunately media reports are relied on for incidents in public diplomacy. In the WikiLeaks affair many state departments around the world were exposed in that the views of their governments, which were wired to the respective capital cities through embassies in advance of state visits, primarily came from the newspaper reports of the respective countries. This paints a bleak picture of the work done in many embassies, but it doesn't change the starting position. It becomes all the more important to answer the questions of how perspectives can be broadened and who is ultimately responsible for the clichés to which not only the local people are reduced.

MEDIA STEREOTYPES: ITALY, GREECE AND FRANCE

How important the solution to this problem is can be seen at the outset using the example of Germany: half a century after the end of Hitler's reign of terror the only German politician the elite in America know is Adolf Hitler. Even Helmut Kohl, who should be known to the American entrepreneurs, politicians, scientists and other participants in the 2002 elite survey, is still not even half as well known amongst the US elite, even though he was in office for three years longer than the dictator at a time when every private household had a TV (see Figure 10.2).

Gerhard Schröder, who had just been re-elected as the German chancellor at the time of the survey, was only known to 12 percent of these Americans. It can be assumed of these Americans that, as politicians, they would want to negotiate contracts with the decision-makers in Europe, as managers discuss investments and scientists drive joint research projects.

The 2002 survey, however, not only covered the American elite, but also people in Idaho, Iowa and Indianapolis. The figures were even worse there: nobody knew who Gerhard Schröder was and only 4 percent knew who Helmut Kohl was, though more than 40 percent still knew who Adolf Hitler was: 47 years after his death. What could be the reason for this? Next to the surveys, Figure 10.2 also shows the continuous analysis data and which politicians were presented to the Americans on the prime-time news broadcasts of ABC, CBS and NBC. It goes without saying that the nation's own representatives dominate, as is the case in every other country. However, the fact that not even

FIGURE 10.2 | **Agenda-setting at its best?**

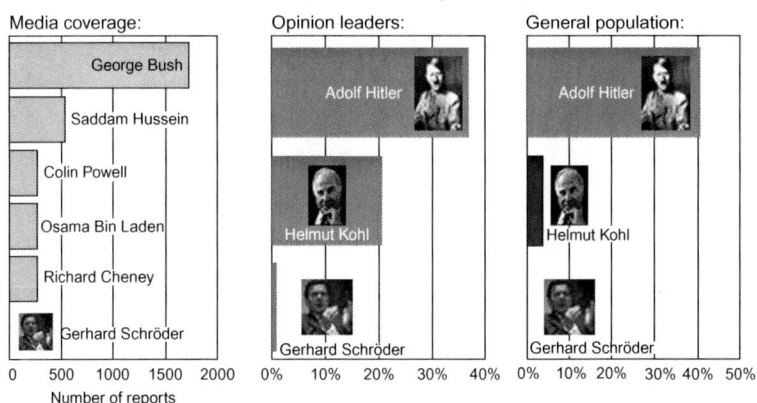

Source: *Bundespresseamt* of the Republic of Germany for official pictures.

one report was devoted to the German Chancellor in the whole of 2002, helps neither German companies to be perceived as business partners in America, nor does it help the Americans. Whoever does not know one of the most important heads of government in the largest economic powers in the world has no chance five years before the collapse of Lehman Brothers, as, according to the "facts" given by one's own TV service provider, it is assumed that money can only be earned on Wall Street. If Americans are not shown life in Frankfurt, Beijing or Tokyo, they will react and make decisions differently to people who know the alternatives. The objection could be raised that, because of the particular atrocities unleashed by the Nazi terror, the American perception of Germans could be justified even 50 years after the end of the Second World War because, ultimately, Adolf Hitler and his followers tyrannized more than just their own nation, and because the dictatorship only came to an end because people in other countries were prepared to fight against them – and paid an immeasurably high price for doing so.

For this reason, using examples from other less parochial countries, the following illustrates that the lack of a media strategy also makes other countries the victims of their own stereotypes – with consequences for tourism, investment and often less favorable results when negotiating bilateral and multilateral contracts. Let us start with Italy (see Figure 10.3).

The picture of the leaning tower in Pisa hardly does justice to the image debacle under which the proud Republic of Italy has had to suffer for a long period of time. Silvio Berlusconi's successor used the first State of the Nation address not only to commit his nation to the required austerity measures but also to present the solution to the dilemma. Mario Monti committed himself to improving his country's image as it was clear that no investor would put his or her money anywhere between Milan and Palermo under a Berlusconian news flow and that a decline in the number of tourists would additionally weaken public revenue.

Within a short period of time, Monti succeeded in gaining the attention of the media worldwide for topics that were necessary to champion Italy – transparent budgeting and verifiable measures instead of judicial scandals, unclear budget promises and permanent involvement in sex scandals.

At the end of 2011, Italy was again on the world stage in the media seeking, together with its EU partners, to repay its huge debt, focusing on the essentials that had been paid off. As financial markets can also be influenced by reputation, Italy was able to obtain better conditions on the money market at the beginning of 2012 than was the case at the end of 2011. No economist would want to justify this based on the changed economic situation alone.

There is also the case of the supposed trigger for the euro crisis, Greece. Whoever thinks of Greece in 2011 and describes the images that are brought

FIGURE 10.3 | The whole picture

to mind must ask the question as to whether the stone-throwing demonstrators are as representative as any idealized Greeks four years ago. With an overall share of 0.03 percent of the information broadcast being on Greece, an attentive follower of the US TV news had no chance of finding out before the crisis what the situation in the country really was. Of the 20 percent of information selected by ABC, CBS, FOX and NBC in the whole of 2009 for events outside of the United States, only 0.03 percent related to events in Athens. Yet Americans were also extensively involved with Goldman Sachs in falsifying the figures years before until the country was allowed to satisfy the Maastricht criteria and thereby enter the euro zone. The heads of the Greek government were educated at Harvard and the majority of the Greek family clan had extensive trade relations with America. Reasons enough to keep one's own population up to date more extensively instead of using the little space mostly for Iraq and Afghanistan where the news flow has not really changed so much as to warrant daily reports (see Figure 10.5).

In Europe the situation was only marginally better. European countries determined the evening prime time headlines when information was provided that was supposed to be important for taxpayers. The exorbitant debt in Athens hardly grabbed any attention in 2009 – although the facts were accessible, the people were left unaware of the problem on their continent. With a 1.5 percent share in all the information on events abroad, the British, French, Italians, Spaniards and Germans were not able to form their own impression from the regular evening TV news. In this way, a cliché of Greece remained

FIGURE 10.4 | Topic structure of Italy's media coverage 2009–11

Only sports and culture with some positive news

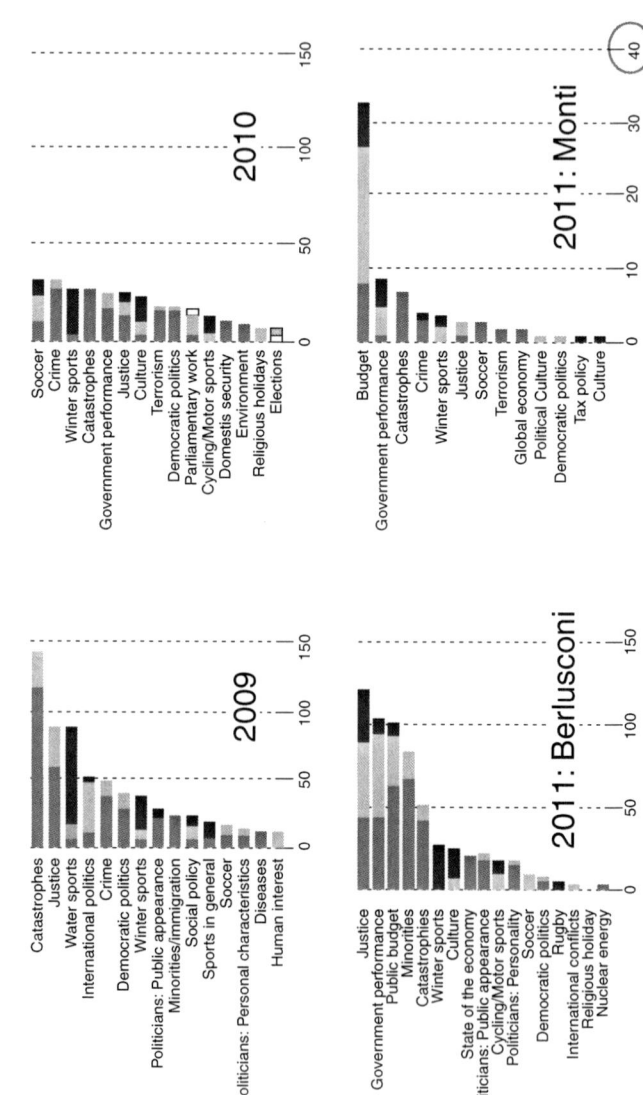

Note: Based on 848/379/741 stories on Italy in US, UK and German TV news programs.

FIGURE 10.5 | **Visibility of Greece in US TV news 2008**

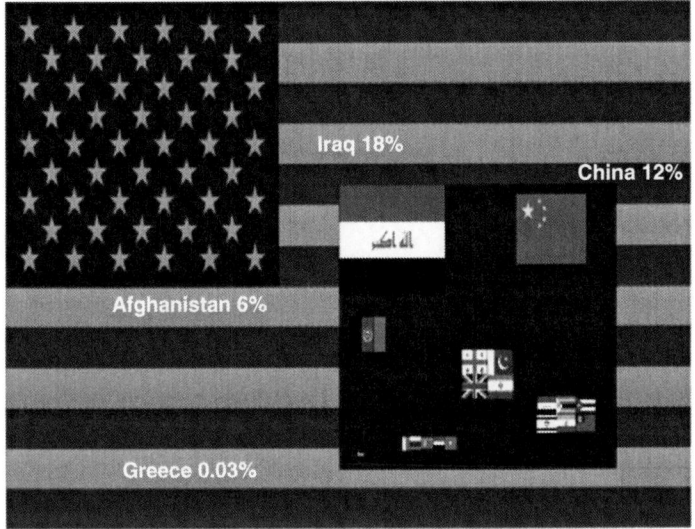

Only 19 countries are above 1% of foreign coverage

> Iraq China and Afghanistan occupied over a third of the available foreign coverage in the US media – the next 16 countries around one quarter. For a country like Greece, a share of 0.03% of *foreign* coverage means it is struggling to gain awareness.

Sources: CBS, ABC, Fox, NBC foreign reports.

in people's minds until its bankruptcy that was quickly replaced by another within only one year of reporting it in 2010 (see Figure 10.6).

Greece's bad image created in 2009 continued through 2011. Of course, not all Greeks defraud their own tax authorities, not all Greeks falsify budgets, not all Greeks retire at age 55, and, especially, not all Greek companies are bankrupt. In fact, it's quite the contrary. The airport in Athens stands as a prime example worldwide for efficient and profitable management. To win over the international media after the 2010/11 debacle, to have the media not only report the scandals but also the successful examples is far more difficult if a continuous and diverse information flow had not been ensured earlier.

The third example is France. It was difficult to believe what one was seeing when opening the daily newspapers and following the TV news in summer 2011. Within just a few days, the image of the entire country changed. Whoever before had given *savoir vivre* the thumbs up and had marveled at not only the elegance of life in Paris, Bordeaux or Strasbourg, but also acknowledged its beauty, was thrown back into the Middle Ages

FIGURE 10.6 | Visibility of Greece in European TV news 2008

Western Europe does slightly better

> In Western Europe, foreign coverage occupies close to 40% of television news. This means the chances are greater for countries to get on the agenda. In 2008 Greece occupied around 1.5 % of this foreign coverage.

Source: Nearly 100,000 reports In French Swiss, Italian, Spanish, UK and German media.

overnight. Thomas Hobbes identified the pattern of behavior before the Enlightenment with his famous "Homo homini lupu" (man is a wolf to [his fellow] man); and little seems to have changed in France, at least in the relationships between men and women, certainly for whoever believes the statements of French men and women in the media after the Strauss-Kahn revelations. Within hours, the sex scandal of the IMF chief related not just to the goings-on in New York and his subsequent arrest, but the statements from his own environment in particular painted a picture of a sick society. Everyone seemed to know that not only this representative of the financial world had a major problem accepting the personal rights of another – in particular if this other person was a woman. The references to earlier presidents and similar patterns of behavior helped neither Strauss-Kahn's nor France's reputation on the whole: under the glare of the global media spotlights it was made clear to everyone that the grand nation had a long way to go to shed its archaic understanding of man and woman. The various individual cases that always come up during scandals were less responsible for the French reputation debacle than the eloquent shoulder shrugging of the French opinion-leaders in politics, the economy and the media that were of the view that they were contributing to the acceptance of the country with an "it's always been like that". If positions are advertised in the future by the OECD in Paris, if the Sorbonne wants to attract foreign students to its undoubtedly excellent education, if Renault wants to increase its share of female management staff from abroad: the change in the image of France that took place in summer 2011 after the Strauss-Kahn scandal would have changed the willingness of people abroad to choose France as their home for their profession. If large countries such as Germany, Italy or France depend on the perception of people abroad, who time and again have the opportunity of adjusting their image through their politicians, companies and universities, what is the situation for smaller countries?

THE MEDIA PERIPHERY: AUSTRIA, BAHRAIN AND VIETNAM

Another European country, though a smaller one, Austria, developed into a strong economy in the 1990s; in particular since the beginning of the new millennium. The fall of the Berlin Wall in 1989 multiplied the relationships between western and eastern Europe, and Vienna skillfully used its geographical advantage. What worked well for the higher levels in the days of the emperors and kings was now replicated on all levels: universities, small, medium and large businesses, cultural sites, sport and tourism, all started to profit from the trips back and forth. But the global headlines were dominated by just one topic: the Kampusch abuse scandal. This overshadowed the perception of the Alpine republic in 2009 and 2010. Only the reporting on the European Football Championships had more coverage than the ongoing revelations of child abuse (see Figure 10.7).

When a second case of child abuse emerged in the aftermath, the cliché seemed to have been perfected: in Austria, committing criminal offences against one's own children was "normal". From a reputational point of view, this was a situation akin to the classical tragedy: every act makes things worse. But the topic cannot be suppressed – even just out of respect for the victim. It is also too late for comprehensive information, as neither the media nor society is prepared for such a discussion in the process. The well-known example of the Catholic Church demonstrates exactly how dramatic an effect silence around a misdeed has when hindsight is applied. The challenges are even greater for a country, as there is no direct institution that can be defined and there is no directly responsible family. Those involved in the legal system are chronically communicatively challenged. Further, statements by heads of governments quickly become meaningless as they can hardly contribute anything verifiably concrete apart from the usual expressions of concern. In such situations, one has no chance if media relations, in the best sense of the

FIGURE 10.7 | Topic structure of Austria's media coverage 2008–10

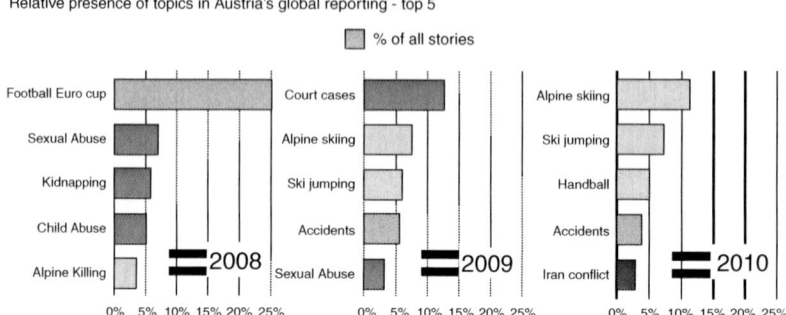

The horrifying news of the Kampusch case was a significant blow to the Austrian image. However, 2010 saw the country's key reputational assets – its successful winter sportsmen and women – back on the agenda.

Note: Based on 1,737 individual reports from Austria or on Austrian protagonists in 30 international TV news programs.

word, have not been nurtured over a long period of time. Continuous dialog with journalists of one's own country as well as the local correspondents at least helps to ensure better presentation of special topics. The creation of clichés can only be controlled *once the media is also willing to present the incident as an individual case that does not seem to fit into the overall reality*. Editors are only prepared to do this if they are continuously constructively supported in their work. This includes everything except sending press releases or emails. Examples include a personal telephone call that is associated with an invitation to an interview or feedback on written articles or TV reports. Whatever entity wants to be perceived as a country must first of all be prepared to perceive those that contribute to the reputation of the country: the journalists. Whoever does not know the interests and needs of the individual participants of a press conference does not need to wonder why there is nothing, or just a little, to read about the next day.

The same applies to countries that are not from the same culture group. With respect to the movements for change in the MENA region, the Arab world was offered a unique opportunity for their diversity to be discovered beyond Islam and terror. But only a few have made use of the opportunity. The Bahrain example clearly demonstrates how even positive developments can have the opposite effect due to incorrect communication patterns.

The kingdom was the first country to decide 100 years ago to initiate changes itself and not wait. Long before the world became aware of

Dubai, those responsible in Manama turned their island into a partner for international corporations. The king made sure that financial interests were taken into account and, unfazed by the global press, appointed women in its government, developed forms of democracy and created a climate of major change and respect between the various religious groups in his country. Compared to other countries in the Gulf region, Bahrain was also recognized accordingly in the media in the US, Europe and Africa (see Figure 10.8).

But these 100 years of change were eclipsed overnight by one decision: instead of continuing to seek dialog and welcoming and supporting the accelerated change in the region and in its own country at the beginning of 2011, the king allowed the hardliners free reign and requested military assistance to deal with the protest movement. Coverage of rolling tanks, wounded demonstrators and pending court decisions turned the image of this country, interested in dialog and development, into its very opposite.

How long do images last when one mentions words such as "Vietnam", "Tiananmen Square" or "Bhopal"? Who would want to plan their holiday trip to those places? Who would even seriously consider investing in a manufacturing plant there? Vietnam, especially, has achieved much since 1975. Similarly to South Africa under Nelson Mandela, the Asians succeeded in treating the deep wounds in such a way that, although nobody could ignore the scars, they were not a stumbling block, either in their country or abroad. The postcards sent by people from Hanoi or Ho Chi

FIGURE 10.8 | **Coverage of King Hamad of Bahrain in international media, 2008–09**

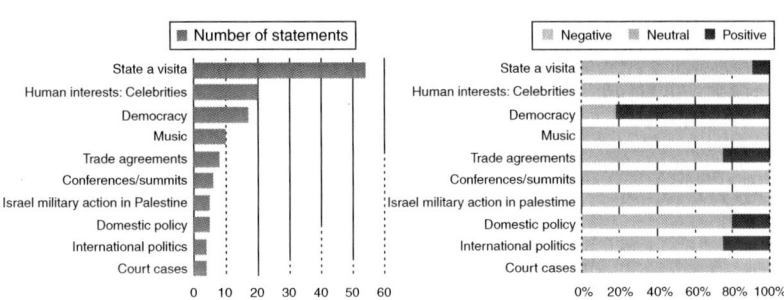

King Hamad is viewed in a positive light. The topic structure is relatively one-sided however. The Democracy issue has the potential to create more positive reputation for the King.

Note: Based on 188 statements.

Minh City and many other cities to people in Boston, Miami or Chicago were not part of a PR campaign, but addressed the deepest desires of the Vietnamese: they wanted to continue to have a relationship with those they had waged war against. While the images of the napalm victims dominated the perspectives in Europe and the United States, the Vietnamese also tried to see the other side. Decisions made personally when assimilating experiences were revised time and again. In the meantime, the country is now one of the so-called "Next 11" (one of the nations from which the global economy not only expects the greatest growth in the next few years but also a better balance of economic powers). Because, in times when the whole world is aware that the US only has a 20.4 percent share in the global economy – compared to Europe with just under 25 percent – alternatives are needed once individual drivers lose their force.

However, Vietnam is not yet visible in the prime time news outside of Asia, so it lacks coverage on its economy, science, sport and politics. Though it is clearly below the perception threshold, Vietnam must continue to fight for recognition of its achievements to date (see Figure 10.9).

FIGURE 10.9 | Visibility of Vietnam in international TV news, 2011

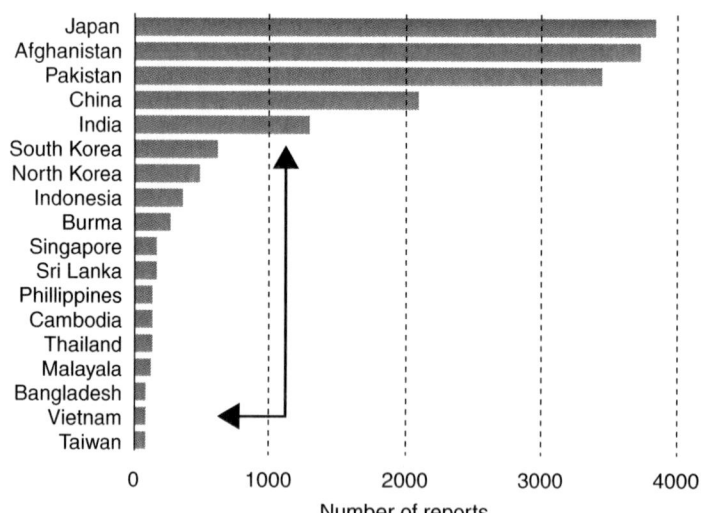

Global TV news focused on Asia in 2011 – but not all countries managed to achieve ongoing coverage in BBC, CBS, TF1 and 69 other leading news shows. Three of the next 11 growth countries stay under the media radar: Philippines, Bangladesh and Vietnam.

Note: Based on 17,248 reports in international TV news programs.

WHAT CAN WE DO?

Reputation follows facts – this doesn't change. So, what are the opportunities for countries that are reduced to clichés? Contrary to many advertising myths, no image can develop against reality in the medium term, let alone the long term. Whoever thinks that they don't need to do their homework will, time and again, fail. This will be made painfully clear to the Greeks in 2012: for three years they have been promising to develop a functioning tax authority. But there were too many promises and not enough action. Correspondingly, the number of those no longer prepared to help the Greeks out of their problem has increased. The Americans, who remain the largest environmental polluters, and in 2008 contributed to the destruction of financial assets, will experience something similar. In 2012, the people in America, but too few outside the United States, know what Goldman Sachs, Citibank and others did to prevent a repeat of their misconduct. Violations against the applicable law of the Securities Exchange Commission (SEC), the state supervisory authority, remain punishable with monetary fines, but repeat offenders are not really spurred on effectively to change their behavior. After all, monetary fines are not paid by the top managers, but by their customers and shareholders, if not the taxpayer in the case of a bailout.

At the height of the anti-American sentiment after the 9/11 terror attacks and the subsequent war in Iraq and Afghanistan, a group met in Washington that wanted (and had) to fight against the stigma. Under the banner "Business for Diplomatic Action", alternative ambassadors were sought that could give America a different image on the other continents than the ugly one painted by the media of George W. Bush, in particular in Europe. The pressure was immense: young Americans were forced to put the Canadian flag on their backpacks when travelling so as not to be drawn into discussions about the actions of their government at every turn. In New York and elsewhere in the US, hotels felt a declining interest for holding important conferences in the country.

The initiators were invited by the State Department to find more ambassadors, although it had always been an American tradition to choose not only career diplomats as ambassadors but deserving personalities from finance and other areas of US society. Even if the posts were given in accordance with the amount of monetary donation provided to the winning president during his election campaign, there is hardly another country that has so many well-known ambassadors that know how to make their country look good in the eyes of the public of the host country and beyond. Nevertheless, in 2004 it appeared to be necessary to send new faces to break the monotony of the perception of America as an imperial power lusting for war. Representatives from other political spectra were considered as it was clear to all that the deep split between America and the rest of the world was no longer a question of a membership book. The 1997 Kyoto Protocol received as little attention under Bill Clinton as it did under his successors.

The diversity of American society should be expressed by the selection of the additional "ambassadors": representatives of the best universities, various industries, etc. Everything that could help the country out of its difficult communication spot was welcome and reduced to a reaction to the terror attacks, in particular in the media, subsequent to political decisions. But, what starts as a good idea so often ends in everyday politics: those responsible in the State Department could not hold sway against the interests of the White House and the whole project ended before it could truly reveal its media power despite all the good will.

Even if this project was not implemented, it still remains a good approach, the idea of which has now been taken up by other countries. What is still missing to achieve success is the obligation to hold sustainable dialog with the various media in the defined target regions. Simply agreeing to advertising campaigns has long not been enough as people doubt the images and content of the TV news and even more so the paid advertisement broadcast before or after – the very spot that is supposed to prove the opposite. Even Henry Ford did not know which dollar from his massive advertising budget would be effective and motivate people to buy his cars and which dollar was wasted money. In 2012, advertising agencies still can't give the Henry Fords of today a better answer. Nevertheless, nine out of ten measures for improving the image of countries end in the simple decision to launch another advertising campaign, without checking its potential effectiveness.

Correctly understood, the Business for Diplomatic Action concept means that CEOs, scientists, sportspeople, etc., in addition to exciting projects, obligate themselves to a clearly defined minimum number of interviews and guest contributions that they give in the key media in selected target countries to actually inform people of the projects. And, similarly to the aid services provided in response to disasters, there must be objective assessments to find out whether the announcements were followed up with relevant deeds. Just as it does nothing for Germany's reputation to make big promises of monetary donations after every tsunami or earthquake and then only actually provide 6 percent of the promised funds, a Business for Diplomatic Action concept can only succeed if all participants actually appear in the daily newspapers, weekly magazines and TV news as agreed and with the relevant topics. Which country then succeeds in breaking through the perception threshold in the relevant target markets can be seen from the increase in its foreign direct investments, the tourists and students lining up for first registration at the country's universities and the earnings that can be generated through this concept.

In conclusion, the example of "Made in Germany" illustrates how a change in reputation is possible – and how important it is to maintain it sustainably instead of resting on one's laurels after tasting the first fruits of success. The Made in Germany label is known to people on all continents and helps companies from the Federal Republic not only to sell their products, but also to obtain a higher price. The reason for this is that the quality is right and that the products manufactured between Garmisch-Partenkirchen and Flensburg last longer than other products that consumers could buy. But the promise of quality radiates beyond the products to include service around the products as well: people can rely on the advice being correct and on time. For a long time now not just companies have benefited from this reputation, but also scientists and sportspeople – even politicians. But who knows the history of Made in Germany? The label was invented by the British after the Second World War, but not with the objective of helping the Germans get back on their feet as quickly as possible after their defeat. In fact, it was quite the contrary. As under apartheid, German companies were forced to stick this label onto their products so that everyone outside of Germany could be warned because everything that was manufactured in Germany after 1945 appeared to be of lower quality. But, as it so often happens in history, when winners believe that they have to stigmatize those they have conquered, the label had the opposite effect to that intended by the British. Customers were rarely scared off. Even more importantly, the German entrepreneurs (there were no managers at that time yet) felt they were honour-bound to do their best. The rest is history. But what happened in 2011? The EU attempted to steal the label from German companies if these companies could not prove that the product was mainly produced in the Federal Republic. This was an unusual understanding of globalization and externalization of success: why shouldn't the people in Asia, Africa or any other continent benefit if they can produce something on behalf of an engineer in Munich at the same quality as the people in Munich? This latest proposal from Brussels is likely to lead to a further reputation loss for the EU authorities.

REFERENCES

Anastasio, P.A., Rose, K.C. and Chapman, J. (1999) "Can the media create public opinion? A social-identity approach", *Current Directions in Psychological Science*, 8(5): 152–5.

Go, Frank (2011) "Impact of a positive peace in a political economy of plenty", in Steve Killelea and Roland Schatz (eds), *Global Peace Report*, Zurich: Innovatio, pp. 5–6.

Lippmann, Walter (1921) *Public Opinion*, New York: Harcourt, Brace & Company.

CHAPTER 11

Do National Green Reputations Matter? The Global Green Economy Index and Implications for Stakeholders in the Green Economy

Jeremy Tamanini

As the field of nation branding and country reputation management evolves, so do the tools available to country brand managers for measuring and evaluating the success, or lack thereof, of their strategic and tactical efforts. Up to this point, measurement frameworks employed different methodologies to look at generalized conceptions of country "brands" or "reputations". In this chapter I introduce the point of view, methodology and results related to the Global Green Economy Index (GGEI), a specialized product designed to assess both the perceptions and performance of 27 national green economies. I will argue that green reputations are an increasingly important factor defining overall country brands and, as a result, national and city leaders face a growing incentive to improve upon or consolidate their "green" reputations.

EXISTING INDICES AND UNDERLYING METHODOLOGIES

As country reputation management functions became more institutionalized within government agencies and bureaucracies, various methods for measuring these efforts emerged. In addition to providing metrics through which country-level managers can assess their efforts, these varied reports serve as a valuable tool for convincing laggard nations that their country brand is underperforming relative to their national peers. Furthermore, these different indices provide increased substance about the field of nation branding to various stakeholders in a synthesized format, indirectly bolstering the interest in and legitimacy of this field.

Established in 2005, the Anholt-GfK Roper Nation Brands Index represents the most comprehensive and wide-reaching tool for countries to measure and monitor their national brand. Measuring approximately 50 nations, the index encompasses the quality and power of each country's brand image by combining the following six dimensions: exports, governance, culture and heritage, people, tourism, and investment and immigration. The resulting brand hexagon produces a visual rendering of the country's brand score and communicates how each of the six dimensions impacts on this overall score. Because these scores are composed of online interviews with citizens in 20 countries around the world, the index can provide both broad and narrow insights into country reputations. The broad view would look generally at the brand hexagon in comparison to other countries and isolate dimensions where these peer nations are outperforming. A more narrow view would analyze how specific countries ranked the nation across these six dimensions and adapt strategy and planning accordingly.

Also established in 2005, the FutureBrand Country Brand Index (CBI) is an annual ranking based on a quantitative research study with about 3,400 international business and leisure travelers. The study includes citizens from 13 countries, whose responses are complemented by qualitative focus groups in around 14 major metropolitan areas. The results are then tabulated into an overall country brand score in the following areas: awareness, familiarity, associations, preference, consideration, decision/visitation and advocacy. While the online interviews underlying these rankings are similar to the Anholt GfK Roper Nation Brands Index, the corresponding focus groups suggest that the CBI methodology may produce more qualitative insights for nations into why their country scored a certain way, particularly in the nations where the 14 cities targeted for these focus groups are located.

In 2008, the East West Nation Brand Index was introduced with an entirely different methodology for measuring generalized conceptions of nation "brands". This index is based on analyzing millions of mentions of countries in news articles on a quarterly basis. The basis for this effort is a proprietary text analysis system whereby positive and negative country mentions, in addition to the "strength" of these mentions, can be cataloged. The underlying philosophy here is that media drives perceptions and the truest way to pinpoint these insights is through a system for organizing the myriad country references in widely read international media outlets.

In early 2010, the Reputation Institute launched Country RepTrak, employing survey interviews and follow-up fieldwork to evaluate the attitudes of G8 citizens about 39 countries included in the report. Referencing earlier tools and systems for measuring reputations developed through the

Reputation Institute, Country RepTrak joins a growing list of tools through which national stakeholders can analyze and track their global reputations. As these indices proliferate, and others like them emerge in the future, nations will benefit from their diverse methodological approaches. Not only is it worthwhile to compare national performance across these different indices, but there is also value in monitoring changes over time within each one. National progress when measured using one methodology may not be realized consistently across these different surveys. Understanding the reasons behind these differences offers country brand managers future opportunities to adjust and refine their strategic and tactical efforts according to a diverse sampling of data-collection methods.

MACRO-TRENDS IN THE GREEN ECONOMY

Climate change and global efforts to combat its negative impacts through binding international treaties and domestic policy mechanisms persist as an urgent and volatile topic in every country around the globe. Stakeholders across the political and economic spectrum stand to gain or lose depending on efforts pursued by national leaders and institutions, meaning that national behavior in this context carries significant risks and rewards for broader country reputations.

Adding to the volatility of this topic, citizens, corporations, cities and countries have always had a complicated and nuanced relationship to all things "green", in part because there is no common, shared understanding of what constitutes "green" in the first place. A color once associated with environmentalism has morphed into the political realm (e.g. the green party), commercial spaces (e.g. green products), places (e.g. green city) and more generalized conceptions (e.g. green brands, green marketing). Similar ambiguity surrounds the precise definition and parameters of a "green economy" today. According to the United Nations Environment Programme, a green economy is "an economy or economic development model based on sustainable development and a knowledge of ecological economics". In more specific terms, a green economy is often defined by six main sectors: renewable energy, green buildings, clean transportation, water management, waste management and land management.

As these definitions become more formalized, public and private actors should be more assertive in defining their relationship to the green economy. Once marginalized to niche "green" parties, some mainstream politicians now address issues of climate change, carbon emissions and green growth with a similar emphasis to other national and global policy issues. With global new investment in renewable energy passing $200 billion in 2010, leaders promote policies tied to green job growth and private sector development through new firms and existing supply chains. Large economies with high contributions to greenhouse gas emissions like the United States, EU and China better articulate their positions in the context of international climate negotiations. And as the global population becomes increasingly urban, city mayors are building smarter infrastructure systems and green buildings. The global green economy will only grow in importance in the years ahead and government leadership will face increased pressure from their constituents and the global community to articulate an honest and responsible position within it.

METHODOLOGY

Accepting the trend that national and city actors will face increasing scrutiny around their role in the global green economy, the creation of the GGEI started with a question: what are the most important areas where government actors have impact that also inform a country's green reputation? Through a series of meetings with an advisory board of practitioners with active roles in the area of climate change policy, cleantech investment and academia, the working group decided on the following four dimensions: leadership, domestic policies, cleantech investment vitality and green tourism.

Leadership is important because of the extensive news coverage lavished on national leaders who have taken a strong position for or against "green" issues and the way in which leadership and national figureheads appear to exert a strong influence on country reputations more generally. The leadership performance index measures the head of state's commitment to green issues, national media penetration, actions through international forums like the United Nations and the extent to which sustainability is embedded in development aid.

Domestic policies matter for two main reasons. The first is that, due to the nascent character of this field, government policy will play a central role in defining the parameters of this market and shaping incentives for new industries to flourish and the consumer subsidies to further their adoption. Second, governments who succeed in getting these domestic policies "right" would likely be rewarded as first-movers and receive positive recognition for it. The policy performance index measures the level of renewable energy contribution in a country, its national success at adopting and implementing best-practice clean energy policies and trending related to greenhouse gas emission reduction.

Cleantech investment is an important complement to domestic policies. If a national market was viewed as attractive from an investment point of view, it might validate the efforts already pursued by national leaders, both through policy and their leadership on the international stage. Also, nations viewed as vital investment targets for cleantech will likely observe a "multiplier effect" over time as the infusion of this capital will highlight new green industries in the country and positively support its green reputation. The cleantech performance index measures weighted cleantech investment volume, sector vitality and the strength of national institutions in promoting cleantech as an investment or export sector.

Finally, green tourism is included to acknowledge the significant contribution made by national tourism bodies to country promotion and the fact that all outsiders experience a country as tourists of some kind, be it business or leisure, and as a result this dimension would impact on a country's green reputation. Furthermore, visitors to a country tend to interact with national infrastructure such as transportation and hotels where opportunities exist to promote sustainability and influence outsider's opinions about a country's commitment to it. The green tourism performance index measures environmental tourism competitiveness, national green tourism accreditation schemes and the strength of national institutions promoting sustainable tourism.

The GGEI measures both the perceptions and performance of national green economies along these four dimensions. The perception data are based on an annual survey sent to non-governmental practitioners working in the green economy globally. In the spring of each year, a new survey is distributed online to a predefined target list of individuals with demonstrated experience in the realms of climate change policy, cleantech financing and entrepreneurship, academia, and international marketing and communications. The final survey results are presented to small focus groups to add further meaning to them.

The index portion of the product measures national green performance on the same four dimensions (leadership, domestic policy, cleantech investment and green tourism) as defined by 37 quantitative and qualitative indicators. These indicators draw upon secondary data sources in the marketplace in addition to qualitative assessments of government efforts or bodies linked to their activities in the global green economy. As an example, a quantitative indicator would be the cleantech investment volume in a country over a given year, while a qualitative indicator would be a scoring of the strength of investment facilitation bodies in promoting cleantech investment internationally.

The 2011 wave of this product tracked 27 countries representing over 90 percent of the global green economy today. They are Argentina, Australia,

Brazil, Canada, China, Denmark, Finland, France, Germany, Iceland, India, Indonesia, Israel, Italy, Japan, Mexico, the Netherlands, New Zealand, Norway, South Africa, South Korea, Spain, Sweden, Turkey, the United Arab Emirates, the United Kingdom and the United States. This country list represents nations with a somewhat developed green economy relative to the rest of the world, and this same list appears in other studies, allowing comparison of these results with other reports, highlighting similarities and differences.

SELECTION OF RESPONDENTS

The targeted nature of the survey's respondents was deliberate. Generally speaking, it would be difficult today to conduct a mass survey about national green reputations. Recently similar studies have been conducted measuring consumer perceptions of commercial "green" products. These surveys often focus on the pricing dimension and issues related to the commonly held perception that green products are more expensive, or deliberately priced higher to garner greater margins to producers. Mass opinions on this issue range from uninformed to passionately supportive or antagonistic. Because of the aforementioned diversity about what being "green" in the commercial or national realm even means, the survey is targeted to qualified practitioners familiar with the nuance of leadership, policy-making, cleantech investment and tourism in the green economy.

In another sense, the targeted approach to this survey and the experts selected to participate is rooted in the point of view many marketers take that resources should be concentrated on "influencer" groups who disproportionately shape overall conversations about brands and other topics. Facing limited resources, proponents of this approach would argue that budgets are most effectively allocated to segments of individuals who tend to shape information and perceptions among peer groups. This approach is even more relevant in the internet age where social media and the ability to establish "one to many" conversations make these influencers all the more important.

In the context of this project, influencers are assumed to be individuals affiliated with the organizations and media entities that define and disseminate opinions and assessments of green issues and how nations interact with them. Efforts were also made to capture feedback from members of active social networking groups dedicated to cleantech, sustainability and other related areas. By focusing on these online communities, the report captured sentiments and perceptions from the people most likely to shape future conversations about national green reputations. The 2011 GGEI realized around 700 responses from an internal database of global green economy practitioners.

RESULTS FOR 2011

The survey and subsequent focus groups revealed both intuitive and some surprising results related to both the perceptions and performance of these 27 national green economies. Generally speaking, a block of northern European nations – anchored by Germany, Denmark and Sweden – have the strongest aggregate green reputations. More surprisingly, the United States and China both have strong perceived green reputations as well, in large part due to their strong performance on the investment dimension of the survey and to a lesser extent their domestic policies. However, the United States and China do not rank as well when considering the performance index results, while Germany, Denmark and Sweden maintain their top positions, joined by New Zealand and Iceland, two smaller economies lacking similar recognition in our expert survey.

More specifically, the four categories of measurement revealed actionable results for nations in a variety of ways, mostly where perceptions fell short of performance, suggesting value in better communications of national merits. In terms of leadership, Germany, Denmark and Sweden continue to dominate the perception side of the GGEI, while nations hosting the annual UN Conference of Parties (COP) summit (i.e. Denmark, Mexico and South Africa) make stronger showings on the performance side. The strong performance of nations like South Africa, Brazil and Mexico, compared to their much weaker recognition from our perception survey, suggests a gap where better communications of national leadership efforts may be justified.

On the policy dimension, experts continue to credit a block of northern European nations with having the best policy frameworks in place to promote renewable energy, sustainable development and emissions reductions domestically; China and the United States to a lesser extent are also recognized here. In terms of performance, nations with concrete success at furthering renewable energy use or reducing emissions perform the best, with nations like Norway and Iceland with high hydropower or geothermal energy portfolios leading the rankings. As the reporting on the 2011 COP17 conference in Durban, South Africa illustrates, rhetoric and reality are two very different things when it comes to green policy and measuring actual results – as opposed to nonbinding targets or goals – renders a more complete picture of national policy performance.

The investment dimension revealed how much market size and economies of scale continue to influence how experts evaluate cleantech investment opportunities and market vitality. Large economies like China, the United States and Germany lead the survey results for this category by wide margins. Yet interestingly, our performance index revealed a different story where, again, Germany, Denmark and Sweden topped the rankings. In considering investment flows as weighed by GDP, the vitality of cleantech markets in each country and a qualitative ranking of national efforts to facilitate cleantech investment these northern European nations again prove to be the most vital green economies, despite offering smaller overall domestic markets as compared to China or the United States.

In the realm of green tourism, New Zealand emerged as the undisputed leader on both the perception and performance side of the GGEI. There shouldn't be anything too surprising about this result. New Zealand invested heavily in its 100 percent "Pure" tourism campaign for the past decade and, while green tourism wasn't necessarily the central element of this effort, the imagery and depiction of the country as offering various natural options for visiting obviously made an impact. Furthermore, New Zealand has one of the more developed accreditation systems for recognizing hotels and tourism operators that adhere to government endorsed codes of sustainability and environmental responsibility, a standard lacking in the majority of the 27 nations measured by the index.

The 2011 wave of this product did measure the main urban area in each of the 27 nations surveyed. The survey asked respondents to select the city most linked to green leadership and sustainable development. The resulting top five cities were Copenhagen, Stockholm, Amsterdam, Oslo and Berlin. The 2011 GGEI did not produce a city index to measure performance of these same cities but the 2012 product, in coordination with emerging analytic tools like the Siemens Green City Index, will feature both a perception and performance measurement for green cities.

MANAGING GREEN REPUTATIONS

As nations and cities become increasingly strategic about green reputation management, how should these efforts be coordinated and what examples do we have of initiatives already underway? Denmark's focus on its national green brand took a step forward with the establishment in 2008 of State of Green, designed to strengthen awareness of the solutions and competencies of Danish business and industry within energy, climate and the environment. South Korea's former Prime Minister Dr Han Seung-soo founded the Global Green Growth Institute (2010) to integrate economic growth and environmental sustainability through models of green growth furthered by public–private partnerships. New Zealand continues to articulate its 100 percent "Pure" brand through extensions like "Pure Advantage" that engage citizens and social media with advancing the country's green brand. And the C40 Cities Climate Leadership Group (2005), a network of large and engaged cities from around the world committed to implementing meaningful and sustainable climate-related actions locally, continues to highlight and coordinate green city branding.

As these examples illustrate, there is unlikely to be one model for countries to follow in the event that national green reputations become a priority and resources exist to "brand" a place along the lines of green growth and sustainability. The GGEI shows that however nascent, the global green economy is very complex and reputations within it are defined by a multitude of factors. The type of political system in place, domestic public opinion, pre-existing energy portfolios or natural resources, market size and overall investment flows, and other local regulations and constituencies vary significantly across the 27 nations currently covered by the GGEI. One size does not fit all, and green reputation management relies upon clearly articulating a broader national strategy related to green growth.

Nations currently dominating the global green economy face the additional challenge of maintaining their leadership as their green economies become more mature, or powerhouse markets like the United States and China begin to catch up in a more meaningful way. The northern European nations currently dominating the GGEI will be challenged to maintain distinct positions. Those countries with low perception values relative to their performance – nations like New Zealand, Israel, South Korea, Brazil and Mexico – have a lot to gain by focusing more on bolstering their green reputation through strategic communications.

For nations and cities working to deal with these challenges, here are some broad questions to consider:

1. What is the green strategy of your nation or city? Who are the industries, leaders and other stakeholders most central to executing this strategy? What relationship does your national green reputation have to the larger country brand or how do efforts based in city government relate to larger national ones?

2. How does your national or city green strategy compare to other countries, particularly those in your immediate geographic neighborhood? How will the character of your national or urban green reputation be distinct?

3. Who will be tasked with managing and promoting this green identity? How will they encompass diverse expertise about policy, investment and tourism and gain support from domestic constituencies? How will city and national stakeholders be coordinated?

4. What is the plan for communicating this green identity and associated green strategy? How do leaders in government and business project the position in breakthrough ways in coordination with a budget-sensitive communications plan?

CONCLUSION

As the field of national reputation management grows and these efforts are understood in a systematic way, nations will begin to define themselves with increased specificity in line with the influences of their domestic constituents and the international markets most important to them. While the green dimension of reputation is but one more specific realm to focus on, it is particularly salient today due to the pace at which citizens and the international community appear to be emphasizing its importance. Nations and cities that lay the groundwork today for intelligent green strategies and develop branding and communications plans to support them will be rewarded with recognition, investment and increased tourism. Countries already viewed as first-movers in this realm must consolidate their positions further in the coming years, defining more narrowly what makes their green brand distinct and the value it provides to the global community at large.

CHAPTER 12

Branding Brazilian Slums through "Freeware" Cultural Production: The Case of Rio de Janeiro

Antonio Paolo Russo

Large cities in Latin America may well have been the cradle of postcolonial national societies, but at least since the beginning of the 20th century they have also concentrated the direst effects of uneven development, becoming the living image of democratic deficit (De Oliveira and Roberts 1996; Hoffmann and Centeno 2003; Davis 2006). The progressive concentration of "urban problems" in those areas also meant that the crisis of the 1990s has hit these areas hardest, accelerating their decline and inducing in some cases a reaction by progressive city governments who started to elaborate strategies for revitalization and regeneration, though, for the most part, these projects remained on paper or gave results below expectations (see Sosa 2010, for the case of Buenos Aires; Segre 2004, for the case of Rio de Janeiro; and Alves 2008, for case of São Paulo).

The recent turn in Latin American politics coincides with a watershed period in which the largest Latin American countries, mostly untouched by the global financial crisis, are growing at "tiger" pace. Brazil had one of the fastest growing economies throughout the 2000s decade, touching yearly rates of 8 percent; Argentina seems to be finally recovering from the debt and inflation problems that plunged the country into a deep social crisis by the mid-1990s and is now following on Brazil's steps; and Colombia, on the way to improving its image as a safe investment location, has boosted its exports of primary resources to levels unseen in this century. Cities like São Paulo, Buenos Aires, Medellin, Porto Alegre and Santiago are not only and not anymore the culmination and gateways of national industrial systems, but are rapidly diversifying their economies and accomplishing their own ways of transition to post-Fordism.

In this favorable context, cities are bound to regain a new type of centrality, in different forms from the postcolonial epoch and in a different relation with the rest of the world than in the past, similarly to what happened in many other European and North American cities in the last decades. This change, of which evident signs are already tangible, has potentially profound social implications and is stirring the debate around claims for a more just urban society. Social movements with the most intense relations with local and national politics are pre-eminently urban and are very active in claiming their "right to the city": the most evident aspects of transition to a post-Fordist economy take place in cities, which concentrate the creative workforce that sustains such economic change.

Tourism development is hardly alien to those transformations, and may even have a positive role in accompanying the process of transition and regeneration of Latin American cities: either for making them open, appreciated and loved to the world, and so triggering new "bilateral" global connections, or because much emphasis is given in official discourses by regional governments and international organizations to tourism development as a "greening", "including", "pacifying" strategy that promises to exert profound effects on the urban reality.

This chapter explores a specific angle of this broad issue, specifically the way in which sectors of the Latin America urban communities that identify with their degraded living settlements – the slums or *favelas* – are negotiating their legitimacy and inclusion as urban stakeholders through a powerful branding of their creative expression. They do so by adopting a new discourse by which the products of creativity, such as popular art, new media and events, are freely produced and consumed by anybody and distributed globally, thus sidestepping the cultural boundaries erected throughout the modern period by the "white" bourgeoisie and their institutional media, and fully embracing a post-Fordist paradigm of acquiring information, recoding and sharing it, but from a grassroots perspective.

These creative products have the potential to reconnect *favelas* to urban development, for instance through tourism, which is increasingly pursuing breaks with such creative landscapes, or through the cultural industries, which may come to integrate them horizontally, achieving multiple objectives, such as inclusion and emancipation, a genuine "sanitization" of slum areas, and a new brand for Latin America as one containing smart and sustainable places based on the recognition and valorization of difference. These insights are based on field research conducted by me in 2010 in Rio de Janeiro, one of the most emblematic places of this "cultural shift" in development politics.

RIO DE JANEIRO: THE WORLD OF *FAVELAS* VS THE CORPORATE TOURIST CITY

The city of Rio de Janeiro is home to approximately 6,100,000 inhabitants. As such, it is the second city of Brazil after São Paulo, the third largest in Latin America and among the world's ten largest cities. Its metropolitan area, including 19 municipalities in the Fluminense region, contains more than 11 million people, ranking it twenty-first in the world. It is the capital of the Rio de Janeiro State, and has been the capital of Brazil from 1822 to 1960.

In the early 20th century, Rio was assuming the traits of a world city, where the taste for high culture and fashion (absorbed from Europe) fused with the rich popular culture of the former African slaves and the descendants of the Portuguese into a kaleidoscopic environment, involving designed streetscapes and manicured natural areas, important theater and musical productions, and a vivid intellectual scene, side by side with the frantic rhythms of samba and a penchant for street life. This unique cultural landscape[1] caught the attention of the world elites and nurtured an imagery that contributes to this date to affirm Rio as a "world brand" and an exotic tourist destination.

In the last 30 years many manufacturers have moved to regions with better access to the market and labor conditions. Besides, key administrative functions were lost out to Brasilía when the capital moved there 50 years ago, breaking down a large part of the "bureaucracy economy" of the city. The end of a 20-year military regime in the mid-1970s put added pressure for economic recovery, but Rio has been lagging behind in the development of advanced services to replace traditional functions, widely overcome by São Paulo as a "global city" well positioned within the web of the knowledge economy.

The problems of urban violence contributed significantly to the decline of Rio's allure, reflecting an objective escalation of criminality which occurred in the 1990s and early 2000s, but also an increasing preoccupation of the middle classes for their personal security, and possibly the mounting pressure by capital and "power coalitions" to eradicate the problem altogether through the forced removal of *favelas*. In fact, as violent crime rates have wavered over recent years, the space they occupy in the media seems to be constantly on the rise. This general feeling of unsafety contributed to chasing away visitors and international investors, and aligned Rio with other Latin American cities in the trend toward the suburbanization and fencing of middle-class livelihoods, eroding substantially the "carioca" traditional lifestyle based on mixedness and street-life.

However, in the last decade things started to change: as Brazil is on the verge of joining the club of the world's economic powerhouses, things for Rio look even rosier. New ambitious projects that should reinforce the economic outlook of the city have been recently presented, channeling the equivalent of some $80 billion of private investments into the state economy (more than half of it in the petrochemical complex) in the 2010–12 period. Only a small part of this investment ($3 billion) will fall on the city proper, but it still represents an important lever for the transformation of the economy and for urban development, like the urbanization of *favelas*.

Tourism is already strong of Rio, but in spite of its natural and cultural assets, already attracting 2.7 million arrivals into the city, it is the oncoming sports mega-events of 2014 (the soccer World Cup, whose final will be played in Rio, and whose headquarters will be based there) and 2016 (Olympics) that promise to represent key turning points for the city economy, for which the successful organization of the Pan American Games of 2007 has produced a demonstrable effect.[2] These events are also expected to achieve a "scale jump" in the international positioning of Rio and enhance its far-from-good transport and accommodation infrastructure with a new airport terminal and an extension of the underground rail network.

Another important *grand projet* is the renovation of the port area which connects the downtown of Rio with its northern shore. This could be considered the realization of the strategic plan "Porto Maravilha" endorsed at the beginning of the 2000s, based on an in-depth analysis of Rio's weaknesses and opportunities in the face of global changes. The plan was designed to create a fresh city brand for Rio, involving the renovation of its waterfront, to be refurbished and partly reconstructed around an "edutainment" complex. The present alignment of political orientations at all three governance levels (national, state and city) has finally given way to the first lot of works, counting on a $1.7 billion financial backup from the federal government, and including all sorts of iconic "cultural" facilities such as a poly-functional building by "starchitect" Santiago Calatrava, high quality apartments, tourist and commercial facilities as well as social housing projects and education and research facilities.

It is nevertheless today acknowledged that progression in the construction of a more solid, "global" economic outlook cannot proceed separate to the solution of the city's dire social problems (Urani 2008), although there is still a strong debate on whether the ongoing "corporatization" of the city should come first and be a lever for the reduction of poverty, or whether the latter issue should be given priority over boosterist development on ethical as well as sustainability grounds.

The first signs of real progress in the reduction of poverty and crime – arguably the result of successful federal policies in the social and cultural fields – have led politicians, private parties and civic organizations to express a consensus that something may finally change for the better. *Favelas* have ceased to be considered illegal settlements, as specifically written down in the 1988 Constitution, and most of them by now have become established neighborhoods with basic city services, though still concentrating dire poverty and social problems.

A more critical appraisal of recent developments suggests that the goal of a more just society may be not so rapidly attained, as processes of eviction of the slummed population are currently intensifying under the pressure of the corporate agenda, echoed louder than ever by the media.

However, we may be witnessing a new phenomenon altogether, rather than a mere amelioration of the living conditions of the worse-off. Award-winning feature movies like the 2002 *Cidade de Deus* (director F. Meirelles) and the 2007 *Tropa de Elite* (J. Padilha) gave global projection to the problems of slums, urban violence, drug wars and class divisions, raising an awareness which is opening the discursive field to first-person accounts of slummed lives and legitimizing the antagonistic stances of *favela*-based social movements. This is also contributing to the development of niche forms of tourism which is interested in allowing people a closer look at what is happening in the "interstices" of the corporate city. Some *favelas* have even started to get equipped to welcome (and in some cases already accommodate) tourists, a radical turn for places that were the epitome of no-go areas for tourists and middle-class residents until very recently. In this way, *favelas* – and especially their human and cultural landscape – are changing into something of a new brand for a more cohesive Rio de Janeiro, which is contested but intriguing. In the next section I will analyze the process by which this brand is being constructed "from the bottom".

THE CULTURAL LANDSCAPE OF *FAVELAS*: BRANDING THE FREEWARE

In the favorable context described above, efforts to brand Rio de Janeiro as a global destination and a "growing" city are intensifying. This also contributes to valorizing the city's exceptional urban landscape. One way this is being done is the "boosterist" refurbishment of its urban infrastructure, and especially its waterfront, and the transformation of the run-down downtown areas (*Centro*) with new functions oriented to a global audience of mobile consumers, investors and corporate workers.

The other (to some extent complementary) strategy is to recuperate and rehabilitate the cultural landscape of Rio and brand the city as one of the most diverse and archetypal monumental capitals of Latin America. In this sense, Rio de Janeiro is interested in submitting its candidature to be included in UNESCO's World Heritage List as a "cultural landscape". This inclusion would represent the highest recognition of the city's universal value as an outstanding example of integration and mutual molding between natural and socio-cultural elements, which is worth preserving in its essential features as a symbol of human achievement. More pragmatically, it would be a way to give this landscape a conservation framework and to have its application monitored according to international standards, especially in view of the history of chaotic expansion of the city and of the new pressures for redevelopment brought about by the oncoming 2014 and 2016 mega-events. This objective raises many questions and expectations. What exactly should be emphasized (and branded to visitors) as "unique" and "worth preserving" is not a trivial question. Political interests and rapidly shifting opportunities are defining the way in which this candidature is presented, and it is possibly the "sensitive" nature of the issue that is delaying the presentation of an actual proposal to UNESCO: after three aborted attempts focusing mostly on physical landscape elements, a new opportunity finally to develop a more integral, dynamic notion of cultural landscape based on intangible elements, comes from the re-enlivened debate on the role of culture as a springboard for inclusive urban development,[3] which is currently under study. This shifting focus is bound to take in multiple elements of the cultural landscape of Rio de Janeiro in the social sphere, their inner diversity and contradictions, and the way they are being put to use and integrated into a city brand which conveys significant meaning.

One of these is certainly the social landscape of poverty and the creative expressions of the narration of – and resistance against – exclusion that has materialized throughout history in specific areas of the city. For instance, Samba originates from the celebrations of former slaves in their very first settlements in downtown districts adjacent to the port, to be later transferred and fused with other musical styles in the industrial suburbs of the Fluminense region. The Carnival is a celebration of diversity and integration and is a challenge to the constituted order introduced by humble workers of Portuguese descent. The bossa nova was a new musical style picked up by intellectuals and artists who opposed conservative values and flourished into a "scene" in middle-class Ipanema. And the celebrated city beaches, with their wide open space appropriated by the city's outcast in wild games, represent the democratic "soccer landscape" of Brazil. However, today, the most pulling creative expressions of antagonism and identity affirmation are concentrated in *favelas*.

Favelas, or slums, are interspersed throughout the city and they also form a unique element of Rio's landscape, an exceptional (and highly creative) form of informal urban settlement developed in the interstices of the "legitimate" city, mostly by urbanization of the seemingly inaccessible peaks that mark Rio's cityscape. Poorly serviced with basic facilities like water, electricity and paved roads, they continue to be an eye-catcher on the way toward renewing the Rio brand in terms of smart and sustainable growth.

Comparing census data (IBGE 2002), the total number of inhabitants of *favelas* in the city was estimated at around 882,000 in 1991 and 1,092,000 in 2001 (a 0.38 percent growth per year). *Favelas* occupy an area of around 37 square kilometers in the city, corresponding to 6.3 percent of its total territory. Their social composition is today more mixed and representative of what is found in the rest of the city than in the past, though distinctively younger, poorer, black and less educated, even compared to the most popular neighborhoods.

The distinctive cultural landscape of *favelas* is highly reflective of the dual discourse by which, on one side, society acknowledges them as a unique social structure and space for consumption, but on the other side still considers it a "world apart": criminal, unhealthy, a space to be cleared out, its inhabitants transferred to other zones for "their own sake" (Corrêa and Queiroz Ribeiro 2001). Their proximity to residential middle-class neighborhoods makes the divisions existing in the Brazilian – and specifically *carioca* – society more evident; hence, as suggested by Albergaria (2010), their reification.

In this context, it is not surprising that the most visible cultural expressions of *favelas* reflect this "oppositional" identity, not even attempting to be inclusive in spite of their increasing popularity with middle-class youth, and maybe this is why they have been so firmly targeted and stigmatized by politics and the media.[4] From this point of view, they constitute a spatially organized form of bio-resistance, by which community organizations and civic movements, and especially the young black groups, develop a new subjectivity (Cocco 2011), whose most poignant aspects (and those which have more chances to achieve, if not straightforward social integration, at least a tangible improvement of living conditions in *favelas*) regard the contemporary cultural and artistic realm.

At the center of this development, there is unbounded connectivity provided by the internet, which promises to overcome the invisible barrier keeping *favelas* segregated. According to Vieira (2008), the internet has created such new relational power that is also changing the way in which the *favela* sees itself and is represented in the mainstream, giving its cultural production a new perspective and mobilizing it globally: it does not have to be legitimized any more by the local institutions and power coalitions, it legitimizes itself through its success and global projection.

Another pillar of this turn is the acknowledgment of "hacker culture" as a form of social activism (Coleman and Golub 2008), affirming the right to acquire, recode and reuse information from digital sources into new collective identities as a form of subversion against the establishment in the industries of culture and representation (see also Castells 2003: 122–4). Especially in the field of music, "neo-artisanal" musical genres, like funk, *tecnobrega* from Pará and the new *electro-forró* of Pernambuco, have emerged as parallel, "low cost" cultural industries, largely based on the illegal acquisition and creative manipulation of musical themes and sources, and not only for the infringement of copyrights, but, more radically, because in most cases electricity and telephone connections in *favelas* are "hacked" from regular lines in the legitimate city (only recently there was a move from the state government to provide most slums with regular wiring, and a plan to provide city center *favelas* with free Wi-Fi connection is being implemented).

These musical products (mostly in the shape of digital files) arrive directly to the consumer and without having to depend on corporate intermediaries. In a matter of minutes, the "funk" produced by youngsters in Rio's *favelas* goes straight to informal street markets in Maputo, Mozambique or other cities in Portuguese-speaking countries, where local youngsters can easily relate to the social issues that it voices. Business is not done through the sale of CDs, which are normally downloaded and reproduced freely, but from live shows. These attract ever larger young audiences into *favelas*, while local DJs perform regularly in clubs in São Paulo, New York, Amsterdam or London, bringing back a "legal" source of income into the feeble *favela* economy and developing all sorts of supply chain networks, from fashion to advertisement and video-art. By making a virtue out of necessity, this model can be seen as a global laboratory of the cultural industries of the future, anticipating global trends in the production, distribution and organization of musical creations. Locally, the turn in representation perspectives also has important symbolic effects: Vieira (2008) notes that successful *funkeiros* are substituting drug lords as "heroes" in the collective imagery of the *favela*'s youth.

The change in the way communities represent and narrate themselves extends to other genres. In music video-clips, feature movies and theater productions, the artists of the *favelas* and suburbs talk about their everyday life, which does not sum up to only violence, drugs and death, as the rest of the urban community tends to think, but touches issues of conviviality, diversity, civic rights and gender parity. An example is the movie *5x Favela, Agora por Nós Mesmos*, which was entirely produced, in every aspect, by *favela* residents. In this movie, only one episode showcases drugs and violence. The winning performance is in fact *Christmas Story* based in the scenic Vidigal community and interpreted by the respected collective *Nos do Morro*. Another example of this global projection is the cooperation established by designers in the Rocinha community with the influential "creative factory" Fabrica.

The creative dynamism of *favelas*, together with the ongoing "regularization" of their situation, has attracted the interest of another important global audience, that of tourists. The issue of poverty or slum tourism acquired visibility in critical studies of tourism (Freire-Medeiros 2009; Williams 2008; Frenzel and Koens 2012). Generally, this literature identifies a paradoxical counterpoint between the stated objective of benefiting deprived communities through the income generated by tourism, and the commodification of poverty, transformed into a "show" for visitors within the framework of "dark tourism" (Stone 2006), though the works quoted above introduce a more optimistic angle of slum tourism as breaking down cultural barriers and raising global awareness.

Rio's *favelas* have been receiving visitors since at least a decade, when "Rocinha tours" started to be advertised on specialized websites and showcased in guidebooks such as Lonely Planet. These tours are strictly limited to groups accompanied by authorized guides and are backed up by NGOs that would "negotiate" visits with local gangs so as to ensure visitors' safety. Visitors are picked up at their South Zone hotels, driven up Rocinha's narrow alleys, and then they get to walk through these "forbidden" places, talk to local activists and simple residents, buy local products and crafts, and possibly enjoy a home-cooked meal, but mainly they have a direct, unmediated impression of a landscape of injustice. For most participants, this is an illuminating (and thrilling) experience; the media coverage of recent episodes of violence, as well as the internationally successful movies featuring *favelas*, have paradoxically turned this sort of "reality tour" into a blockbuster instead of scaring tourists away. It should be said that there are very few other places where this type of experience is offered with a similar level of professionalism and safety. Rio's *morros* (hills) also have an inherent attractiveness due to their location and views, which shantytowns in say Mexico City or São Paulo don't have, and also a certain joyful "ambience" that most slums lack.

The attractiveness of slums is now extending to other aspects than "voyeurism" or awareness-raising: community organizations are setting up their own proper visitor attractions, like interpretation centers and *"favela* museums", but also cultural venues and events, small-scale festivals, dance gigs, street markets, workshops and courses, research and educational centers, as well as an embryonic tourism infrastructure, like small guesthouses and tourist restaurants, bank offices, and public transport. These resources are accessible to independent visitors, who today venture to *favelas* in increasing numbers without a guide or big concerns for their safety.

The success of visits to *favelas* has started a fashion of sorts: every weekend the South Zone youth virtually flocks to Rocinha to take part in "funk dances" and other events. Other poor areas of the immense suburb of Rio – like Madureira, the cradle of Samba schools; or Vigário Geral, with its very active "black" music and dance schools; and the municipality of Nova Iguaçú, an epicentre of grassroots theater products – have started to be visited by small numbers of unorganized tourists, moved by curiosity for a "genuine" encounter with local contemporary culture, but also by the large exposure that finally the independent media and the Web are giving to these "niches" in the cultural aspect of this great city. No "official" tourist leaflet showcases these attractions, but an increasing number of tourists are today familiar with these creative brands and are willing to engage with the reality they define.

Wrapping up, *favelas* may continue to be criminalized especially by the conservative media as "illegal" settlements reproducing violence. Yet, by involving approximately a million people, and providing unprecedented opportunities for disadvantaged youth groups that "officialist" cultural stances would never give, they cannot be neglected any more as places of creative expression, as neither can the reality that such expressions portray and the claims advanced through it by local activists.

The development and consolidation of a global cultural brand for Rio as a creative city, though, needs intuitional support in terms of urban policy: removing slums by evictions, "normalizing" the cultural scene through heavy police surveillance and sanctioning hacker activities goes in the opposite direction of dissolving these creative impulses, or, worse, leaving them at the mercy of the criminal gangs.

CONCLUSIONS: SOFT-BRANDING DIVERSITY FOR SUSTAINABLE DEVELOPMENT

According to Mike Davis (2006), the formation and criminalization of slums in the developing world (but not exclusively) is today one of the most problematic aspects of contemporary urbanization and a phenomenon that elucidates a global model of development which pursues the interests of corporate agendas against the legitimate rights of the working classes of the world. In his work he presents the formation of urban slums as germane to the unregulated exploitation of cheap manpower to feed the growth agendas of capitalism, mostly with the complicity of malleable national governments.

This position is not without critics (for instance, see Angotti 2006 and Capel 2007) whose main angle is the fact that slums are not just hopeless spaces but are also liberating important opportunities for personal emancipation, organized resistance and the creative reconfiguration of lives which challenge "from the margin" the agendas of institutions and corporations, coherently with the transformation of a society triggered by the post-Fordist turn.

The case of Rio de Janeiro's *favelas* and their burgeoning creative economy is an illustration of this trend: criminalized by the media, sanctioned by institutions, controlled by criminal gangs, the slummed population has nevertheless managed to elaborate, and most importantly diffuse, their own cultural languages using the opportunities found in the "breaches" of the system and making themselves visible to a global audience: not only the physical and legal breach that *favelas* per se represent, but also the economic breaches of copyright infringement, hacking and de-intermediation. This is feeding a whole new value chain that is finally presenting a real development opportunity for an excluded sector of the urban population and a consumption filière "at the margin" which successfully negotiates a new, positive collective identity for the urban poor. This global, almost "ageographic", brand is also picked up locally by the "traveling audiences" represented by tourists, legitimizing the role of *favelas* and their cultural landscape as attractions in the context of a world destination like Rio de Janeiro. In this new context urban juvenile cultures and their "violent" practices are not anymore an element of "danger" to tourism, with negative implications on the construction of the tourist city, but a force of socio-spatial reconnection and diversification.

The cultural landscape of Rio de Janeiro that I have presented has unlimited resources for generating solutions to exclusion and poverty, especially if the main stewards of such landscape, its communities, are actively involved in the process of negotiation and affirmation of this brand, which could become a "soft" undertone by which Rio projects a global image of a historical and at the same time contemporary, but also open, cohesive and diverse cultural capital of Brazil. If this strategy prevails over corporate agendas, it could become a model to be exported and adapted in many other Latin American cities.

NOTES

1. This term, introduced by geographer Carl Sauer in 1925, refers to the process of fashioning "from a natural landscape by a culture group. Culture is the agent, the natural area is the medium, the cultural landscape the result" (Sauer 1925). In the case of this study, the medium should be understood as the urban area; indeed "urban cultural landscapes" are a preservation category for UNESCO.
2. While the occupancy rate went down a good 10 percent in the last decade, it caught up slightly in 2010 to an estimated average annual rate of 75–77 percent, and Rio, as mentioned above, is leading again the ranking of the most visited cities. Visits to all the main attractions have increased during the last year, as have international arrivals at the airport (up 10 percent in the same period).
3. After a lengthy discussion culminated with the preparatory works for the annual general meeting held in Brasilía in July 2010, UNESCO is now willing to consider "urban cultural landscapes" as a new category of cultural landscape characterized by "human" elements which are inherent to an urban society.
4. Herschmann (1997) discusses the process by which the local and national media, by presenting urban juvenile violence in an ideologically biased way, amplifying it and reifying poverty, also opened important spaces of "negotiation" around conflictive issues by glamorizing violence, and so brought about a legitimacy of such cultural languages – and from there, an acknowledgment of the problems that inspire them – by turning them into a cultural commodity (he makes this case for the "funk" musical movement born in Rio's *favelas*).

REFERENCES

Albergaria, D. (2010) "Motivações e consequências sociais das reformas urbanas no Rio", *ComCiência: revista mensal eletrônica de jornalismo científico*, 118.

Alves, G. da Anunciação (2008) "O papel do patrimônio nas políticas de revalorização do espaço urbano", *Scripta Nova: Revista Electrónica de Geografía y Ciencias Sociales*, 12: 270(136), www.ub.es/geocrit/sn/sn-270/sn-270-136.htm.

Angotti, T. (2006) "Apocalyptic anti-urbanism: Mike Davis and his planet of slums", *International Journal of Urban and Regional Research*, 30(4): 961–7.

Campbell, T. (2003) *The Quiet Revolution: Decentralization and the Rise of Political Participation in Latin American Cities*, Pittsburgh, PA: University of Pittsburgh Press.

Capel, H. (2007) "El debate sobre la construcción de la ciudad y el llamado 'Modelo Barcelona'", *Scripta Nova: Revista Electrónica de Geografía y Ciencias sociales*, 11(233), www.ub.es/geocrit/sn/sn-233.htm.

Castells, M. (2003) *The Internet Galaxy: Reflections on the Internet, Business and Society*, Oxford: Oxford University Press.

Cocco, G. (2011) "As biolutas e a constituição do comum", *Revista Global*, 14, www.revistaglobalbrasil.com.br/?p=651.

Coleman, E.G. and A. Golub (2008) "Hacker practice: Moral genres and the cultural articulation of liberalism", *Anthropological Theory*, 8(3): 255–77.

Corrêa do Lago, L. and L.C. de Queiroz Ribeiro (2001) "A divisão favela-bairro no espaço social do Rio de Janeiro", *Cadernos Metrópole*, 5: 29–47.

Davis, M. (2006) *Planet of Slums*, London: Verso.

De Oliveira, O. and Roberts, B. (1996) "Urban development and social inequality in Latin America", in J. Gugler (ed.), *The Urban Transformation of the Developing World*, Oxford: Oxford University Press, pp. 253–313.

Freire-Medeiros, B. (2009) "The favela and its touristic transits", *Geoforum*, 40(4): 580–8.

Frenzel, F., and K. Koens (forthcoming) "Slum Tourism: Developments in a young field of interdisciplinary tourism research", *Tourism Geographies*, 14(2).

Herschmann, M. (1997) "Mídia e culturas juvenis: o caso da glamourização do funk nos jornais cariocas", in Menezes, Philadelpho (ed.), *Signos plurais. Mídia, arte, cotidiano na globalização*, São Paulo: Experimento.

Hoffman, K. and M. Centeno (2003) "The lopsided continent: inequality in Latin America", *Annual Review of Sociology*, 29: 363–90.

IBGE (2002) *Censo Demográfico 2000*, Rio de Janeiro: IBGE.

Sauer, C.O. (1925) "The morphology of landscape", *University of California Publications in Geography*, 2(2): 19–53.

Segre, R. (2004) *Rio de Janeiro Metropolitano: añoranzas de la "Cidade Maravilhosa"*, São Paulo: Vitruvius.

Sosa, V. A. (2010) "Planificación urbana y políticas de representación, el patrimonio como recurso de renovación urbana y espacio de confrontación en el casco histórico de Buenos Aires", *Scripta Nova, revista electrónica de geografía y ciencias sociales* Vol. XIV, 331(71), www.ub.edu/geocrit/sn/sn-331/sn-331-71.htm.

Stone, P.R. (2006) "A dark tourism spectrum: towards a typology of death and macabre related tourist sites, attractions and exhibitions", *Tourism*, 54(2): 145–60.

Urani, A. (2008) *Trilhas Para o Rio: Do Reconhecimento da Queda a Reinvençao do Futuro*, Rio de Janeiro: Capus.

Vieira, M. (2008) "Internet muda a cultura da periferia carioca", *Grandes Reportagens: Megacidades*. São Paulo: O Estado de Sao Paulo.

Williams, C. (2008) "Ghettourism and voyeurism, or challenging stereotypes and raising consciousness? literary and non-literary forays into the favelas of Rio de Janeiro", *Bulletin of Latin American Research*, 27(4): 483–500.

Chapter 13

Improved Public Infrastructure and Sustainable Place Branding

Keith Dinnie

In his superbly written book *Soft City*, novelist and travel writer Jonathan Raban makes the following observation: "in our city, it is easy to drift into a privacy of symbols, a domain of subjective illusions made concrete by the fact that two or three people have gathered together to conspire in them" (Raban 2008, p. 143). Raban was referring to the behavior of individual citizens and their means of engaging with a vast and labyrinthine metropolis that can be overwhelming if not tamed through certain psychological approaches. But his observation may also be applied to the unhealthy power exercised by small coteries of politicians and marketing professionals who take it upon themselves to decide upon the symbols and "subjective illusions" that are used in branding cities. Crass slogans and risible logos emerge, and taint the whole concept and practice of branding places. To counter the usual over-emphasis on slogans, logos, PR and advertising, in this chapter I show how sustainable place branding can be conducted not by superficial communications techniques, but by tangible improvements in public infrastructure that benefit all those who work in the city or visit it or invest in it.

Improved public infrastructure should logically go hand in hand with sustainable place branding. Enhancing the public infrastructure of a city, region or other type of place should improve the perceived image of such places in the eyes of target audiences such as investors, tourists and residents. However, until recently the two topics have tended to follow parallel academic paths, with public infrastructure studied in the domain of urban design, development and regeneration (Arimah 2005; Grossman 2010; Meijer *et al.* 2011) and place branding studied in the field of marketing (O'Shaughnessy and O'Shaughnessy 2000; Kotler and Gertner 2002).

But this separation of research streams may be nearing an end. An encouraging evolution over the past few years has been the creation of new academic journals such as the *Journal of Town and City Management*, the *Journal of Place Management and Development* and *Place Branding and Public Diplomacy*, which bridge the divide between the fields of urban development and place branding. Such journals provide a platform for academics and practitioners to share their findings from conceptual and empirical work that explicitly recognizes the link between urban development and place branding. For example, the role of place branding in sustainable development has been examined by Maheshwari *et al.* (2011), who review the evolution of the place branding concept from the perspectives of regeneration, growth and sustainability, specifically in the context of the city of Liverpool's year as European Capital of Culture in 2008. In a case study of the Ghanaian capital Accra, Spio (2011) also underlines the need to address infrastructure challenges such as road networks, electricity and water supplies, and housing supply in order to provide a solid foundation for developing a city brand. The integration of the sustainability concept into place branding represents a highly promising area for future research.

INFRASTRUCTURE AND THE CITYSCAPE

The determinants of infrastructure spending by cities constitute an under-researched area that would benefit from a sustainable place branding approach and perspective. Arimah (2005) draws upon the United Nations Human Settlements Programme's global urban indicators database to attempt to identify the determinants of infrastructure spending in the cities of developing countries, concluding that intercity variations in infrastructure spending derive from differences in the macroeconomic environment, urban growth rate, quality of governance and financial capacity of municipal governments. Although Arimah's study focuses on urban infrastructure spending, it does not contain an explicit place branding dimension; the determinants of infrastructure spending are identified, but the paper's scope does not extend to analyzing the consequences of the place brand image of the alluded to infrastructure spending. Place branding scholars may need to take the initiative in establishing an integrated approach to the analysis of infrastructure spending effects upon place brand image, given that place branding is a younger, less established field of study and practice than urban development from an economic perspective.

The immaterial of marketing and the material of the cityscape need to come together as interlocking facets of services and brand strategy (Govers and Go 2009, pp. 68–72). Cities may be considered as complex multidimensional servicescapes. As with most services, the constant challenge is how to brand the intangible. In the broad domain of services marketing,

Bitner (1992) elucidated the impact of physical surroundings on customers and employees, yet there has been surprisingly little application of the "servicescape" construct to the branding of places. With the importance of the experiential dimension of brands now widely acknowledged, the relevance of fusing branding strategy and the tangible assets of cities assumes great importance. Go and Govers (2011, p. xiv) offer a conceptualization of this perspective by stating that "the representation of culture and its ensuing discourse between the cultural landscape and the experiential landscape informs our basic understanding of nature, offering new models that provide a bridge to the immaterial world".

CITIES AND THE EXPERIENCE ECONOMY

Cities represent an important platform or stage for the experience economy. Pine and Gilmore (1999) have emphasized the theatrical aspect of the experience economy, a perspective applied to the field of destination management by Morgan *et al.* (2009, p. 201) who delineate "an approach to services management through theatrical metaphors of staging, casting and performance". With their dynamism and diversity, cities clearly form a rich environment for the theatre of the experience economy.

Tangible urban facilities such as movie theaters, bars, museums, art galleries and trendy shops constitute a valuable asset for cities seeking to craft a city brand that appeals to the affluent creative class, which is generally considered to represent an attractive target audience for city branding initiatives (Boschma and Fritsch 2009). The competitiveness of cities may partly be determined by the aesthetics of their urban environment as evidenced in a city's architecture, streets, parks, water systems, lighting systems, signposting, and so on (Parjanen *et al.* 2011). Applied to these tangible elements of the city, the techniques of branding are, according to Clegg and Kornberger (2010, p. 7), "a way of managing the city as a medium and controlling the production and circulation of meaning". One might question the use of the verb "controlling" in this context, as the production and circulation of meaning lie only partly within the control of policy-makers; however, Clegg and Kornberger rightly draw attention to the need to at least attempt to manage the meaning associated with place brands.

CASES

One of the largest infrastructure developments that could have a significant effect on place brand image is the King Abdullah Financial District

(KAFD) project in Riyadh, Saudi Arabia. Scheduled for completion in 2013, KAFD is intended to become Riyadh's new city center, offering the city's first public transportation, pedestrian zones and a network of air conditioned skywalks between the towers. Major financial organizations such as the Capital Markets Authority, Tadawul Stock Exchange and Samba Bank will relocate to the newly created district, which will also contain residential units, retail space, three hotels, a convention center, an aquarium and a science museum. The scale of this investment in the city's infrastructure will not only radically transform the essence of the urban environment, it will also help Riyadh to emerge more clearly as a distinctive city brand rather than being known simply as the capital of Saudi Arabia.

Another example of infrastructure investment that should result in improvements in place brand perceptions concerns the Arnhem/Nijmegen region in the Netherlands. The region's web portal (www.coolregion.nl) provides an extensive introduction to the area, and established communication tools such as Twitter, Facebook and a printed magazine are already intensively used to promote the city-region brand. Yet the most powerful driver of changes in perceptions of this city-region brand will probably be the infrastructure investment in a complex water and urban design project near Lent, across the river from Nijmegen's city center. The project synthesizes the constant challenge of managing high water levels in the Netherlands with the more universal aims of urban development, and as such it has attracted visits by interested delegations from countries including Korea and France. A new city island will emerge in the basin of the River Waal, with facilities there and in the surrounding areas being developed on the basis of an inclusive approach whereby input is sought from all local stakeholders. By literally channeling development into the existing urban area, the green spaces in the surrounding area can remain green rather than being developed. The sustainability dimension of the project is explained by local alderman Jan van der Meer: "we can fit a bustling piece of city here. And the best part is, Nijmegen is one of the few cities in the Netherlands that, in terms of population, is expected to continue to grow until 2040. Additional housing construction can best be done in cities, specifically to maintain the green spaces in the surrounding areas. Our plans enable us to do that" (*Arts Meets Science* 2012).

The examples of KAFD in Riyadh and the Arnhem/Nijmegen city region illustrate the way in which cities can strengthen their respective place brands, not through the superficial techniques of marketing communications, but by making real tangible changes to the essence of their urban environments. A city brand needs to be rooted in reality rather than existing merely in a bubble of spin and manipulation. Several cities have focused their brand-building attention on the need to address the challenges of tangible evidence instead of relying only on marketing communications. The Indian city of Ahmedabad, for example, has invested in significant developments such as the Sabarmati Riverfront Project and the launch of the city's Bus Rapid Transit System (Nair 2011). These infrastructure developments signal the city's commitment to an environmentally responsible approach that makes a real improvement to the quality of life of Ahmedabad's citizens. Musa and Melewar (2011) similarly demonstrate how the development and improvement of infrastructure and services in Kuala Lumpur contributes to the strengthening of that city's brand, as well as showing how the creation of the new cities of Putrajaya and Cyberjaya also contribute to enhancing the Malaysian nation brand. Musa and Melewar (2011, p. 164) emphasize the sustainable dimension of these city developments: "the city design of Putrajaya is unique with its blend of Islamic and modern architecture. The street lights and the several bridges were built beyond their utilitarian purposes. Also known as the 'City in a Garden', 60 per cent of its land area is covered with greenery, open spaces and parks, and a 600 hectare man-made lake".

Even cities that have benefited from the high profile media attention associated with the hosting of the Olympic Games have gone on to further strengthen their city brands through infrastructure investment rather than relying solely on the steadily fading glow of having once been an Olympic host city. Belloso (2011) underlines how the city of Barcelona did not achieve its current strength only through hosting the 1992 Olympic Games, but also by investing in a profound transformation of the city through the creation of a new transport infrastructure, the establishment of more universities and the modernization of the public health and education systems. Apart from the Olympic Games (Schreiner and Go 2011), the other major international sporting event that cities and nations compete to host is the FIFA World Cup. As with being a former Olympic host city, being a former FIFA World Cup host city brings undeniable benefits in terms of brand awareness. But that brand strength needs to be nourished post-event. Two Asian metropolises, Seoul and Tokyo, hosted games during the 2002 tournament and have gone on to invest significantly in sustainable place branding initiatives. The city of Seoul has integrated sustainable infrastructure investment into its city branding strategy, particularly through the Han River Renaissance Project and the City Recreation Project (Kim and Kim 2011). In Tokyo, one of the most densely built up urban environments in the world, the concept of creating new green spaces has gained increasing recognition through the beneficial effects of roof gardens and vertical gardens, and recovering rivers and urban bays (Braiterman 2011).

Public infrastructure may be viewed as a key dimension of urban design, with the potential to create positive city-brand-related associations amongst residents, investors and tourists. For example, in a study of the Parque dos Nações in Lisbon, Portugal, Aelbrecht (2010) identifies spatial, social and experiential conditions that are conducive to the social interactions between people that are part of the fabric of city life. A similar emphasis on the importance of sustainable urban design is provided by Meijer *et al.* (2011), who describe the work undertaken by the Dutch Working Group on Sustainable Urban Development, a group comprising experts from the professional fields of urban design, urban planning and landscape architecture. They conclude that a new approach to urban design is required, with a focus on spatial systems within a flexible design that allows for future adjustments.

One specific aspect of urban design that has been largely overlooked by place branding researchers is the role played by lighting in an urban environment. Cities such as Curitiba in Brazil and Bogotá in Colombia have invested in improved lighting to enhance the quality of urban life in those cities. Formal recognition for cities that have integrated a creative approach to the use of lighting in the urban environment is provided by the city.people.light awards, an annual competition run in partnership by Philips and the Lighting Urban Community International Association whose aim is to demonstrate the contribution that lighting can make to the well-being of those who live in, work in or visit a city or town. The awards criteria include how a lighting project adds to the cultural and architectural heritage of a city, its night-time identity and environmental contribution.

The city of Valladolid in Spain was awarded the first prize in the 2011 competition. Rotterdam in the Netherlands came second and Kanazawa in Japan came third. Marc de Jong, CEO of the Professional Luminaires business within Philips Lighting, commended the city of Valladolid in the following terms: "Valladolid shows that lighting has become more than simply a means of ensuring security and visibility; it is now regarded as an essential part of a city's cultural identity" (www.luciassociation.org). Runner-up Rotterdam was praised for a project that transformed Atjehstraat, a previously crime-ridden street, into a rejuvenated area through innovative lighting, whilst the other runner up, Kanazawa, received recognition for its use of a lighting sequence representing the history and culture of the city. Kanazawa's lighting project not only expands the visible hours for tourism but also enhances the landscaping of tourist areas, thus contributing to the tourist economy of the city.

CONCLUSIONS

I have sought to throw light on the somewhat undervalued role that public infrastructure can play in sustainable place branding. I have attempted to demonstrate that city branding should not be conceptualized simply in terms of marketing communications, but that a deeper significance should be attached to the tangible evidence of good urban design. Improved public infrastructure guided by the principles of urban design can contribute powerfully to the achieving of city branding objectives such as attracting residents, investors and tourists. I have shown how cities as diverse as Valladolid, Riyadh and the Arnhem/Nijmegen city region have invested in improved public infrastructure in ways that should enhance their city brands as much, if not more so, than simply relying on marketing communications tools such as logos, slogans and advertising campaigns.

REFERENCES

Aelbrecht, P.S. (2010) "Rethinking urban design for a changing public life", *Journal of Place Management and Development*, 3(2): 113–29.

Arimah, B.C. (2005) "What drives infrastructure spending in cities of developing countries?", *Urban Studies*, 42(8): 1345–68.

Arts Meets Science 2012: Arnhem Nijmegen City Region Magazine (2012) "Nijmegen embraces the Waal: metamorphosis down by the river", pp. 24–6.

Ashworth, G.J. and Kavaratzis, M. (2011) "Why brand the future with the past? The roles of heritage in the construction and promotion of place brand reputations", in Go, F.M. and Govers, R. (eds), *International Place Branding Yearbook: Managing Reputational Risk*, Basingstoke: Palgrave Macmillan.

Belloso, J.C. (2011) "The city branding of barcelona: a success story", in Dinnie, K. (ed.), *City Branding: Theory and Cases*, Basingstoke: Palgrave Macmillan, pp. 118–23.

Bitner, M. (1992) "Servicescapes: the impact of physical surroundings on customers and employees", *Journal of Marketing*, 56(2): 57–71.

Boschma, R. and Fritsch, M. (2009) "Creative class and regional growth: empirical evidence from seven European Countries", *Economic Geography*, 85(4): 391–423.

Braiterman, J. (2011) "City Branding through New Green Spaces", in Dinnie, K. (ed.), *City Branding: Theory and Cases*, Basingstoke: Palgrave Macmillan, pp. 70–81.

Clegg, S.R. and Kornberger, M. (2010) "An organizational perspective on space and place branding", in Go, F.M. and Govers, R. (Eds), *International Place Branding Yearbook: Place Branding in The New Age of Innovation*, Basingstoke: Palgrave Macmillan.

Dinnie, K. (ed.) (2011) *City Branding: Theory and Cases*. Basingstoke: Palgrave Macmillan.

Go, F.M. and Govers, R. (2011) *International Place Branding Yearbook: Managing Reputational Risk*. Basingstoke: Palgrave Macmillan.

Govers, R. and Go, F.M. (2009). *Place Branding: Glocal, Virtual and Physical Identities, Constructed, Imagined and Experienced*, Basingstoke: Palgrave Macmillan.

Grossman, S.A. (2010) "Elements of public–private partnership management: examining the promise and performance criteria of Business Improvement Districts", *Journal of Town and City Management*, 1(2): 148–63.

Kim, Y.K. and Kim, P.E.-P. (2011) "Seoul city branding: the case of Seoul's international brand communication", in Dinnie, K. (ed.), *City Branding: Theory and Cases*, Basingstoke: Palgrave Macmillan, pp. 190–8.

Kotler, P. and Gertner, D. (2002) "Country as brand, product, and beyond: a place marketing and brand management perspective", *Journal of Brand Management*, 9(4): 249–61.

Maheshwari, V., Vandewalle, I. and Bamber, D. (2011) "Place branding's role in sustainable development", *Journal of Place Management and Development*, 4(2): 198–213.

Meijer, M., Adriaens, F., van der Linden, O. and Schik, W. (2011) "A next step for sustainable urban design in the Netherlands", *Cities*, 28(6): 536–44.

Morgan, M., Elbe, J. and Curiel, J.E. (2009) "Has the experience economy arrived? The views of destination managers in three visitor-dependent areas", *International Journal of Tourism Research*, 11(2): 201–16.

Musa, G. and Melewar, T.C. (2011) "Kuala Lumpur: searching for the right brand", in Dinnie, K. (ed.), *City Branding: Theory and Cases*, Basingstoke: Palgrave Macmillan, pp. 162–8.

Nair, S.K. (2011) "The City Branding of Ahmedabad". In Dinnie, K. (ed.), *City Branding: Theory and Cases*, Basingstoke: Palgrave Macmillan, pp. 106–11.

O'Shaughnessy, J. and O'Shaughnessy, N.J. (2000) "Treating the nation as a brand: some neglected issues", *Journal of Macromarketing*, 20(1): 56–64.

Parjanen, S., Harmaakorpi, V. and Kari, K. (2011). "The aesthetics challenge", in Morgan, N. Pritchard, A. and Pride, R. (eds), *Destination Brands: Managing Place Reputation*, 3rd edn, Oxford: Elsevier, pp. 117–28.

Pine, B.J. and Gilmore, J.H. (1999) *The Experience Economy: Work is Theatre and Every Business Is a Stage*, Boston, MA: HBS Press.

Raban, J. (2008) *Soft City*, London: Picador. [First published 1974 by Hamish Hamilton.]

Schreiner, W. and Go, F.M. (2011) "Blessing or Burden: Do Major Sports Events Hosted by Developing Countries Have an Impact on Reputation? A Case Study of the 2010 FIFA World Cup in South Africa", in Go, F.M. and Govers, R. (eds), *International Place Branding Yearbook 2011*, Basingstoke: Palgrave Macmillan, pp. 133–46.

Spio, A.E. (2011) "The city branding of Accra", in Dinnie, K. (ed.), *City Branding: Theory and Cases*, Basingstoke: Palgrave Macmillan, pp. 99–105.

CONCLUSION

Frank M. Go and Robert Govers

In 2009, in order to understand the paradoxes, find answers to place brand puzzles and search for a paradigm, we embarked on a journey together with a set of contributors. They gracefully accepted our invitation to explore how "disruptive innovation", reputation and sustainability are likely to cause both the deconstruction and the construction of the place branding process. Their ideas have been captured in the three volumes of this Yearbook series so far. The premise was that place brand managers require a more sophisticated grasp of how to grow, collectively, potential innovation through smart "coordination" of government, market and civil society to achieve a balanced-centric performance in terms of equity, efficiency and effectiveness (see Figure C.1). In an attempt to reflect the current status, we will conclude this series with three debates and a brief research agenda, linking effectiveness/reputation/consumption, efficiency/innovation/production and equity/sustainability/critical studies.

THREE MAIN DEBATES

The purpose of the following sections is to review three scientific and societal debates that hang over branding in the spatial context, including the questioning of its usefulness and viability. These are captured under three headings: consumption, production and critical studies (Lucarelli and Berg 2011, p. 22).

Consumption

The exponential scaling of cities implies the expansion of wealth and by extension consumption in urban areas. Brands and branding are inextricably and geographically entangled in terms of "their value and meaning in material, discursive and symbolic ways" (Pike 2009, p. 628) amongst others through spatial circuits of consumption around which the first debate revolves, one of the most important characteristics being the complex relationship between demand and supply based on the dynamics of consumers' perceptions, values, attitudes and expectations. Accordingly participation in consumption is subject to cultural filters, which may change over time,

FIGURE C.1 | **Model of balanced centricity as a priority for future place branding**

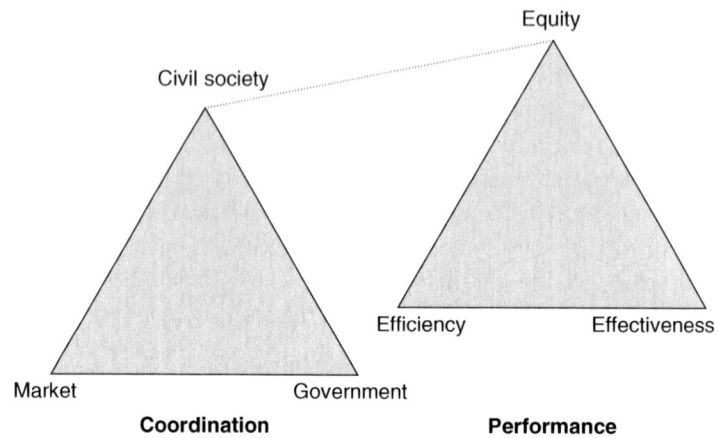

Source: Authors' model based on art of triangle management model by Van Tulder (1999, p. 25).

and to the evolution of marketing, as Vargo and Lusch (2004, p. 3) have written. In terms of the marketing paradigm, consumption is considered an exploitative process. There exists a wide range of actors in transition whose knowledge, attitudes, structures and practices represent different degrees of understanding and sophistication about place marketing and branding. In the multitude of topics the former and latter can become easily overwhelming in terms of topics, concepts, theories and examples. Hence the need is to present the material so that decision-makers can apply the concepts that are relevant to place-specific issues that clarify in what stage in the life cycle the territory operates and comprehend the concomitant challenges this unleashes and where they are going in the formation and advancing of place branding.

The overview presented by Vargo and Lusch (ibid.) summarizes the evolution of distinct stages. Actors who discover that their territory has attractive characteristics typically increase the availability in a specific location, resulting eventually in a boom and maximum exploitation, which renders the resource/product less attractive and valuable in time, which, in turn, leads to decline. This approach to place marketing resembles the features noticeable in the classical and neo-classical economics school (1800–1920) – based on a regime of adding utility-value and value-in-exchange through manufactured, standardized output – and the views of the school of early and formative marketing theory (1900–50), which held that transaction output and institutional marketing performance "provided time and place utility" (ibid.). Both these were anchored in knowledge from an objectivist epistemology view which assumed that it is possible to develop the "knowledge is truth" perspective (McAdam and McCreedy 2000), i.e. the notion that knowledge is derived from intellectual knowledge consistent across cultures and time. Consequent to the conditions of conspicuous consumption, the marketing management school of thought (1950–80) developed the philosophy that "customers do not buy things but need or want fulfillment". Accordingly, marketing involves consumption. However, "value is determined in the marketplace and such 'embedded value' must therefore have usefulness" (ibid.), resulting in a differential competitive advantage. This view recognizes that knowledge is, in part, socially constructed.

From 1980 onwards a defining shift took place in the paradigm of marketing as a continuous economic and social process, which Vargo and Lusch coined as the service dominant (S-D) logic (2004). Instead of regarding knowledge as a discrete object, Vargo and Lusch (2006) refer to S-D logic as knowledge from the practice-based epistemology characterized by the following. First, it emphasizes "service" (singular) to connote a process aimed at thinking and doing something for someone (p. 282). Second, it considers the relationship between service and good, beyond their binary relationship. Third, it seeks "resource integration for all economic entities" (p. 284). Fourth, it aims for the co-creation of value as distinguished from co-production (p. 284). Fifth, networks and the interaction between actors (Suchman 2003) play a key role in value creation exchange (p. 284). Finally, but not least, it holds that the "market place can falsify market hypotheses" (Vargo and Lusch 2004, p. 3), i.e. render knowledge contestable. By extension, it challenges claims that, for example, a marketing campaign could effectively build place brand image (Govers 2011, p. 228) and reinforces the notion that the practice-based perspective of knowledge is actually embodied in people, culturally embedded and socially constructed. Considerations of the contestable nature of knowledge is most relevant to place branding because, first, humans typically need to make inferences and judgments, due to the characteristics of the place brand, notably inseparability, ambiguity and variety. Second, it gives entities affordance "to learn about their actions and find ways to better serve their customers and to improve financial performance" (Vargo and Lusch 2004, p. 3).

Footloose industries and a low degree of dependency on local resources lend credence to the argument that cities "only exist when they have an audience" (Boisen *et al.* 2011, p. 135). Moreover, it resonates with the marketing approach, which turns our attention toward the issue of who the specific place users are. Kotler *et al.* (1999) listed four categories: (i) visitors, (ii) residents and employees, (iii) businesses and (iv) industry; to which Van den Berg *et al.* (2005) added a fifth category: export markets and investors. These stakeholders play different roles, have different backgrounds and contrasting agendas. In order to establish critical mass one needs to map their divergent mental pictures and subsequently bring about a measure of accommodation between the actors concerned in order to bridge the three gaps in the branding model (Govers and Go 2009, p. 41).

Mental world of brands

A more empirical stream of analysis in the consumer research tradition has focused on image perception, projection and choice modeling (Govers and Go 2009). In particular, the "mental world of brands" of Franzen and Bouwman (2001) conveys how brand images involve the human mind and memory. Brand image is defined as "perceptions about a brand as reflected by the brand associations held in memory" (Keller 1993, p. 3; Gwinner 1997; Gwinner and Eaton 1999). Brand associations can be derived from a variety of sources, including product use, place consumption or information derived from other sources (e.g. advertising, packaging, word-of-mouth). Relevant for place branding is how brands become associated through sponsorship activities of special events (Keller 1993). More specifically, selected value-associations linked with the 2012 London Olympics may get linked, subsequently, with sponsorship brands in the consumers' memory (Gwinner 1997). Value-associations refer to the psychological and social value that brands may have to consumers. This can be either emotional value or self-expressive value. Consumers may derive certain emotional benefits from value-associations, e.g. linked to the unique and favorable feelings of attending the 2012 London Olympics, which may enhance the potential for brand image transfer (Gwinner 1997; Smith 2004). Laden with positive attributes and value-associations, such as favorability, uniqueness and strength, brands are typically perceived as rendering high quality and receive high consumer scores and therefore of great interest to corporate sponsors.

Keller (1993) indicates that brand knowledge is an important variable influencing the brand image transfer process. In sponsorship, brand knowledge is defined as the brand associations about the sponsor in relation to the sponsored entity that consumers hold in their memory. Brand knowledge consists of brand recall and brand recognition. Brand recall is "the ability to name (typically unprompted) the brands involved in a given sponsorship" (Smith 2004, p. 463) and an often-used mode to find out how successful the sponsoring of a particular event has been. Put differently, the more respondents recall a particular sponsor of a significant special event, the more successful the latter would consider its sponsorship. For instance, a study of the 1992 Olympics revealed that 88 percent of the respondents recalled at least one out of four commercials presented by a specific sponsor (Stipp and Schiavone 1996). This evidence serves to strengthen sponsors' perceptions that the Olympics afford a lever to establishing potential brand recall among a multi-billion global television audience. The economic value of an event like the Olympics is typically predicated on the media attention that the event obtains (Mules and Faulkner 1996). While the effects of an event's image on a destination's image have not been demonstrated convincingly, evidence from the sponsorship literature suggests that the strongest benefits to brand image will accrue when consumers perceive a meaningful match between the image and the event and that of a destination (Gwinner and Eaton 1999). This implies the need to specify what is meant by match-up and "what constitutes an appropriate basis for selecting and using events to obtain a desired effect on the destination's image? (Brown *et al.* 2004, p. 284). As consumers' knowledge of brands involves associative networks that have been found to be relevant descriptors of brand image (Keller 1993) the pairing of two brands images into the image of one brand can strengthen its association set sharing "common elements with the association set of the brand with which it is paired" (Gwinner and Eaton 1999, cited by Brown *et al.* 2004, p. 284). Also, evidence presented by Peracchio and Tybout (1996) and Gwinner and Eaton (1999) suggests that consumers with strong psychological schematas, such as elaborate amounts of interconnected product knowledge, are likely to be less impacted on by the inconsistencies in communication compared to consumers who possess weak psychological schematas. Whereas the Olympic Rings stand as symbols of hope of global cooperation, international understanding and the bonding of individuals through the medium of sports, there is no guarantee of the symbolic image transfer to the host country. For example, China recognized the reputational risks associated with the 2008 Games and dedicated a security budget that reportedly exceeded US$1 billion. The news items which affected the reputation of China and the Chinese people based on the Olympics, included in particular the images of the 2008 earthquake in Sichuan, footage of victims trapped under buildings and news that 86 giant pandas were safe, have been captured in minute-by-minute updates by government-owned media. The *China Daily*, the biggest Chinese, English-language newspaper, confronted a vice minister over school collapses and got a straight answer. Such candor and access contrasts with China's media lockdown during the 2008 Tibetan riots. What has been the media impact in the post-Beijing 2008 Olympics era on the host country? The main contribution, conclude Zeng *et al.* (2011), has been an enhancement of the understanding about China on a worldwide scale. But the breadth and attribution of China's image appears to have remained relatively stable. Therefore, it cannot be concluded that the 2008 Olympics improved China's telecast national image, directly. However, indirectly the international media have raised interest in the host country. Particularly it has helped to define China's telecast national image more clearly than before.

While the presentation of place associations from the past can be tangled up in a branding narrative, it is the human memory that must interact and recall brands. Put differently the conception of brand value capturing becomes increasingly a multilayered driven process, involving three overlapping relationships. In turn, these require a regime of coordination aimed at converging the agendas of the established hierarchical and national/local government (laws and control), the civil society (voice and collective action) and market (rivalry and prices). These should result in, first, network processes "as the simultaneous co-existence of social interrelations and interactions at all spatial scales from the most local level to the global" (Massey 1993, p. 155); second, "value and meaning of brands occur[ring] in material, discursive and symbolic ways throughout spatial circuits" (Pike 2009, p. 628) of consumption and regulation, amongst others; third, the raising of the question: how can we make sense of the demands of smart growth branding in the complex and ever-changing world in which we perform? The logic and mechanisms that drive sustainable development can be considered a stage-by-stage process in which operators learn and understand that brands can endanger a destination's cultural, social and natural capital through inappropriate commodification, but that they can also help protect it by building incentives" (Stronza 2001, cited in Gnoth 2007, p. 345). Therefore, in Gnoth's terms, decision-makers should consider that:

> Processes of commodification are punctuated by a series of crises that trigger responses that move the destination forward. The triggering mechanism is often the tensions between the scaling of tourism which requires the physical growth of the destination and a subsequent loss of meaning and the alienation of people from their cultural symbols, including the damage to the destination brand as a publicly owned asset. (2007, p. 354)

However, destination marketers and package tour operators are typically more interested in satisfying tourists. They are therefore keen to understand consumer needs, attitudes, interests and behavior as their starting point and less interested in arguments as to why the publicly owned assets of the destination brand matter to their own business growth. Theories of

Conclusion

marketing must be supported by scientific evidence, and for this purpose Gertner performed a meta-analysis to "unfold and configure the literature on 'place marketing' and 'place branding' published in the last two decades" (2011, p. 92), though the author found it impossible to conduct such an investigation because the "scarcity of empirical as well as the fragmentation literature engages with topics investigated, impedes the development of a meta-analysis of multiple studies dealing with a set of related research hypotheses and their combined results, our original goal" (ibid., p. 100). But doesn't his study try to compare studies involving a "place marketing" approach, which (should) differ in content and construct from "place branding"? The former takes an "outside-in", comparative, relatively static approach and the geographical and historic context as a given. This leads to ignoring the potential relevance of: first, the "selective nature of place branding and the layering of spatial identities" (Boison et al. 2011); second, the need for unraveling the place branding field from place marketing as distinct domains in order to create an effective overarching place competitive identity (Govers 2011, p. 227); third, the need to identify the significant structural functional barriers that follow on from the previous points that one would typically expect to encounter in the place brand implementation stage in particular, e.g. the integration of stakeholders. The assumption is that integration depends on a durable model, but regimes of rivalry and flexibility contest this. For example, Anderson (2009) chronicles how increasingly businesses profit by giving something for nothing as a mechanism to compete. And Kelly (1997) refers to the new rules in the economy as drivers of flexibility. Their perspectives are corroborated by integrated marketing communications (IMC) theory. While the issues surrounding IMC are aimed at creating and maintaining brands, these ultimately failed, because its procedures were ill-equipped to overcome significant structural functional barriers which contributed importantly to the rapidly decreasing effectiveness of IMCs (Percy 1997). Therefore, we have tried to argue that taking an interactive, multilayered approach in the context of complex networks (Go and Govers 2010, p. xxix) should be more appropriate for managing place branding and yielding co-creative value propositions.

Muniz and Schau (2007, cited by Chandler and Vargo 2011, p. 37) portray knowledge as a resource derivative "through networks that center on a brand in communities". Similarly, changing contextual challenges are broadening the body of knowledge, including consumer relationships within geographical network perspectives. These network relations are significant because most economic activity occurs in cities, particularly through goods and service consumption, and they contain associations about places, products, artifacts or other people as encoded in psychological schemata (Atkinson *et al.* 1987, cited by Govers 2011, p. 229). Moreover, many of today's urban consumers often have personal relationships to brands. Therefore the "object of the brand and the process of branding are geographical in at least three ways" (Pike 2009, pp. 619–20):

> first, brands are entangled in inescapable spatial associations … Second, branded objects and branding processes are themselves geographically differentiated and uneven in, for example, their manifestation, representation, visibility, fixity and mobility throughout the spaces, places and temporalities of economy, society, culture and polity … Third, the entanglements of brands and branding are not only geographically differentiated in their own right but they intertwine with spatially uneven development because their underlying dynamic of differentiation is predicated on the search for, exploitation and reproduction of economic and social inequalities over space and through time.

Hallworth and Evans (2008 p. 209) provide competing explanations for brand underperformance and causal factors for economic underperformance. While brand strategies have been popularly touted as fundamental to success in the context of a fragmented world, relatively little attention has been paid in the brand literature to the argumentation based on the direction of causality (Fan 2006). More specifically, what evidence-based research exists which proves that a strong place brand derives from the competitive advantage consequent to systematic economic growth or, reversely, to an effective branding process? In this context Fan's argument (2006, pp. 12–13) is especially relevant to ours and therefore follows verbatim below:

> Nation branding should be distinguished from nation brand as there is not necessarily a direct link between the two. A nation's "brand" exists with or without any conscious efforts in nation branding, as each country has a current image to its international audience, be it strong or weak, clear or vague. In theory nation branding could help a nation to improve its image; in reality there are many other factors that affect the image and perception of the country, resulting in only a marginal role for nation branding. Anholt (2002) calls for the poor countries in the Third World to use nation branding in developing their economies, but they first have to find or make something to sell: a product or service which is competitive in the marketplace. To achieve this, they need investment, technology and know-how far more than they need nation branding. Without a good product, branding would work to no avail. There is rather a chicken-and-egg situation here. How can nation branding help a country's image building if it is plagued by war, poverty, crime or terrorism? The image problem of a

nation or place is often the reflection of some more serious political and socio-economic troubles in that area. Facial make-up will not help a cancer patient feel healthy.

Brand knowledge as creative resource

More recently conceptual transitions have led to the S-D logic lexicon in association with the goods-dominant logic (Vargo and Lusch 2006, p. 286). Experiences, value-creation networks and co-creation are part of this new lexicon. In turn, the latter has become visible in the literature, amongst others, in the category of event-marketing, in particular as a new breed of communication strategy, involving target audiences as active participants and an instrument to boost brand performance. Whelan and Wohlfeil (2006) suggest that event-marketing facilitates customer engagement with the brand through informal dialogs and personal first-hand brand experiences. Experiential brand interaction between internal and external brand representatives can sustain consumer brand relationships, as they co-produce added value. Such relationships are built on trust and an emotional bond between the brand and the consumer, facilitated through brand values (ibid.). Their observations resonate with Fyrberg and Juriado (2009, p. 506) who demonstrate the importance of interaction between brands and network actors as integrators within S-D logic. Following Vargo (2009), Warnaby (2009, p. 418) elaborated the applications of the foundational premises of S-D logic in the place marketing context and suggests that place branding may provide some development of S-D logic in the literature (Brodie *et al.* 2006).

Zimmerman (1972) indicates that "brand knowledge is a creative resource that evolves in response to the behaviors of actors". Together, actors that maintain favorable, strong and unique brand associations expand the potential of brand knowledge as a resource. For most actors, brand knowledge is a resource that cannot be controlled because it is neither owned nor is it unilaterally controlled. As a resource, brand knowledge can provide, among other things, benefits such as product familiarity, uncertainty reduction or higher price premiums (for firms) (Zimmerman 1951, cited in Chandler and Vargo 2011, p. 37). Accordingly, in a knowledge-based economy the concepts of "contextualization and value-in context" (Chandler and Vargo 2011, p. 35) play an increasingly important role on the branding research agenda. Vargo and Lusch (2008) elaborated on how to derive a user-centric classification of organizational operant resources – resources that are the fundamental source of competitive advantage in that they represent the comparative ability to cause the desired change that drives competition.

Foundational premises of service dominant logic

The above observations and terms suggest that, rather than using a supply or demand perspective, we look at the broader, multilayered context in which place branding is embedded through the lens of the value creating networks. Against the backdrop of the ubiquity of information and communication technologies (ICTs) place brands can be positioned on the decentralization continuum with regard to the extent that their stakeholders feel informed, networked, empowered and participative (Prahalad and Ramaswamy 2004) in making decisions that matter to them, with a speed and intensity which are likely to undermine place brands that remain hierarchically organized. Warnaby (2009) suggests that the knowledge domain lacks a traditional theory to accommodate the "context specificity of places", which can be widened and deepened by way of the emerging S-D logic of marketing (Vargo and Lusch 2008, p. 7), composed of ten foundational premises (FPs) as follows:

FP1 Service is the fundamental basis of exchange.

FP2 Indirect exchange masks the fundamental basis of exchange.

FP3 Goods are distribution mechanisms for service provision.

FP4 Operant resources are the fundamental source of competitive advantage.

FP5 All economies are service economies.

FP6 The customer is always a co-creator of value.

FP7 The enterprise cannot deliver value, but only offer value propositions.

FP8 A service-centered view is inherently customer orientated and relational.

FP9 All social and economic actors are resource integrators.

FP10 Value is always uniquely and phenomenologically determined by the beneficiary.

The above terms and definitions can be elaborated by the foundational premises of the S-D logic, thereby providing a rethinking of the role of place branding and developing a new lexicon in support of levering the dynamics of social and economic actors as resource integrators. With the idea in mind that value is unique and determined phenomenologically by the beneficiary (FP10) we argue that the S-D logic can be applied to catalyze, manage and monitor change within a framework that both "hard" scientists and "soft" social scientists are prepared to access in their role as social and economic actors and resource integrators (FP9) to build a service centered theoretical framework (FP8) for developing smart growth place branding aimed at attaining sustainability.

Production

The second major debate has focused on the aspect of competitive identity of place and brand building equity, including name awareness, image and loyalty, derived from an overarching strategy and policy, which is supply driven, as opposed to demand driven (Govers 2011, p. 230). While globalization is both creating and undermining the construction of place, "here" and "there" remain central elements of the human condition. Therefore, what occurs in space production as seen through the Lefebvrian (1991) lens impacts on the social construction of place, its local population, culture, heritage, etc. In turn, this "inside-in" perspective to questions of place branding production under conditions of internationalization is affected by the need to formulate "inside-out" policies and strategies by various stakeholders, including government, local policy-makers, professionals and consultants, and the private sector. Against this backdrop, a first approach to building the actors' bargaining power or the requisite capability for influencing the rules of rivalry is that of Ruigrok and Tulder (1995), which is most relevant to place branding strategy. These authors refer to the framework of "industrial complexes", which they coin the "centers of gravity". Also, they point to Piore and Sabel's (1984) important contribution to the debate on the restructuring of production through their argument that the expansion of flexible specialization networks of interdependent smaller firms, for example in the Italian region of Emelía-Romagna, could serve as a best practice model to other industries and countries. Following this logic, other researchers such as Askegaard and Kjeldgaard (2007, p. 138) contend that flexible networks would contribute to "creating sustainable small scale production and consumption relations" beyond standardized Fordist production, and that "branding may have become the dominant production of culture in a globalizing cultural economy" (ibid., p. 146). As place brands and the place branding process develop they tend to evolve gradually from a quasi-stable condition through an interval of accelerated transition to re-emerge in a new state with qualitatively different features (Martens and Rotmans 2001, cited by Raskin *et al.* 2002).

Why place branding nurtures the wealth of nations

A second body of literature addresses the economist's perspective. Porter's (1998) view on the clusters and the new economics of competition has been much cited, but to what extent is his argument sound? In order to find out, we refer in this section to Glaeser and his colleagues (1992). They used data on employment growth between 1956 and 1987 for the six most important industries in 170 metropolitan areas in the United States to test three theories of what they called "dynamic externalities". The externalities were basically knowledge spillovers from one person or group to another, and the theories were different views about the institutional structure that best facilitated the spillovers. More rapid employment growth would occur in cities with the best institutional structure for growth. Nowlan (1997, pp. 111–13) chronicled their main findings as follows:

> One theory was that of Michael Porter, whose book on *The Competitive Advantage of Nations* had been published in 1990. Porter's research suggested that competitive firms within a concentrated single-industry cluster provided the best structure for successful growth.
>
> Another theory was associated with several economists from Alfred Marshall, a turn-of-the century Cambridge (UK) economist through Harvard's Kenneth Arrow to Paul Romer, the MAR theory. This theory, like Porter's, was that single-industry clusters were most conducive to the spread of knowledge but that the incentives to produce knowledge were less among competitive firms than among monopolists or near-monopolists. New knowledge is costly to create and competitive firms can't as easily hang on to the benefits as monopolists, so they don't as easily hang on to the benefits as monopolists, so they don't as readily incur the costs of research.
>
> The third theory that Glaeser et al. tested was that of Jane Jacobs. This was that new ideas and knowledge spread about most readily in cities with competitive, not monopolistic, businesses and with a diversity of business. Unlike Porter and MAR, diversity not single-industry clusters was important. The results of the study were that competition was more conducive to growth than monopoly and that a diverse city economy is better than one with a concentration of a few industries. The evidence is thus negative on MAR, mixed on Porter, and consistent with Jacobs. (Glaeser et al. 1992)

So the evidence rules in favor of Jacobs (1984). By extending her thoughts to Fan's critique (2006) the following question, especially relevant in times of constraints, emerges: Shouldn't the center of gravity of investment in branding migrate from the national scale toward the urban scale? In this way the knowledge of the place branding process can become understood, theoretically, as a more place-selective entity. In turn, this would give affordance to connecting the characteristics of knowledge from a practice-based epistemology, i.e. linking knowledge embedded in practice – culturally embedded and socially constructed – with explicit knowledge.

These dimensions converge in Jacobs's observations about the economies of cities that have been embraced in the "new growth" theory. In summary, Jane Jacobs's perspective relates to transforming imports through a variety of material socioeconomic and symbolic interventions to exports, which finance more imports. The practice-based epistemology of knowledge, culturally embedded and socially constructed, are characteristics relevant for place branding. In turn, these coincide with Anholt's (2002, p. 235) view, albeit beyond the urban scale, that "culture plays an essential role in the process of enriching a country's brand image, in driving the process from the initial shorthand of media communications towards a fuller and more durable understanding of the country and its values".

Images of organizations

A third body of literature addressed strategic theory underpinning our understanding of issues, in particular the contextual challenges the place branding process faces. The disruptive context has brought about imbalances which can be understood by the application of framing, if governments and corporations demonstrate the capability "to achieve recurrent purposeful emergence". Thereby, Normann distinguishes three possible levels of *outcome*: "adaptation and correction, i.e. continuous improvement within a frame breaking reconfiguration, structural change of the business to match paradigmatic change in the environment, and recurrent purposeful emergence or the capacity and preparedness to achieve frame-breaking reconfiguration when required" (Normann 2001, p. 241).

Amid Mintzberg's eloquent contributions to the strategic literature is the construct of configuration theory. This aspect is highly relevant to place branding because value creation takes place in networks, which in turn are situated in a constellation (Normann and Ramirez 1993). Configuration theory examines how network members use interrelated variables, rather than a single organizational attribute (such as location or genre), for "getting it all together" and subsequently "follow a path to success" (Mintzberg 1989, p. 95). Following Mintzberg, we define configuration "as a system in which it makes sense to refer to a network of interrelationships" (ibid., p. 96), due to its central role in interaction in value creation and exchange (Lusch and Vargo 2006, p. 285). Transportation and information technologies have created new spaces that trigger our senses, such as TV channels, the internet and simulated environments. From the audience perspective these different spaces have become interwoven in intricate patterns that afford individuals an inclusion in multiple worlds. For instance, people travel while phoning home and watching a billboard movie clip (Go and Van Fenema 2006) that, for example, is promoting the Olympics. In the multilevel, multi-actor context of the summer and winter Olympics, and their accompanying infrastructures designed for mass televised audiences and the consumption by stadium and television spectators, configuration theory presents a lever to understand complex interfacing of hard (infrastructural, facilities) and soft (mental, symbolic functions). In turn, such understanding can be used for mapping the relationship between the event and spectators, particularly in terms of how images associated with the Olympics can be transferred, possibly strengthened, enhanced or changed to the benefit of the host city (Brown et al. 2004, p. 279). In turn, configuration theory raises a two-pronged issue: first, to what extent do organizers opt for a basic form of organization drawing only on a single attribute in a Darwinian-like response to intense competition for audiences, which is part and parcel of the mega-event market? Second, to what extent are mega-event organizers drawn "toward configuration in order to achieve consistency in their internal characteristics to create synergy" in the host place branding process and "to establish a fit with their external contexts" (Mintzberg 1989, p. 96)?

From the sociological perspective Molotch (1976) conceives both mega-events and their accompanying infrastructures metaphorically as elements of the "growth machine" for economic investment and urban/regional regeneration, whether as prestige projects or localized anchor projects, possibly tied to shopping malls or sport parks. Such projects often leave legacies behind in the form of parks, sport facilities, student housing and public transport improvement. Also, they provide satisfaction for participants (competition, pride), standing organization (image), traders (turnover), host country (status), governments (tax revenues) and the event managers and staff (satisfaction, prestige and income). Intimately linked to transnational capital flows as opposed to community relations, mega-events such as the Olympics and the Tour de France built substantially on protocols, organizational procedures and routines in order to mitigate the risk of dependencies on the host city's organization, facilitative infrastructure and the logistics supporting the event. The local circumstances can strongly influence the image of events, thereby impacting not only on the event branding but also on the special event image being transferred onto the place brand.

From an organizational change perspective Gareth Morgan (1986) advocates that every user has an implicit picture of an organization or a mental brand image of what it is like. His "images of organization" framework of metaphors suggests that an organization can be seen differently by different people, but also can be seen in different ways by any one person. If multiple images are used of, for example, a city, much greater understanding may be gained from the psychological schematas of stakeholders and users alike, which would have great utility, because cities are many things at once. Accordingly, such multiple images may reveal new ways of seeing (Morgan 1986), e.g. place brand images that prior to investigation may not have been apparent. Morgan generated eight possible images of organizations: (1) machines; (2) living organisms; (3) brains; (4) cultures; (5) political systems; (6) psychic prisons; (7) systems in flux and transformation; and (8) instruments of domination. These images provide potentially fresh perspectives that can aid decision-makers to make sense of where they are in the place branding process and the limitations of their place brand knowledge vis-à-vis the surrounding world.

Critical Studies

In the avalanche of literature of critical perspectives, the third major debate has been drowned out to a significant extent. Our aspiration here is to pay heed to this observation by examining place branding from a critical perspective, based on academic arguments. For example, Wilkinson and Pickett (2010, p. 219) claim, consistent with the "anti-growth" camp view, "that there are ways of improving the quality of life in rich countries without further economic growth". However, their (2010, p. 275) views have attracted both thoughtful criticism and strident political attacks from the "pro-growth" camp. This dichotomy adds to the differing objectives a cast of actors in different roles, from different backgrounds and often with contrasting agendas, which renders smart growth place branding a controversial value proposition.

Why look at claims about ethics of place branding?

In 1962 Rachel Carson's *Silent Spring* helped to ignite the start of the worldwide sustainability movement. Since the World Commission on Environment and Development conceptualized the notion of "environmental sustainability" in 1987, lots of attention has been given to the concept by the media, policy-makers, politicians, business managers, activists and the public at large (Goodland 1995). Sustainability's triple bottom line, economic, environmental and social, engulfs many aspects of current branding concerns. Government legislation, consumer demands for sustainable products and services have moved businesses, professional associations and local authorities "to develop codes of ethical conduct" and address the undesirable consequences of place branding, including "social inequality and environmental damage" (Insch 2011, p. 151). Looking at claims about ethics and related codes of conduct is justified because such research perspectives have the potential to advance our knowledge of place branding, which is inseparable from practice. In turn, the latter affects directly or indirectly the everyday of urban users and can potentially aid in guiding their sustainable behavior. The issues of sustainability and place brand presentation have so far been developed largely in isolation from one another, resulting in binary responses to the process of economic restructuring that affects trade transactions, technology transfer and capital flows. These are symptomatic of the intensification of competition, whereas in the context of supranational governance and consequent multilayered interaction, place branding poses many challenges for the analysis of multi-stakeholder collaboration.

Who are we? Redrawing borders and national identity

Recent developments in the "New World Order" have challenged the established national borders (Castells 1993). As Anderson (1996) indicates, borders are both institutions and process markers and agents of identity. National identity is a fundamental force and remains the bedrock of many political, economic and social activities. The ambivalence in the "borderless" European Union (EU) demonstrates ambiguous identities because economic, cultural and linguistic factors pull citizens in different directions.

This is also true politically as they may display only a weak identification with Europe and its supranational institutions. At the supranational scale recent policy formation has focused on the EU proposition to understand smart and inclusive growth. While one may agree or not with this "smart growth" policy or question the required investment vis-à-vis the advantages it touches on, the realm of place branding practice therefore should not be ignored by researchers. The EU proposition can be broken down into three crucial dimensions. First, the EU's Europe 2020 growth strategy indicates that there is a *process* at play. Whether seen as formal or informal, rational or irrational, this process proceeds through a number of stages and is driven by a myriad of factors, including demand, supply and capability. These stages impact, directly or indirectly, on the place branding decision-making process.

Second, the EU smart specialization strategies aim at ensuring that "research and innovation resources reach a critical mass and are supported by targeted interventions in human resources, knowledge infrastructures and suitable conditions for business" (EU Regional Policy for Smart Growth in Europe 2020). The same also indicates the intention for developing policy to suit a place-specific *context*.

Third, the idea that three mutually reinforcing priorities should help EU member states to deliver high levels of employment, productivity and social cohesion signal that place branding and its related efforts should result in a concrete *output*.

Conclusion

Governance designed to activate co-decisional processes can help establish a delicate balance between stakeholders (Hatch and Schultz 2010, cited by Go and Govers 2011, p. xxv). It allows stakeholders to advance their understanding both in terms of the process and areas of potential conflict so as to establish the critical mass needed for smart growth place branding. In essence, a sense of purpose represents a vital source and positioning of the smart growth brand in a manner which addresses issues that matter to stakeholders and will go quite some way to getting them to participate in the decision-making process. How can stakeholders understand their surrounding world? Following Shaw and McCombs (1977) the mass media appear stunningly successful in telling them what to think about. It is, therefore, relevant to understand how media coverage impacts on stakeholders, particularly in terms of how they mentally order and organize their world. Holt (2002, pp. 70, 72) coveys how the "modern cultural engineering paradigm premised upon a consumer culture … granted marketers cultural authority … consumers are beginning to break down marketers' dominance by seeking out social spaces in which they produce their own culture, apart from that which is foisted on them by the market [allowing] people to continually rework their identities, rather than let the market dictate identities for them". This shows that the nation and its traditions and big business are often popularly perceived in isolation from one another. But underneath the veneer the branding techniques that commercial and territorial actors apply are not quite as separate or different as they appear at first sight. For example, Hansen and Machin (2008, p. 792) found that "Getty's images are designed in the first place to foster greater consumption of products and services" as opposed to fostering a cultural paradigm of branding designed to influence and guide sustainable behavior.

This illustration opens up several lines of thought regarding the relationships of the codes of ethical conduct in pursuit of sustainability and business, politics and consumers. Nicholas Ind (2004) suggests that businesses account for 51 of the largest 100 economic entities in the world and therefore branding should have a wider social perspective in order to sustain its continued relevance. In *Living the Brand* Ind points to two main living brand characteristics. These are operating with openness and integrity. In turn, these can be assessed by answering a set of criteria posed in the form of questions. First, does branding ignite people's passions (both stakeholders and customers)? Second, does it focus on relevant issues? Third, does it deliver on the promise? Fourth, does it contribute to people's happiness? Fifth, does it contribute to cultivating happiness in organizations? Finally, does it create a sense of community? At the political scale, governments' attempts consciously to "shape a specifically-designed place identity and promote it to identified markets, whether external or internal, has been a prevailing trend" as "old as civic government itself" (Kavaratzis and Ashworth 2005, p. 506).

Global flows, their propensity to impact on interconnectedness, and the characteristics of process, growth and mobility have all intensified. Yesteryear's structures have turned into processes, as opposed to solid systems with government mandates. Instead, in the "New World Order" wealth is gained from experiments with the cycle of creative destruction (Schumpeter 1980 [1934]). As we saw earlier, knowledge networks comprise network nodes of business, government or organized civil society groups, and individuals pursue value-in-context. Typically, they would use the success criteria of provenance associations as core value propositions to enable them to configure the potential place umbrella brand values themselves (Iversen and Hem 2008). In light of this it is relevant to observe that multi-stakeholders from a wide range of backgrounds, and backgrounds often with conflicting agendas, often constrain the coordination regime, thereby frustrating local public, private and nonprofit sector collaboration on developmental issues which is a prerequisite to achieving mutually beneficial smart growth outcomes. Eshuis and Edelenbos (2009, p. 272) highlight the significance of these common powers in the context of urban/regional regeneration and branding as follows: "a brand tends to receive more support if it is a result of co-production by the stakeholders involved". Holt's (2002) dialectical theory of consumer culture and branding resonate with Gnoth (2007, p. 13), who views destinations as open systems evolving as living entities. He goes on to say that "commoditizing a destination's cultural, social and natural values" harbors both difficulties and dangers. He writes:

> place branding can assist in utilizing and managing a destination's attractions to its advantage, both commercially and with the aim of sustainability. By having developed a model that makes the value system that constitutes place central and transparent to a branding approach, and by systematically seeking to reflect that system in the destination brand, tourism operators receive an incentive that can benefit themselves as well as the destination in its development. The open system of place, its historicity and evolving rather than managed or manufactured reality explains the absence of clear owners of destination brands. By linking the success of destination development to its capital base, tourism operators and researchers have the opportunity knowledge of creating new approaches to effective sustainable development.

The knowledge derived from a value system can be characterized as socially constructed, embedded in place branding practice and multi-dimensional, i.e. the tacit and explicit knowledge of business, civil society and government are inseparable and needed for improving place brand performance. Pike observes (2009, p. 621) that "the spatial and multifaceted nature of brands, for example, makes them simultaneously 'economic' as goods and services in markets, 'social' as collectively produced, circulated and consumed objects, 'cultural' as entities providing meanings and identities, and 'political' as regulated intellectual properties, financial assets and traded commodities". These ideas provide an appropriate illustration as how to consider multiple dynamics that can result in contestable knowledge which may feed contradictions among stakeholders closely linked in remit to the pursuit of place branding decision-making.

Place brands and space: a reciprocal relationship

Following on from Andy Pike (2009) we assume that "brands mutually constitute and shape each other" at the economic scale through the consumption of market commodities and, simultaneously, through the social construction of knowledge. As such knowledge circulates and configures a constellation for considering a path of "smart growth" in the place branding context, the question is immediately raised: What arguments would provide justifications to opt for "smart growth" branding?

The received answers are derived from different disciplines and practices. From both a marketing perspective and brand perspective, the overarching justification is user-centric (including consumers and citizens). Their participation would be subject to understanding the value derived from smart place brand offerings. This raises another query of import: Why would urban users contribute to smart growth policy? This question can be answered in a pragmatic way (e.g. the pursuit of "saving valuable time" or reduced bureaucracy-induced aggravation) and an aesthetic way (e.g. "keeping the city beautiful and livable"). The former motivated Miller and Hoel (2002, p. 1) to justify smart growth as a label for "a range of regulatory, financial, and educational practices that may help to coordinate transportation planning and land development within an integrated manner". From a *socio-psychological* viewpoint the latter justify smart growth policies as a means "for achieving a better quality of life by reducing traffic gridlock through incentives for transit- and pedestrian oriented communities built under new urbanist principles" (Audirac 2005, p. 135). She writes:

> To this day, the promise of enhancing quality of life via incentives for more livable communities and simultaneously fostering economic growth seems primarily oriented toward the tastes of ICT workers and executives and the more affluent households. However, as restructuring authors point out, the much touted

vibrancy of smart growth communities also depends on low-wage, service temp workers from nearby digitally deprived communities. (Ibid., p. 137)

Inclusiveness implies reciprocity and focuses on the issue of how social and economic stakeholders can be transformed into resource integrators and place brand beneficiaries. There is a myriad of motives behind smart growth. While derived from different disciplines these are inextricably interlinked within society and the economy when placed in "everyday" space, as determined by work, learning, recreational and other activities. From a *socio-economic* perspective smart growth is justifiable for purposes of competing in the international market and collaborating in ways to gain a critical mass of support against acceptable transaction costs. In both the categories of competition and collaboration, place branding requires a leadership discourse from the political arena that helps to elaborate both relevant "ideas" and the infrastructure needed for effectively developing into a center of smart growth through innovation which would serve to reinforce the traditional role of brands as fundamental to value creation under regimes of rivalry (Klaus and Maklan 2007, p. 120). Such rivalry conditions raise issues of conceptualization resulting in the intersections of three overlapping relationship paradigms. These are: first, a legislative framework of a distinctly top-down and established relationship between national, state and local government; second, "a participatory relationship between those initiating and those recipient of development or change"; third, an "overlying framework involving finance" (Orbasli 2000, p. 100).

Accordingly, place brand performance assessment necessitates the application of a balanced and smart growth approach involving the tradeoffs in group decision-making. Presently, emerging resource scarcity and climate change focus attention on exploring concepts and new growth theory (Romer 1986; Lucas 1988), which highlights the role of knowledge in enabling growth and justifying the European Commission proposition of smart growth communities and inclusiveness from a *political and ideological* perspective, in particular when viewed as a path toward developing "an economy based on knowledge and innovation" and sustainability as "promoting a more resource efficient, greener and more competitive ... and inclusive, high-employment economy delivering social and territorial cohesion" (European Commission 2010).

Soft and hard components shaping brands

Vargo and Lusch's (2008, p. 7) third foundational premise invites us to recognize "goods as distribution mechanisms for service provision". Accordingly, in the place brand framework the challenge is to frame the hard properties (e.g. infrastructure and architecture) within value propositions (FP7) that matter to consumers who manifest their desire to participate as co-creators of value (FP6). For purposes of pulling things together, reference to the idea of discourse is relevant. Discourse is the frame of reference of the participants that determines the way they think and act, and therefore how the organization and those in it function. For instance, Chris Mabey and Tim Freeman (in Chapter 1) introduce discourse as a theoretically informed way to explore the role of leadership in the place branding context. Foucault (1977) built on early 19th-century British philosopher Jeremy Bentham's theoretical design for a prison building which created a situation in which governments exercise identity and image management to shape and maintain control over the rising expectations of stakeholders.

Giovanardi (2012, p. 30) challenges the hard–soft binary in traditional place marketing discourses and encourages researchers to consider the "functional and representational dimensions interconnected in every brand and even more in every place brand". His conceptualization implies the need to bridge a dialectical tension between the space of place, as experienced by humans, rooted in historically evolved spatial organization, and the global space of flows consisting of goods, people, symbols and electronic impulses (Castells 1996, p. 412). Analysis of transportation and information technologies has transformed human interaction with spaces, as well as challenging the "local–global" binary. Presently, human interaction, the including and excluding in the perspective of multiple spaces, encompasses the information space, mental space and social space (soft) and material (hard) space (Go and van Fenema 2006, cited by Govers and Go 2009, p. 6) – including the infrastructure of urban spaces. These lead to complex if not chaotic patterns challenging the mind–body dichotomy that is inherent in the objectivist epistemology of knowledge. The new technologies enabling mobility to bodies and minds offer unprecedented access to "other" worlds, cultures and spaces, and refer to creative cities, probably the most often referred to soft power dimension since Richard Florida launched his discourse (2002). But his critics struggle with his discourse, e.g. Peck (2005, p. 768) opines that "creativity strategies subtly canalize and constrain urban-political agency, even as their material payoffs remain extraordinarily elusive". From a research viewpoint intriguing issues arise: How can researchers conceptualize the new spatial arrangements? What patterns are emerging? How can dynamic spaces change existing places and affect their branding? According to D' Andrea *et al.* (2011, p. 158): "this realization of mobility as a complex, diverse and multidimensional phenomenon calls for care with methodological frameworks sensitive to complexity ... From micro to macro, as experience and structure, this effort to structure the very process of enquiry emerges from the need to examine a variety of spatial, social and cultural possibilities".

In such a wider, inclusive framework Audirac (2005, p. 120) examined the spatial implications of the information age and found that the "form of cities is spatially more loose and fragmented, dynamically becoming more polycentric and complex, and fast dispersing and de-concentrating". If this were true, it might represent another question: To what extent can one regard place branding as a selective, integrated and viable practice? When considered in the broadest terms, place branding aims at a great variety of objectives, driven by external forces, e.g. positioning the place in the media under conditions of "intense competition for tourists, investments and businesses" (Avraham 2000, p. 363); "creating sustainable small-scale production–consumption relations, and, therefore local cultural sustainability" (Askegaard and Kjeldgaard 2007, p. 138); or leveraging ICT-intensive methods to produce regional network agglomeration economies (ibid.) as sources of growth.

But how can we know whether or not the latter would promote smart growth place brands? Since the early 1980s the time-sensitive logic of computer mediated work has been altering the ways knowledge workers approach their tasks (Zuboff 1982), signaling a shift in work structure from co-located to mobile work styles. This discourse has driven the new order of business conduct which, in turn, has shaped organizations, management styles and human lives. Audirac (2005, p. 132) recapitulates its possible consequences for the urban fabric as follows:

> In the information age, the tension between urban centrifugal and centripetal forces, influenced by the ICT revolution, favors overall urban dispersion but not the death of cities. The synergies between ICT-enhanced supply chains and the automobile and airplane society are deepening the need for high speed accessibility to virtual and physical places. This has ushered a rise in demand for swift intermodalism, fast mobility, and state-of-the art digital connectivity, resulting in increased congestion costs for cities and a tendency for agglomerative activities to spatially recombine into new clustered patterns of metropolitan dispersion and deconcentration ... However, as overwhelmed network capacities restrict the fast tempo logic of information age business models, new waves of businesses and population deconcentration are likely to ensue.

Audirac's observations pose challenges to the metropolitan smart growth agenda and trigger critiques of scholarly thinking of Taylorist-driven supply chains and market-driven subjects by Sevin (2011) amongst others, who argues that these dominant approaches and definitions of place branding limit the thinking of scholars. A corollary of these movements is that they contribute to divisiveness and exclusion in society. He justifies his *critical theory-induced* approach by underscoring that it is difficult to even discuss ethical issues at a conceptual level within the market-driven approach in order to expose widely ignored issues and redefines place branding through a communicative action model composed of two steps. Step 1 highlights *legitimacy* and *inclusion* as ethical concerns in a domestic communicative action; while step 2 enters the *consistency* issue which arises between the messages in the domestic and international arena. The debate regarding soft and hard components reminds us of the disputes about the goods (tangibility) and services (intangibility) in the knowledge domain of service marketing. Within this context it helps to note that place brands are dynamically linked to the experience economy. Hence the unraveling of the place brand serves to identify its fundamental role as the "signifier" of service exchange (FP1), drawing on operant resources as source of competitive advantage (FP4) of social and economic actors (FP9) who operate with a view to be customer orientated and relational (FP8) and must respond to ethical issues of legitimacy, inclusion and consistency so as to offer justifiable and relevant value propositions (FP7).

Brands, semiotic space and urban experiences

The public policy literature, a third body of knowledge, having documented the decreasing influence of the nation-state, demonstrates the importance of the local initiative in urban economic restructuring (Wilson *et al.* 1997). The presence of technologically, organizationally sophisticated and resourceful transnational corporations may contribute to a new learning process, benefiting from location specific externalities (Porter 1998), associated with local and regional economies. Branding can be levered for attracting consumers to a brand (Van Ham 2001; Anholt 2002; Buer 2002).

However, there are risks associated with creating a brand, as there is an unspoken promise to consumers that their trust in the brand will be respected. This leaves the brand owner exposed to considerable reputational risk (van Ham 2001; Buer 2002). Consequently, learning is relevant, if need be, to revamp the brand. Olins (1999, p. 255) provides a powerful example of how the British "House of Saxe-Coburg-Gotha was re-launched as the House of Windsor during the First World War when Germany was the enemy".

Strong forces such as globalization and ICTs have altered the reputational landscape and increased transparency and risk exposure (Go and Govers 2011, p. xxv), reminding stewards that they have to be vigilant. The knowledge embodied in material, social and political dynamics is neither owned nor "unilaterally controlled" and therefore "cannot be controlled"

(Chandler and Vargo 2011, p. 37). In short, "brand promises are not made in isolation" (Buer 2002). This is exemplified, among others, by the complex of international media, which affords better-educated and informed citizens and consumers to demand a higher level of corporate social responsibility and ethics (Egri and Ralston 2008). In the integrated framework for brand co-creation based on Prahalad and Ramaswamy's (2004) building blocks of dialog, access, transparency and risk, brand governance (Hatch and Schultz 2010) accordingly faces multilevel, multi-actor and multisector challenges. The result is a complex of fuzzy boundaries, not just in a territorial sense but also in terms of the role of both public and private actors in, for example, operating the place brand as an "umbrella" (Kavaratzis and Ashworth 2005; Iversen and Hem 2008). First, the multisector challenge involves the issue of how to include a multitude of stakeholders efficiently and equally for mutually beneficial development. Second, the multi-actor challenge concerns the question of how the relevant spatial structure is linked to the "place-specific circuits of power linked to society, economy and the state" (Yüksel *et al.* 2005). Third, the multilevel challenge addresses a branding issue involving, particularly, the geographic, macro-, meso- and microscales.

Peter van Ham (2008, p. 126) explains how the academic discourse on soft power enabled place branding to acquire "its proper, still awkward place". Nye (2006, p. 256) defines soft power as "the ability to alter the behaviour of others by using attraction techniques, rather than by coercion or obligation, in order to achieve the needs of the individual or the group", while Olins (1999), referring to countries and companies trading identities, asserted that their primary roles remain fundamentally different. For example, Hakala *et al.* (2010) refer to an anecdotal saying in Finland, that "Finland cannot benefit Nokia but Nokia can benefit Finland". In this case and following Fan's (2006) argument the direction of causation seems clear: "the nation brand could emerge as a result of the success of a national industry" (Hakala *et al.* 2010, p. 63). The multilayered challenge in brand governance is also evident in the staging of transnational mega-events involving issues of the safety and security of international spectators. Based on empirical insights into the 2006 FIFA World Cup in Germany, Klauser (2011, p. 3204) conveys how:

> the tightly enclosed fan zones addressed not only the need to regulate public life during the event, but also served temporarily to reconfigure urban space in the interest of visibility and branding for FIFA's commercial partners. FIFA was in full control of the brands and billboards displayed in the official fan zones, thus exemplifying the intimate relationship between the opportunities and the vulnerabilities associated with urban space at the sport mega event. Following a combined

security and branding rationale, fan zones provide a secured space for the collection and integration of individual spectators into commercialized spheres of emotions and analogous rituals, moving beyond the traditional stadium in restructuring and appropriating urban space more generally.

DEFICIENCIES

When assessing the three debates above a bit closer, two parallels emerge. Though closely linked in remit and domains of investigation, there are few cross-references amongst the various disciplines or from one debate to the other, even though many issues appear to have a connection. Gertner (2011, p. 100) lamented that the fragmentation of the topics investigated impedes the development of a meta-analysis of multiple studies dealing with a set of related research hypotheses and their combined results. But the research issue Gertner encountered may have been flawed because it seems to ignore the "context specificity of place", thereby overlooking the "inseparability" of place which gives "life" to the place brand, including the dynamism derived from its mobility and governance. The latter is central to urban politics and influences place branding. Therefore, brand equity building, including name awareness, reputation and loyalty, require a supply-driven analysis as opposed to a demand driven one (Govers 2011, p. 230). The deficiency of "place brand impact measurement" is another impediment to advancing place branding and place brand knowledge.

The Deficiency of Definition: What Is Being Branded?

The place branding concept refers to branding studies in the context of cities, regions and nation-states. However, the properties of each differ markedly, which renders definition ambiguous and comparison hard, if not impossible. At the level of the nation, the same has resulted in confusion over what is being branded. In the debate as to whether France can be rebranded, Wally Olins wrote in marketing terms, whereas academic Michel Girard wrote about France the nation "from a historical and cultural perspective" (Fan 2006, p. 11). At the regional level, "region" is usually defined as "an administrative division of a country" and is often used to signify the governance of policies to assist processes of economic development (Cooke and Leydesdorff 2005, p. 6). But there also other definitions; for instance the region can also be understood as "a unit for geographical, functional, social or cultural reasons" (ibid.). So, what exactly is meant in studies by region branding is often unclear. Also, the layering of spatial identities (Boison *et al.* 2011) requires new spatial interactions at new scales and with new research approaches. In this framework mobility is a concept akin to the notion of place, the "dynamic equivalent of place" (Creswell 2006, p. 3). Along these lines, the findings by D' Andrea *et al.* (2011, p. 156) signal a significant challenge for the "systematic unbundling and formalization of research protocols, methods and analysis that can integrate macro and micro components, rather than allowing these to continue developing separately".

The Deficiency of "Place Brand Impact Measurement"

Many claims referred to in the literature suffer to a certain extent from a mixture of analysis, description and prescription. They also lack the evidence to underpin the former. Furthermore, Keller and Lehmann (2006, p. 754) remark that researchers have been preoccupied "with brand extensions and some of the processes that lead to the development of brand equity. By contrast, there has been relatively limited effort directed toward exploring the financial, legal, and social impacts of brands". The branding of place requires substantial investments. While considerable resources are allocated to place marketing and branding efforts, so far the research has not been able to measure the impact (Jacobsen 2009; Zenker and Martin 2011). In the 1976 film *All the President's Men*, two journalists investigate the Watergate scandal for the *Washington Post*, heeding the advice from 'Deep Throat' to follow the money trail. They obtain, subsequently, the evidence they had been searching for earlier, but to no avail. Similarly, researchers should follow the foreign direct investment flows as Jacobsen (2009, p. 70) did in an attempt to "identify the place brand actuators which contribute to (more) efficient place brands". The measurement of fiscal flows would then contribute to the more "efficient and effective use of taxpayers' money" (Zenker and Martin 2011) and be seen to be both highly relevant to place branding research and practice in the wake of the financial meltdown and current economic crisis.

REFERENCES

Anderson, B. (1996) *Imagined Communities: Reflections on the Origin and Spread of Nationalism*, London: Verso.

Anderson, C. (2009) *Free: How Today's Smartest Businesses Profit by Giving Something for Nothing*, New York: Hyperion.

Anholt, S. (2002) "Foreword", *Brand Management*, 9(4–5): 229–39.

Askegaard, S. and Kjeldgaard, D. (2007) "Here, there, and everywhere: place branding and gastronomical globalization in a macromarketing perspective", *Journal of Macromarketing*, 27(2): 138–47.

Conclusion

Audirac, I. (2005) "Information technology and urban form: challenges to smart growth", *International Regional Science Review*, 28(2): 119–45.

Avraham E. (2000) "Cities and their News Media Images", *Cities*, 17(5): 363–70.

Berg, L. van den, Pol, P.M.J., Winden, W. van and Woets, P. (2005) "European cities in the knowledge economy", *Urban Studies*, 44(3): 525–49.

Boisen, M., Terlouw, K. and van Gorp, B. (2011) "The selective nature of place branding and the layering of spatial identities", *Journal of Place Management and Development*, 4(2): 135–47.

Brodie, R.J., Glynn, M.S., and Littel, V. (2006) "The service brand and the service dominant logic: missing fundamental premise or the need for stronger theory", *Marketing Theory*, 6(3): 363–79.

Brown, G., Chalip, L., Jago, L. and Mules, T. (2004) "Developing brand Australia: examining the role of events", in N. Morgan, A. Pritchard and R. Pride (eds), *Destination Branding: Creating the Unique Destination Proposition*, 2nd edn, London: Elsevier Butterworth Heinemann.

Buer L. 2002. "What have public affairs and advertising got in common?", *Journal of Public Affairs*, 2(4): 293–95.

Castells, M. (1993) "European cities, the informational society and the global economy", *Journal of Economic Social Geography*, 84(4): 475–85.

Castells, Manuel (1996) *The Rise of the Network Society, The Information Age: Economy, Society and Culture, Vol. I.* Cambridge, MA: Oxford, UK: Blackwell. [2nd edn 2000.]

Chandler, J.D. and Vargo, S.L. (2011) "Contextualization and value-in-context: how context frames exchange", *Marketing Theory*, 11(1): 35–49.

Cooke, P. and Leydesdorff, L. (2005) "Regional development in the knowledge-based economy: the construction of advantages", *Journal of Technology Transfer*, 31(1): 5–15.

Cresswell, T (2006). *On the Move: Mobility in the Modern World*, London: Routledge.

D' Andrea, A., Ciolfi, L. and Gray, B. (2011) "Methodological challenges and Innovations in Mobilities Research", *Mobilities*, 6(2): 149–60.

Egri, C.P. and Ralston D. (2008) "Corporate social responsibility: a review of international management research from 1998 to 2007", *Journal of International Management*, 14: 319–39.

Eshuis, J. and Edelenbos, J. (2009) "Branding in urban regeneration", *Journal of Urban Regeneration and Renewal*, 2(3): 272–82.

EU Regional Policy for Smart Growth in Europe (2020) http://ec.europa.eu/regional_policy/sources/docgener/informat/2014/smart_specialisation_en.pdf.

European Commission (2010) "EUROPE 2020: a European strategy for smart, sustainable and inclusive growth", European Commission, Brussels, 3 March, http://ec.europa.eu/europe2020/index_en.htm.

Fan, Y. (2006) "Branding the nation: what is being branded?", *Journal of Vacation Marketing*, 12(1): 5–14.

Florida, R. (2002) *The Rise of the Creative Class and How It's Transforming Work, Leisure, Community and Everyday Life*, New York: Basic Books.

Foucault, M. (1977) *Discipline & Punish: The Birth of the Prison*, London: Allen Lane.

Franzen, G. and Bouwman, M. (2001) "The mental world of brands: mind, memory and brand success", Henley-on-Thames, Oxfordshire: World Advertising Research Centre.

Fyrberg, A. and Juriado, R. (2009) "What about interaction? Networks and brands as integrators with service dominant logic", *Journal of Service Management*, 20(4): 420–32.

Gertner, D. (2011) "Unfolding and configuring two decades of research and publications on place marketing and place branding", *Place Branding and Public Diplomacy*, 7(2): 91–106.

Giovanardi, D. (2012) "Haft and sord factors in place branding: between functionalism and representationalism", *Place Branding and Public Diplomacy*, 8(1): 30–45.

Glaeser, E.L., Kallal, H.D., Scheinkman, J.A. and Shleier, A. (1992) "Growth of cities", *Journal of Political Economy*, 100: 1126–52.
Gnoth, J. (2007) "The structure of destination brands: leveraging values", *Tourism Analysis*, 12(5/6): 345–58.
Go, F. M. and Fenema, P. van (2006) "Moving bodies and connecting minds in space: a matter of mind over matter", in Clegg, S.R. and Kornberger, M. (eds), *Space, Organizations and Management Theory*, Malmö: Liber and Copenhagen Business School Press, 64–78.
Go, F.M. and Govers, R. (eds) (2010) *International Place Branding Yearbook 2010: Place Branding in the New Age of Innovation*, Basingstoke: Palgrave Macmillan.
Go, F.M. and Govers, R. (eds) (2011) *International Place Branding Yearbook 2011: Managing Reputational Risk*, Basingstoke: Palgrave Macmillan.
Goodland, R (1995) The concept of environmental sustainability, *Annual Review of Ecology and Systematics*, 26: 1–24.
Govers, R. (2011) "From place marketing to place branding and back", *Place Branding and Public Diplomacy*, 7: 227–31.
Govers, R., and Go, F.M. (2009) *Place Branding: Glocal, Virtual and Physical, Identities Constructed, Imagined and Experienced*, Basingstoke: Palgrave Macmillan.
Gwinner, K. (1997) "A model of image creation and image transfer in event sponsorship", *International Marketing Review*, 14(3): 145–58.
Gwinner, K. and Eaton, J. (1999) "Building brand image through event sponsorship", *Journal of Advertising*, 28(4): 47–57.
Hakala, U., Lemmetyinen, A. and Gnoth, J. (2010) "The role of nokia in branding finland-companies as vectors of nation branding", in Go, F.M. and Govers, R. (eds), *International Place Branding Yearbook Place Branding in the New Age of Innovation*, Basingstoke: Palgrave Macmillan, pp. 55–65.
Hallworth, A. and Evans, S. (2008) "Managing a third division city: negative parochialism as a restraint on urban success", *Journal of Place Management and Development*, 1(2): 199–213.
Ham, P. van (2001) "The rise of the brand state: the postmodern politics of image and reputation", *Foreign Affairs*, 80(5): 2–6.
Ham P. van (2008) "Place Branding: The State of the Art", *Annals of the American Academy of Political and Social Science*, 616: 126–49.
Hansen, A. and Machin, D. (2008) "Visually branding the environment: climate change as a marketing opportunity", *Discourse Studies*, 10(6): 777–94.
Hatch, M.J. and Schultz, M. (2010) "Towards a theory of brand co-creation with implications of Brand Governance", *Branding Management*, 17(8): 590–604.
Holt, D. (2002) "Why do brands cause trouble? A dialectical theory of consumer culture", *Journal of Consumer Research*, 29(6): 70–90.
Ind, N. (2004) *Living the Brand: How to Transform Every Member of the Organization into a Brand Champion*, London: Kogan Page.
Insch, A. (2011) "Ethics of place making", *Place Branding and Public Diplomacy*, 7(3): 151–4.
Iversen, N.M. and Hem, L.E. (2008) "Provenance associations as core values of place umbrella brands: A framework of characteristics", *European Journal of Marketing*, 42(5/6): 603–26.
Jacobs, J. (1984) *Cities and the Wealth of Nations: Principles of Economic Life*, New York: Viking Penguin.
Jacobsen, B.P. (2009) "Investor-based place brand equity: a theoretical framework", *Journal of Place Management and Development*, 2(1): 70–84.
Kavaratzis, M. and Ashworth, G. (2005) "City branding: an effective assertion of identity or a transitory marketing trick?", *Tijdschrift voor Economische en Sociale Geografie*, 96(5): 506–14.

Keller, K.L. (1993) "Conceptualizing, measuring, and managing customer-based brand equity", *Journal of Marketing*, 57(January): 1–22.

Keller K.L. and Lehmann, Don (2006) "Brands and branding: research findings and future priorities," *Marketing Science*, 25(6): 740–59.

Kelly, K. (1997) "New rules for the new economy", *Wired*, http://library.isb.edu/digital_collection/New_Rules_for_the_New_Economy.pdf.

Klaus, P. and Maklan, S. (2007) "The role of brands in a service dominated world", *Journal of Brand Management*, 15(2): 115–22.

Klauser F. (2011) "The exemplification of 'fan zones': mediating mechanisms in the reproduction of best practices for Security and Branding at Euro 2008", *Urban Studies*, 48(15): 3203–19.

Kotler, P., Asplund, C., Rein, I. and Haider, D. (1999) *Marketing Places: Europe*, London: Pearson.

Lefebvre, H. (1991) *The Production of Space*, Oxford: Blackwell.

Lucarelli, A. and Berg, P.O. (2011) "City branding: a state-of-the-art review of the research domain", *Journal of Place Management and Development*, 4(1): 9–27.

Lucas, R.E. (1988) "On the mechanics of economic development", *Journal of Monetary Economics*, 22: 3–42.

Lusch, Robert F. and Stephen L. Vargo (2006) *The Service-Dominant Logic of Marketing: Dialog, Debate, and Directions*, Armonk, NY: M. E. Sharpe.

Massey, D. (1993) "Power-geometry and a progressive sense of place", in Bird, J. Curtis, B. Putnam, T. Robertson, G. and Tickner, L. (eds), *Mapping the Futures: Local Cultures, Global Change*, London: Routledge, pp. 59–69.

McAdam, R. and McCreedy, S. (2000) "A critique of knowledge management: using a social constructivist model", *New Technology, Work and Employment*, 15(2): 155–68.

Miller, J.S. and Hoel, L.A. (2002) "The 'smart growth' debate: best practices for urban transportation planning", *Socio-Economic Planning Sciences*, 36: 33–40.

Mintzberg, H. (1989) *Mintzberg on Management Inside Our Strange World of Organizations*, New York: The Free Press.

Molotch, H. (1976) "The city as a growth machine: toward a political economy of place", *The American Journal of Sociology*, 82(2): 309–32.

Morgan, G. (1986) *Images of Organization*, Newbury Park, CA: Sage.

Mules, T. and Faulkner, B. (1996) "An economic perspective on special events," *Tourism Economics*, 2(2): 107–18.

Normann, Richard (2001) *Reframing Business: When the Map Changes the Landscape*. Chichester: John Wiley & Sons.

Normann, Richard and Rafael Ramirez (1993) "From value chain to value constellation: designing interactive strategy", *Harvard Business Review*, 71: 65–77.

Nowlan, D.M. (1997) "Jane Jacobs among the economists", in Allen, M. (ed.), *Ideas That Matter: The Worlds of Jane Jacobs*, Ontario: The Ginger Press.

Nye, J. (2006) *Soft Power: The Means to Success in World Politics*, New York: Public Affairs.

Olins, W. (1999) "Trading identities: why countries and companies are taking each others' roles", *Corporate Reputation Review*, 3(3): 254–65.

Orbasli, A. (2000) *Tourists in Historic Towns Urban Conservation and Heritage Management*, London: E & FN Spon.

Peck, J. (2005) "Struggling with the creative class", *International Journal of Urban and Regional Research*, 24(9): 740–70.

Peracchio, L. A. and Tybout, A. M. (1996) "The moderating role of prior knowledge in schema-based product evaluations", *Journal of Consumer Research*, 23(December): 177–92.

Percy, L. (1997) *Strategies for Implementing Integrating Marketing Communication*, Chicago, IL: NTC Business Books.
Pike, A. (2009) "Brand and branding geographies", *Geography Compass*, 3: 190–213.
Piore, M.J. and Sabel, C. (1984) *The Second Industrial Divide*. New York: Basic Books.
Porter, M.E. (1998) "Clusters and the new economics of competition", *Harvard Business Review*, 76(6): 77–90.
Prahalad, C.K. and Ramaswamy, V. (2004) *The Future of Competition: Co-Creating Unique Value with Customers*, Boston, MA: Harvard School Business Press.
Raskin, P., Banuri, T., Gallopin, G., Gutman, P., Hammond, A., Kates, R. and Swart, R. (2002) *Great Transition: The Promise and Lure of the Times Ahead*, Boston, MA: Stockholm Environment Institute.
Romer, P.M. (1986) "Increasing returns and long run growth", *Journal of Political Economy*, 94: 1002–38.
Ruigrok, W. and Tulder, Rob van (1995) *The Logic of International Restructuring: The Management of Dependencies in Rival Industrial Complexes*, London: Routledge.
Schumpeter, J.A. (1980 [1934]) *The Theory of Economic Development*, Oxford: Oxford University Press.
Sevin, E. (2011) "Thinking about place branding: ethics of concept", *Place Branding and Public Diplomacy*, 7(3): 155–64.
Shaw, D.L. and McCombs, M. (1977) *The Emergence of American Political Issues: The Agenda Setting Function of the Press*, St Paul, MA: West Publishing.
Smith, G. (2004) "Brand image transfer through sponsorship: a consumer learning perspective", *Journal of Marketing Management*, 20(3/4): 457–74.
Stipp, H. and Schiavone, N.P. (1996) "Modeling the impact of Olympic Sponsorship on corporate image", *Journal of Advertising Research*, 36(4): 22–28.
Suchman, L. (2003) "Organising alignment: the case of bridge building", in Nicolini, D., Yanow, D. and Gherardi, S. (eds), *Knowing in Organizations: A Practice-based Approach*. London: M. E. Sharpe, pp. 187–203.
Tulder, R. van (1999) "The boundaries of redrawing organizations", in van Tulder, R. (ed.), *Redrawing Organizational Boundaries*, Rotterdam: Sviib/Department of Public Management, Erasmus University.
Vargo, Stephen L. (2009) "Toward a transcending conceptualization of relationship: a service-dominant logic perspective", *Journal of Business & Industry Marketing*, 24(5/6): 373–9.
Vargo, S.L. and Lusch, R.F. (2004) "Evolving to a new dominant logic for marketing", *Journal of Marketing*, 68(Jan): 1–17.
Vargo, S.L. and Lusch, R.F. (2006) "Service-Dominant Logic: What it is, What it is not, What it might be", in Robert F. Lusch and Stephen L. Vargo (eds), *The Service-Dominant Logic of Marketing: Dialog, Debate, and Directions*, Armonk: M.E. Sharpe, pp. 43–56.
Vargo, S.L. and Lusch, R.F. (2008) "Service-dominant logic: continuing the evolution", *Journal of the Academy of Marketing Science*, 36: 1–10.
Warnaby, G. (2009) "Towards a service-dominant place marketing logic", *Marketing Theory*, 9(4): 403–23.
Whelan, S. and Wohlfeil, M. (2006) "Communicating brands through engagement with 'lived' experiences", *Journal of Brand Management*, 13(4/5): 313–29.
Wilkinson, R. and Pickett, K. (2010) *The Spirit Level: Why Equality is Better for Everyone*, London: Penguin.
Wilson, P.A., Moulaert, F. and Demaziere, C. (1997) "Urban restructuring and local response", in Moulaert, F. and Scott, A. (eds) *Cities, Enterprises and Society on the Eve of the 21st Century*, London: Pinter.

Yüksel, F., Bramwell, W. and Yüksel A. (2005) "Centralized and decentralized tourism governance in Turkey", *Annals of Tourism Research*, 35(3/4): 859–86.

Zeng, Guojun, Go, F.M. and Kolmer, Christian (2011) "Beijing Olympics 2008 impact on China's image formation in international TV coverage: a media content analysis perspective", *International Journal of Sports Marketing & Sponsorship*, 12(4): 319–36.

Zenker, S. and Martin, N. (2011) "Measuring success in place marketing and branding", *Place Branding and Public Diplomacy*, 7(1): 31–42.

Zimmerman, E.W. (1972) *World Resources and Industries: A Functional Appraisal of the Availability of Agricultural and Industrial Materials.* New York: Harper & Row.

Zuboff, S. (1982) "New worlds of computer-mediated work". *Harvard Business Review*, Sept/Oct: 142–52.

INDEX

Notes: **bold** = extended discussion or term highlighted in text;
f = figure, n = endnote/footnote, t = table.

ABC [US network]   151, 153, 155n
academia   70, 167, 168
academic perspective   xxii–vi, xxviii–xxix, 24
academics   xiv, 136, 188
accountability   16, 49, 94
accounts of leader, follower, context   **38**
Accra   188, 194
activists   37, 70, 114, 209
actors and groups   35f
added utility-value   196
added value   *see* value-added
additional 'ambassadors' (USA)   **161–2**
administration   20, 23, 219
administrators   48, 50
advertising   48, 60, 65, 67, 82, 161, 181, 187, 198
advertising agencies   57, 162
advertising campaigns   193
  'marketing campaigns'   95, 197
  'media campaigns'   64, 81
  'tourism campaigns'   57
Aelbrecht, P.S.   192, 193
aerospace   97, 98, 114
affluence   189, 213
Afghanistan   153, 155f, 160f, 161
Afghanistan War   149
Africa   3, 59, 63, 159, 163
  see also Middle East
African Growth Opportunities   121
'age of crisis'   x
ageing population   134
agencies   41, 49
agency [power to act]   41
agenda-setting   49, 124, 148, 150, 151f, 184, 200, 224
agglomeration advantages   11

agriculture/farming   69, 82
agro-food   97
Ahmedabad   16, 191, 194
AIESEC (Romanian student organization)   142
air quality   53, 137, 139
air transport   114
air-conditioned skywalks   190
airports   177, 185(n2)
Al Jazeera   149
Albergaria, D.   180, 185
Alenia Aeronautica   98
alienation   48, 52, 200
All the President's Men (1976)   220
Alves, G. da A.   174, 185
Alvesson, M.   34, 43
ambiguity   **6**, 197, 210, 219
American Marketing Association   7
American Planning Association (APA)   69, 70, 73, 74
Amsterdam   xii, 171, 181
  see also Dutch Delta Metropolis
Anastasio, P.A.   **148–9**, 163
Anderson, B.   210, 220
Anderson, C.   201, 220
Angotti, T.   184, 185
Anholt, S.   xii, 12, 36, 43, 46, 54, 72, 74, 133, 143, 202, 207, 220
  launched notion of nation-branding (1997)   23
Anholt-GfK Roper Nation Brands Index (2005–)   165
anthropology   72
'anti-growth' camp   **8–9**
apartheid   163
Arab world   xxvii, 147, 158

Index

architects xxi, 70, 177
architecture xvi, 4, 133, 138, 189, 191, 192, 215
Argentina 168, 174
Arimah, B.C. 188, 193
Aristotle 147
Arnhem-Nijmegen region xxix, **190**, 193
arrests 110, 156
Arrow, K. 206
art 97, 189
Ashbrook, T. 129, 130
Asia 3, 65, 163
Askegaard, S. 205, 220
Assche, K. van **xv**, xviii, **xxiii–iv**, 9, 25, **69–77**
asset creation 16
association football 82, 109, 110, 121, 125, 154f, 157, 158f, 177, 218–19, 223
  see also European association football tournament
Association of Greater Manchester Authorities 115
Athens (C5 BC) 21
Athens Airport 155
Atlanta 65
'Atlantic Gateway' 105, 114
audience characteristics (crisis communication) **60–3**
  audience knowledge and place's former image **60–1**
  audience type and size **61–2**
  audience's sources **62–3**
  proximity-distance between target audience and place **62**
  social-political environment and essential values **63**
audiences xxiii, 120, 197, 202, 207
  competition for 208
  see also target audiences
Audirac, I. **216**, 213–14, 221
Aurora (brand) 98, 99, 100, 102
austerity 83, 103, 152
Austin, J.E. 95, 101
Australia xviii, 53–4(n2), 168, 221
  department stores ('Manchester' cotton and fabric goods) 105
Austria 147
  geographical advantage 157

media stereotypes **157–8**
topic structure in media coverage (2008–10) 158f
Avraham, E. **xv, xxiii**, 25, **56–68**
awareness 155n, 171, 178, 182, 191
awareness (Spinoza) 49

Baceanu, I. 136, 139
Bahrain xxvii, 147, **158–9**
Balibar, E. 47, 54
Baltic Sea 18
Bangladesh 160f
bankruptcy 84, 155
Barcelona xviii, xix, 83, 193
  'most powerful global brand' 84
Barcelona Olympics (1992) 82, 191, 199
Barton Aerodrome (1928–) 114
BBC 114, 160n
Beaumont, C.E. 69, 70, 74
becoming **38**
Beijing 11, 17, 152
Beijing Olympics (2008) 199, 225
being **38**
Belloso, J.C. 191, 193
Benfield, F.K. 70, 74
Bengston, D.N. 69, 74
Benoit, W.L. 57, 67
Bentham, J. 215
Berg, L. van 198, 221
Berg, P.O. 22, 28
Berlin xxvii, 147, 157, 171
Berlusconi, S. 152, 154f
Berthon, P. 18, 26
Bertone (car designer) 98
best practice 11, 92(n1), 167, 205, 223
Better Life Initiative (OECD) x
Beunen, R. **xv**, xviii, **xxiii–iv**, 25, **69–77**
beyond place branding **xxii–iii, 45–55**
  enabling people to connect **50–1**, 53–4(n2)
  living with participation **47–50**, 53(n1)
  see also place branding
Bhopal 159
bias 93, 98, 149, 185(n4)
bicycles 53, 139
big business 39–40, 211
'Big Society' (UK) 113, 117(n2)
Bilbao 82, 138

Index

billing systems   126–7t, 127
Binnie, J.   108, 117
bio-diversity   150
bio-resistance   180
bio-technology   97
Birmingham   xvi, xviii–xix, 111, 113
Bitner, M.   189, 193
black groups   180
BlackBerry   111, 150
Bogotá   192
Boisen, M.   **18–19**, 26
Bordeaux   155
Boston (Massachusetts)   xix, 21, 160
Boston, J.   108–9, 117
bottom-up dissatisfaction   103
boundaries   xxii, **18**, 24, 36, 41, 44, 47, 50, 72, 150, 175, **210–13**, 218, 224
  'borders'   2
  institutional, professional, territorial, community   34
Bouwman, M.   198, 221
'brains' metaphor   25
brand associations   37, 198
brand characteristics (Ind)   **211–12**
brand co-creation   218, 222
brand equity   7, 219, 220, 223
brand governance   222
  challenges (multilayered, multilevel)   218
brand image   198, 199, 222
  see also place image
brand knowledge   **198–9**
  as creative resource   **203**
  definition   198
brand leadership
  four readings   **33–44**
  see also place leadership
brand literature/branding literature   14
  direction of causality   202
Brand Management (journal)   2
brand managers   46
  see also place brand managers
Brand Manchester   **105–9**
'brand mission'   xi
brand name
  'ideally linked to organization's identity'   7
brand performance/
    underperformance   202, 203
  see also place brand performance

brand promises   133, 218
brand recall   198–9, 200
brand recognition   198
brand repair (proactive)   **103–18**
brand research
  state-of-art   xiii, xiv
brand sustained through proactive repair: Manchester   **xxv–vi**, **103–18**
  Brand Manchester   **105–9**
  chapter subject matter   104
  Cottonopolis to Madchester   **105–9**
  'research topic of some significance'   117
brand-building   205
  beyond control of organizations   46
  changing processes   46
branding   **4**, 42, 44, 195, 211
  conceived as form of communication   33
  'death'   46
  'dominant production of culture in globalizing economy'   205
  impacts (economic, socio-cultural, political)   14
  international audiences   16
  'more than marketing'   72
  precisely defined (business management literature)   81
  problem   **45–7**
  research agenda   203
  terminology   **7–8**
  see also place branding
branding Brazilian slums: Rio de Janeiro   **xxviii**, **174–86**
  field research (2010)   175
  'freeware' cultural production   xxvi, **174–86**
  strategy outlined 'could become a model'   184
branding investment
  center of gravity   206
branding model
  'three gaps'   198
branding strategy/brand strategies   202
  green design and (Bucharest)   **132–44**
brands   13, 33, 41, 42, 93, 100, 136, 142, 195, 212, 217, 218
  almost 'ageographic'   184
  'built'   42

brands – *continued*
  costs of creation and maintenance 71–2
  'critical research queries' 22
  definition 71
  experiential interaction 203
  glocal 17–18
  impact (financial, legal, social) 220
  impact on aspirations **111–12**
  interaction with stakeholders (co-creation of meaning) 46
  literature **220–5**
  mental world **198–203**, 221
  'new semiotic spaces' 22
  riots and **111–12**
  salient attributes 8
  'selective promises' 46
  socially responsible management 52, 54
  'spatial and multifaceted nature' (Pike) 213
  success factor 140
  sustained through proactive repair (Manchester) **xxv–vi, 103–18**
  terminology **7–8**
  see also place brands
brands and branding
  'geographical entanglement' (Pike) 13, 14
Brands and Branding (Simmons, no date) 136
brands, semiotic space, urban experiences **217–19**
Brasilía 176, 185(n3)
Braun, E. 14, 26, 105, 117
Brazil xxvii, 53, 147, 169, 192
  economic growth rates 174
  federal government 177–8
  GGEI 169, 170, 172
  military regime 176
  slum-branding **174–86**
  'soccer landscape' 179
  'world economic powerhouse' 177
Brazil: Constitution (1988) 178
bread 98, 107
Bridgewater Canal (1761–) **106**
broadcasting organizations 149
Brodie, R.J. 203, 221
'broom fascism' 113
Brown, G. 199, 221
Brussels 64

Bucharest xvii
  'city of contrast, diversity, change' 138
  design-led environmental brand strategy 141, 142–3
  environmental problems xxvi, 138, 139f
  personal space 139
  'strata of its society' 138
Bucharest: green design and branding strategy xxiv, **xxvi, 132–44**
  Bucharest's environmental problems in citizens' opinions 139f
  chapter purpose 133
  conclusions and recommendations **141–3**
  'gemstone turned into diamond' **xxvi, 132–44**
  international trends **132–3**
  key findings **137**
  key question, aim, objectives **135**
  literature review 135
  observational research 136, 139
  problem and motivation **133–5**
  theory 136
Bucharest: green design and branding strategy: methodology
  Stage 1: discovery and planning **135–6**
  Stage 2: investigation **136**
  Stage 3: analysis and integration **136**
  Stage 4: conclusions **136**
Bucharest: Palace of Parliament 138
Bucharest: Town Hall 136
Bucharest Brand **137–41**
  common vision required 143
  'general panorama' **134**
  positive factors 134
  'raw, unpolished product' 138
  'two sides' **138**
Bucharest story **133**
Buenos Aires xx, 174, 186
buildings 17, 85, 87, 139, 166, 167
Bundespresseamt (FRG) 151n
Burby, R.J. 70, 74
Burchell, R.W. 69, 70, 74–5
Burdett, R. 52, 54
bureaucracies 164
bureaucracy 213
'bureaucracy economy' 176
Burma 160f
'*burqa*' discussions 150

Index

Burson-Marsteller's Brand Vulnerability Index (BVI) 104, 117
Bush, G. 151f
Bush, G.W. 161
business 19, 185, 212, 213
Business for Diplomatic Action 161, 162
business elites 1
business environment 23, 122
business hubs 121
business leaders xi, 173
business management literature 81
business managers 209
business organizations 137, 141
business relocation 134
'business-as-usual' approach 59
businesses 7, 37, 47, 51, 69, 93, 97, 120, 123, 142, 157, 198, 216

C40 Cities Climate Leadership Group 53, 172
Cairo 17
Calatrava, S. 177
Cambodia 160f
Cambridge University 206
Cameron, D. 107
Canada xvi, 140, 161, 169
cantons xiv, 49
CAP [crisis, audience, place] analysis 58
capability 36, 210
Capel, H. 184, 185
capital 5, 39, 168, 208
capital accumulation xiii, 5, 22
capital cities 150
capital flows 19, 208, 210
capitalism 1, 9, 22, 72, 184
 late 108
 multi-national 118
car designers 98, 100
car-pooling 53
carbon emissions see emissions
care ('feminine ethics') 87
carioca lifestyle 176, 180, 186
Carnegie Mellon University 122
cars/automobiles 139, 216
 'automotive industry' (Turin) 97–8
 love affair with 52–3
 parking 112, 116
Carson, R. x, xi, 7, 209

Cartmell, M. 104, 117
case studies xiii, xiv, **xxiv–vi, 79–144**
 case A: sex and city (Spain) **xxiv, 81–92**
 case B: common agenda for place-branding: Made in Torino **xxv, 93–102**
 case C: brand sustained through proactive repair: Manchester **xxv–vi, 103–18**
 case D: social media: insight into 'public mood' of places: Johannesburg **xxvi, 119–31**
 case E: Bucharest: green design and branding strategy **xxvi, 132–44**
Castells, M. 181, 185
casualties
 origin-nationality (crisis characteristic) **59**
Catholic Church
 'silence around misdeeds' 157
causality/causation
 cyclical 34
 direction 2, 202, 218, 222
CBS 151, 153, 155n, 160n
Celestial Seasonings 96
'centers of gravity' (Ruigrok and Tulder) 205
central government 39, 85, 103, 104, 105, 110, 115
CEOs 40, 96, 162, 192
Certeau, M. de 6, 26
Chandler, J.D. 201, 203, 221
Cheney, R. 151f
Cheshire 114
Chester 114
Chicago 160
child abuse 150, 157, 158f
children 45, 88, 107
China xix, xxvii, 147, 155f, 160f, 167, 169
 cities (contribution to global GDP) 15
 GGEI 169, 170, 171, 172
 image formation 199–200, 225
 Olympic security budget 199
 water shortages 3
China Daily 199
Christmas Story 182
Cidade de Deus 178
Citibank 161

Index

cities xi, xiv, xxvii, xxviii, 1, 5, 27, 29, 33, 46, 58, 67, 73, 130, 147, 165, 166, 175, 184, 219, 222, 223
- artistically creative 21
- brand projection 7–8
- branding budget 82
- business diversity (spread of new ideas and knowledge) 206
- 'centers of excellence' 97
- 'complex multidimensional servicescapes' 188–9
- congestion costs 216
- 'critical research queries' 22
- diseconomies 21
- economic power 15, 28
- European typology 15, **19–21**, 26
- experience economy **189**
- 'external' versus 'internal' 137
- form (Audirac) 216
- global green economy (questions) **172–3**
- global system **15**
- 'golden ages' 1
- green strategy 172
- historical growth 15
- implementation of climate-related actions 172
- 'inability to keep pace with their growth' (responses) **16–17**
- loss of identity 17
- multiple images **208–9**
- 'new growth' theory 207
- openness to world 19
- planning failures 48
- promotion as good business location 96
- rationally-conceived 47
- renaissance through smart growth branding 2
- resource-scarce 3
- scaling and sustainability 9
- sex and (Spain) **81–92**
- small and medium-sized 17
- 'smaller' 18
- socio-cultural and political dynamics 19
- 'sustainable reputation' 96
- technologically innovative 21
- twenty-two of twenty-five largest (measured by GDP) located in developed economies 18
- see also sustainable cities

'citizen journalism' 120
citizens 48, 49, 50, 52, 53, 81, 85, 90, 93, 94, 96, 116, 123, 124, 140, 142–3, 165, 166, 172, 187, 213, 218
- feedback system 121
- needs and wants 45
- participation 25
Citizens Band radio 111
citizenship xxiv, 89
city branding xv, xxiv, 132, 135, 141
- definition (Bucharest) 137
- implementation (eight factors) (Braun) **14**
- 'important question' 15
- literature 136
- 'masculine' versus 'feminine' thinking **87–9**
- new paradigm (ethics of care) **88–9**
- objectives (importance of infrastructure) 193
- re-conceptualization 13
- shift (Spain) **85–7**
- Spain **81–92**
- 'wider definition' 81
city brands
- negative image 17
- responses **14–22**
city economy (Bucharest) 137, 141
city and enterprise
- mutual dependence **94–5**
city governments xiv, 89, 174
city hubs: centers of gravity in global value chain **11–22**
- diagnosing metropolitan growth **14–22**
- potential city brand responses **14–22**
- smart growth (relevance to place branding) **13–14**
city management
- sustainable activities 132
city managers 88, 89, 92(n1), 138
- technological innovation 17
city mayors 167
city politics 6
city size 83
'city of urban innovation' 21
city.people.light awards 192

Index

city-regions   93, 115
   Arnhem-Nijmegen (Netherlands)   **190**
cityscape   **188–9**
Cityscope (MGI)   15, 16, 18, 21, 28
civic movements   180
civic pride   134
civic rights   182
civil disturbances   xxvi, 25
civil society   86, 90, 195, 196f, 200, 212, 213
civilization   27
Clark, G.   15, 19, 26
classical economics   196
classifications and taxonomies   34
'cleantech investment' (GGEI)   167, **168**, 169, 170, 171
   see also renewable energy
Clegg, S.R.   189, 193
climate   97, 171
climate change   x, xi, 2, 14, 53, 94, 140, 141, 142, 166, 167, 168, 214, 222
Clinton, W.J.   162
clusters/clustering   2, 11, 19, 22, 97, 98, 100, 102, 205, 206, 216, 224
CNN   65
co-creation   203
   place images   93
co-creative improvement process   25
co-decisional processes   211
Co-operative movement   107
Co-operative Wholesale Society (1872–)   107
co-production   197
coal   106
Coca-Cola   65
Cochrane, A.   108, 116, 117–18
codes of conduct   209, 211
coffee   54(n2), 98
coffee shops   **50–1**
   'fuse private and public space'   51
cognitive resources   149
'Coke Town' (Dickens)   105
collaboration   214
collaborative learning   36, 41
collective action   14, 36, 90, 95, 200
'collective individuality' (Balibar)   47
Colombia   174, 192
Combined Authority (Manchester, 2011–)   115

combined perspective   xxvi, xxix
commodification   **72–3**, 182, 212
   triggering mechanism   200
common agenda for place-branding: Made in Torino)   **xxv**, **93–102**
   chapter purpose   94
   common agenda for industrial tourism (realizing an image fit)   94, **95–7**
   conclusion   **100–1**
   discussion partners   94, **102**
   fundamental trends   **94–5**
   literature review and interviews   94
   'Made in Torino: Tour the Excellent'   94, **97–100**
common policy agenda
   requirements   95
communication   33, **45–6**, 89t, 95, 99, 133, 137, 150, 162, 173
   prevailing medium   5
   'superficial techniques'   187
communication centers   93
communication inconsistencies   199
communication strategy   203
communication technologies   14
communicative action model   217
communism   133, 138
communities of interest   50
communities of place   48
community organizations   180, 182–3
community projects
   well-marketed   42
community   37, 71, 74, 137, 141, 211, 221
compact discs   181
companies/firms   xi, 1, 2, 11, 20, 57, 60, 93–4, 97–8, 100–1, 152, 155, 157, 163, 167, 203, 223
   'best structure for growth'   206
   competitive   206
   'consultation and cooperation' model   94
   independent, smaller   205
   service-oriented   95
   see also corporations
company museums   93
company tours   95–9
'company visits'
   five categories (Turin)   98
   terminology   96
compassion   45, 47

competition   102, 120, 206, 210, 214, 216, 224
  'new economics' (Porter)   205, 224
  'something for nothing'   201, 220
competitive advantage   24, 81, 82, 197, 202, 203, 217
Competitive Advantage of Nations (Porter, 1990)   206
competitive identity   201
competitiveness   2, 11, 44, 168, 189, 202
complexity   17, 21, 25, 28, 33, 71, 81, 116, 150, 172, 188, 195, 200, 201, 208, 215, 216
'comprehensive planning'   70
computer-mediated work   216
concepts   xiv
conceptual models   33, 44
conferences   161
configuration
  definition (Mintzberg)   207
configuration theory   **207–8**
congestion   21, 116, 138, 139f
Congressional ballot   122
'connection based purpose' (Austin)   95
consensus   86, 87, 95–6
conservation   179
consistency issue   **217**
conspicuous consumption   112, 197
'constituencies'   123–4, 172
construction magnates   39
constructivist discourse   38
consultants   xiv, xxix, 136, 205
consumer attitudes   200
consumer behavior   60
consumer confidence   122
consumer culture   211, 222
consumer perceptions   33, 169
consumer power   209
consumer research tradition   198
consumer subsidies   167
consumerism   51–2
consumers   12, 71, 95–7, 99, 163, 178, 195, 199, 203, 211, 213, 217, 217
consumption   xiii, 13, 22, 50, 53–4(n2), 180, **195–205**, 211, 213, 216
  brand knowledge as creative resource   **203**
  foundation premises of service dominant logic   **204–5**
  mental world of brands   **198–203**
  new means   4
  'significantly exceeds resources'   51
  spatial circuits   195
consumption-based model
  'not sustainable' (Hakim)   52
consumption experience   82
container shipping   114
content analysis
  computer-supported   12
context   3f, **4**, 5–6, 10–12, 24, 33, 36, **38**, 45, 49, 89, 104, 119, 121, 124, 126, 129, 175, 178, 180, 184, 188, 195, 201, 202, 213, 217, 219, 221
  'broader, multilayered'   204
  city branding   **14**
  developing policy to suit a place-specific   **210**
  'glocal'   8
  multilevel, multi-actor   207–8
  'scalable influence' (salience)   19
  urban   16
  urban governance   **14**
'contextualization'   203, 221
contracts   152
conviviality   182
Coombs, W.T.   57, 68
coordination   195, 196f, 200
coordination problem (Haiti)   49
coordination regime   212
Copenhagen   171
copyright infringement   181, 184
core-periphery   3
Cornell University Library   130
corporate branding domain   24
corporate brands   95, 99
  two-way relationships with place brands   96–7
corporate citizenship   94, 96
corporate communications   117
corporate headquarters
  location   36
corporate social responsibility (CSR)   95, 142, 218
  'good corporate citizenship'   99
corporate workers   178
corporate world   48

Index

corporations 166, 184, 207
    'international corporations' 159
    'multinational companies/
        corporations' 116, 133
    'transnational corporations' 217
    see also companies
corporatization 117, 177
Cottonopolis xxv, **105–7**
countries xi, xiv, xxvii, 7, 46, 67, 147, 166, 223
    see also nations
country brand managers 164
Country RepTrak (Reputation Institute, 2010–) 165–6
country reputation management xxviii, 164
country reputations
    'broad view' versus 'narrow view' 165
courage 45, 47
courts [of law] 71
craft products, 182
'crawl' (internet) 120
creative cities 215
'creative class' 51, 189, 221, 223
'creative destruction' cycle (Schumpeter) 212
'creative factory' Fabrica 182
creative hubs 2
creative industries 95, 115
    new 37
creative innovative city 21
creative resources
    brand knowledge **203**
creative talent 133
creativity xxvii, 47–8, 132, 147, 175
Creswell, T. 220, 221
crime 56, 110, 121, 154f, 178, 180, 192, 202
criminality xxvi, 107, 116, 176
criminalization 183–4
crises
    long-term versus short-term 59
    unexpected 56
crisis acknowledgement **57–8**
crisis characteristics
    duration **59**
    geographic scale **58**
    origin-nationality of casualties **59**
    stage **59–60**
    type of threat and scale of damage **60**
crisis communication and sustainable place-marketing **xxiii**, **56–68**
    audience characteristics **60–3**, 67
    chapter purpose 56–7, 67
    place characteristics **63–7**
    tailor-made solutions required 56–7, 67
    theoretical background **57–8**
crisis management
    strategic approach 57, 68
critical discourse 34, 35f, **39–41**, 43
    'dualist' 39
    see also dialogic discourse
critical management research 43
critical studies 195, **209–19**
    brands, semiotic space, and urban experiences **217–19**
    claims about ethics of place-branding **209–10**
    place brands and space (reciprocal relationship) **213–14**
    redrawing borders and national identity **210–13**
    soft and hard components shaping brands **214–17**
critical theory-induced approach (Sevin) **217**
cross-boundary learning xxii, 25, 33
cross-boundary working 36
Cruise Baltic,
    inter-territorial branding 18, 28
cuisine 13, 138
    see also food
cultural capital 200
cultural context 6
cultural diversity 19
cultural environment 41
cultural equipment 82
cultural events 86
cultural groups 42
cultural identity xiii
'cultural industry model' (Russo) xxviii, 25
cultural institutes and foundations xiv
'cultural landscape'
    Sauer 176, 185(n1)
    UNESCO 179, 185(n3)
cultural languages 184

cultural policy   8
cultural sites   157
cultural theorists   2–3
cultural tourism   5
culture   xi, 29, 38, 40, 46, 50–1, 62, 63, 64, 70, 72, 99, 134, 139, 140, 154f, 165, 175, 178, 183, 185(n4), 189, 192, 197, 202, 205, 211, 212, 213, 215, 219
  'essential role in enriching country's brand image' (Anholt)   207
  modernist and postmodernist   53–4 (n2)
  parallel, 'low-cost' industries   181
  participatory   47
  representation 'indivisible from place branding'   1
  sustainability   216
culture brands   105
'cultures' metaphor   25
Cummings, D.   122, 130
Curitiba   53, 192
customer 'always co-creator of value' (Vargo and Lusch, FP6)   204, 215
customer attitudes   120
customer engagement   203
customers   7, 47, 51, 99, 161, 189, 193, 197, 211, 217, 223, 224

D'Andrea, D.   215–16, 220, 221
'dark tourism' (Stone)   182, 186
Darlington, K.   123, 131
Darwinian-type approach   xiii, 208
data deficiencies   99
  public mood research   119
David, J.   50
Davis, M.   183, 185
de-industrialization   33
de-industrialized cities (sub-category of European city)   **20**
death   181, 186
debtor cities   18
debtor states   18
decentralization continuum   204
decision-makers   59, 64, 150, 151, 196, 200, 209
decision-making   xxvii, 66, 67, 88, 119, 121, 148, 152, 204, 210, 211, 213, 214
deconstruction   38
Deetz, S.   34, 43

'Deep Throat'   220
deficiencies   **219–20**
  definition (of what is to be branded)   **219–20**
  place brand impact measurement   **220**
democracies   62, 66, 72–3
democracy   16, 48–9, 82, 154f, 159, 159f
democratic deficit   174
democratic discourse   117
democratization   47, 48, 53
demography   65, 128, 132
demonstrators   153, 159
Denmark   169, 170, 171
Denmark: 'State of Green'   171
Denver International Airport   17
design/designers   48, 100, 141, 142
destination brands   33, 43, 44, 200, 212, 221, 222
  leverage   43
destination images   199
  negative   56, 57
destination managers   194
destination marketing   57, 81–2
determinism   41
Detroit   21, 29
developed economies/regions   19
  'industrialized countries'   59
  largest cities (by GDP)   18
developers   70, 71, 73, 85, 104
developing countries   19, 62, 183, 188, 193
  cities (contribution to global GDP)   15
development aid   167
development policies   71, 175
DG Regio   115
dialectic interaction
  'hard' technology/infrastructure versus 'soft' concepts   4
dialog   46, 89
dialogic discourse   34, 35f, **37–9**, 42
  see also discourse
Dickens, C.J.H.   105, 118
digital media   115, 216
Dinnie, K.   xii, **xv–xvi**, **xxix**, 25, **187–94**
direct debits   141
direct democracy   49, 54
disasters   162
  man-made   14
  natural   14, 56

Index

discourse xxii, 24, 33, 38, 41, 117, 189, 214, **215**, 216, 218
   permeability 35
   viewpoints **34–5**
   see also functionalist discourse
disease 9
   see also epidemics
Disney World 29
Disparities
   city responses **16**
'disruptive innovation' 195
distance 4
'distance dispersion' (Fenema) 5
distributed leadership **37**
diversity **6**, 47, 182
Dodds, P. 124, 130
domestic policies (GGEI) **167**, 168, 169, 170
'domestic reputation management' 119
   see also public mood
Downs, A. 69, 70, 71, 73, 75
Dual Citizen Inc. xx, xxvii
dualism 39, 42
Dubai 12, 114, 159
Duncan, J.B. 69, 76
dust 138, 139f, 139
Dutch Delta Metropolis **11–12**
'dynamic equivalent of place' 6
'dynamic externalities' (Glaeser et al., 1992) 206
'dynamic hub' **11**
dynamism/energy **6**, 21, 47

Early, D. 10, 26
East West Nation Brand Index (2008–) 165
Eaton, J. 199, 222
ECO-Civica/EcoCivica 136, 141
Eco-Europe/Eco-EUROPE 140, 143
ecological economics 166
ecology x, 10, 137
economic actors 204–5, 217
economic crisis (current global) 10, 18, 25, 83, 88, 103, 109, 112, 123, 174, 220
economic development 9, 102, 105, 147, 166, 219
   ministries xiv
'economic discoveries' (terminology) 96

economic diversification 174
   Turin 97–8
economic dynamic 3f
economic geography 28
economic growth 2, 5, 15, 82–3, 130, 160, 202
   'fetish' (Hamilton) 51–2, 54
   inclusive 210
   Kondratieff wave theory 1
   'powered by cities' worldwide 132
   'problem of dominance' 51
economic power 64
   eastward shift (C21) 8, 18, 19
economics xiv, 1
Economist, The 133
economists xxvii, 1, 148, 152, 205, 206, 223
economy, the 202, 213, 214, 218
Edelenbos, J. 212, 221
education x, 20, 45, 87, 191
   see also higher education
education hubs (Knight) 21, 28
educational attainment 180, 218
effectiveness 15, 100, 195, 196f
   doing 'right' things 'right' xxix, 14
efficiency 195, 196f, 220
   doing things 'right' xxix, 14
Egypt xxvii, 66, 147
eighteenth century 107
Eilat (Israel) 58, 66
'either-or' thinking 34
elections 108, 148, 161
electricity 60, 132, 180, 181, 188
electro-forró 181
electronic mail 49, 111, 158
Eleventh International Agenda-Setting Conference (2010) 150
Eleventh of September (2001) 63, 64, 161
elites 1, 16, 25, 151, 176
elitism 41
emancipation 40, 43, 175, 184
'embedded value' 197
emerging markets 9, 16, 119, 121
emigration 17
   see also immigrants
Emília-Romagna 205
emissions 129, 134, 170
   'carbon emissions' 22, 95, 139, 141, 166
   'greenhouse gas emissions' 167

emotion 88, 120, 121, 123, 129, 140, 144, 198, 203, 219
empiricism 15, 188, 198, 201
employees 19, 39, 47, 51, 95, 96, 99, 134, 189, 193, 198
  safe and healthy environment 97
  see also 'labor (cheap)'
employers 96
employment 19, 84, 95, 97, 206, 210, 214
  green growth 167
empowerment 41, 49, 204
enabling people to connect **50–1**, 53–4(n2)
Endicott, E. 70, 75
energy [power supply] 52, 171, 172
energy efficiency 132, 139
England 105
  punitive sentencing (2011) 111
  riots (1981) 104, 111
  riots (2011) **110–12**, 118
  see also United Kingdom
England: North-West 115, 116
  see also North-West Regional Development Agency
Enlightenment 156
enterprise cannot deliver value, but only offer value propositions (Vargo and Lusch, FP7) 204, 215, 217
entrepreneurship 33, 85, 163, 168
environment x, 4, 10, 47, 48, 52, 69, 70–1, 94, 97, 126–7t, 127, 138, 139f, 154f, 171, 192, 222
environmental activists/lobbies 70, 114
Environmental Brand Strategy (Bucharest) 136
environmental campaigns
  design-led 141
environmental design 133, 135–6
environmental education 140–1, 142
environmental governance 139
environmental legislation 140
environmental monitoring equipment 140
environmental regulation 130
environmental scarcity 3, 27
environmental sustainability 209
environmentalism 51
epidemics 56, 58, 64
  see also plague
epistemology 4, 5, 34, 39, 41

emergent versus fixed **34**, 35f
  objectivist 215
  practice-based 6, 197, 206–7
equity (doing 'right' things) xxix, 14, 85
equity (fairness) 195, 196f
Eshuis, J. 212, 221
established capitals (sub-category of European city) **20**
ethics 112, 217, 218
  place-branding **209–10**
ethics of care 87, 88, 90
  new paradigm for urban policies and city branding **88–9**
'ethics of concept' (Sevin) 224
ethics of justice 88, 90
Euro zone 82, 152, 153
Eurocities Questionnaire 82
Europe 9, 62, 65, 70, 82, 151, 159, 160, 161, 175, 176
Europe 2020 strategy 210, 221
  smart, sustainable, inclusive growth 21
European association football tournament
  Euro (1996) 109
  Euro (2008) 223
  see also FIFA World Cup
European Capital of Culture 105, 188
European Commission 15, 19, 21, 26, 214, 221
European Green City Index 134, 139
European Union xxiv, 69, 152, 167
  capitals 134
  'further reputation loss' 163
  Maastricht criteria 153
  new member-states 20
  smart specialization strategies 210
Evans, S. 202, 222
event-marketing literature 203
everyday life 5, 26, 123, 181–2, 221
exchange 204, 207
expansion by grace of import-replacing 'master economic process' 21
experience economy 94, **189**, 194, 217
experiences 73, 82, 93, 203, 224
expertise 50, 71, 173
experts 49, 72, 92(n1), 147, 169, 170, 171, 192
'explosive' import replacement 1, 24
exports 1, 2, 20, 36, 165, 168, 198, 207

Index

Facebook (2004–) 49, 111, 120, 136, 190
   see also media
Factiva/Dow Jones search engines 122
factories 66, 96, 105
Factory Records 108
false consciousness **39**
family 87, 96, 153, 157
Fan, Y. **202–3**, 206, 218, 221
fan zones 218–19, 223
fashion 176, 181
favela museums 183
favelas (slums) xxviii, 175, 180
   5x Favela, Agora por Nós Mesmos (motion picture) 182
   branding the freeware **178–83**, 185(n3–4)
   'burgeoning creative economy' 184
   census data (1991, 2001) 180
   cultural landscape **178–83**, 185(n3–4)
   'new brand for more cohesive Rio de Janeiro' 178
   'oppositional' identity 180
   'unique element of Rio's landscape' 180
'feeds' 120
Fenema, P. van 5, 26, 207, 215, 222
FIAI [*Fabbrica Italiana Automobili Torino*] 100, 102
   factory tours 98–9
   'more than twenty thousand visitors a year' 98
FIFA World Cup 191, 194
   2002 (Seoul/Tokyo) 191
   2006 (Germany) 218–19
   2010 (South Africa) 121, 194
   2014 (Brazil) 177, 179
   see also mega-events
film cities 86
film industry 97
finance 214
financial assets 161
financial cities 86
financial institutions 103
financial markets 152
financial performance 197
financial services 19
financial transactions, 'controlled by twenty-five cities' 15

Finland 169, 218, 222
First International Conference on Economic Degrowth and Ecological Sustainability and Social Equity (Paris, 2008) 52
first-mover advantage 167, 173
fixed propositions 36
flagship projects 82, **84–5**
Flanders 12
'flashmobs' 111, 113
Florence 21
Florida (USA) 12
Florida, R. 215, 221
Fluminense region 179
Flyvbjerg, B. 105, 118
focus groups 136, 165, 168, 170
food x, 96, 140, 182
   see also cuisine
foot-and-mouth epidemic
   'crisis limitation by geographical scale' 58
Ford, H. 162
Ford, J. **38–9**, 40, 43
Ford, K. 48, 54
Fordism 205
foreign direct investment 15, 81–2, 162, 220
   see also investment
Foucault, M. 47, 54, 215, 221
Fox 153, 155n
Fox, N xii
frame-breaking reconfiguration (Normann) 23
France 116, 138, 147, 169, 190, 219
   media stereotypes **155–7**
   riots (2005) 111
   television news coverage of Greece 153
Frankfurt 57, 152
Franzen, G. 198, 221
fraud 155
Freeman, T. **xvi, xxii**, 25, **33–4**, 215
'freeware' cultural production
   branding Brazilian slums **174–86**
Freire, J.R. 19, 26
friends/friendship 47, 96
Friends of High Line (New York) 50
'frugal innovation' (Hakim) 52

functionalism 221
functionalist discourse 34, 35f, 38, 40–3
  leadership, place branding, place leadership **36**
  see also image-repair discourse
functionalist leadership research 40
'functions of city economics' 21
funk/*funkeiros* 181, 183, 185(n4)
  see also music
Fushun 16
future 49, 71, 93, 166, 181, 192, 196f, 223
future generations 51, 94, 132, 137
Futurebrand Country Brand Index (CBI, 2005–) 165
fuzziness **6**
Fyrberg, A. 203, 221

G8 citizens 165
Galbraith, J.K. 8
Galileo Avionica 98
gangs 182, 183, 184
gap between principles and 'just place brand' practice xxix
garden cities 191
gardens 192
gateways (sub-category of European city) **20**
Gehry, F. 138
'gemstone turned into diamond'
  green branding strategy (Bucharest) **xxvi, 132–44**
gender xxiv, 2, 87, 88, 182
General Architecture for Text Engineering (GATE) 125
general public 209
genetics 87, 123
gentrification 51, 53–4(n2), 87
geographic isolation 58
geographic scale (crisis characteristic) **58**
geography 4, 5, 9, 23, 62, 72, 13, 29, 172, 195, 218, 219
  object of brand and process of branding **201–2**, 224
  see also economic geography
geothermal energy 170
German Chancellors **151–2**
Germany 116, 143, 157, 162, 217
  GGEI 169, 170, 171
  reputation **163**
  stories on Italy in television news (2009–11) 154f
  television news coverage of Greece 153
  visibility of Greece in television news (2008) 156f
Germany: FIFA World Cup (2006) 218–19
Gertner, D.
  meta-analysis of place branding literature 201, 219, 221
'getting it all together' 14
getting policies 'right' 167
Getty's images 211
Ghana 188
Giddens, A. 4, 26
Gihring, T.A. 70, 75
Gilmore, J.H. 189, 194
Giovanardi, D. 215, 221
Girard, M. 219
Giugiaro, G. 98
Giuliani, R. 50
Glaeser, E.L. **206**, 222
Glasgow 17
global cities/world cities 176
  disparities **16**
global economy/world economy x, 16, 25, 154f, 160
Global Green Economy Index (GGEI) **xxvii–viii**, xx–xxi, xxviii, 25, 164, **167–73**
  database 170
  list of countries tracked 168–9
  methodology **167–9**
  quantitative and qualitative indicators 168
  questions for nations and cities **172–3**
  reality versus rhetoric 170
  results (2011) **170–1**
  selection of respondents **169–70**
  'targeted approach' 169
Global Green Growth Initiative 172
global media cities 118
Global Reporting Initiative (GRI) 11, 27
global value chain 2
  city hubs (centers of gravity) **11–22**
globalization xiv, 14, 19, 81, 89t, 94, 118, 140, 141, 163, 205, 217, 220
  versus local identity 12

Index

glocal approach   17–18
Gnoth, J.   xii, 33, 43, 200, 212
   functional, experiential and symbolic dimensions of destination brands   33
Go, F.M.   ii, x, **xii**, **xvi–xvii**, **xxvi**, **xxix**, **1–29**, 57, 82, 91, 117, 143, 150, 163, 188–9, 193–4, **195–225**
Golder, S.   124, 130
Goldman Sachs   153, 161
goods/products   71, 99, 120, 182, 204, 215, 217
   'distribution mechanisms for service provision' (Vargo and Lusch)   204, 214–15
   transport   17
goods and services   1, 36, 201, 213
   'products and services'   7, 52, 97, 202, 209, 211
goods-dominant logic   12, 203
Google   47
Gotham, K.F.   72, 75
governance   xxiv, 47, 71, 73, 133, 165, 188, 211, 219
   multi-level   24
   supranational   210
government agencies   xiv, 164
governmental sectors   137
governments   xix, xxvii, 11, 39, 41, 48, 50, 51, 66, 70, 99, 103, 107, 111, 141, 142, 148, 150, 159, 171, 177, 195, 196f, 199, 200, 205, 207, 208, 211–12, 213, 214, 215
   impact on country's green reputation (most important areas)   167
   inability to react faster than citizens to crisis   49, 53(n1)
   role   47
   top-down policy   109
Govers, R.   ii, x, **xii**, **xvii**, **xxix**, **1–29**, 57, 82, 91, 117, 143, 188–9, 193–4, **195–225**
Graham, B.   137, 143
Gramon-Suba, I.   **xvii**, **xxvi**, 25, **132–44**
'grant coalition'   109
Greater London Assembly (GLA, 2000–)   104
Greater London Council (abolished 1985)   104
Greater Manchester   114
Greater Manchester Council (abolished 1985)   115
Greater Manchester Local Enterprise Partnership   115
Greece   147, 155f
   'bad image' (2009–)   155
   functioning tax authority promised   161
   media stereotypes   **152–3**, **155**, 156f
   visibility in European television news (2008)   156f
   visibility in US television news (2008)   155f
green branding strategies
   variable success (reasons)   135
green buildings   166, 167
green cities   **171**
green city branding   xxvi, 136, **137**, 172
   strategy   140
   success factors   **140–1**
'green' concept (evolution)   **166**
green design   **xxvi**, **132–44**
   see also Bucharest
green economy   97
   'ambiguity' of concept   166
   macro trends   **166–7**
   stakeholders   **164–73**
green identity   173
green parties   166
green reputations: national   **xxvii–viii**, **164–73**
   conclusion   **173**
   existing indices   **164–6**
   macro trends in green economy   **166–7**
   managing green reputations   **171–3**
   methodologies   **164–6**, **167–9**
   more than one model   172
   results (2011)   **170–1**
   selection of respondents   **169–70**
   starting question   167
green spaces   134, 138, 190, 191–2
   see also parks
green tourism (GGEI)   167, **168**, 169, 170, 171, 173
Grint, K.   38, 43
gross domestic product (GDP)   x, 171
   global (contribution of cities)   15

gross national product 45
groups 46
'growth coalitions' (USA) 109
growth figures 45
'growth machine' 208
growth machine theory 1
Guardian 103, 110, 111, 118, 130(n1), 144
Gufram 98, 99, 102
guilt motive x
Gustanski, J.A. 70, 75
Gwinner, K. 199, 222

hacking 181, 183, 184
Haiti earthquake (2010) 49
Hakala, U. 218, 222
Hakim, A.M. 52, 54
Hall, Sir Peter 7, 21, 27
Hallworth, A. 202, 222
Halton 114
Ham, P. van xii, 218, 222
Hamad, King (Bahrain)
   coverage in international media (2008–9) 159, 159f
Hamburg: Intelligent Cities Expo (2011) 143
Hamilton, C. 51–2, 54
Hammond, R. 50
Han Seung-soo, Dr 171–2
Hankinson, G. 24, 27, 43
   principles for destination brand management 33, 44
Hanoi 159
Hansen, A. 211, 222
Harding, N. **38–9**, 43
Harvard University xx, xxi, 153, 206
Harvey, D. 2–3, 5, 27
Hatch, M.J. 211, 222
heads of government 157
health x, 20, 45, 126–7t, 127, 137, 191
heartbeat 9
hearts and minds 8
Hem, L.E. 12, 27
'here' versus 'there' 205, 220
Herschmann, M. 185(n4), 186
Heynen, N.C. 72, 76
hierarchical command and control 16

hierarchical professional silos 36
hierarchical structural authority
   lacking 37
higher education 20, 114
   see also universities
Hildreth, J. 72, 75
historians 1
history 9, 22, 23, 43, 71, 141, 142, 179, 192, 215, 219
Hitler, A. 151, 151f, 152
Ho Chi Minh City 159–60
Hobbes, T. 47, 156
Hoel, L.A. 213, 223
Hofstede, G. 90, 91
Hollywood 21
Holm, E.D. **xvi, xxii–iii**, 25, **45–55**
Holt, C. **xvii, xxvi**, 25, **132–44**
Holt, D. 211, **212**, 222
   dialectical theory of consumer culture and branding 212
Homer-Dixon, T.F. 3, 27
Homo homini lupu (Hobbes) 156
hotels 19, 20, 65, 84, 134, 161, 168, 182, 190
   accreditation systems 171
   occupancy rates 185(n2)
House of Windsor 217
housing x, 69, 188, 190
HS2 high speed railway 105, 113
   see also railways
Huambo 16
hub cities 17
   see also city hubs
Hulbert, J.M. 18, 26
Huxley, J. 15, 19, 26
human capital 13, 36, 97, 134
human resources 210
humanistic perspective 5, 29
Hurricane Katrina (2005) 13, 48
hydropower 170

Iceland 169
   co-created processes 49, 50
   financial crisis (2008) 49
   GGEI 169, 170
   new constitution (open approach) 49
Idaho 151
ideas 7, 8, 37, 47, 49, 214

Index

identity 2, 5–8, 11, 33, 34, 38, 43, 44, 71, 81, 82, 108, 116, 137, 138, 140, 180, 184, 192, 201, 205, **210–13**, 215, 219, 223
  contestation of boundaries 'central' 18
  glocal 12, 27
  local (versus globalization) 12
  physical 17
  regional 24
  spatial 19, 26
  virtual 17
ideology 39, 40, 43, 52, 62, 185(n4), **214**
IE Business School 83
'ignoring crisis' strategy 59, 61–2
image/s xi, 12, 23, 25, **39**, 45–6, 71, 82, 98, 100, 137, 141, 123, 133, 160–2, 187, 188, 197, 199, 205
  France (change, summer 2011) **156–7**
  negative 17
  of organizations **207–9**
  versus reality (New Orleans) 13
  up-to-date 95
image fit 94, **95–7**
image gap 93
image management 215
image perception, projection, and choice modeling 198
image problem 202–3
image-repair discourse 57, 67
  see also interpretive discourse
image-restoration strategies xxiii, 57, 67
'Images of Organization' (Morgan) 24–5, 28, **208–9**, 223
IMF 156
'immediate commentary opinion' 120
immigrants/immigration 15, 62, 107, 165
  see also migrants
imports 1, 207
in-groups versus out-groups **149–50**
inclusion **217**
inclusivity 41
income distribution 22
income equality 13
Ind, N. **xvii–xviii, xxii–iii**, 25, **45–55, 211–12**, 222
India xxvii, 147, 160f, 169
Indianapolis 151
individual liberty 5
individual responsibility 49
individualism 63
individuality 47
individuals 38, 40, 46, 51, 88, 89, 187, 212
  connected 48
  true interests **39**
Indonesia 160f, 169
'industrial complexes' (Ruigrok and Tulder) 205
industrial heritage tourism **93**
industrial revolution 109
industrial tourism xix, xxv, 25, 94, 95, 102
  common agenda (realizing an image fit) 94, **95–7**
  cost-efficiency (versus other forms of marketing and PR) 96
  defined **93**
  'instrument of co-branding' 96–7
  'key question' (for companies) 96
  Turin case-study **97–100**
industrial tourists
  difficult to count 99
industrialization 59, 105
industries 94, 162, 167, 172, 206
  footloose 197
  and nation brands (direction of causation) 218, 222
  new 7
  new green 168
  'sustainable reputation' 96
industry 19, 20, 198
  negative image 96
inequalities 43
  economic 4, 13, 202
  income and occupational 16
  social 4, 13, 16, 202, 209
  wealth and poverty 22, 28
'influencer' groups 169
'influencers' 121
information 8, 67, 149, 175, 198, 216
information and communication technologies (ICTs) xvi, 97, 115, 126, 204, 213, 217
information technologies 2, 16, 207, 215, 221
infrastructure 9, 20–1, 25, 40, 53, 60, 84, 105, **113–15**, 126–7t, 127, 137, 138, 168, 177, 183, 208, 214, 215

infrastructure – *continued*
  'boosterist' refurbishment (Rio de Janeiro) 178
  and cityscape **188–9**
  'smarter systems' 167
  spending determinants 188
  sustainable place-branding **187–94**
  see also public infrastructure
'infrastructure marketing' (Kotler et al., 1999) 17, 28
'infrastructure of love' 140
'inner-directed mnemonic city' (Graham) 137
innovation 1, 20, 33, 44, 48, 54, 106, 132, 195, 214
  'master economic process' 21
  social and technical 115–16
innovativeness 11, 12
institutional theory 1
institutions 3, 9, 46, 52, 83, 141, 181, 184, 206
  governmental and economic 47
  supranational 210
integrated marketing communications (IMC) theory 201
integrity/character 45, 52, 211
intellectual capital 35, 47, 114–15
intellectual knowledge 197
intellectual life 176
intellectual property 213
intellectuals 179
inter-disciplinary approach 24–5, 213, 214
inter-territorial branding 18, 19
interaction 4, 37, 46, 50, 53, 201, 203, 210, 215, 221
Interbrand 140, 143
International Association for Advancement of Artificial Intelligence (AAAI) Conference on Weblogs and Social Media (2010) 122
International Expo Zaragoza (2008) 84
international hubs (type of European city) **19–20**
international marketing xiv, 168
International Meeting Destinations 11
internationalization 205
internet 7, 17, 49, 50, 112, 113, 117(n2), 120, 122, 128, 131, 134, 165, 168, 170, 183, 185, 186, 207

relational power 180–1
internet age 169
interpretive discourse 34, 35f, **36–7**, 41–2, 43
  see also critical discourse
interviews 84, 85, 90, 112, 136, 162, 165
  time allocated (bearing on survey results) 119
Intuit (company) 47
investment xiv, xxviii, 2, 3, 5, 84, 147, 151, 152, 165, 167, 168, 174, 177, 190, 202, 208, 216, 220
  green 173
  inward financial 33
  lacking 17
  public 4
  see also foreign direct investment
investors xi, xxvi, xxix, 1, 47, 57, 60, 83, 93, 96, 123, 133, 134, 142, 176, 178, 187, 192, 193, 198
'involvement theory' 95
Iowa 151
Iraq 153, 155f, 161
Irwell River 106, 109
Islam 158, 191
Israel xv, 58, 62, 66, 169
  GGEI 169, 172
Italy xii, xvii, 99, 100, 147, 169, 205
  'huge debt' 152
  media stereotypes **152**, 154f
  television news coverage in Germany, UK, USA (2009–11) 154f
  television news coverage of Greece 153, 156f
Iveco 98
Iversen, N.M. 12, 27
Iwakura mission (1872) 105

Jacobite uprising (1745–6) 107
Jacobs, J. 1, 28, **206–7**, 222, 223
Jacobsen, B.P. 220, 222
Japan xvi, 160f, 169, 192
Jerusalem 65
Jessop, B. 72, 75
Johannesburg
  'public mood' of places **119–31**
  social media **119–31**
Johnson, S. 48, 54

Index

Jong, M. de 192
Journal of Place Management and Development 188
Journal of Town and City Management 188
journalism (mirrors public mood) 129, 130
journalists xiv, 120, 158, 220
journals xv–xx, 2
Juriado, R. 203, 221
justice 89t, 154f
justice ('masculine ethics') 87

Kampusch, N. 157, 158f
Kanazawa (Japan) 192
Kant, I. 150
Kantianism 88
Kaptein, M. 94, 101
Kavaratzis, M. 33, 43, 44
Keller, K.L. 198, 220, 223
Kelly, E.D. 69, 70, 76
Kelly, K. 201, 223
Kennedy, R.F. 45, 51, 53
Kenya 49
Ketter, E. **57–8**, 62–3, 67, 68
'key industries' 98
keywords 125, 126
Kinder Scout (mass trespass, 1932) 107
Kjeldgaard, D. 205, 220
Klauser, F. 218–19, 223
Knight, J. 21, 28
knowledge 13, 14, 42, 47, 49, 56, 201, 215
  contestable nature 197
  'does not move in frictionless way' 9
  embedded in practice 206
  explicit 206, 213
  practice-based perspective 197
  robustness 24
  social-construction 197, 212, 213
  tacit 213
  terminology, definitions, conceptualizations, theory 24
knowledge hubs (sub-category of European city) **19**, 21
knowledge infrastructures 210
knowledge networks 2, 212
knowledge spillovers 206
'knowledge is truth' perspective 197
knowledge workers 216

knowledge-based economy 2, 94, 105, 115, 176, 203, 214, 221
knowledge-sharing xxii, 25, 33
Knowles, E.M. 104, 118
Kohl, H. 151, 151f
Kondratieff wave theory 1
Kornberger, M. 189, 193
Kotler, P. 17, 28, 198, 223
Kraetke, S. 115, 118
Kuala Lumpur 194
Kuala Lumpur: Putrajaya Garden City and Cyberjaya 191
Kunczic/Kunczik, M. 61, 68
Kyoto Protocol (1997) 162

L'Hospitalet de Llobregat 84
labor (cheap)
  unregulated exploitation 184
  see also skilled labor
labor conditions 176
labor costs 134
Labour governments (UK) 116
Labour Party (UK) 108
lakes 99, 191
Lambooy, J.G. 25, 28
Lancashire 105
land 3, 86, 166, 213
land use 10, 69, 71
Landes, D. 9, 22, 28
language 6, 37, 125, 128–9, 181, 184, 199
Las Vegas: New York-New York casino 6
Lash, S. 53(n2), 54
Latin America xxviii, 15, 174, 184
  'South America' 65
Lavazza (coffee producer) 98
law 85, 161, 200
Layard, R. 8
leaders **36**, **37**, **38**, 40, 172
  see also national leaders
leadership **33–44**, 126–7t, 127, 172, 215
  changing context 36
  constitutive theory (Grint) 38
  GGEI **167**, 168, 169, 170
  'performative nature' 38
  socially and culturally reconstructed 35f
  traditional models 41

Index

leadership: place branding, place leadership
   critical discourse **39–41**
   dialogic discourse **37–9**
   functionalist discourse **36**
   interpretive discourse **36–7**
leadership competencies/skills 36, 38, 43
leadership discourse 214
leadership identity 42
leadership practices **37**
leadership research
   individualized approaches 36
leadership studies 36
Lecce (brand) 98
Lee, F. 132, 143
Leeds 17, 111
Lefebvre, H. 6, 28, 205, 223
   critical analysis of space and place 38
legal ethics 88
legal system 157
legislation 209
legislative framework 214
legitimacy 8, 175, **217**
legitimation 73, 164, 178, 181, 184, 185(n4)
Lehman Brothers 84, 152
Lehmann, D. 220, 223
leisure 221
leisure tourists 96
Lemmetyinen, A. 18, 28
Lent (Nijmegen) 190
Leuven University xvii
Leviathan (Hobbes, 1651) 47
Libya xxvii, 147
life sciences 97, 105
'life of soul' (Plato) 87
lighting systems 189, 192
Lighting Urban Community International Association 192
'limiting crisis by geographical scale' (media strategy) 58
line-drawing process 72
linguistic identity 8
Lippmann, W. 148, 163
'liquid modernity' 23
Lisbon: *Parque dos Nações* 192
Little, S.E. xii, **xviii**, **xxv–vi**, 25, **103–18**
Liverman, D. 71, 76
Liverpool 108, 111, 188
Liverpool Airport 114
Liverpool First agency 105
Liverpool and Manchester Railway **106**
Living the Brand (Ind, 2004) **211–12**, 222
'living organism' metaphor 25
living with participation **47–50**, 53(n1)
living standards 128
Lo Ming-Chien x**viii**, **xxiii–iv**, 25, **69–77**
'local' 5
local authorities 11, 66–7, 93, 99, 116, 209
local communities 11, 36, 94
local development 25
Local Docklands Development Corporation 39
'local enterprise partnerships' 103
local government/s 71, 85, 90, 94, 108, 115, 121, 200, 214
local identity 8
local leadership **66–7**
local politics 70, 71
   participation **48–9**
local-global binary (challenged) 215
locale 35f, **37**
'localism' xxv, 110, 115
location 1, 35f, **36**, **65–6**, 93, 102, 128, 196, 207
   core versus periphery 65–6
locomotives 105, 106
'locum' 35f, **38**
'locus' 35f, **39**
Logan, J.R. 94, 101
logistics 97, 208
logo/s xi, 7, 12, 13, 25, 81, 187, 193
London 21, 57, 64, 115, 116, 181
   brand image (2011 damage) 103
   civil unrest (August 2011) 110, 111, 123
   pre-Olympic environment 116
   well-established brand (greater durability in crisis events) 61
   see also Greater London
London: Brixton riots (1981) 111
London: Crossrail project 113
London: Isle of Dogs 39–40
London: 'Olympic Borough of Hackney' 116
London Olympics (2012) 103, 198
   'most sustainable Games ever' 7
London: orbital motorway (M25) 114
London School of Economics 110, 111

Index

Lonely Planet guidebooks 182
looting 110, 111
Los Angeles 17, 64, 87
'Love Manchester' campaign (2011) **112–13**, 117(n1–2)
loyalty 205, 219
Lucarelli, A. 22, 28
Lury, C. 72, 76
Lusch, R.F. 8, 24, 29, **196–7**, 203, **204**, 207, 224
    third foundational premise 204, 214–15

Maas, W. 12, 28
Mabey, C. **xviii–xix, xxii**, 25, **33–44**, 215
Machin, D. 211, 222
'machine' metaphor 25
Macmillan, H. 104
macro trends
    green economy **166–7**
macroeconomic environment 188
macromarketing 220
Macy, M. 124, 130
Madchester **108**
'Made in Germany' **163**
'Made in Torino: Tour the Excellent' (2005) **97–100**
magazines 162, 190
Maheshwari, V. 188, 194
Malaysia 160f, 191
Malthus, T.R. 8
management 23, 216
Manama 159
Manchester
    brand-management 116
    Caribbean immigrants 107
    city centre facilities 112
    civil disturbances (2011) **109–15**, 116, 117(n1–2)
    civil unrest (brand response, 2011) 104
    congestion charges 114
    Cottonopolis to Madchester **105–9**
    IRA bombing (1996) 105, 109, 110
    new infrastructure, new momentum **113–15**
    Olympic bids (1996, 2000) 108–9
    parallel narrative (social infrastructure) **106–7**
    path dependence 105
    'physical and cultural transformation' 108
    rioters (2011): categories 110–11
    riots (1981) 107, 110, 111
    riots ('political', 1981) versus 'criminal' (2011) 107
    riots and brands **111–12**
    road-charging (abortive referendum) 116
    'second-tier city' (UK) 115
    sustaining brand through proactive repair **103–18**
    see also Greater Manchester
Manchester: Commonwealth Games (2002) 108, 109
Manchester: 'Gay Village' 108, 117
Manchester: Haçienda nightclub (1982–) 108
Manchester: M&S (world's biggest) 109
Manchester: Market Street shopping area 113
Manchester: Metrolink light-rail system 109, 116
Manchester: Moss Side **107–8**
Manchester: Museum of Science and Industry 106–7
Manchester: orbital motorway (M60, 2000) 113
Manchester: People's History Museum 107
Manchester: 'Ringway' 114
Manchester: Rusholme 107
Manchester: St Peter's Square massacre ('Peterloo', 1819) 107
Manchester: Trafford shopping center 114
Manchester Airport 114
Manchester City Council 110, 112–13, 114, 116
    slogan 109
Manchester City FC 109
Manchester City Region 115
'Manchester Mela' 116
'Manchester Moment' 113
Manchester Ship Canal (1894–) **106**, 114
Mandela, N. 159
Mansfeld, Y. 60, 68
manufacturers/manufacturing 95, 176, 196
Maputo 181
marginalized groups 16, 40, 89
market access 176

market commodities   213
market regions   17
market share   66
market structure   13
market-driven approach   217
market-driven subjects   216
marketing   xiv, 3, 13, 23, 26, 54, 63, 66, 71, 84, 95, 104, 188, 196–8, 204, 213, 219
   'less than branding'   72
   literature   220–5
   non-place   17, 29
   beyond physical goods and services   33
   precisely defined (business management literature)   81
   service-dominant logic   17
   waste-minimization   96
marketing communications   46, 193
   leveraging of collective symbolic values   17
   versus 'real tangible changes'   190–1
marketing management school of thought   197
marketing professionals   187
marketing theory   197
   'key assumption'   7
   scientific evidence   200–1
markets   1, 33, 195, 196f, 200, 211, 212
   competitive global   18
   international   173, 214
   multi-layered   19
   national   168
Marshall, A.   206
Maskell, P.   36, 44
Massachusetts   49
Massachusetts Institute of Technology (MIT)   21
Massey, D.   5, 7, 28
master plans   86, 86f
May, P.J.   70, 74
Mayes, R.   40, 43, 44
mayors   xiv, 117
McCombs, M.   150, 211, 224
McKinsey   21
McKinsey Global Institute (MGI)   15, 16, 18, 21, 28
McLuhan, M.   5, 28
Mecca   65
Medan   16

Medellín   174
media   xxvii, xxviii, 28, 51, 64, 68, 71, 81, 89t, 104, 113, 115, 123–4, 126–7t, 127, 129, 148, 162, 163, 165, 167, 176, 178, 180, 182–4, 185(n4), 207, 209, 211, 216, 218
   'new media'   175
   'scale of blood'   59
   see also newspapers
media content analysis   199–200, 225
media coverage   151f
   influencing factors   59, 61, 62
media credibility   62
media perception   147
media periphery
   Austria, Bahrain, Vietnam   **157–60**
media relations   67, 157–8
media stereotypes: Italy, Greece, France   **151–7**
media strategy
   'directly affected' by resource-availability   64
   restorative   **56–68**
Media Tenor International   xix
media unity
   overwhelming impact on public opinion   **149–50**
medical tourism hubs   21–2
Meer, J. van der   190
mega-cities   16, 21
mega-events   4, 64, 86, 98
   hosting/bidding to host   82, 85, 86, 108–9
   see also Olympic Games
mega-projects   105, 113, 118
Mehrhoff, W.A.   70, 76
Meijer, M.   192, 194
Meirelles, F.   178
Melewar, T.C.   xii, 191, 194
memory   198, 200, 221
Memphis (Tennessee)   21
men   37, 87, 88, 107, 156
'mental shortcuts'   149
'mental world of brands' (Franzen and Bouwman)   **198–203**, 221
mentality   143
mercoCIUDAD   83–4, 90, 92(n1)
'Mersey Corridor'   105

Index

Mersey River 106
Mersey-Humber motorway (M62) 113–14
Merseyside
  'negative connotations' 105
metaphysics 42
metropolitan areas 206
  salient characteristics 15
metropolitan county authorities 104, 115
metropolitan growth **14–22**
Mexico 3, 61, 169, 170, 172
Mexico City 182
Miami 160
micro-economics of space 1
micro-macro relationships 4
Middle Ages 155–6
middle class 51, 54(n2), 176, 179, 180
Middle East 65, 68, 147
  MENA 158
  see also sub-Saharan Africa
'middleweight' cities **16**
migrants/migration 3, 107
  see also emigration
Milan 152
Miller, J.S. 213, 223
mind–body dichotomy (challenged) 215
Minnesota xv, xviii, 73
Mintzberg, H. 207, 223
Miró, J. 82
Missouri 73
Mitchell, M. 135
mobile telephones/cellphones 111, 150
mobility 24, 215, 220, 221
  'dynamic equivalent of place'
    (Creswell) 220
'model of balanced centricity' xxix
'modern cultural engineering paradigm'
    (Holt) 211
modern industrial centers (sub-category of
    European city) **20**
modernist credo 50
modernity 63
modernization 191
Molotch, H.L. 94, 101, 208, 223
'money trail' ('Deep Throat') 220
Monitor Group 121, 130
Monti, M. 152, 154f
morality/morals 47, 87
Morgan, G. 24–5, 28, **208–9**, 223

Morgan, M. 189, 194
Morocco 12
morros 182
Moscow 17, 134
motion pictures 181, 182
motorways 113–14, 139
'Mount Prospect' 6
Mozambique 181
Mozilla (company) 47
multi-culturalism 63, 118
multi-dimensionality 212, 215
multi-disciplinary perspectives xxix, 119
  sustainable place branding xiv, **xxii–iv**,
    31–77
multi-discourse approach **34–5**
multi-layered interaction 210
multiplier effect 168
Mumbai 17
Munich 163
municipal government 37
  financial capacity 188
'municipal socialism' 104, 108
municipalities 66–7, 176, 183
  larger versus smaller 48–9
murder 60–1
Murgeanu, R. 136, 137, 138–9
Musa, G. 191, 194
museums 86, 134, 140, 189, 190
mushrooms 1, 25
music 13, 64, 108, 176, 179, **181**, 183
  live shows 181
  'neo-artisanal' genres 181
  see also funk
mycelium/mycelia 1, 25

name awareness 205, 219
narcotics 178, 181–2
narratives 7, 37, 71, 72, 73–4, 87, 105, 107,
    181
  hidden 40
nation-brand
  distinguished from 'nation-branding'
    (Fan) **202–3**
  success (direction of causation) 218,
    222
nation-branding xv, 25, 164, **202–3**, 221
  notion launched by Anholt (1997) 23
  theory versus reality 202

'nation-international order' binary 7
nation-state 3, 19, 217, 219
National Association for Environmental Protection (Romania) 142
National Association of Home Builders (USA) 71, 73, 76
national borders **210–13**
National Environment Protection Agency (Romania) 136
national green reputations see 'green reputations: national'
National Health Service (Romania) 141
national identity **210–13**
national leaders 167, 168
  see also leaders
national service hubs (sub-category of European city) **20**
nationalism 58, 220
nationality 'blurred' 2
nations xxviii, 1
  global green economy (questions) **172–3**
  green strategy 172
  and traditions 211
  wealth and poverty 22, 28
  see also countries
natural capital 200
natural resources 10
natural sciences 4–5
natural systems 34
nature xv, 72
Nazareth 65
Nazi terror 152
NBC 151, 153, 155n
'negative parochialism' 17
'negotiation' spaces 185(n4)
'neighbor of choice' 94
neighborhoods 33, 70, 72, 73
Nelson, A.C. 69, 76
neo-classical economics 196
neo-liberalism 72, 108
nested brands 116
Netherlands xii, xv–xvii, xix, 169, 194
  infrastructure investment **190**
Netherlands: Working Group on Sustainable Urban Development 192
networking 22, 33, 36, 48, 115

networks xiii, 13, 18, 25, 28, 38, 41, 108, 118, 140, 142, 181, 197, 199–201, 203, 207, 216, 221
  flexible specialization 205
  'lacking in hierarchical structural authority' 37
  relational (constructing and levering) 24
  'simultaneously enable and restrict' 16–17
  value-creating 204
new economy 201, 223
'new eyes' (Proust) 23
'new growth' theory 207, 214
New Holland (car manufacturer) 98
New Labour 108
New Orleans 13
  city planning (failure post-Katrina) 48, 54
New Public Management 108–9
New World Order 210, 212
New York xx, 6, 93, 156, 161, 181
  local government debt (impact on services and perceptions) 112
  post-11 September strategies 63, 64, 65
New York: Broadway shows 64
New York: High Line Park 50
New York: Manhattan 50
New York: Meatpacking District 50
New York: Wall Street 123, 152
New Zealand 117
  GGEI 169, 170, 171, 172
  world-leading sustainable tourism 7
New Zealand: 'Pure Advantage' 172
New Zealand: 'Pure' tourism campaign 171, 172
Newburn, T. 111, 118
Newig, J. 124, 130
news 150, 165, 167
  see also television news
news corporations: headquarters 64
newspapers 112, 122, 155, 162
  see also press
'Next Eleven' xxvii, 147, 160
Nieman Reports 129, 130
nineteenth century 105, 106, 107, 138, 176, 215
Niro Investment Group 141–2
noise 96, 139
Nokia 218, 222

Index

Nolon, J.R. 71, 73, 76
non-governmental organizations 70, 104, 117, 136, 140–1, 182
non-profit sector 10, 50, 212
Norberg, J. 9
Normann, R. 23, 28, 223
  'three possible levels of outcome' **207**
North America xix, 65, 175
  cities (contribution to global GDP) 15
  urban landscape 18
North of England Co-operative Wholesale Industrial and Provident Society Limited 107
North Korea 160f
North-West Regional Development Agency (NWDA)/abolition (April 2012) 114, 115
Norway xii, xvi, 169, 170
Nos do Morro (collective) 182
Nottingham 17
Nowlan, D.M. **206**, 222
Nye, J. 218, 223

Obama, M. 125
O'Connor, B. 122, 130
objectification process 73
objectivist epistemology 14–15, 197
objectivity 36, 137, 149
'Occupy' movement 103, 123
OECD x, 157
Offer, A. 8
Olins, W. 218, 219, 223
Olympic Games 86, 191, 207–8
  1992 (Barcelona) 82, 191, 199
  1996 (Atlanta) 108
  2000 (Sydney) 108
  2006 (Turin) 98
  2008 (Beijing) 199, 225
  2012 (London) 7, 103, 116, 198
  2016 (Brazil) 177, 179
  see also association football
Olympic Rings 199
'one-size-fits-all' approach xxiii, xxvi, 25
ontology 4, 6, 38, 39, 41, 42
operant resources 24, 25, 203, 204, 217
opinion leaders 151f

opinion polls/survey 124, 127, 129
  high costs 127
  traditional 122, 129
organisms,
  size versus rate of growth 9
organizational change perspective 208
organizational life,
  social, symbolic, cultural aspects 41–2
organizations xvii, 7, 11, 25, 37, 38, 41, 43, 46, 57, 71, 93, 216, 223
  boundaries 224
  charts 83
  images **207–9**
  multiple (and occasionally contesting) **42**
  network forms 44
organized resistance 184
'organizing capacity' concept 95
Osaka 105
Osama Bin Laden 151f
Oslo 171
Otgaar, A. x**ix**, **xxv**, 25, **93–102**
  discussion partners **102**
other, the xxvii, 148
outcome/s 3f, **4**
outsourcing 104, 116
overpopulation 121

Padilha, J. 178
Pakistan 160f
Palermo 152
Pan-American Games (2007) 177
Pankhurst family 107
Papagheorghiu, E. 136, 138
Pará 181
paradigms, social and organizational inquiry 34
parents and sons 88
Paris xxvii, 17, 57, 64, 65, 93, 133, 138, 147, 155
  well-established brand (greater durability in crisis events) 61
Paris: Sorbonne 157
parks 50, 51, 189, 191, 208
  'national parks' 107
  see also green spaces
Parliament (UK) 106
parliamentary reform 107
participation **47–50**, 53(n1)

participative philosophy (city planning) 48
participatory relations 15
partisan rights 35f
partners [business collaborators] 47
passengers 17, 20
Pastiglie Leone 98
patents 9
path dependence xxv, 105, 117
patriarchy 87
patriotism 58, 63
Pechlaner, H. 96, 102
Peck, J. 72, 76, 215, 223
pedestrians 190, 213
Peel Holdings 104, 114, 118
Pennine valley 106
pens 98, 99
people 94, 165, 215
Peracchio, L.A. 199, 223
perception 2, 12, 33, 58, 60, 73, 82, 84, 90, **93**, 98, 112, 123, 132, 133, 135, 137, 141, 143, 147, 157, 160–2, 164–5, 168–72, 187, 190, 195, 199, 202
   international public 46
   shaped by stereotypes **148–50**
performance 164, 168, 171, 196f
   identification of gaps 36
   measures 14
Pernambuco 181
persuasion 71
   'central' versus 'peripheral' routes (Anastasio et al., 1999) 149
persuasiveness 133
Philippines 160f
Philips 192
Philips Lighting 192
Pickett, K. 8, 13, 29
Pied Piper 150
Piedmont 99, 102
Pike, A. 13, 29, **202**, 213, 224, 224
Pine, B.J. 189, 194
Pininfarina (car designer) 98
Piore, M.J. 205, 224
Pisa
   'known only for its tower' xxvii, 147, 148f, 152
   'whole picture' 153f
Pizam, A. 60, 68

place 28, 29, 44, 220
   'articulated moments in networks of understandings' 39
   competitive identity 205
   'context specificity' 219
   'cultural and symbolic' articulations 37
   epistemological perspective 4, 5
   'essence' 36, 40
   four readings of brand leadership **33–44**
   image restoration **56–68**
   ontological perspective 4
   organizational, community, regional 42
   'performative nature' 38
   'produced' 42
   'self-contained arena' versus 'unbounded, open, hybrid in character' 7
   social construction 205
   space and **4–7**
   'unstable and unfixed nature' 40
   ways to define **4–5**
place: intrinsic characteristics **6**
   ambiguity **6**
   dynamism **6**
   fuzziness **6**
   inseparability **6**
   susceptibility **6**
   variety and diversity **6**
place brand equity
   impact measurement 25
   investor-based 222
place and brand leadership: four readings **xxii, 33–44**, 215
   chapter purpose 41
   four discourses 35f
   multi-discourse approach **34–5**
'place brand impact measurement' 219
   deficiency **220**
place brand managers 104, 195
place brand strategy
   environmental design-led 25
'place brand strategy gap' (Govers and Go) 138
place brand symbolism
   and inter-relating socio-cultural, economic, and political dynamics 2, 3f
place branding xv, 26, 54, **71–3**, 123, 196, 203–5, 212, 214, 219, 224
   and beyond **xxii–iii, 45–55**

Index

common agenda (Torino case study) **93–102**
conceptual evolution 188, 194
'confusion in use of term' 81
considered as form of place management 33
dynamism 24
'embedded through lens of value-creating networks' 204
ethics **209–10**
'inside-in' perspective 205
'inside-out' policies and strategies 205
literature xxiv, 73, 201, 220, 221
meaning 7
micro-, meso- and macro-perspectives (interlocking) 7, 12, 13, 19, 22–3, 218
model of balanced centricity 195, 196f
'nurtures wealth of nations' **205–7**
paradigm-development (requirements) 24
versus 'place marketing' 45
problem **45–7**
relevance of smart growth **13–14**
relevance of sustainability 10–11
research and practice 220
'selective, integrated, and viable practice' 216
'should result in concrete output' **210**
'site for generative construction of difference' **38**
spatial dimension (versus commercial-type branding) 24
state of art 222
strategy 25
'superficial and short-termist' 45
sustainable xiv, **xxii–iv**, **31–77**
sustainable (improved public infrastructure) **187–94**
techniques, methods, tools xiv
'three trends' 45
'uncovering pre-existing reality' 36
unravelling **2–11**
and urban development 188
see also place marketing
Place Branding: Glocal, Virtual and Physical Identities (Govers & Go, 2009) xvii, 12, 27

place branding practice 23–4, 210, 212
place branding process 205, 206, 207
integrated, balanced, centric 22
political battlefield 25
Place Branding and Public Diplomacy (journal) xv, xvii, xviii, 2, 188
Place Branding Yearbooks (Go & Govers) 195
(2010) *Place Branding in New Age of Innovation* ii, x, xi
(2011) *Managing Reputational Risk* ii, x, xi, 117
(2012) *Managing Smart Growth and Sustainability* x, xi
book organization **xxii–xxix**
conclusion **xxix**, 13, 25, **195–225**
objectives **xiii**
overview **xiv**
research agenda 195
target audience **xiv**
'the what of our story' 24
place brands xi, 95, 105, 117, 210
case studies (part two) xiii, xiv, **xxiv–vi**, **79–144**
complexity 17
dwelling place **2–11**
efficiency 220
metaphorical thinking (Lambooy) 25
and networks 'as inseparable as mushrooms and mycelia' 1
'reciprocal relationship' with space **213–14**
soft and hard components **214–17**, 221
themes (part three) xiv, **xxvii–xxix**, **145–94**
two-way relationships with corporate brands 96–7
as 'umbrella' 218
see also smart growth
place characteristics
inherent 5
location **65–6**
national–international status **63–4**
regime and local leadership **66–7**
resource availability **64–5**
tourism life-cycle **66**, 196
type and variety of tourist attractions **65**
place identity **71–3**

place identity, its projection, perceived image of consumers
  triadic tension   12
place image
  co-creation   93
  distance of new from existing one (Avraham and Ketter)   58
place leadership   xxii, 42
  policy and practice   41
  'relatively under-theorized'   33
  research   43
Place Management and Development (journal)   2
place managers   52, 53
place marketing   xiv, 2, 8, 95, 196
  defined   **7**
  literature   201, 221
  versus 'place branding'   45
  sustainable   **56–68**
  see also 'planning, preservation and place branding'
place power
  visible and accessible versus hidden and inaccessible   63–4
place-making
  multi-actor process   38
place-shaping projects   41
  context (historical, political, ideological)   43
'place-specific circuits of power' (Yüksel *et al.*, 2005)   16, 29
placelessness   5, 29
plague   58, 63
  see also disease
planet (Earth)   52, 94
planning   xxiii–iv, 21
  rebranded   **69–71**
planning, preservation and place-branding   **xxiii–iv, 9, 69–77**
  chapter purpose   69
  place branding, place identity, and smart growth   **71–3**
  smart growth as rebranded planning   **69–71**
  see also sustainable place marketing
Platform for Bucharest (2008)   140, 143
Plato   87
police   112, 117, 183

policing   107, 108, 110
policy-makers   70, 93, 100, 123, 189, 205, 209
policy-making
  democratic   25
  top-down, government   25
political capital   33
political dynamic   3f
political economy   163, 223
political opinion   122
political perspective   **214**
political situation
  'increasing complex' (Boisen *et al.*, 2011)   18
political system   25, 172
political will   133
politicians   xxvii, 37, 47–50, 73, 85, 120, 123, 148, 151, 166, 178, 187, 209
politics   5, 24, 39, 40, 43, 44, 48, 54, 95, 109, 148, 160, 162, 174, 180, 203, 211, 213
pollution   9, 21, 96, 134, 138–41, 150, 161
population   3, **15**, 66, 83, 84, 97, 133, 143, 167, 176, 216
Porter, D.R.   69, 70, 76
Porter, M.   100, 102
Porter, M.E.   205–6, 224
Porto Alegre   174
ports   20, 106
Portugal   192
Portuguese descent   176, 179
positivism   40
post-colonial epoch   174, 175
post-Fordism   174–5, 184
post-industrial activities   xxviii, 20
post-industrial conurbations   17
post-modern theories   51, 53–4(n2), 54
post-modernity   27, 50–1
post-war era (1945–)   70, 105, 107, 152, 163
poverty   3, 9, 13, 22, 28, 150, 178, 179, 183–4, 185(n4), 202
  'deprivation'   111
  'economic hardship'   56
poverty tourism   182
Povey, K.   xii
Powell, C.   151f
Powell, W.   36, 44

Index

power (political)   1, 29, 34, 35, 35f, 41, 47, 64, 187, 218
   covert dynamics   43
   'place-specificity'   11–12
   'silo-oriented regime'   16
'power coalitions'   176, 181
'power distance' (Hofstede)   90
practical contributions   56–7
practitioner's perspective   xxii, xxvi, xxvii, xxix
   'practical perspective'   xxiii
practitioners   xiv, xxii, 23, 24, 71, 81, 167, 170, 188
   non-governmental   168
pragmatism   179, 213
Prahalad, C.K.   218, 224
Presidential Administration   140
press   224
press conferences   67, 158
press releases   158
   see also print media
prestige   1, 208
Preston   105
price/s   163, 200
price premiums   203
pricing dimension   169
print media
   international coverage   121
   see also social media
prisons   215, 221
'privacy of symbols' (Raban)   187
private sector   10, 19, 85, 94, 100, 108, 118, 121, 166, 167, 205, 212
privatization   114, 116
privilege, power, partisan knowledge (contested arena)   39
'pro-growth' camp   **9**
processes   3f, **4**, 5, 24, **210**, 212
production   xiii, 13, 22, 50, 96, 189, 195, **205–9**, 216
   images of organizations   **207–9**
   small-scale   205
   wealth of nations (nurtured by place branding)   **205–7**
production: 'theatre of production'   51
productivity   21, 210
products and services   see goods and services

professional associations   70, 209
professional development   134
Professional Luminaires   192
professionalism   182
professionals   205
profit motive   71, 116
profits   4, 94
'progress', 'best way to measure'   x
'promise-of-value'   7
ProNature   141
Proust, M.   23, 29
psyche   39
'psychic prisons' metaphor   25
psychology   22, 23, 36, 163, 187, 198, 199, 201, 208, **213**
public attention   124, 130, 131
public diplomacy   150
   see also Place Branding and Public Diplomacy
public infrastructure (improved): and sustainable place-branding   **xxix**, **187–94**
   cases   **189–92**
   chapter purpose   187, 193
   conceptual work   188
   'future research'   188
   separation of research streams 'nearing an end'   187–8
   see also social infrastructure
public mood   xxiv, **123–4**, 130(n1), 131
   definition (Rahn et al., 1996)   123
   robust database required   119
public mood: Johannesburg   **119–31**
'public mood' index   25
public officials, integrity   45
public opinion   66, 103, 122, **123–4**, 129, 130, 151f, 163, 169, 172
   media unity (overwhelming impact)   **149–50**
   traditional surveying versus focus on social media   120
public policy literature   217
public relations (PR)   59, 60, 65, 67, 83, 96, 160, 187
   FIAT   98
   international   68
public safety   218–19

public sector 10, 19, 20, 22, 85, 142, 166, 212
public services
  deterioration 121
  quality 48–9
public transport 52, 104, 126–7t, 127, 190, 208
  electric and biofuel-driven 53
  see also transport
public–private partnerships xxiv, 85, 97, 100, 137, 141, 172, 193
'putting city on map' 87, 89t

qualitative focus groups 165
qualitative indicators 168
qualitative ranking 171
qualitative research
  'public mood' 119
  versus quantitative methods 40
quality 97, 100, 163, 198
quality of life x, xiii, xxiii, xxvi, 10, 21, 45, 53, 132–3, 134, 137, 139, 140, 142, 191, 213
  urban 192
quantitative indicators 168
quantitative research 165
questionnaires 92(n1), 136
Quilley, S. 108, 109, 116, 118

Raban, J. 187, 194
Radulescu-Dobrogea, N. 136, 139
Rahn, W. 123, 131
railways 50, 51, 86, 105, **106**, 109, 113, 116, 177
Ramaswamy, V. 218, 224
Ramirez, R. 207, 223
Raskin, P. 205, 224
re-invented capitals (sub-category of European city) **20**
real estate 12, 50, 83, 85, 86
realism 95
'reality' 34
reality 36, 70, 123, 150, 158, 175, 183, 190–1, 202, 212
  nature **39**
  versus negative media images 62–3
  social constructions 40
'reality tour' 182

rebranded planning **69–71**
'recurrent purposeful emergence' (Normann) 23
recycling 97, 134, 140, 141
Red Sea 58
regime type **66–7**
regional branding 23
regional cluster scale 2
regional development agencies 103
regional governments xiv
regional growth and sustainability 33
regional market centers (sub-category of European city) **20**
regional network agglomeration economies 216
regional poles (type of European city) 19, **20–1**
regional public service centers (sub-category of European city) **20**
regions [sub-national] xiv, xxvii, 33, 46, 58, 73, 82, 85, 98–100, 103, 108, 147, 187, 217, 219
  definitions 219
  regeneration 8, 208, 212
regions [supra-national] 18
regions [unspecified],
  'internal functional integration' 24
regulation 200
regulations 172
reification 180, 185(n4)
relational capital 37
religion 2, 8, 47, 61, 62
religious sites 65
Relph, E. 5, 29
Remembrance of Things Past/In Search of Lost Time (Proust, 2003 edition) 23, 29
Renaissance 21, 48
renewable energy 97, 166, 167, 170
  see also 'cleantech investment'
rent 84
rent-seeking 116
representational spaces **39**
representationalism 221
representations of space **39**
reputation/s 36, 66, 71, 100, 123, 147, 152, 158, 161, 194, 195, 219

Index

Austria 157
France 156–7
'internal' place brands 122
national green **164–73**
sustainable 96
reputation indices 45
Reputation Institute 165–6
reputation management 124, 129
'reputation of place' measurement 119
reputational change 163
reputational risk x, 2, 10, 12, 104, 199, 217
research 24, 27, 34, 87, 177, 206
research centers (sub-category of European city) **20**
research institutes 11, 115
researchers xiv, 23, 71
residents xxix, 37, 39, 60, 66, 70, 73, 93, 95, 97, 98, 123, 142, 187, 192, 193, 198
  high-quality 57
resource allocation 41
resource availability **64–5**
resource integrators 204–5
resource scarcity x, 21, 214
restaurants 20, 134
retirement age 155
return-on-investment 85
'right to city' 175
'right to roam' (2005–) 107
Rio de Janeiro
  basic facts 176
  beaches 179
  branding Brazilian slums **174–86**
  carnival 179
  city brand 177
  cultural niches 183
  favelas versus corporate tourist city **176–8**, 185(n1–2)
  'freeware' cultural production **174–86**
  global brand as creative city 183
  'global destination' 178
  investment 177
  'most visited cities' 185(n2)
  'scale jump' expected 177
  social problems 177–8
  soft-branding diversity for sustainable development **183–4**
  suburbanization 176
  'world brand' 176
  'world destination' 184
Rio de Janeiro: *Centro* 178
Rio de Janeiro: Ipanema 179
Rio de Janeiro: Madureira suburb 183
Rio de Janeiro: Nova Iguaçú 183
Rio de Janeiro: Porto Maravilha 177
Rio de Janeiro: Rocinha 182, 183
Rio de Janeiro: South Zone 182, 183
Rio de Janeiro: Vigário Geral 183
riots and brands **111–12**
Riots Communities and Victims Panel (England, 2011) **110–12**, 118
Ripberger, J. 124, 127, 131
risk/s 61, 71, 90, 166, 208, 217, 218
  global 14
  see also reputational risk
rivalry conditions 214
rivers 192
Riyadh xxix, 193
Riyadh: Capital Markets Authority 190
Riyadh: King Abdullah Financial District (KAFD) **189–90**
Riyadh: Tadawul Stock Exchange 190
roads 72, 106, 180, 188
Rocky Mountains 17
Rode, P. 52, 54
Rogers, R. 84
Romania xvii, 133, 141
  see also Bucharest
Romania: Direction of Culture, Education and Tourism 136
Romania: Ministry of Regional Development and Tourism 136
Romanian Bank of Development 142
Romanian Commercial Bank 142
Rome 65
Romer, P. 206
Rosenbaum, M. 10, 29
Rossi (beverages) 98
Rotterdam xii, 105
  'uses femininity as branding strategy' 87
  see also Dutch Delta Metropolis
Rotterdam: Atjehstraat 192
Rotterdam: Erasmus University xvi, xix, xx
Rotterdam School of Management (RSM) xvi, xvii, xx

Ruigrok, W.   205, 224
Russian Federation   xxvii, 147
Russo, A.P.   **xix, xxviii**, 25, **174–86**

Sabel, C.   205, 224
Saddam Hussein   151f
Salford rioting (2011)   110, 112
Salford: Media City UK   114, 115, 116
Salkin, P.E.   71, 73, 76
Salman, S.   135, 144
samba   176, 179, 183
Samba Bank   190
San Francisco Bay Area   21
Santa Fe (Mexico)   16
Santa Fe Institute (SFI)   9
Santiago (Chile)   174
São Paulo   17, 174, 176, 181, 182, 186
Saragossa   83, 84
SARS epidemic   64
satellite towns (sub-category of European city)   **21**
Saudi Arabia   65, **189–90**
Sauer, C.O.   185(n1), 186
savoir vivre   155
'scale of blood' (propensity of media to cover a crisis)   59
scale and scope advantages   11, 15
scandals   152, 155
Scandinavia   48
scarce resources   35f, 95
scarcity   3, 27
Schatz, R.   **xix–xx, xxvii**, 25, **147–63**
Schreiner, W.   **xx, xxvi,** 25, **119–31**, 194
Schröder, G.   151, 151f
Schultz, M.   211, 222
Schumpeter, J.A.   9, 212, 224
science   xviii, 20, 105, 160
scientists   48, 151, 162, 204
'sea of homogeneity'   8
sea-and-sun tourism   61, 65
Securities Exchange Commission (SEC)   161
segmentation   128, 169
Segre, R.   174, 186
Seisdedos, G.   x**x, xxiv**, 25, **81–92**
self-identity   4, 26
semiotic space   **217–19**
'sense-and-response' feeling   121

sentiment analysis   120, 125, 127
Seoul   194
Seoul: City Recreation Project   191
Seoul: FIFA World Cup (2002)   191
Seoul: Han River Renaissance Project   191
Seoul Media city   114
'service' [helpfulness]   46, 197, 204
service economies (all economies)   204
service exchange   217
service flow analysis   13
service quality   163
service-centered framework   204, 205
service-delivery   89
service-dominant (S-D) logic (Vargo and Lusch)   8, 29, 197, 203, 221, 223, 224
  foundational premises   **204–5**
services   20, 115, 116, 217
  see *also* goods and services
services marketing   188–9
servicescapes   188–9, 193
Sevin, E.   216–17, 224
sex and the city **xxiv**, **81–92**
  city-branding models   89t
  city-branding shift   **85–7**
  conclusion   **90**
  duality on urban management tools   86f
  ethics of care   **88–9**
  from flagship projects to white elephants   **84–5**
  implications   **89–90**
  interviews (semi-structured)   83, 84, 85, 90, 92(n1)
  'masculine' versus 'feminine' thinking and city branding   **87–9**
  methodology   **83–4**, 92(n1)
  new paradigm   86, 87
  new paradigm for urban policies and city branding   **88–9**
  sample cities (listed)   83
  Spanish cities: from now on, what?   **82–3**
  themes   83
  trend analysis   83
Shackleton, Lord   x
Shaw, D.L.   150, 211, 224
Sheller, M.   52–3, 55
shops/shopping malls   189, 208
Sichuan earthquake   199
Siemens Green City Index   171

Index

Siemens index of environmental governance (2010) 134, 144
'signature' architecture 4
Silent Spring (Carson, 1962) x, xi, 209
Simmel, G. 5
Simmons, J. 136, 138
Simon, J. 9
Sinatra, F. 87
Singapore 12, 160f
   healthcare reforms (1980s) 21–2
   high cost of media campaign (post-SARS epidemic) 64
   medical tourism hub 21–2
site 10
Skeggs, B. 108, 117
skilled labor xviii, 82
skilled workforce hubs 21
   see also workers
skills 13, 41, 42, 47, 48
slaves 176, 179
Sloan Business School (MIT) 21
slogans 187, 193
slum tourism 182
slums 183–4
   see also favelas
small countries 5
smart growth xi, xxiv, **4**, **8–10**, 26, 40–2, 180, 205, 210, 212–13
   characteristics 10
   combination of planning and place-branding 74
   cost-saving, revenue-making promises 70
   factors **14**
   impacts 'limited' 71
   metropolitan agenda (challenges) 216
   'myriad of motives' 214
   networked 12
   'no single definition' **9–10**
   obstacles (USA) 70
   'overlapping interests' **69**
   place branding, place identity, and **71–3**
   potential for place-branding 'vast' 73
   as rebranded planning **69–71**
   relevance to place branding **13–14**
   unity of vision 'crucial' 71–2
   US versus European perspectives 70
   'way to integrate environmental and development policies' 71
smart growth branding 200
   renaissance of cities 2
smart growth literature 69, **70**, 221, 223
   mostly American in origin 9–10
smart growth place branding 211
smart growth place brands 216
   see also brands
Smith, A. 1, 9
Smith, S. 123, 131
SMS 49
soccer see association football
social actors 204–5, 217
social capital 37, 44, 200
social class 51, 53(n2), 62, 87, 123, 178, 179, 180
social cohesion 52, 137, 210
social consensus 34, 35f, 36, 37
social 'dissensus' 34, 35f
social exclusion 81, 179, 184, 217
social identity **149**, 163
social inclusion 19, 214
social inequality 4, 13, 16, 202, 209
social infrastructure **106–7**
   see also infrastructure
social interaction 37, 50, 53
   see also interaction
social justice/injustice 3, 4, 13, 41, 178, 182
social media xxii, xxv, 2, 8, 49, 104, 111–13, 115–16, 119–20, 169, 172
   analysis 'poses myriad challenges' **128–9**
   flow of information and influence 124
   'municipalization' xxvi, 117
   role **123–4**
   'sense-and-response' feeling 121
   surveys 'value for money' 121
   see also television
social media: insight into 'public mood' of places: Johannesburg **xxvi, 119–31**
   conclusion **129**
   database 121
   discussion **128–9**
   existing research **122**
   methodology **124–5**, 129
   'possible business model' 121
   reasons for focus on social media **120–1**
   research goal 121, 125, 129

social media: insight into 'public mood' of places: Johannesburg – *continued*
  research project (academic and pragmatic relevance) 121
  results **125–8**
  theory 121
  top category issues (extended proximity) 125–6, 127t, 127
  top category issues (near proximity) 125, 126, 126t, 127
social movements 175, 178
social policies 88, 89t, 90, 154f
  'living laboratory' 84
social relations 42, 150
social sciences 4–5
  'new lens of ubiquity' 23
social scientists 205
social systems 9, 23, 34
social world 34, 39
socialist realism 133
socialization 48
societal structure 50
societal trends 8
society 4, 26, 34, 52, 95, 141, 157, 185, 202, 213, 214, 216, 218, 219
socio-cultural dynamic 3f
socio-economic conditions 86–7, 94, 203
socio-economic perspective **214**
socio-political environment **63**
socio-psychology **213**
socio-spatial diversification 184
sociology 23, 124, 208, 223
Soft City (Raban, 2008 edition) 187, 194
soft power xiii, 215, 223
  definition (Nye) 218
soft urbanism xxii, xxiii, **50–1**
soft-branding diversity
  Rio de Janeiro **183–4**
software 26, 120, 125, 129
Somalia 56
Sosa, V.A. 174, 186
soul versus body (Plato) 87
South Africa xx, xxvii, 147, 159, 169, 170
South Africa: FIFA World Cup (2010) 121, 194
South Korea 114, 160f, 169, 171–2, 190
  see also Seoul

Southeast Asia 85
space/s 13, 22, 28, 29, 42, 86f, 193, 202, 215, 216, 222
  'everyday' 214
  multi-sector xiii
  multiple 215
  and place **4–7**, 38–9
  private and public 50
  private and public 'fused by coffee shop' 51
  'reciprocal relationship' with place brands **213–14**
space production 205, 223
Spain xix, xx, 169, 192
  'budget deficit and economic weakness' 83
  city branding **81–92**
  city branding (affected by financial crisis) 83
  economic boom 82
  high-speed train 86
  modernization program 82
  sex and city **81–92**
  television news coverage of Greece 153, 156f
Spanish cities **82–3**
  'economic asphyxia' 83
  town planning 'main engine for economic growth' 85–6
spatial commodification **72–3**
spatial planning
  'about drawing conceptual boundaries' 72
spatial practice **39**
specialized poles (type of European city) 19, **20**
spectators 208, 218–19
Spinoza, B. de 49, 54, 55
Spio, A.E. 188, 194
Spirit Level (Wilkinson and Pickett, 2010) 13, 29
spiritual proximity 62
sponsorship 222
sponsorship brands **198–9**
sport 64, 154f, 157, 160, 162, 199, 208
Squires, R.H. 70, 75
Sri Lanka 160f

Index

stakeholders 1, 2, 5, 8, 11, 12, 14, 19, 22, 43, 53, 72, 90, 93–5, 98–101, 119, 121, 140, 142–3, 150, 175, 198, 201, 204, 205, 208, 210–15, 218
  green economy **xxvii–viii, 164–73**
  mindset 136
  needs and wants 46
Stanford University 130
star projects 86, 89t, 90
Starbucks 54(n2)
state, the 218
State of European Cities 19
state fragility 10
state governments [sub-national] 214
state power xiii, 5
state role 109
state visits 150
statehood,
  shifting scales 24
statistics 128, 138, 143
stereotypes 19, 25, 58, 61, 63, 65, 89t
  overcoming risk of **xxvii, 147–63**
  shaping of perception **148–50**
stigma 161, 163, 180
Stilolinea (brand) 98
stock markets 122
Stocker, K.P. 57, 68
Stockholm 21, 171
Stoke-on-Trent 17
Stone, P.R. 182, 186
Stough, R. 41, 44
Strasbourg 155
strategic communications 172
  facilitation of sustainable place-branding **147–63**
strategic market forces perspective 27
strategic urban plan (SUP) 86f
Strauss-Kahn, D. **156–7**
streets 176, 183, 189, 191
structural functional barriers 201
student housing 208
students 21, 49, 108, 142, 162–3
sub-region 37
sub-Saharan Africa 3, 130
  see also Africa
'subjective illusions' (Raban) 187
subjectivist thinking 34
subjectivity 35, 129, 180

sun (Miró) 82
suppliers 95, 100
supply and demand 195, 204, 205, 210, 219
supply chains 104, 167, 181
  ICT-enhanced 216
supra-national levels 3–4
supra-national sector 8
susceptibility **6**
sustainability xxvi, **4, 10–11**, 26–7, 36, 40–3, 69, 81, 167, 168, 171–2, 177, 195, 205, 210, 211, 214
  combination of planning and place-branding 74
  definitions **10**
  delivery **51–3**
  'leading paradigm in competitiveness of cities' 94
  rhetoric 'often exceeds action' 51
  small-scale production–consumption relations 216
  UN definition (1987) 10, 29
sustainability movement x–xi
Sustainable Cities (Canadian NGO) 140
sustainable cities 136
  'long-term vision' 137
  see also urban areas
sustainable development xxi, xxvi, 132, 140–1, 166, 170, 191, 200, 212
  Brundtland definition (1987) 51
  common vision (definition) 95
  soft-branding diversity (Rio) **183–4**
sustainable growth 9, 180
sustainable place branding xxix, 25
  facilitation **147–63**
  improved public infrastructure **187–94**
  see also beyond place branding
sustainable place marketing **56–68**
sustainable urban development (SUD) 94, 96–7
Sweden 169, 170, 171
'swift intermodalism' 216
Switzerland xviii, xxiii, 49, 156f
Swyngedouw, E. 72, 76
Sydney 53–4(n2)
symbolic city brand value propositions 3f
symbols xi, 215
synergies xiii, 37, 69, 208, 216
Syria xxvii, 147

'system of illusions' (Govers & Go) 138
'systems in flux and transformation' metaphor 25

Taba (Egypt) 66
Taiwan 160f
Tamanini, J. **xx–xxi, xxvii–viii**, 25, **164–73**
target audiences **xiv**, 37, 56–61, 63, 187, 189, 203
    proximity-distance from crisis location **62**
    see also audience characteristics
'taste makers' industry 98
taxation 140, 161, 208
taxpayers 39–40, 153, 161
taxpayers' money 46, 220
Taylorism 216
technology 2, 20, 21, 105, 106, 202
    advanced 62
    clean 167
technology transfer 19, 210
tecnobrega 181
telecommunications 60
telephones 158, 181
    see also mobile telephones
television 111, 151–2, 207, 225
    global audience 199
    see also Twitter
television news 162
    coverage of Austria (2008–10) 158f
    France (2011) 155
    visibility of Greece (selected European countries, 2008) 156f
    see also news
terrorism x, 56, 58, 63, 147, 158, 162, 202
'text' 34
text message 111
TF1 160n
Thailand 160f
Thales Alenia Space 98
Thatcher, M.H. 108, 115
The Hague see Dutch Delta Metropolis
theater/s 99, 134, 176, 181, 183
theatrical metaphors 189
TheInfrastructurist 140, 144
theory xiv, xxiii, xxix, 33, 41, 56–7, 87, 121
Third World 202
3M (company) 47
'Tiananmen Square' 159

Tibetan riots 199
Tickell, A. 72, 76
time 4, 5, 13, 29, 34, 52, **59**, 60, 61, 122, 123, 141, 149, 163, 166, 168, 195–7, 202, 213, 216
time-saving devices 16
Tokyo 152
    green spaces 191–2
Tokyo: FIFA World Cup (2002) 191
top-down approach 214
top-down legislative framework 15
Torino see Turin
Tour de France 208
tourism xiv, xvi, xxviii, 2, 11, 12, 13, 20, 25, 27, 33, 36, 56–7, 98, 103, 134, 136, 147, 152, 157, 159, 165, 175–7, 200
    adoption of destination-marketing 81–2
    niche forms 178
    sustainable 7
tourism business network 18
tourism crisis management 68
tourism industry life cycle **66**
tourism infrastructure 183
tourism operators 212
tourist attractions 66
    type and variety **65**
tourist destinations 67
    former image (effect on present image) **60–1**
tourist industry 40
tourists xi, xxvi, xxix, 37, 47, 58, 59, 60, 93, 97, 123, 142, 162, 184, 187, 192, 193, 216
    demographic characteristics 65
    see also visitors
tours for newspeople 67
town planning 85–6, 129
'trackers' 122
trade unions 11
'traditional modernist thinking' 50
traffic 126–7t, 126–7, 213
transaction costs 95, 214
transformation poles (sub-category of European city) **20**
transparency xxiii, 46, 49, 152, 212, 217, 218
    'openness' xxiv, 211

Index

transport 16, 17, 105, 139, 177
  motor car versus 'more environmental forms' 53
  sustainable 97
  see also public transport
transport hubs
  'gateway, flagship, symbol' (Warnaby) 17, 29
transport infrastructure 47, 106, 191
transportation 1, 60, 69, 166, 168, 207, 215
'traveling audiences' 184
trends 33, 44
triangle management model (van Tulder) 196f
Triple P (People, Planet, Profit) Bottom Line 94
Tropa de Elite 178
Trouble with City Planning (Ford, 2010) 48, 54
Trunfio, M. 22, 27
trust 13, 48, 90, 140, 141, 149, 150, 203, 217
truth 36, 39, 133, 142
  performative theory 38
  singular, objective, universally applicable (rejected) 38
tsunamis 162
Tuan Yi-Fu 5, 6, 29
Tufts University (Massachusetts) 49
Tulder, R. van 94, 101, 196n, 205, 224
Tunisia xxvii, 147
Tuqan, Y.T. 49, 55
Turin xvii
  basic facts 97
  co-branding (city and industries) 97
  common agenda for place branding **93–102**
  image 98
  industrial tourism **97–100**
  meetings, incentives, conferences, exhibitions 99
Turin Province: Chamber of Commerce 97, 98, 100–1
Turismo Torino 97, 99, 102
Turkey 29, 169
Tuscany 73
twentieth century 21, 81, 107, 133, 174, 176

twenty-first century 157
Twitter xxi, 111, 119–22, 125–6, 128, 130
  'global trending map' 113
  see also Facebook
Tybout, A.M. 199, 223

uncertainty 115, 203
'uncertainty avoidance' (Hofstede) 90
unemployment x, 17, 83, 107
United Arab Emirates xvii, xxi, 169
United Kingdom xii, xvi–xviii, 12, 58, 105, 115, 163, 169
  gap between income equality and trust 13
  general election (1983) 108
  recession (late C19) 106
  regional policy 109
  stories on Italy in television news (2009–11) 154f
  television news coverage of Greece 153, 156f
  umbrella city brandings versus sub-brands 14
United Nations xxi, 167
  UN Conference of Parties (COP) 170
  UN Environment Programme 166
  UN Human Settlements Programme database 188
  UNESCO xvii, 179, 185(n1, n3)
  World Heritage List xvii, 179
United States xii, xviii, xxiv, 12, 45, 69, 109, 115, 149, 159, 160, 167, 224
  comprehensive spatial visioning (lacking) 70
  elite knowledge of German politicians (2002 survey) 151
  employment data (1956–87) 206
  gap between income equality and trust 13
  GGEI 169, 170, 171, 172
  image of Israel 62
  'imperial power' perception 161–2
  knowledge (lacking) of German personalities 151f, **151–2**
  place branding 'useful for implementing smart growth' 71
  planning (described) 70
  pollution 161

United States – *continued*
  presidency 162
  presidential approval ratings 122
  presidential elections (monetary donations) 161
  selection of additional 'ambassadors' **161–2**
  society and politics 13
  stories on Italy in television news (2009–11) 154f
  television news (visibility of Greece) 153, 155f
  'voluntary simplifiers' 52
United States: Environmental Protection Agency 70–1
United States: State Department 161, 162
universities xv–xxi, 108, 115, 134, 157, 162, 163, 191
  see also education
University of Salford 114
urban areas/locations xiii, 9, 171, 192
  competitiveness 85, 95
  economic restructuring 217
  energy, transport, and water systems 17
  evolution (regional characteristics) 19
  'more just' society 175
  post-modern life 50–1
  problems 174
  projected percentage of world population (2050) 132
  reconstruction and development 9
  regeneration 8
  size (relation to growth rate) 9
  see also cities
'urban cultural landscape' (UNESCO) 185(n1)
urban design xxix, 187, 193
  sustainable 192, 193, 194
urban development 129, 175, 188, 190
  inclusive 179, 185(n3)
  and place-branding 188
urban experiences **217–19**
urban governance 6, **14**, 19, 103
urban growth 188
  consumption-driven 22
  sustainable 81
  'universal law' 9

'urban hinterworld' (Kraetke) 115
urban innovation
  'four main stages' (Hall) 21, 27
urban integration 8
Urban Land Institute (ULI/USA) 10, 29, 71, 73, 76
urban management 81
urban parks 50
urban planning xvi, 8, 192
urban policy 183
  'living laboratory' 84
  new paradigm (ethics of care) **88–9**
urban regeneration 85, 208, 212, 221
urban regime theory 95
urban software 89t
urban spaces 215, 218–19
  infrastructure (soft and hard) 22
urban sprawl 69, 70
urban strategy 90
urban studies 66
urban transformation 84
urban transportation planning 213, 223
urban violence 176, 178
urban vision 12, 28
urbanity
  humanistic aspects 52–3
urbanization 9, 15, 24, 167, 180, 183
Urry, J. 2–3, 52–3, 55
user-centricity 213
  classification of organizational operant resources 203
Ushahidi 49
utilitarianism 88, 105, 191
Utrecht see Dutch Delta Metropolis

Vaggione, P. **xxi**, 25, **81–92**
Valladolid xxix, 193
  lighting as 'essential part of cultural identity' 192
value
  co-creation 197, 204, 224
  effects of planning 69
  'uniquely and phenomenologically determined by beneficiary' 204
value-added 12, 100, 203
value-associations 198
value chains 12, 184, 223
value constellations 207, 223

Index

'value-in-context' 16, 203, 212, 221
value-creation 21, 47
value-in-exchange 196
value propositions 8, 23, 204, 217
value systems 212
values/norms 58, 150, 195
  abstract 88
  essential **63**
values-in-place 73
Vargo, S.L. 8, 24, 29, **196–7**, 201, 203, **204**, 207, 221, 223, 224
  third foundational premise 204, 214–15
variety **6**
Venice 65
Vidigal community 182
Vieira, M. 180, 181, 186
Vieira, R. 10, 29
Vietnam xxvii, 147
  image versus achievements since 1975 159
  media stereotypes **159–60**
  visibility in international television news (2011) 160f
Vina del Mar 16
violence 27, 61, 68, 110, 111, 181–4, 185(n4)
'Virtual Tourism Destination Image' (Govers, 2005) 12, 27
vision xi, 42, 71
  planning and preservation 25
visitor centers (sub-category of European city) **20**
visitor numbers 45
visitors 96, 133, 198
'vital cities' 11
'voluntary simplifiers' 52
voter turnout 117
VW Blue Motion 7

Waal River 190
Wales 12
  see also United Kingdom
war 56, 202
War Child 7
Warnaby, G. 17, 29, 203, 204, 224
Warrington 114
Warsaw 134

Washington DC xviii, xx, 161
  high cost of media campaign (post-11 September 2001) 64
Washington: Pentagon 138
Washington: White House xxvii, 147
Washington Post 220
waste 137, 138, 139, 141, 166
water 3, 72, 106, 139, 140, 166, 180, 188–90
Watergate 220
'We Love MCR' day (26 August 2011) 113
wealth 9, 20, 22, 28, 195, 212
  'economic prosperity' 66
wealth of nations 222
  'nurtured by place-branding' **205–7**
Wealth of Nations (Smith) 1, 28
weather 60, 125
  see also climate
weblogs/blogs 111, 120, 122, 126
websites 62–3, 125, 182, 190
Weitz, J. 69, 77
well-being 45, 48, 66, 142
  disconnect between increased material wealth and happiness 52
  'enhanced possibilities' 51
Western Europe 18
Whelan, S. 203, 224
'where' 4
Where Good Ideas Come From (Johnson, 2010) 48, 54
'white elephants' **84–5**, 86, 90
WikiLeaks affair 150
Wilkinson, R. 8, 13, 29
wisdom 45, 47
wit 45, 47
Wohlfeil, M. 203, 224
Wolfsburg: Volkswagen Autostadt 93
Wolfsfeld, G. 64, 68
women 37, 87, 88, 156, 159
  suffrage movement 107
'word-of-mouse' 6–7
word-of-mouth 6–7, 123, 198
work 221
work structure 216
workers 37, 179
  low-wage, service, temporary 214
workforce qualifications 134
working class 87, 184
  see also employees

World Commission on Environment and Development (1987) 209
 Brundtland Report (1987) 51
world/international politics xiv, 154f, 223
World War One 217
World Wide Web 7
world-cloud software 125
Worsley 106
'Writer and Co' 136

Yemen xxvii, 147
young people/youths 99, 108, 110, 111, 180, 181, 183, 185(n4)
Yüksel, F. 16, 29

Zeng Guojun 199–200, 225
Zimmerman, E.W. 203, 225
Žižek, S. 108, 118
zoning 70, 71
Zovanyi, G. 69, 77
Zukin, S. 2–3, 5, 29